BURIAL IN
EARLY MEDIEVAL
ENGLAND AND WALES

THE SOCIETY FOR MEDIEVAL ARCHAEOLOGY
MONOGRAPH SERIES: NO. 17

BURIAL IN
EARLY MEDIEVAL
ENGLAND AND WALES

Edited by
Sam Lucy and Andrew Reynolds

The Society for Medieval Archaeology
London
2002

ISSN 0583–9106
ISBN 1 902653 65 3

PUBLISHED BY THE SOCIETY FOR MEDIEVAL ARCHAEOLOGY

PRODUCED IN GREAT BRITAIN BY MANEY PUBLISHING
HUDSON ROAD, LEEDS LS9 7DL, UK

CONTENTS

PREFACE AND ACKNOWLEDGEMENTS

This volume *Burial in Early Medieval England and Wales* is the result of a conference held in April 1999 at University College London under the aegis of the Society for Medieval Archaeology. The event, organized by Sam Lucy and Andrew Reynolds, was intended to bring together archaeologists working on material across the Anglo-Saxon period in an attempt to redress the balance of research which has concentrated to date on the cemeteries of the early Anglo-Saxon centuries.

The papers published here reflect the increasing variety of approaches to the study of early medieval mortuary remains. New perspectives are provided on long established research topics in early Anglo-Saxon archaeology, but the volume gives equal weight to the middle and later Anglo-Saxon periods with the presentation of much new material.

The London conference was organized with the assistance of Henry Escudero, Alex Langlands and Simon Roffey, whose assistance is greatly appreciated. Particular thanks are due to those senior colleagues who agreed to act as chairs and discussants for each of the three days of the conference: Dr John Blair, Dr Tania Dickinson, Dr Bruce Eagles, Professor James Graham-Campbell, Dr Catherine Hills and Professor David Hinton. Amongst this group are a number of prominent contributors to the volume *Anglo-Saxon Cemeteries, 1979*, published in 1980 and edited by Philip Rahtz, Tania Dickinson and Lorna Watts.[1] One of the principal purposes of the present collection of papers was to attempt to provide a broad review of cemetery studies twenty years after this important event.

Certain papers presented at the London conference, by Mark Corney, Chris Loveluck, John Blair, Mark Blackburn and Kristin Bornholdt, and Birthe Kjølbye-Biddle, are not published here as they are to appear elsewhere. These colleagues are thanked for their participation and the influence of their contributions is reflected in the contents of this book. Additional papers were offered by Helen Gittos, Dawn Hadley and Nick Stoodley and the volume provides a rounder coverage for their work. The cover was designed by Alex Langlands.

Inevitably, there are aspects of the subject which are not covered in the book, but the intention from the outset was to re-examine broader themes and new approaches and it is hoped that this aim has at least partially been fulfilled.

---

[1] P. Rahtz, T. Dickinson and L. Watts (eds.), *Anglo-Saxon Cemeteries 1979* (BAR Brit. Ser., 82, Oxford, 1980).

LIST OF CONTRIBUTORS

Professor Martin Carver, Department of Archaeology, University of York
Christopher Daniell, Pastforward, York
Dr Helen Geake, Archaeology and Environment Division, Norfolk County Council
Helen Gittos, The Queen's College, University of Oxford
Dr Dawn Hadley, Department of Archaeology and Prehistory, University of Sheffield
Professor John Hines, School of History and Archaeology, Cardiff University
Dr Sam Lucy, Department of Archaeology, University of Durham
Dr David Petts, Northumberland County Council
Dr Andrew Reynolds, Department of Archaeology, King Alfred's College, Winchester
Dr Julian Richards, Department of Archaeology, University of York
Dr Nick Stoodley, Department of Archaeology, University of Nottingham
Dr Victoria Thompson, Department of English and Related Literature, University of York
Dr Martin Welch, Institute of Archaeology, University College London
Dr Howard Williams, Department of Archaeology, Trinity College, Carmarthen

Burial in Early Medieval England and Wales:
Past, Present and Future

By SAM LUCY *and* ANDREW REYNOLDS

The review presented here does not attempt to provide an exhaustive discussion of early medieval cemetery archaeology (5th to 11th centuries) past, present and future, but rather a commentary on aspects which we consider important with regard to the longer term study of the subject. We do not, for example, cover the issue of lingering Christianity in sub-Roman Britain. An overview of this length can only really flag up a range of issues, themes and debates rather than critically assessing each in turn. Nevertheless, we have attempted to summarize certain aspects of the development of early medieval burial archaeology, and to provide a historical narrative for others. Some suggestions for future research directions are considered towards the end of the paper.

PAST: BIAS AND EMPHASIS IN EARLY MEDIEVAL BURIAL ARCHAEOLOGY

EARLY ANGLO-SAXON CEMETERIES AND FURNISHED BURIALS

Until very recently, the study of early medieval burial rites in England and Wales meant the study of remains largely in eastern England dating to the early Anglo-Saxon period — roughly the 5th to 7th centuries A.D. Consisting of both inhumations and cremations, often furnished with grave-goods such as jewellery and other personal ornaments, containers and weapons, such burials have been discovered and written about extensively over the last 150 years. Indeed, the very fact that burials of this date often contain grave-goods can explain a great deal of this bias. Traditionally, archaeology of this period was seen as a way of fleshing out the meagre historical sources. Written sources are particularly scarce and of varying reliability for the 5th to 7th centuries, while the burial archaeology is particularly rich. For both the Christian period (from the 7th century), and for western Britain in the 5th to 7th centuries, with their largely unfurnished burials, the potential of archaeology for adding detail to social understanding was not perceived as strongly, and thus these sites have not been given the archaeological attention that we might expect today.

As well as showing a bias towards the study of the earlier material, early archaeologists also seem to have been influenced by pervading historical frameworks in their interpretations of that material. Indeed, the over-riding influence on the interpretation of early Anglo-Saxon cemeteries since the middle of the 19th century can be argued to be the concept of migrations from the Continent — the 'Germanic' background of the 'Anglo-Saxon' burial rite. The early linking by archaeologists such as Charles Roach Smith and Thomas Wright of this class of site to the Venerable

Bede's renowned statement regarding the continental origins of the Angles, Saxons and Jutes ensured that searches for parallels between English and continental material of the 5th and 6th centuries was the mainstay of early Anglo-Saxon archaeology for many decades.[1] When these parallels were found (for they certainly exist), they were taken as proof of the presence of incoming migrants. While such interpretations can be debated (and certainly are being — see Lucy and Williams *infra*), the effect of this dialogue was to focus attention on the recovery of grave-goods from these early sites. In the absence of detailed documentary sources for this early historic period, archaeologists working in the first half of the 20th century (particularly the 1920s and 1930s), such as E. T. Leeds and J. N. L. Myres, thought that the artefacts found in these graves could be used to trace the progress of Anglo-Saxon invasions across the country, and the emergence of the kingdoms which were historically well known by the 8th century.[2] Much effort was therefore put into arranging the artefacts found, especially the brooches (for these seem to exhibit the most variation over time), into ethnically significant types and then into chronological sequences. While some of the underlying assumptions governing these chronologies can be challenged (the idea that brooch-types start with simple forms, becoming more complex or 'developed' over time), they remain broadly accepted today.

SUTTON HOO AND THE 7TH CENTURY

For the first two decades of the 20th century in eastern England, 5th- and 6th-century burials were thus the focus of attention, with later remains largely unrecognized. New discoveries affected the way the 7th century was viewed, however. T. C. Lethbridge's excavations at Burwell and Shudy Camps in the late 1920s and early 1930s demonstrated one type of 7th-century burial, which came to be known as 'Final Phase'.[3] Another type of 7th-century burial came to light in the late 1930s, with the discovery and initial excavation of the Sutton Hoo ship burial. By chance untouched by earlier grave robbers, this stunningly rich grave, with goods from all over Europe and beyond revolutionized archaeological impressions of the 7th century A.D. in Britain. The wealth contained within the grave offered a vivid picture of the resources available to the 7th-century elite, while the cosmopolitan nature of the grave-offerings indicated the strength of pan-European links between members of those elites. Further research into the burial assemblage and burial practices at the site has shown the deliberate selection of aspects of the burial from a vast region: the Scandinavian-linked use of ship burial; the gold and garnet style ultimately of eastern-European origin; the Egyptian bowls; the Merovingian coinage. Another effect of the Sutton Hoo discoveries was to focus attention on to the issue of Christianity. Were the Christian artefacts in the Mound One grave — the baptismal spoons, for example — an indication of royal or elite conversion? How might new converts in the 7th century have been buried?

---

[1] C. Roach Smith, *Collectanea Antiqua, Etchings and Notices of Ancient Remains Vol.* 1 (printed for the subscribers, 1850); T. Wright, *The Celt, the Roman and the Saxon* (London, 1852).

[2] E. T. Leeds, *The Archaeology of the Early Anglo-Saxon Settlements* (Oxford, 1913); J. N. L. Myres, *Anglo-Saxon Pottery and the Settlement of England* (Oxford, 1969).

[3] T. C. Lethbridge, *Recent Excavations in Anglo-Saxon Cemeteries in Cambridgeshire and Suffolk: A Report* (Cambridge, 1931), 47–70; ibid., *A Cemetery at Shudy Camps Cambridgeshire: Report of the Excavation of a Cemetery of the Christian Anglo-Saxon Period in* 1933 (Cambridge, 1936).

What (if any) are the archaeological indicators of Christianity? It is only recently though that such questions have been considered to be of interest.[4]

INTO THE CHRISTIAN PERIOD

Yet, as noted above, the material attributes of a significant proportion of burials of the early period, particularly those found in eastern England in the 5th and 6th centuries, has ensured a scholarly bias towards the study of these remains. In part, there was an element of 'treasure hunting' involved in the earlier researches, but the focus on the pre-Christian period was also partly due to the cultural visibility of furnished burials and the perceived ease with which archaeologists were able to interpret and categorize the material that they found. Until recently, interest in the burial archaeology of the Christian period was thus limited to an explanation of why furnished burial came to an end rather than examining longer-term trajectories in the development of burial customs and religion. This latter factor is mirrored in the terminology used by E. T. Leeds, and subsequently followed almost without question, which considered the end of furnished burial as a 'Final Phase';[5] a choice of words which arguably defines the interests of Leeds and his successors as being centred on the 'Pagan Saxon Period'. Subsequently, much writing and research has addressed the nature of the conversion of Anglo-Saxon societies to Christianity and in particular the ways in which such a process might be represented in the burial record. Bede's descriptions of the Conversion process, and in particular the chronology of that process, were linked, frequently uncritically, to archaeological material and a seemingly consensual sequence of events was adhered to throughout the development of the 'Final Phase' model from the 1930s to the 1980s. It is now realized, however, that burial customs within the pagan period were not static phenomena in themselves. Close examination of the dating of the latest furnished burials has extended Bede's documented chronology of the Conversion from the 680s to the 730s. In view of the recent identification of Christian period field cemeteries (see below) it is now possible to chart a virtually seamless development in burial rite throughout the Anglo-Saxon period exhibiting aspects of both continuity and change. In essence, Leeds and his successors effectively drew a line under the study of early medieval burial archaeology, which led to the great imbalance in both knowledge now extant and field research.

Besides the availability of evidence and the specialized interests of many early scholars, there was (and still is) a widely held belief that, once converted, the English buried their dead in a uniform fashion, without grave elaboration, and in clearly defined cemeteries represented by the parish and larger church cemeteries in the modern landscape. These two issues are largely responsible for the chronic lack of study of burial customs in England from the 8th to 11th centuries. The assumption of simple uniformity, of supine, oriented burials without objects or elaboration, can no longer be upheld. During the 1960s and 1970s excavations at Winchester Old Minster (Hampshire) in particular revealed a complexity in burial rite which has since been

---

[4] For the most up-to-date summary of the contribution of Sutton Hoo studies to early medieval archaeology, see M. O. H. Carver, *Sutton Hoo: Burial Ground of Kings?* (London, 1998).

[5] E. T. Leeds, *Anglo-Saxon Art and Archaeology* (Oxford, 1936), 96–114.

both confirmed and elaborated upon by excavations elsewhere.[6] The Biddles' efforts at Winchester brought a new dimension to the study of early medieval burial archaeology in terms of the realization of the complexity and character of the available evidence for the Christian period. Yet, despite the exciting and varied material revealed amongst the Old Minster burials, work on Christian period cemeteries and burial rites has remained fragmented on a site-by-site basis.

The divided nature of the study of Anglo-Saxon archaeology has also contributed to the scholarly bias toward the early material. Until recently, early Anglo-Saxon archaeology was studied in almost total isolation with little regard to longer term processes both within individual categories of material and in the wider social context. It is also the case that an understanding of burial archaeology is related to the research agenda of the 'settlement' archaeologist. During the 1960s and 1970s it was perceived that the abandonment of upland settlements in the 7th century led to settlement in river valleys and the establishment of patterns of rural landscape which were to persist into modern times. This view of events thus maximized the cultural differences between the pagan and Christian periods. So-called pagan Anglo-Saxon burials were therefore more suitable for academic study in contrast to Christian populations with which a common cultural thread could be traced, at least ideologically. There is increasing evidence to support the emerging view that early Anglo-Saxon cemeteries are often close to the settlements that they served (see Reynolds this vol.), in the manner of later medieval villages, and thus the development of settlement patterns throughout the Anglo-Saxon period chips away at one of the major pillars of support for the compartmentalized study of early medieval burial archaeology.

A further assumption that has underpinned what we might call the separationists' view, is that unaccompanied inhumations, particularly in cemeteries containing demonstrable 7th-century burials, are broadly contemporary with associated furnished burials. In truth, this fact is far from established and the characteristics of an emerging group of 7th- to 9th-century cemeteries, considered variously in this volume, are indistinguishable from many of the unaccompanied inhumations from later 'early Anglo-Saxon' cemeteries.

On a more practical level, the degree of access for archaeological research into Christian cemeteries is dictated more often by chance discovery than intentional research design. Whilst this might provide a random sample of material, there is still a range of issues that could be resolved through more focussed active research. What the study of Christian period cemeteries lacks in this respect, however, is partly redressed by the wealth and quantity of data relating to the landscape context of Christian burial. Yet, it still remains a fact that the landscape archaeology of both pre-Christian and Christian burial is a neglected area of research with much potential for enquiry.

SPANNING THE DIVIDE: THE DEVELOPMENT OF LANDSCAPE ARCHAEOLOGY

Recent decades have seen the development and rapid growth of landscape archaeology into a mainstream approach to studies of the past. In many respects it

---

[6] B. Kjølbye-Biddle, 'Dispersal or concentration: the disposal of the Winchester dead over 2000 years', 210–47 in S. Bassett (ed.), *Death in Towns: Urban Responses to the Dying and the Dead, 100–1600* (Leicester, 1992), at pp. 222–4.

now stands as the principal approach serving to provide contexts for research into many different themes and issues that were previously studied in their own right. In particular, early medieval burial archaeology is a late arrival into the landscape archaeologists' scene. The study of settlement patterns has been largely the preserve of historical geographers, economic and social historians and archaeologists whose concerns were usually with post-Conquest issues and clearly defined in the context of medieval rural settlement studies. Their concern with settlements and fields left little room for the archaeology and geography of burial in the landscape. It is not the intention to provide an exhaustive review of approaches, but Desmond Bonney's work in particular marks a watershed in terms of the way in which burial data suddenly became relevant to the 'settlement' archaeologist,[7] even if much of his pioneering work has been succeeded as new ways of thinking and new discoveries have emerged. In fact, the history of Bonney's work, and that which it both provoked and inspired, leads us into the current scene in landscape studies where it is realized that burial data are often used uncritically in narratives about landscapes. The move toward incorporating burial data into landscape studies led to a situation whereby elements of landscape were reduced to symbols on maps with little attempt to sift through the data to establish their reliability or character. Archaeologists are beginning to emphasize once again the importance of characterizing rather than simply plotting archaeological material.

In summary, the bias towards furnished cemeteries and the subsequent neglect of both Christian-period burial archaeology and earlier western British burial traditions has resulted from a variety of factors, including: the effects of a historical agenda, namely that of Bede writing in the first half of the 8th century; a contemporary ideological view of pre-Christian England as a foreign past; and a series of reactions by archaeologists to these influences resulting in varying degrees of unqualified assumption. Further factors requiring consideration here are those of excavation and publication and some comments are provided below.

EXCAVATION

Excavations of early medieval cemeteries have always exhibited a wide variety of skill and attention to detail, although more standardized methodologies now characterize British archaeology. Even in the 19th century, one can find examples of sites excavated with care and attention, with detailed plans prepared, and a great deal of contextual information recorded, but (most) other sites have fared far worse, with extensive destruction often preceding discovery of the cemetery. With the exception of the later 6th- and 7th-century barrow cemeteries like Sutton Hoo (Suffolk) and the sites on the downs of Kent, Surrey, Sussex and the Isle of Wight, early medieval cemeteries are rarely marked on the surface. Their discovery is thus something that usually occurs by chance (although in recent years the advent of archaeological investigations in advance of building works has gone some way to ameliorating this). From quarrying and railway-construction in the 19th century, to the building of motorways, industrial estates and housing developments in the 20th century, the recovery of early medieval remains was largely dependent on the goodwill and patience

---

[7] See, for example, D. Bonney, 'Early boundaries and estates in southern England', 72–82 in P. Sawyer (ed), *Medieval Settlement: Continuity and Change* (London, 1976).

of the contractor. Excavation tended to be organized on a rather haphazard basis, with local volunteers and university staff often lending a hand to rescue the disturbed remains. Even if a competent excavation could be carried out, post-excavation work, including analysis of the remains and the writing-up of the site, was reliant on patchy funding, and on expert goodwill.

Nowadays, the situation has improved somewhat, although some drawbacks are still present. With the move to developer-funded excavation, archaeological units put in tenders for site investigations and excavations. This usually involves predicting what will be found. If a cemetery turns up unexpectedly, the successful unit may well find that its costing is now an under-estimate, as cemetery excavation is these days an expensive business, especially if the potential of environmental sampling is fully explored. Even if the cemetery is known, the contract often goes to the unit putting in the lowest tender, leading to a similar situation where the potential for research work is tightly constrained by lack of funding.

PUBLICATION

Recent publication has been kind to the study of burial practice not only in the later Anglo-Saxon world, but also in Scotland, Wales and Ireland. The publication of pre-Conquest Christian-period cemeteries at York Minster, St Oswald's Priory in Gloucester, Whithorn (Dumfries and Galloway), and Raunds (Northamptonshire) amongst many others, has indeed marked a coming of age for the study of early medieval cemetery archaeology.[8] It still holds true, however, that synthesis of the evidence for the later period is at an early stage of development, although there are preliminary discussions by Richard Morris and Warwick Rodwell, amongst others, and more latterly those published by Elizabeth O'Brien in 1996 and Christopher Daniell and Victoria Thompson in 1999 which stand as excellent summaries of the period in their own right.[9] The student of Christian-period burial customs is more fortunate now than even five years ago, but the quantity of information currently available is still small and largely undigested in comparison with that from early cemeteries. The later material is only just beginning to be published on a site by site basis, with limited cross-comparisons between aspects of the data from the better known excavations. To a large extent the complexity of urban excavations, where the majority of Anglo-Saxon Christian-period cemeteries have been recorded, has led to a delay in publication, a situation unacceptable to some, but partly a function of under-funding, the (unavoidable) short-sightedness of the 'Rescue' years and the lack of a model for the publication of post-Conversion cemeteries.

[8] D. Phillips and B. Heywood, *Excavations at York Minster Volume 1*, ed. M. O. H. Carver (London, 1995); C. Heighway and R. Bryant, *The Golden Minster: The Anglo-Saxon Minster and Later Medieval priory of St Oswald at Gloucester* (CBA Res. Rep., 117, York, 1999); P. Hill, *Whithorn and St Ninian: The Excavation of a Monastic Town, 1984–91* (Stroud, 1997); A. Boddington, *Raunds Furnells, The Anglo-Saxon Church and Churchyard* (English Heritage Archaeol. Rep. 7, London, 1996).

[9] R. Morris, *Churches in the Landscape* (London, 1989); W. Rodwell, *The Archaeology of the English Church* (London, 1981); E. O'Brien, 'Past rites, future concerns', 160–2 in J. Blair and C. Pyrah (eds), *Church Archaeology: Research Directions for the Future* (CBA Res. Rep., 104, York, 1996); C. Daniell and V. Thompson, 'Pagans and Christians: 400–1150', 65–89 in P. Jupp and C. Gittings (eds.) *Death in England: An illustrated history* (Manchester, 1999).

Unlike the later largely unfurnished cemeteries, early Anglo-Saxon cemeteries have fortunately normally been published in a useful way. Unless the circumstances of excavation meant that the graves were not excavated individually, the norm has been for a site report consisting of a minimum of descriptions of the grave-goods, general discussion of the site and a grave catalogue, listing grave-goods and very often the positioning of the body and skeletal information, where that evidence survived. Even 19th-century excavations sometimes attained these standards, for example those by J. R. Mortimer at Cheesecake Hill and Garton (both East Riding of Yorkshire), which were published with grave-by-grave descriptions and lavishly illustrated plates of the grave-goods.[10]

One problem has, however, been the length of time between excavation and publication. Typical of this are Vera Evison's excavations of Dover Buckland (Kent), conducted in the 1950s, yet not published until 1987.[11] Other sites remain unpublished, often due to the death of the original excavator (Sonia Hawkes's excavations of Finglesham (Kent), being a case in point). It may be that the high standards now expected for site reports of this kind, with full contextual discussions, detailed descriptions and analyses of the grave-goods, mean that publication of some earlier excavations is now practically unattainable. Perhaps a more pragmatic solution is that adopted by Catherine Hills and East Anglian Archaeology, whereby the Spong Hill (Norfolk) excavations were published as a series of quickly produced grave catalogues, with a full synthesis and discussion scheduled to follow. A worry with developer-funded excavations that has recently emerged is, however, that the obligation to publish is being over-ridden by financial issues. While some larger units can afford the staff time to produce high-quality site reports, others seemingly cannot, and the reports are produced as internal documents only.

Despite this, recent developments in excavation and publication are adding to a growing body of information about early Anglo-Saxon cemeteries, although that information remains in rather a scattered form. Summaries of older excavations can be found in Audrey Meaney's invaluable Gazetteer published in 1964,[12] but information about sites excavated in the 1960s and later has to be pieced together from the publications that do exist, various county sites and monuments records (some in a more useful form than others), developers' reports and various collections of information that have been compiled for research purposes, such as MAs and PhDs. A national, computerized database for this type of site, indeed for all early medieval cemeteries, could be an invaluable research tool.

PRESENT: THE CURRENT STATE OF KNOWLEDGE

THE IMPACT OF THEORY

Theoretical developments in archaeology have had an impact on understandings of the early medieval burial rite, albeit in rather limited ways. Some might say that for the early period at least, the general thrust of the majority of work remains broadly

---

[10] J. R. Mortimer, *Forty Years Researches in British and Saxon Burial Mounds of East Yorkshire* (London, 1905).
[11] V. I. Evison, Dover: *The Buckland Anglo-Saxon Cemetery* (London, 1987).
[12] A. L. Meaney, *A Gazetteer of Early Anglo-Saxon Burial Sites* (London, 1964).

SAM LUCY AND ANDREW REYNOLDS

culture-historical, with attempts to refine the definition of Anglian, Saxon and Jutish material, its distribution and changes over time. Concomitantly, material from Wales and other parts of western Britain is often presented in contrast to this largely furnished burial rite as typifying the 'native' or 'sub-Roman' burial rite. Indeed, refining typologies and chronologies remains a central part of early Anglo-Saxon studies, despite some worries about the usefulness of this effort. While knowing the date of manufacture of an artefact is always of interest, the vagaries of archaeological deposition and preservation mean that manufacture and deposition can often be far distant in time. An early 6th-century brooch can be passed through the generations and deposited in a late 6th-century context, for example. Of how much value is it to know that the brooch was manufactured in the 510s, as opposed to the 530s? Such a brooch would display few traces of how it had been used in the intervening period — archaeological evidence would only exist as to how it was last used — in the late 6th-century burial rite.

So-called 'processual' methodologies had little impact on the interpretation of early medieval cemeteries, despite their strong influence on excavation techniques and methodology. Although Christopher Arnold tried to correlate burial wealth with the varying political power of different kingdoms,[13] in general little attention was paid. Post-processual approaches, with their focus on symbolism and structure had a greater influence, for the burial rite itself seems more amenable to such interpretations. Pader demonstrated strong gender- and age-structuring of the burial rite at three early Anglo-Saxon East Anglian inhumation cemeteries,[14] while Richards demonstrated similar correlations with the form and decoration of cremation urns.[15] Härke's extended study of the inhumation weapon burial rite has highlighted its highly symbolic nature,[16] and Stoodley has come to similar conclusions regarding burial with a jewellery assemblage.[17]

The outcome of these and similar studies is that it is no longer enough to study aspects of burial rites, or artefact types in isolation. It is the selection of particular rites and artefacts, and their combination at any one point in time that gives any specific burial its meaning.

THE IMPACT OF SCIENCE

New sorts of information have also been feeding into the interpretative process. While scientific dating has not yet had the same dramatic impact on the chronological frameworks of this period as it has had, for example on prehistory, there are potentials

---

[13] C. J. Arnold, 'Stress as a stimulus to socio-economic change: England in the seventh century', 124–31 in C. Renfrew and S. Shennan (eds.) *Ranking, Resource and Exchange* (Cambridge, 1982).

[14] E.-J. Pader, *Symbolism, Social Relations and the Interpretation of Mortuary Remains* (BAR Brit. Ser., 130, Oxford, 1982).

[15] J. D. Richards, *The Significance of Form and Decoration of Anglo-Saxon Cremation Urns* (BAR Brit. Ser., 166, Oxford, 1987).

[16] H. Härke, ' "Warrior graves"? The background of the Anglo-Saxon weapon burial rite', *Past and Present* 126 (1990), 144–8; ibid., 'Changing symbols in a changing society: the Anglo-Saxon weapon burial rite in the seventh century', 149–65 in M. O. H. Carver (ed.) *The Age of Sutton Hoo* (Woodbridge, 1992); ibid., *Angelsächsische Waffengräber der 5. bis 7. Jahrhunderts* (Cologne and Bonn, 1992).

[17] N. Stoodley, *The Spindle and the Spear: a critical enquiry into the construction and meaning of gender in the early Anglo-Saxon burial rite* (BAR Brit. Ser., 288, Oxford, 1999).

that are starting to emerge. Radiocarbon dating has proved extremely useful for those western British sites that are largely unfurnished, and thus hard to date by traditional means. The development of high-resolution radiocarbon dating offers the potential of very accurate dating of the early 5th century and the whole of the 7th century, when the calibration curves are steep enough to allow it. While no burial has yet been shown to date to the early 5th century using this technology, Scull's case study of the Buttermarket cemetery in Ipswich (Suffolk) shows its potential for challenging object-based chronologies and, at long last, offering an independent check for them.[18]

Better understandings of the vagaries of organic preservation also mean that archaeologists can be more critical when presented with partial evidence. Awareness of the impact of different soil-types and drainage on the preservation of human and animal skeletal material, for example, can account for differential preservation on the same site, and even mysterious 'empty graves', with grave-goods but no body. In such cases, phosphate analysis can indicate the former presence of human or animal remains, even where these have been completely dissolved by acidic soils. This is especially important in areas such as Wales, Cornwall and the sands of Suffolk, where bone rarely survives, leading to vast under-representations in the burial record. Knowing that the archaeological evidence for burial is likely to consist only of faint grave-cuts greatly increases the chances of finding such evidence. More recently, chemical analyses of human bone have started to reveal the trace-elements which remain after burial: elements which can start to indicate where those people originated from, possibly a more definite way of studying processes such as population movement and migration.[19]

More sophisticated appreciation of skeletal evidence can also add to detailed knowledge of burial practices. While work on inhumed bone has continued at a steady rate since the mid-20th century, albeit in a far more critical manner these days, it is really in the study of cremated material that major advances have been seen. While just decades ago, cremated bone was generally thought to be uninformative (to the extent that it was often discarded), work by such specialists as Jacqueline McKinley has transformed the way this material is viewed. It is now recognized that cremated bone, while greatly affected by heat, distorts in predictable ways, and that sex, age, trauma and indications of illness can be discerned surprisingly often, as McKinley has shown in her work on the Spong Hill cremations.[20] Similarly, Julie Bond's work on cremated animal bone from similar cremation cemeteries has pointed to the sheer wealth, in animal form, which was often associated with this burial ritual in the 5th and 6th centuries.[21]

Finally, the success of ancient DNA extraction offers an entirely new source of evidence for students of early medieval cemeteries. While destructive (usually a whole tooth needs to be crushed in order to extract the DNA) and rather expensive, the

---

[18] C. Scull and A. Bayliss, 'Radiocarbon dating and Anglo-Saxon graves', 39–50 in U. von Freeden, U. Kock and A. Wieczorek (eds.) *Wölker an Nord- und Ostsee und die Franken* (Bonn, 1999).
[19] J. Montgomery, P. Budd and J. Evans, 'Reconstructing lifetime movements of ancient people: a Neolithic case study from southern England', *European J. Archaeol.*, 3 (2000), 407–22.
[20] J. McKinley, *The Anglo-Saxon Cemetery at Spong Hill, North Elmham. Part VIII: The Cremations* (East Anglian Archaeol., 69, Gressenhall, 1994).
[21] J. Bond, 'Burnt offerings: animal bones in Anglo-Saxon cremations', *World Archaeol.*, 28 (1996), 76–88.

possibility of assigning biological sex to immature or ambiguous remains, or identifying familial relationships within cemeteries, opens up a whole new series of research questions and possibilities. Christine Flaherty's suggestion of a female buried with a spear, and males buried with annular brooches, at West Heslerton (North Yorkshire), is an example of the radical challenges to our perceived notions of gender-linked grave furnishing which extended use of this technique might bring.[22]

THE EARLY ANGLO-SAXON PERIOD: INVENTING A NEW BURIAL TRADITION

From the middle of the 5th century, burial practices in eastern England mark a disjuncture in many respects with what came before. In the re-adoption around this time of both cremation, and often lavishly-furnished inhumation (when compared with the relative austerity of 4th-century burial in Roman Britain), an ideological realignment can be seen. Different areas of the country can be seen to adopt varying facets of a broadly north European/Scandinavian burial practice. The burial of cremations inside decorated hand-made pottery urns reflects the dominant practice in north-eastern Germany; the use of cruciform and square-headed brooches suggests links with southern Scandinavia, while Kent shows heavy borrowing from more southerly 'Frankish' burial customs, with the use of wheel-thrown vessels and distinctive brooch- and weapon-types. What is slowly being accepted (and indeed was recognized long ago by the likes of Leeds and Myres) is that the situation in eastern Britain is a complicated one. While Bede painted a clear-cut picture of a Britain divided neatly into territories whose populations could trace their origins back to these distinct continental districts, modern archaeology now shows that this was a vast over-simplification. Bede's 8th-century view more accurately reflected the political situation of his own day than that represented by the 5th and 6th-century burial archaeology.

The present distributions of distinctive artefacts such as cruciform brooches and saucer brooches, while showing concentrations in the 'traditional' Anglian and Saxon areas, also show a blurring over a much wider area. There are no strong demarcations between the distributions of different brooch-types, and only a few artefacts (such as sleeve-clasps) show a tightly bounded area at all. It is becoming increasingly difficult, in the face of a rapidly-expanding information base, to continue to think about the 5th and 6th centuries in eastern Britain as consisting of highly-distinctive ethnic communities, in the way that Bede would have had us believe. Indeed, the idea that the artefact-types themselves are significant in ethnic terms is one that is increasingly challenged. Few now would accept the proposition that the wearing of Germanic brooches was exclusively confined to people of Germanic origin: it is now recognized that material culture is used more actively and imaginatively than this. In recent years the potential of grave-goods, when viewed in combination with the skeletal and other archaeological evidence, for shedding light on the social, rather than political-historical aspects of past societies, has been highlighted.[23]

[22] C. Flaherty, 'The use of DNA analysis of human skeletal remains in early Anglo-Saxon England to examine sex and kinship', paper presented at the 64th Annual Meeting of the Society for American Archaeology, 26 March, 1999 (Chicago).
[23] Stoodley, op. cit. in note 17; S. Lucy, *The Early Anglo-Saxon Cemeteries of East Yorkshire: An Analysis and Re-interpretation* (BAR Brit. Ser., 282, Oxford, 1998).

The past twenty years have also discovered a variety of ways of elaborating individual burials. From the ring-ditches surrounding inhumations at Spong Hill, to the 'cremation houses' found by Alec Down and Martin Welch at Apple Down (West Sussex), there seem to have been a variety of ways in which specific graves could be distinguished.[24] Burial position and orientation could also be used. More analysis is needed, looking at all aspects of the burial rite, in order to judge possible reasons why those individuals were distinguished and not others.

As well as looking at individual burials, cemetery composition and location are now receiving more attention. The distribution of cremation and inhumation burials within a mixed-rite cemetery is often of interest. At Spong Hill, for example, the inhumations were confined to the north-eastern corner of the site, largely within an enclosure, while the far more numerous cremations spread to the south and west. At Castledyke, Barton-on-Humber (North Lincolnshire), the single cremation from the site was deposited in a ditch that demarcated the edge of the otherwise inhumation cemetery.[25] The choice of cremation over inhumation is still a poorly-understood one, but it seems to have socially-symbolic overtones.

The placing of the cemetery in the landscape also seems to have been determined by a number of factors. An important one was the pre-existence of other features. The high percentage of these cemeteries which re-use existing prehistoric or Roman sites or monuments is forcing a re-evaluation of the significance of cemetery location.[26] Similarly geographical features such as height and visibility seem to have played a role, at least in the East Riding of Yorkshire.[27] One issue that has, as yet, received little attention is the longevity of many of these early cemeteries, several of which are now known to remain in use from the 5th until at least the 7th century. The reasons for the foundation and eventual abandonment of these sites deserve exploration.

WALES AND THE WEST, 5TH TO 7TH CENTURIES

The contextualized study of early medieval burial practice in Wales and western Britain has only really begun within the last two decades. As more of these largely unfurnished sites are excavated, and are scientifically dated to the 'sub-Roman' period, the sheer variety of burial practices in these areas is being revealed. Within the large 'community' cemeteries, such as Poundbury (Dorset),[28] distinctive features such as the longevity of use (the last phase of burial lasting from the 4th to possibly the 6th century), the age-related use of cist-burial, and the clustering of graves around other 'special' burials have highlighted the complexity involved in supposedly uniform Christian cemeteries. More recently, the problems of distinguishing unfurnished non-Christian from unfurnished Christian burial practices have been noted. Many early

[24] C. Hills, K. Penn and R. Rickett, *The Anglo-Saxon Cemetery at Spong Hill, North Elmham. Part III: Catalogue of Inhumations* (East Anglian Archaeol., 21, Gressenhall, 1984); A. Down and M. Welch, *Chichester Excavations VII: Apple Down and the Mardens* (Chichester, 1990).

[25] G. Drinkall and M. Foreman, *The Anglo-Saxon Cemetery at Castledyke South, Barton-on-Humber* (Sheffield, 1998).

[26] H. Williams, 'Ancient landscapes and the dead: the reuse of prehistoric and Roman monuments as early Anglo-Saxon burial sites', *Medieval Archaeol.*, 41 (1997), 1–32.

[27] Lucy op. cit. in note 23.

[28] D. E. Farwell and T. I. Molleson, *Poundbury. Volume 2: The Cemeteries* (Dorset Archaeol. Nat. Hist. Soc. Mon. 11, Dorchester, 1993).

cemeteries in Wales, for example, have roots in the prehistoric past, with either continuity or re-use of former sites and monuments. While these sites may end up 'Christianized', their status in this early period is unclear.[29] As well as questions of conversion and religious practice, therefore, are also issues concerning the landscape contexts of these sites, their development over time and the micro-structures which they exhibit internally.

CONTINUITY AND CHANGE: THE 7TH–11TH CENTURIES

In the past, scholars working on English material assumed a very straightforward process to have occurred with the conversion to Christianity. Far more attention was paid to understanding patterns in the material culture of 7th-century inhumation cemeteries than to attempting to address the issue of what followed. Ultimately, the search for an explanation for the virtual disappearance of objects with human burials during the course of the late 7th and early 8th centuries sought a clear chronological horizon, one provided by Bede's *Ecclesiastical History*. Bede's chronology for the conversion of the English is clear and unequivocal, although a pattern of reversion to paganism was common following the succession of an initial convert king.

A purely archaeological approach to Christian period burial in England in particular, was developed in earnest at Winchester, under Martin Biddle, although the complexities of the Winchester excavations has meant a long gestation period for the final publication which is expected soon. Academic syntheses have remained few and largely confined to brief discussions of comparanda in the context of individual cemetery reports. Examples of the latter include Castle Green, Hereford (Herefordshire).[30] This situation remained largely the case until the Final Phase issue was tackled again in the context of the work of Richard Morris, Andy Boddington and Helen Geake.[31]

England in the 7th to 9th centuries — continuity and change

Anglo-Saxon high-status barrow burial   The emergence of a well-defined class of high-status barrow burials throughout the 7th century and perhaps into the first quarter of the 8th century marks a radical change in the way that the identity, or rather memory, of a wealthy elite became expressed in their mortuary remains. For the first time a concept of geographical 'otherness' is brought into play, seemingly as part of a broader package of reactions to the development of an increasingly ranked society and the growth of the extent of territory controlled by individual kings. Territorial expansion, initially from the scale of small social groups inhabiting the so-called 'micro-kingdoms' described by Stephen Bassett,[32] arguably provided the catalyst for the development of

---

[29] N. Edwards and A. Lane, 'The archaeology of the early church in Wales: an introduction', 1–11 in N. Edwards and A. Lane (eds.) *The Early Church in Wales and the West* (Oxbow Mon. 16, Oxford, 1992); H. James, 'Early Medieval cemeteries in Wales', 90–103 in ibid.

[30] R. Shoesmith, *Excavations at Castle Green, Hereford* (CBA Res. Rep., 36, London, 1980).

[31] Morris, op. cit. in note 9; A. Boddington, 'Models of burial, settlement and worship: The Final Phase reviewed', 177–99 in E. Southworth (ed.), *Anglo-Saxon Cemeteries: A Reappraisal* (Stroud, 1990); H. Geake, *The Use of Grave-Goods in Conversion-Period England, c. 600–c. 850* (BAR Brit. Ser., 261, Oxford, 1997).

[32] S. Bassett, 'In search of the origins of Anglo-Saxon kingdoms', 3–27 in S. Bassett (ed.), *The Origins of Anglo-Saxon Kingdoms* (Leicester, 1989).

the complex social systems necessary to consolidate initial military conquests. The increasing distance in ideological terms between ruler and subject is manifested to begin with in the isolated high-status barrow burials. Sutton Hoo, with its impressive array of high-status burial rites presumably bears witness to the concept of dynasty and this aspect of perceived permanence of kingship is further revealed in the investment of wealth in grand residential and ritual settlements.

The minster cemeteries and lesser burial grounds Documentary sources for the nature of burial between the 7th and 9th centuries are so rare that archaeological evidence is the prime source for our understanding of the period between the Conversion and the advent of parish churches, at least with regard to the burial loci of the mass of Middle Anglo-Saxon populations (from the later 7th to 9th centuries). The locations of many early minsters is known from documentary sources, but where their cemeteries have been excavated there is a tendency for later burials to dominate the record and for higher status burials to be found in apparently disproportionate numbers at certain sites — if the minster cemeteries were intended to accommodate all. What seems more likely during this period is that the minster cemetery provided for the burial of a proportion of the inhabitants of their *parochiae*, but that many, if not most, were buried in rural cemeteries, perhaps unenclosed, but possibly quite substantial if the example at Chimney in the minster *parochia* of Bampton (Oxfordshire), is anything to judge by.[33]

Hamwic (Southampton) presents a rather different model for cemetery development. There, St Mary's minster is presumed to date from the foundation of the trading settlement at the end of the 7th century. At present, however, ten separate burial sites have been recorded within the limits of the Middle Anglo-Saxon settlement (Fig. 1),[34] which indicates that even within the confines of a dense settlement a similar dynamic may have existed between minster and dependent cemeteries as was seemingly the case in the countryside. One major difference, though, is the manner in which many of the Hamwic burial plots were rapidly encroached upon by the expansion of the settlement rather than remaining in use to a later period in the manner of the rural cemeteries. The short life of the Hamwic burial plots indicates a period of rapidly changing geography for the inhabitants of the town and forms a distinct break with earlier burial traditions centred upon long-lived community cemeteries. Perhaps the earlier Hamwic cemeteries represent a period of uncertainty, with newly arrived families founding burial plots of a similar type to those found in the countryside, but this time in a proto-urban context. The rapid demise of these burial plots may indeed chart the success of St Mary's in obtaining a burial monopoly of the kind Martin Biddle has suggested for the Old Minster at Winchester.[35] A similar pattern of 7th-century burials overlain by 'proto-urban sprawl' is to be found at Ipswich, where the

---

[33] S. Crawford, 'The Anglo-Saxon cemetery at Chimney, Oxfordshire', *Oxoniensia*, 54 (1989), 45–56.
[34] A. Morton, 'Burial in middle Saxon Southampton', 68–77, in Bassett op. cit. in note 6, esp. fig. 6.1; P. Andrews, *Excavations at Hamwic: Volume 2* (CBA Res. Rep., 109, York, 1997), 203 and 252. A tenth, apparently high-status, cemetery has recently been found within the confines of Hamwic, but no details are yet available.
[35] M. Biddle, 'The archaeology of the church: a widening horizon', 65–71 in P. Addyman and R. Morris (eds.), *The Archaeological Study of Churches* (CBA Res. Rep., 13, London, 1976), at p. 69.

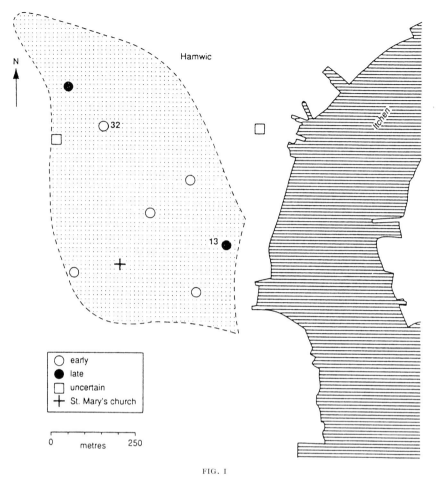

FIG. I

Burial sites in Hamwic (after Morton op. cit. in note 34, fig. 6.1).

chronology of the Buttermarket cemetery has been tightly defined and where the settlement appears to develop more rapidly in the early 8th century than previously considered.[36] It can be argued here, as an alternative to the burial monopoly model, that socio-economic factors exerted a stronger force than either the sanctity of a burial plot or the influence of a local minster and that, if anything the minsters benefited from urban development rather than dictating burial regimes.

The countryside appears less affected by changes if at least some of the unfurnished or poorly furnished burials from conversion period cemeteries are accepted as evidence of continuity from the pre-Christian to the Christian period. Given the similarities between certain conversion period burials and those found in demonstrably later field cemeteries only an intensive programme of radiocarbon

[36] Scull and Bayliss op. cit. in note 18, 48.

dating of such burial remains will advance our understanding of the full sequence of events.

A further area of interest in this discussion is the relationship between high-status barrow burials and early minster churches. Whether the barrow burials themselves represent pagans or Christians is an open-ended question, but a current topic of debate nevertheless. Apart from Taplow (Buckinghamshire), where parch-marks show clearly the outline of a possible early church,[37] high-status barrow burials are not normally associated with churches. Again this aspect might be seen as representing a sector of society in a transitional period, an existing burial rite (barrow burial) used for the last time in a climate of steady conversion to Christianity.

The isolation of high-status barrow burials in 7th-century England occurs up to and during the early development of both Hamwic and Ipswich. The emergence of kings and the founding of ports of trade seem to have ended an ancient burial tradition for important families and for proto-urban dwellers. The inhabitants of Hamwic, for example, can only previously have known fields and open landscape. The confines of a plot in places such as Hamwic, where rubbish was disposed of close to wells and latrine pits, followed by the loss of a family or small community burial plot, perhaps a generation later, further limited the continuity of earlier traditions.

This part of the discussion has ended by considering elements of differences at the beginning and end of the 7th century. Ultimately it seems that if the Final Phase was played out anywhere, it was in the form of elite barrow burials and in proto-urban burial plots. The degree to which the conversion itself affected burial patterns is an ongoing debate but one that has seen the role of religious conversion played down in terms of influence on burial rite. At the present time it seems best to accept Christianity as one of the many factors involved in the development of the society and landscape observed by the time of the Domesday Survey.

England in the 9th to 11th centuries — towards a geography of burial

The development of landscape archaeology over the last 25 years in particular has seen a movement away from artefact-based studies to an exploration of the relationships between different burial sites in a topographical context. In the Middle and Late Anglo-Saxon periods documentary sources shed light for the first time on territorial frameworks and this aspect introduces a third dimension into the research agenda. Rarely are early Anglo-Saxon cemeteries themselves ranked in terms of social importance, apart from the so-called 'princely' burials, and it is widely accepted that early Anglo-Saxon cemeteries reflect the totality of the social scale for their respective settlements, whether excavated or presumed. Equipped with knowledge of territorial patterns as well as excavated evidence, it is possible to develop an understanding of the texture of the later landscape in a way that is simply not possible for earlier periods. The sources are far better in terms of quality and quantity from the 10th century and it is from this period that a clear model for the geography of burial can be mapped out, with the additional aid of charter bounds.

[37] D. Stocker and D. Went, 'The evidence for a pre-Viking church adjacent to the Anglo-Saxon barrow at Taplow, Buckinghamshire', *Archaeol. J.*, 152 (1995), 441–54.

Excavations have revealed a complex micro-geography in the context of churches and churchyards, with the church itself forming a focus for high-status burials, with decorated stone covers, which surely represent the burials of those of thegnly rank, at least in a rural context as at Wharram (East Riding of Yorkshire) and Raunds (Figs 2 and 3).[38] The urban minster cemeteries seem to have contained a wider variety of high-status burial rites, such as at York Minster and Winchester Old Minster, although virtually all excavations at such major churches have been partial and in immediate proximity to the church in question. Ultimately there is no means other than full excavation of establishing the complete demographic profile of these sites. The extraordinary range of burial-types encountered in the high-status cemeteries are individually well known, but the sites are not yet all fully published. Charcoal burials, corpses with various arrangements of stones about the body, burials within sarcophagi or with grave-covers, or within wooden coffins or chests, are some of the more remarkable burial types, but the evidence requires a full analysis before firmer conclusions can be drawn: charcoal burials, for example, are also known from lesser churches, such as at St Mary's Church, Little Oakley (Essex).[39]

The cathedral cemetery at North Elmham (Norfolk), provides a contrast to the other excavated minster cemeteries owing to the simple uniformity of burial rite practised there, but also in terms of the comparatively large area excavated (Fig. 4).[40] A total of 196 burials in 186 graves was found with parts of at least ten other individuals whose graves had probably been disturbed. Burials were made in increasing density closer to the church with much intercutting of graves. Towards the cemetery boundary the graves are more dispersed with open spaces on the western side of the enclosure. This aspect indicates a geographical patterning of burial location, presumably according to status, where social scale can be charted by proximity to the church.

There are two notable exceptions to the mass of burials, however, which lead us to consider the development of burial geography outside the confines of consecrated space. The first (Burial 171), appropriately, lies buried on the line of the cemetery boundary itself, neither within nor without the cemetery. The stratigraphy was unhelpful in establishing the relationship between the filling of the boundary ditch and the burial, but this might suggest that the two were perhaps contemporary. What Burial 171 indicates is that a concept of exclusion was in place and that it was expressed in relation to physical boundaries with additional ideological significance. Of further interest, the individual concerned was an adult male, but he had been either murdered or executed, to judge by the fact that he had suffered multiple cuts to the head and neck. Whether a judicial execution victim or a murder victim, and the latter seems more likely given the existence of specific execution cemeteries at this time, the burial place of the victim clearly bears out the use of space as a means of expressing status. The existence of execution cemeteries at this period further reduces the likelihood of a

---

[38] R. D. Bell and M. W. Beresford, *Wharram Percy: The Church of St Martin*. Wharram a Study of Settlement on the Yorkshire Wolds. Volume 3. (Soc. Medieval Archaeol. Mon., 11, London, 1987), 58–9, fig. 11 and pl. VI A; A. Boddington, op. cit. in note 8, fig. 11, 106–9.
[39] M. Corbishley, 'Excavations at St Mary's Church, Little Oakley, Essex 1977', 15–27 in *Four Church Excavations in Essex* (Essex County Council Occasional Paper 4, Chelmsford, 1984) at p. 21 and fig. 14.
[40] P. Wade-Martins, *Excavations in North Elmham Park 1967–72* (East Anglian Archaeol., 9, Gressenhall, 1980), 185–91.

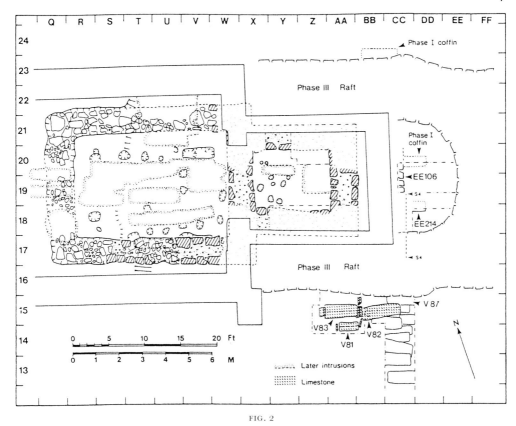

FIG. 2

St Martin's Church, Wharram Percy, North Yorkshire, showing the location of Late Anglo-Saxon burials with stone covers (after Bell and Beresford op. cit. in note 38, fig. 11).

judicial interpretation for Burial 171, and the man's liminal location might suggest that the circumstances of his death were either peculiar or unknown. The second burial (10) lies just outside the cemetery boundary. This individual presents an equally interesting case in that the adult male interred within the grave had a chronically distorted left knee, with a thickened femur and tibia. The orientation of the corpse was reversed, in contrast to 'normal' Christian burials, with the head to the east. There has been no comprehensive study of physically differently able individuals in early medieval cemeteries to examine social attitudes. Evidence from Raunds in the form of the burial of a tuberculosis/poliomyletis victim (Burial 5218), however, shows that people with different physical abilities could also be buried within the confines of the cemetery —in this case close to the north boundary of the churchyard.[41] It seems that local responses determined the nature of burial in such cases rather than a more widespread model.

Raunds is also notable for its so-called eavesdrip child burials, a phenomenon recognized at a growing number of sites such as Cherry Hinton (Cambridgeshire) and

[41] Boddington, op. cit. in note 8, fig. 25 and 41–2.

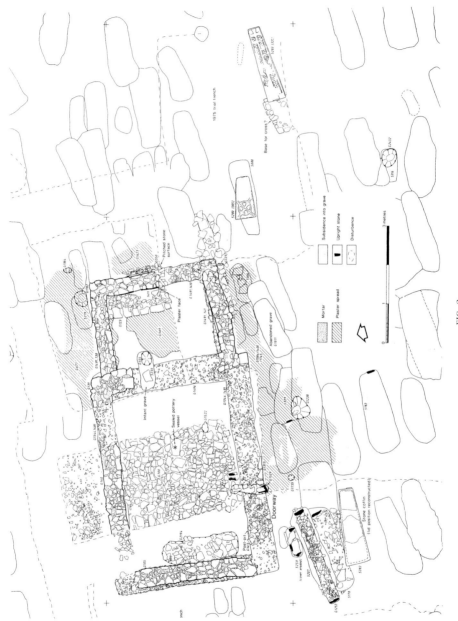

FIG. 3

The Late Anglo-Saxon church at Raunds Furnells (Northamptonshire), showing the location of burials with stone coffins and covers (after Boddington op. cit. in note 8, fig. 10).

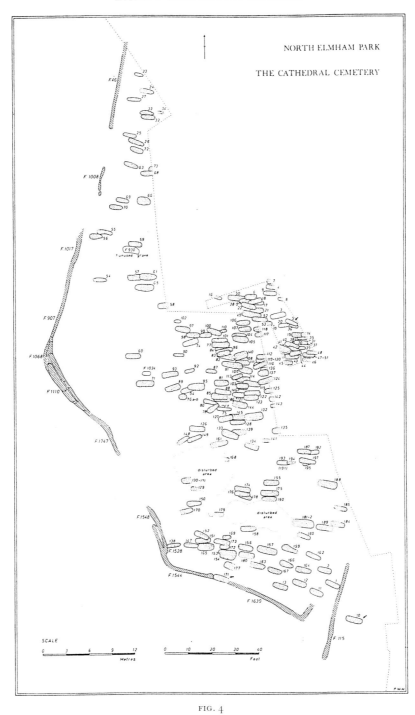

FIG. 4

The Late Anglo-Saxon Cathedral cemetery at North Elmham illustrating burial geography—
particularly burials 171 and 10 at the southern end of the cemetery (after Wade-Martins
op. cit. in note 40, fig. 158).

Compton Bassett (Wiltshire).[42] This rite is a further variation in the Late Anglo-Saxon burial repertoire and emphasizes once again the use of space in relation to the church as an expression of status. Now that gender archaeology is established, the time for wide ranging cemetery analysis, where populations are examined in all manner of contexts, has arrived.

Estate fragmentation and the growth of rural manors: the development of parish churches and churchyards   The concept of estate fragmentation, where large Middle Anglo-Saxon 'multiple estates' were granted away principally by charter from the late 9th century is now a broadly accepted model for the development of the English landscape into its medieval form.[43] Where parish churches fit into the scheme has become increasingly clear over the last decade or so largely owing to the efforts of John Blair, who is to publish a full account of the process in his forthcoming study of the Anglo-Saxon church.[44] Whichever model of landscape development one chooses to follow for the origins of the medieval landscape, it remains that parish churches are closely associated with manorial sites and that, where sites have been sufficiently excavated, churches belong to a secondary phase of manorial development. The rise of the thegnly classes can be charted using the archaeological evidence for their residences, which feature in the archaeological record from the later 9th century onward. Based upon archaeological evidence, three basic lines of development can be traced for rural cemeteries and churchyards (with examples):

Archaic — a cemetery which accompanies a rural settlement. The lifespans of individual cemeteries may vary considerably, with some in use during the pagan period, some transitional and some later in origin. Archaic-type cemeteries of the Christian period are without churches and can remain in use perhaps as late as c. 1200 and the latest phase of parish church origins. Examples of such sites include Mawgan Porth (Cornwall), Bramford (Suffolk) and Shepperton Green (Greater London).[45]

Adaptive — these cemeteries are identical to those of archaic type prior to the building of chapels or churches in the 10th century. Examples of church structures erected upon existing cemeteries can be observed at Barton-on-Humber (North Lincolnshire) and Capel Maelog (Powys).[46] A 10th-century or earlier origin is apparent for this type of cemetery, which continues in use on into the medieval period. Sites in

[42] Ibid, 55–7, fig. 68, p. 69; J. Bradley and M. Gaimster, 'Medieval Britain and Ireland, 1999', *Medieval Archaeol.*, 44 (2000), 235–354, at 252; A. Reynolds and S. Roffey, 'Excavation and structural recording at St Swithin's Church, Compton Bassett, Wiltshire, 1999', in preparation.

[43] D. Hooke, *The Landscape of Anglo-Saxon England* (Leicester, 1998), 46–54; A. Reynolds, *Later Anglo-Saxon England: Life and Landscape* (Stroud, 1999), 65–110.

[44] J. Blair, *The Church in Anglo-Saxon Society* (Oxford, forthcoming).

[45] R. Bruce-Mitford, *Mawgan Porth. A Settlement of the late Saxon period on the north Cornish coast. Excavations 1949–52, 1954, and 1974* (English Heritage Archaeol. Rep., 13, London, 1997). For Bramford, see B. Nenk, S. Margeson and M. Hurley, 'Medieval Britain and Ireland, 1995', *Medieval Archaeol.*, 40 (1996), 234–318, at 285; R. Canham, 'Excavations at Shepperton Green, 1967 and 1973', *Trans. London Middlesex Archaeol. Soc.*, 30 (1979), 97–124.

[46] W. Rodwell and K. Rodwell, 'St Peter's Church, Barton-on-Humber, excavation and structural study, 1978–81', *Antiq. J.*, 62 (1982), 283–315; W. Britnell, 'Capel Maelog, Llandrindod Wells, Powys: Excavations 1984–87', *Medieval Archaeol.*, 34 (1990), 27–96.

this category are less clearly defined in chronological terms than Archaic- or Pioneer-type cemeteries.

Pioneer — these cemeteries are newly founded as secondary developments of thegnly-type residences during the 10th century. In certain cases a period of time is observed between the foundation of the manorial complex, the building of a chapel and, finally, the earliest burials. This process is best seen as reflecting a period prior to the acquisition of burial rights and when estate churches were being built within the context of long established places of burial. Examples include Raunds, Portchester Castle (Hampshire) and Trowbridge (Wiltshire).[47]

Archaic-type Christian burial grounds simply follow long established patterns of small burial plots either within or adjacent to settlements. Adaptive-type burial grounds presumably illustrate a process whereby a local lord has appropriated an Archaic-type cemetery for the construction of an estate church. Pioneer churches are those built as wholly new ventures whose parishioners would be required to break with earlier burial traditions once burial rights had been obtained by the new church.

Execution cemeteries and the socially excluded   The redefinition of burial geography that occurred from the late 9th through to the 12th century was framed within an administrative structure that finds its origins in the period of Alfred. Burial rite and location had become clearly formulated during the 10th century for the mass of the population but a new class of cemetery came into being which was designed purely to receive the corpses of those who had, for various reasons, forfeited the right to burial in consecrated ground.[48] Amongst the latter group are those executed for committing a range of capital crimes as well as certain individuals whose misdeeds precluded them from churchyard burial even though they might have died in otherwise normal circumstances. The burial of social outcasts in specific cemeteries can be followed in the archaeological record in the form of groups of burials displaying traces of trauma. Typically such a burial ground contains about 30 to 40 individuals with a few females amongst them. A proportion of decapitations is common as are hands tied behind the back or to the front and indicative of hanging. The graves are normally shallow, although they may be deeper in the case of prone or decapitated corpses, and the cemeteries are nearly always sited upon barrows or linear earthworks which coincide with the boundaries of hundreds or, in a number of cases, counties. A classic site is that at Stockbridge Down (Hampshire).[49]

An early phase of the separation of a suspicious or perhaps judicially tried individual from the 'normal' place of burial can be seen in the context of several Middle Anglo-Saxon settlements (see Reynolds this vol.). There is also, albeit limited, support from 8th- and 9th-century charter bounds to suggest the existence of at least a

---

[47] For Raunds, see Boddington op. cit. in note 8. B. Cunliffe, *Excavations at Portchester Castle 2: Saxon* (Soc. of Antiq. Res. Rep., 33, London, 1976); A. Graham and S. Davies, *Excavations in Trowbridge, Wiltshire, 1977 and 1986–88* (Wessex Archaeology Rep., 2, Salisbury, 1993).

[48] A. Reynolds, *Anglo-Saxon Law in the Landscape*, (unpublished PhD thesis, University of London, 1998); ibid. this vol.

[49] N. Hill, 'Excavations on Stockbridge Down 1935–36', *Proc. Hampshire Field Club Archaeol. Soc.*, 13 (1937), 247–59.

few clearly marked deviant burial grounds. The regularized pattern of execution sites and deviant burial grounds, which can be observed in both the archaeological and documentary material from the 10th century, clearly finds a local context in the reorganization of landscape that accompanied the origins and growth of the manor from the late 9th century. The Grand Plan, however, would appear to have been one of royal design, a product of the increasingly efficient machinery of Late Anglo-Saxon governance.

FUTURE: THE WAY FORWARD

Rather then viewing the Conversion to Christianity as a defining episode in the development of burial customs, it can be argued that the Conversion period sits awkwardly astride a complex period of change, marked earlier and later in the period by equally complex developments. With the newly increased quantity and range of published material relating to early medieval Christian cemeteries the future for their understanding can only be bright. There is now sufficient material available for a series of detailed studies of funerary practice in early medieval burial archaeology, ideally at least some of these will examine themes and issues over an extended time-frame without reference to traditional period divisions of the material.

For the early Anglo-Saxon period, dating frameworks are now quite well-defined (although high-resolution radiocarbon dating offers the potential to answer some interesting 5th- and 7th-century questions). Within these earlier sites, the interesting questions which are now emerging are those connected with social identities, rather than political processes. To what extent are burial rites localized? How are people of different ages, genders and social status treated within the broad outline of the 'Anglo-Saxon' burial rite? Can any of the people buried within these sites be shown to have come from overseas (something which trace element analysis may soon start to shed light on), or is it our conceptions of ethnicity and cultural antecedents which need re-examination?

Archaeology offers the possibility of challenging entrenched historical frameworks. Perhaps the most stimulating aspect of the recent work on early medieval cemeteries is that they are shedding light on aspects of past social lives which were never recorded in historical documents: the treatment of the dead by the living; the complexity of the burial rite, and the way that it illuminates what must have been highly complex social relations. Although burial rites are not, and cannot be, a direct mirror of life in this period, they do offer much information, when interpreted with a critical eye. One thing that we would argue here, is that it is pointless to think of the past in terms of bounded groups which probably never existed. One aspect that we would argue here, is that it is questionable to think of the past in terms of bounded groups which perhaps never existed.

The chronological aspects of the scheme of developments in burial location and burial rite in the Christian period require further support from scientific dating techniques and selected research excavation in order to clarify issues of chronology. The dating of churchyard boundaries and of unaccompanied burials in 7th century and later unfurnished cemeteries is of particular concern. We also need to start looking in earnest at the landscape contexts of burial from the 5th to 11th centuries. While a good beginning has been made in this respect, there is still much work to be done.

Burial archaeology of the Christian period at least, requires analysis in relation to known territorial frameworks in order to approach the settlement-cemetery dynamic in greater depth and to examine notions of liminality and land demarcation.

Finally, Christian-period cemeteries are in need of a model for publication, but this is difficult without a uniform approach to cemetery excavation with all of its attendant difficulties. Even though the nature of the evidence as excavated and recorded may differ between sites, publication in a similar catalogue format to early cemeteries is highly desirable. Otherwise the researcher can be left with the task of piecing back together the grave and its contents from specialist reports and illustrations spread across several sections of a report.

As a closing comment, we hope that the discussion presented above has provided a first attempt at a long-term overview and that colleagues continuing to work on the burial archaeology of early medieval England and Wales will approach, refine and revise at least some, if not all, of the issues that we have considered.

Cemeteries and Boundaries in Western Britain

By DAVID PETTS

The archaeology of early medieval Wales and other parts of the west of Britain and Ireland is frequently synonymous with the archaeology of early Christianity, to such an extent that 'Early Christian' is frequently used as a descriptive epithet for western Britain and Ireland in the period stretching from end of Roman rule in the area to the onset of the ravages of the Vikings.[1] Whilst it is arguable whether a period should be labelled on the basis of the dominant religion, it is undoubtedly the case that the growth of Christianity was an important phenomenon in this period.[2]

The material expression of this new religious practice is seen in the Christian inscriptions carved on gravestones[3] and the growth of churches, monasteries and other ecclesiastical sites.[4] However, these aspects of worship are sometimes presented as if they are part of a coherent package of religious practices, introduced into the area by missionary saints, and undergoing relatively little development until the 8th century. One of the most important aspects of this 'package' of attributes is the enclosed cemetery. The concept was first outlined by Charles Thomas in his seminal work *The Early Christian Archaeology of North Britain.* It is worth quoting his description of what such a site entails:

> But alongside these sprawling open cemeteries there are others which are enclosed, by a rude stone wall, by a low bank with an external quarry-ditch, even (as with monasteries) by some pre-existing earthwork: and these enclosed burial-grounds are invariably oval or circular in plan.

> There is growing evidence that these cemeteries, *in particular the enclosed ones* [my emphasis], antedate any other form of Christian structure in the countryside of post-Roman Britain, and can thus be viewed as the primary field-monuments of insular Christianity.[5]

Thomas is certainly right to suggest that such cemeteries show some of the best evidence for early Christianity in western Britain, but the position of enclosed

---

[1] H. Mytum, *The Origins of Early Christian Ireland* (London, 1991); K. H. Hughes, *Early Christian Ireland: Introduction to the Sources* (London, 1972); V. Nash-Williams, *Early Christian Monuments of Wales* (Cardiff, 1950).

[2] Mytum, op. cit. in note 1; M. O. H. Carver, 'Conversion and politics on the eastern seaboard of Britain; Some archaeological indicators', 11–40 in B. Crawford (ed.), *Conversion and Christianity in the North Sea World* (St. John's House Papers No 8, St. Andrews, 1998).

[3] E.g. Nash-Williams, op. cit. in note 1; E. Okasha, *Corpus of the Early Christian Inscribed Stones of South-West Britain* (Leicester, 1992); R. A. S. Macalister, *Corpus Inscriptionum Insularum Celticarum*, I (Dublin, 1945).

[4] C. Thomas, *The Early Christian Archaeology of North Britain* (Edinburgh, 1971); N. Edwards, 'Identifying the archaeology of the early church in Wales and Cornwall', 49–62 in J. Blair and C. Pyrah (eds.), *Church Archaeology: Research Directions for the Future* (CBA Res. Rep., 104, York, 1996); I. Fisher, 'The west of Scotland', 37–41 in Blair and Pyrah op. cit. above.

[5] Thomas, op. cit. in note 4, 50.

cemeteries in the developmental scheme must be questioned. Thomas himself in more recent work, following on from the work of Diane Brook,[6] has admitted that:

Curvilinear cemetery enclosures, at any rate in western Britain and southern Scotland, are probably 'secondary' within a 'primary' phase only; sixth-seventh century features rather than fifth-sixth century features. It is also clear that some of them were being modified from older secular enclosures, and possibly being laid out for the first time, as late as the ninth and tenth centuries.[7]

Others have also begun to probe the role of enclosures associated with ecclesiastical sites. Dark has noted that there is little evidence for elaborate multi-vallate enclosures surrounding monasteries from before the 8th century,[8] whilst Carver has questioned whether the large ditched enclosures associated with some Scottish ecclesiastical sites, such as Iona (Argyll and Bute) and Portmahomack (Highland), should be interpreted as originating as monastic *valla*, in the light of increasing evidence for the prehistoric origins of these enclosures.[9] Taking a wider view, and encompassing all of Britain, John Blair has also questioned the distinctiveness of the topography of western British monastic sites, particularly the sub-circular shape of the enclosure.[10] It is taking this increasing unease about the role of enclosures on ecclesiastical sites in western Britain as a point of departure that I want to question the very existence of early Christian (i.e. pre-c. A.D. 800) enclosed cemeteries.

ENCLOSURES

Although this paper focuses on the use of enclosures in specifically religious contexts it is important to remember that enclosures were a fundamental element of early medieval settlement topography. Irish raths and ring-forts,[11] northern Welsh hut-groups,[12] Cornish rounds,[13] Scottish duns[14] and multi-vallate and nucleated hillforts from all regions[15] were characterized by the presence of a surrounding boundary, be it a ditch, bank or hedge. Such boundaries were clearly a major part of the repertoire of built space in these areas, and as such, ecclesiastical and religious sites

[6] D. L. Brook, *Early Christian Archaeology of the Southern Marches of Wales* (unpublished PhD Thesis, University of Wales Cardiff, 1992).
[7] C. Thomas, 'Christianity at Govan: But when?', 19–26 in A. Ritchie (ed.), *Govan and its Early Medieval Sculpture* (Stroud, 1994).
[8] K. Dark, *Discovery by Design: The Identification of Secular Elite Settlements in Western Britain* A.D. 400–700 (BAR Brit. Ser., 237, Oxford, 1994), 39–40.
[9] Carver, op. cit. in note 2, 23; Fisher, op. cit. in note 4, 38.
[10] J. Blair, 'Anglo-Saxon minsters: a topographical review', 226–66 in J. Blair and R. Sharpe (eds.), *Pastoral Care Before the Parish* (Leicester, 1992).
[11] N. Edwards, *The Archaeology of Early Medieval Ireland* (London, 1990), 11–33.
[12] E.g. P. J. Fasham, R. S. Kelly, M. A. Masson and R. B. White, *The Graenog Ridge: The Evolution of a Farming Landscape and its Settlements in North-West Wales* (Aberystwyth, 1998).
[13] A. Preston-Jones and P. G. Rose, 'Medieval Cornwall', *Cornish Archaeol.*, 25 (1986), 135–85.
[14] S. M. Foster, 'Before Alba: Pictish and Dál Riata power centres from the fifth to late ninth centuries AD', 1–31 in S. Foster, A. Macinnes and R. Macinnes (eds.), *Scottish Power Centres from the Early Middle Ages to the Twentieth Century* (Glasgow, 1998); I. Armit, *The Archaeology of Skye and the Western Isles* (Edinburgh, 1996), 159–78.
[15] Dark, op. cit. in note 8; L. Alcock, 'The activities of potentates in Celtic Britain, AD 500–800: a positivist approach', 22–47 in S. T. Driscoll and M. R. Nieke (eds.), *Power and Politics in Early Medieval Britain and Ireland* (Edinburgh, 1988).

were no different from their secular counterparts. Whilst Dark has persuasively argued that ecclesiastical sites were almost always univallate, in contrast with multi-vallate secular elite settlements,[16] single ditches and banked enclosures were also found on a wide range of non-elite settlement types, such as Cornish rounds.[17]

Although on many of these sites, the enclosure may have had some functional role in keeping out both human and animal intruders it is clear that the purpose of well-defined boundaries went beyond the practical and had a symbolic dimension. Boundaries could be used as indicators of status and, as Hingley has noted, the boundary itself could come to have a significant ritual status as a liminal zone.[18] The presence of boundaries defining temple enclosures (the *temenos*) in Roman Britain indicates that the use of a boundary to separate the sacred from the profane has a long tradition in Britain, preceding the introduction of Christianity.[19]

So is it possible to distinguish between different types of boundaries in early medieval Britain? One distinction that needs to be made clear is the difference between boundaries that enclose entire monastic settlements (including all concomitant cemeteries, churches and domestic occupation) and enclosures that function purely to define and separate graveyards and cemeteries from the wider world. Whilst it is possible to find early evidence for monastic *valla*, there is no evidence that enclosures were put in place around cemeteries alone for specifically Christian reasons much before the 9th century. It is the blurring of these two types of ecclesiastical enclosure that has served to muddy the issue of the origin and date of the first enclosed cemeteries.

The area within a monastic vallum did not just contain the church and cemetery, but all the structures within the ecclesiastical establishment, such as houses, oratories and probably agricultural structures. They undoubtedly had some functional purposes; in early medieval society the banks and ditches of monasteries may have acted as real physical defences against both local attack and, from the 9th century, Viking raiding.[20] Despite their physicality, such enclosures served to mark a wider conceptual division between the sanctified enclosure of the monastic establishment and the outside world. In the words of Lisa Bitel, 'The monastery's walls and markers sent a message across the Christian landscape: the saint dwells here with the monks'.[21] The monastic boundary may also have indicated other divisions such as the areas of legal sanctuary,

[16] Dark, op. cit. in note 8.
[17] Preston-Jones and Rose, op. cit. in note 13.
[18] R. Hingley, 'Iron Age settlement in the Upper Thames Valley' 72–88 in B. Cunliffe and D. Miles (eds.), *Aspects of the Iron Age in Central Southern Britain* (Oxford, 1984); R. Hingley, 'Boundaries surrounding Iron Age and Romano-British settlements', *Scottish Archaeol. Rev.*, 7 (1990), 96–103.
[19] B. Jones and D. Mattingley, *An Atlas of Roman Britain* (Oxford, 1990), 290–5.
[20] J. R. Davies, 'Church property and conflict in Wales AD 600–1100', *Welsh Hist. Rev.*, 18/3 (1997), 387–406.
[21] L. Bitel, *Isle of the Saints: Monastic Settlement and the Christian Community in Early Christian Ireland* (Chicago, 1990).

possibly derived from parallels with the cities of refuge (*ad refugium*) of the Old Testament.[22]

PROBLEMS WITH THE ARCHAEOLOGY

One of the biggest problems for archaeologists, whether looking at Celtic religious foundations or the earliest Anglo-Saxon churches, is the intractability of the archaeological material. On both sides of Offa's Dyke there is a relatively high level of continuity of use on church sites. Sites available for large open-area excavations such as Raunds (Northamptonshire) and Capel Maelog (Powys) are exceptional.[23] In most cases archaeological work takes the form of watching briefs, evaluations and small-scale interventions.[24] This means it is often very difficult to get a full picture of the long-term development of a cemetery site.

A second problem, particularly in Wales and the West, is the relative paucity of datable material culture. Whilst some sites, such as the cemetery at the parish church of St Materiana at Tintagel (Cornwall), and the monastic site of Whithorn (Dumfries and Galloway), have produced datable high-status imports in the form of A, B, D and E ceramics and fine glassware, such finds are relatively uncommon, and often restricted to certain areas.[25] Allowing for the usual problems of residuality and the possibility of ditches being recut and banks removed, it is extremely difficult to date cemetery enclosures on artefactual evidence alone. The other method used frequently for dating purposes is radiocarbon dating — unfortunately the period between the late 5th and mid-6th centuries is one which produces wide distributions of possible dates due to a plateau on the calibration curve between A.D. 450 and A.D. 530; close dating of sites using such techniques is just not possible for this period.[26]

It is also important to mention a factor that does *not* date a cemetery, namely the presence of Class I early Christian inscribed stones. These grave markers, bearing inscriptions in Latin, Ogham, and frequently both, are broadly dated to the period A.D. 400–700.[27] However, their substantial appearance belies their mobility within the

[22] W. Davies, 'Adding insult to injury: power, property and immunities in early medieval Wales', 137–64 in W. Davies and P. Fouracre (eds.), *Property and Power in the Early Middle Ages* (Cambridge, 1995); W. Davies '"Protected space" in Britain and Ireland in the Middle Ages', 1–19 in B. Crawford (ed.), *Scotland in Dark-Age Britain* (St John's House Paper No. 6, St Andrews, 1996); H. Pryce, *Native Law and the Church in Medieval Wales* (Oxford, 1993), 163–203.

[23] A. Boddington, *Raunds Furnells: The Anglo-Saxon Church and Churchyard* (London, 1996); W. J. Britnell, 'Capel Maelog, Powys: Excavations 1984–7', *Medieval Archaeol.*, 34 (1990), 27–96.

[24] E.g. A. Preston-Jones, 'Road widening at St Buryan and Pelynt churchyards', *Cornish Archaeol.*, 26 (1984), 153–78.

[25] J. Nowakowski and C. Thomas, *Tintagel Churchyard Excavations at Tintagel Parish Church, North Cornwall Spring 1990: An Interim Report* (Truro, 1990); J. Nowakowski and C. Thomas, *Grave News from Tintagel: An Illustrated Account of Archaeological Excavations at Tintagel Churchyards, Cornwall 1991* (Truro, 1992); P. Hill, *Whithorn and St Ninian: The Excavation of a Monastic Town 1984–91* (Stroud, 1997).

[26] S. Bowman, *Radiocarbon Dating* (London, 1990).

[27] The extent to which it is believed possible to date these stones more precisely varies widely; for two contrasting viewpoints compare K. Dark, 'Epigraphic, art-historical and historical approaches to the chronology of Class I inscribed stones', 51–61 in N. Edwards and A. Lane (eds.), *The Early Church in Wales and the West* (Oxbow Mon., 16, Oxford, 1992), and C. Thomas, *And shall these mute stones speak? Post-Roman Inscriptions in Western Britain* (Cardiff, 1994).

landscape. Elizabeth Okasha's gazetteer of inscribed stones in Cornwall and south-western England has shown how frequently such stones could be moved, sometimes significant distances,[28] and that very few stones are found certainly *in situ*. In some cases they were re-used for building material [29] and in others moved to their present position by concerned antiquarians or the local priest. One even seems to have been used to adorn a summerhouse![30] It is very difficult to prove that such a stone in a churchyard is in its original position. Even when this can be demonstrated, the only thing that this dates is the erection of the stone itself, and it certainly cannot be used to establish a date for any surrounding enclosure.

A further difficulty can occur in establishing an ecclesiastical, rather than a secular, context for an enclosure, particularly without detailed exploration of the site, as secular factors may cause the creation of apparent enclosures around an ecclesiastical nucleus. In Wales one potential factor in creating large, seemingly monastic, enclosures is the pattern of land-holding known as *tir corddlan*, a variant of hereditary land, shared as gardens (*gerddi*),[31] which appears to have taken the form of land disposed round a central nucleus. In some cases it appears that an enclosed church (*llan*) or cemetery (*mynwent*) could have formed such a nucleus and it is recorded that 'the measure of a *corflan* [*sic*] was a legal acre in length with its end to the grave-yard (*mynwent*)'.[32] According to Glanville Jones the appearance of *tir corddlan* could be a series of strips of land arranged in a radial fashion around a central point, usually a churchyard. A strong fence to prevent access to the cultivated area by grazing livestock would then surround this land.[33] In some cases, according to the Welsh law-book, *Llyfr Iorweth*, this boundary could also act to define the area of sanctuary around a *clas* (a hereditary community of canons).[34] This pattern of land-holding could thus create a large outer enclosure around an ecclesiastical focus, which was not ecclesiastical in origin or function, but served to define a nucleal area of agricultural land. This means that it is not possible to assume that apparent enclosures around churches, particularly when only plotted through aerial photography or in relict field boundaries, represent monastic enclosures. Enclosures formed by such radial strips of land can be seen at Castlemartin and Jeffreyston (both Pembrokeshire) (Fig. 1),[35] and some of the very large enclosures plotted from aerial photographs in south-western Wales, which have been suggested as being ecclesiastical in origin may also represent such patterns of *tir corddlan*.[36]

---

[28] Okasha, op. cit. in note 3, 5.

[29] E.g. Okasha, op. cit. in note 3, nos. 11, 12.

[30] Okasha, op. cit. in note 3, no. 48 (St Endellion).

[31] G. R. J. Jones, 'Forms and patterns of medieval settlements in Wales', 155–70 in D. Hooke (ed.), *Medieval Villages: a review of current work*, (Oxford University Committee for Archaeol. Mon., 5, Oxford, 1985).

[32] A. R. William, *Llyfr Iorweth* (Cardiff, 1960), 44.

[33] Jones, op. cit. in note 31.

[34] William, op. cit. in note 32.

[35] J. Kissock, '"God made nature and men made towns": post-Conquest and pre-Conquest villages in Pembrokeshire', 123–38 in N. Edwards (ed.), *Landscape and Settlement in Medieval Wales* (Oxbow Mon., 81, Oxford, 1997), esp. pp. 133–5.

[36] T. James, 'Air photography and ecclesiastical sites in South Wales', 62–76 in Edwards and Lane, op. cit. in note 27.

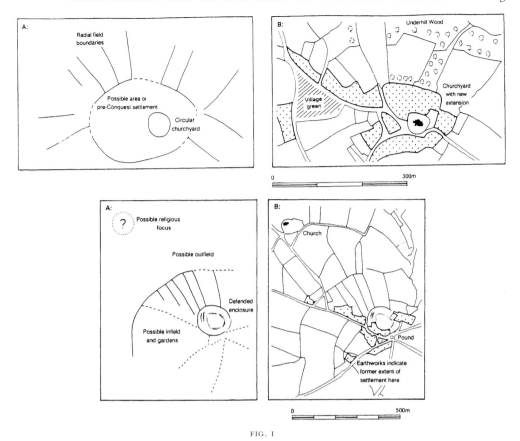

FIG. I

Examples of apparent enclosures around an ecclesiastical site (above) and a secular site (below), possibly caused by *tir corddlan* (after Kissock, op. cit. in note 35).

Conversely ecclesiastical boundaries need not have been defined by a continuous physical marker, such as a bank or a ditch. As is clear from Irish sources, simple stone crosses could mark ecclesiastical areas.[37] In the case of Kildare the bounds were reputedly laid invisibly by Brigit. In other cases the boundary could be as insubstantial as a hedge; Bangor, the name of monasteries in Co. Down and Gwynedd, means 'wattle enclosure', perhaps similar to the hedge surrounding the monastery at Oundle (Northamptonshire).[38]

A final problem is the distinction between the re-use of prehistoric enclosures to surround cemeteries and the *de novo* construction of enclosures purely to define sanctified ground. There are undoubtedly some early examples of cemeteries placed in re-used structures, but it is important to question, in the light of the archaeological evidence, whether there is any reason to believe that these sites are specifically

[37] Bitel, op. cit. in note 21, 63.
[38] Eddius Stephanus, *The Life of Bishop Wilfrid*, ed. and trans. B. Colgrave (Oxford, 1927), Ch. 67.

Christian. It will be argued below that in Ireland there are clear pre-Christian precedents for the placement of inhumation graves in re-used prehistoric enclosures.

The fact of the matter is that there is virtually no convincing evidence for the enclosure of simple cemeteries, in Britain, before the 8th century. The list of well-excavated early medieval British cemeteries without evidence for any enclosures is remarkable, including Plas Gogerddan (Ceredigion); Tandderwen (Denbighshire); Cannington (Somerset); Henley Wood (Somerset); Ulwell (Dorset) and Capel Eithin (Anglesey) amongst others.[39] One obvious argument against this being significant is that all these sites could be failed cemeteries. These sites may have survived to be well excavated in the 20th century, precisely because they never developed into more complex sites, but the clear sequences known from sites such as Capel Maelog suggest this is not the case.[40]

MONASTIC ENCLOSURES

Excavation on monastic sites has failed to reveal any evidence for the subdivision of space, serving to define areas specifically for burial, from before the 8th century. One site that has been argued as representing an early curvilinear cemetery is the monastic site of Llandough (Vale of Glamorgan).[41] This site probably had its origins in a late Roman villa, and the earliest burials from the cemetery are of late Roman date: one burial contained a Roman brooch (Colchester Derivative; 1st century A.D.), three contained Roman glass beads, and five were buried with iron hobnails, a distinctive late Roman burial rite.[42] The earliest medieval burials were from Area I, and the excavators have suggested that these were part of an early curvilinear cemetery, in use from the 5th/6th centuries (Fig. 2). One burial was radiocarbon-dated to A.D. 420–590. This curvilinear cemetery is postulated on the basis of a line of burials on a SW.–NE. alignment, along the north-western edge of Area I, changing to the east to a more regular W.–E. alignment. Whilst this may define an edge to the early burial area at this site, 'no physical barrier such as a fence, wall or ditch was detected'.[43] There is no division between the early burials with a pre-8th-century date (as defined by the C14 date and the presence of Bi ware), and the later burials of the 9th to 11th century (on the basis of C14 dates).

At Whithorn, although the excavators recognized an inner precinct and an outer zone, there was no distinct or formal boundary. They also comment on the

    [39] K. Murphy, 'Plas Gogerddan, Dyfed: a multiperiod burial and ritual site', *Archaeol. J.*, 149 (1992), 1–39; K. S. Brassil, W. G. Owen and W. J. Britnell, 'Prehistoric and early medieval cemeteries at Tandderwen, near Denbigh, Clwyd', Archaeol. J., 148 (1991), 46–97; P. Rahtz, 'Later Roman cemeteries and beyond', 53–64 in R. Reece (ed.), *Burial in the Roman World* (CBA Res. Rep., 27, London, 1977); L. Watts and P. J. Leech, *Henley Wood: The Romano-British Temple and Post-Roman Cemetery: Excavations by E. Greenfield and others between* 1960–8 (CBA Res. Rep., 99, London, 1996); P. W. Cox, 'A seventh century inhumation cemetery at Shepherd's Farm, Ulwell, near Swanage, Dorset', *Proc. Dorset Nat. Hist. Antiq. Soc.*, 110 (1988), 37–41; S. White, 'Excavations at Capel Eithin, Gaerwen, Anglesey, 1980: first interim report', *Trans. Anglesey Antiq. Soc. Field Club* (1981), 15–27.
    [40] Britnell, op. cit. in note 23.
    [41] A. Selkirk, 'Llandough', *Current Archaeol.*, 146 (1996), 73–7.
    [42] R. Philpott, *Burial Practices in Roman Britain: A Survey of Grave Treatment and Furnishing* (BAR Brit. Ser., 219, Oxford, 1990), 165–75.
    [43] A. Thomas and N. Holbrook pers comm.

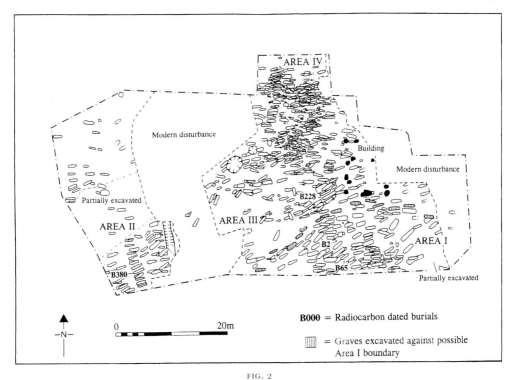

FIG. 2

Cemetery at Llandough. Note the lack of any boundary between the earliest burials (Area I) and the later burials (Areas III and IV).

insubstantial nature of the boundaries that could be recognized in Period I (c. perhaps A.D. 400–730).[44] Excavations on the site by the York Archaeological Trust have shown how the use of one area could move from burial to metalworking and back to burial again. Burial areas, although formalized to some extent, could fall in and out of use with an ease that suggests that there was no sense that cemeteries were permanently sacred or sacrosanct. An example of this can be seen at Whithorn, where the burial area retracted in the later Anglian period (c. 845–1000) and was replaced by a series of wattle buildings.[45]

   These subdivided monastic enclosures appear not to have had simple one-stage plans, but show some evidence of evolution. Berllan Bach, Bangor (Gwynedd), possibly part of Deiniol's monastery, was partially excavated in the 1980s. The first phase of this site consisted of a cemetery of simple inhumation graves placed in N.–S. rows, on the same alignment as the later cathedral. The excavations failed to reveal any boundary to this cemetery. However these graves were cut by a ditch, perhaps defining a rectilinear enclosure, which in turn was cut by a later medieval cross ditch. The earlier ditch produced C14 dates from material from the lowest fills of A.D. 650–990

[44] Hill, op. cit. in note 25.
[45] Hill, op. cit. in note 25, 48–9.

and A.D. 893–1160. Clearly the enclosure dates to the 8th century or later, and post-dates the foundation of the cemetery.[46]

Another cemetery site with a late enclosure is known from the Priory of St John and St Teulyddog, Carmarthen (Carmarthenshire). This site had several phases of occupation, beginning with a small quantity of Roman material of an uncertain character. The second phases consisted of three intercutting ditches, one with a C14 date of A.D. 735 ± 60. The third phase consisted of a series of burials; some of which had a 13th-century date. Thus although the enclosure, if in indeed that is what the ditches represented, was anterior to the burials, these burials are of an 8th-century or later date. Yet again there is no indication of a pre-8th-century enclosed cemetery.[47]

Increased internal complexity can also be seen on smaller monastic or hermitage sites from Ireland. At Reask (Co. Kerry), the early medieval occupation was multi-phase.[48] The initial enclosure contained both occupation deposits and a series of graves, dated to the 5th and 6th century by artefactual and C14 evidence. In the second major phase, a drystone church was constructed, and a dividing wall was built across the site, separating the church and burials from the areas of occupation. At Church Island (Co. Kildare), there was also a combination of occupation layers and religious activity, in the form of a cross-decorated stone, a church and graves.[49] The site was only enclosed by a stone wall in the third phase of occupation. In both cases the erection of enclosures and the separation of the church and cemetery from domestic occupation came late in the sequence of events.

The evidence from these monastic sites suggests that internal layout of monastic sites appears to have become more complicated from the 8th century. Before this period, although the space within ecclesiastical sites had some level of internal organization it was not formalized by the use of internal boundaries. The increased formalization of space served not only to define cemeteries, but also other areas within the outer enclosure, marking out areas of occupation, craft and industry and agricultural processing.

ENCLOSED CEMETERIES

If monastic sites show an increase in internal organization, often separating cemeteries from other areas, in the 8th century, then it is also only in this period that we first start to see evidence for simple enclosed cemeteries. The evidence presented for enclosed cemeteries preceding this period is not convincing.

For example, one burial site that has been presented as an enclosed cemetery is the burial site at Atlantic Trading Estate, Barry (Vale of Glamorgan) (Fig. 3).[50] Forty-five burials, dug into wind-blown sand, are known from this site. Like Llandough the

---

[46] D. Longley, 'Excavations at Bangor, Gwynedd', *Archaeol. Cambrensis*, 144 (1995), 52–70.
[47] T. A James, 'Excavations at the Augustinian Priory of St. John and St. Teulyddog, Carmarthen 1979', *Archaeol. Cambrensis*, 134 (1985), 120–61.
[48] T. Fanning, 'Excavation of an early Christian cemetery and settlement at Reask, County Kerry', *Proc. Royal Irish Acad.*, 81C (1981), 3–172.
[49] M. J. O'Kelly, 'Church Island near Valencia, Co. Kerry', *Proc. Royal Irish Acad.*, 59C (1958), 57–136.
[50] R. Newman, 'Atlantic Trading Estate, Barry', *Archaeol. Wales*, 25 (1985), 37–8; R. Newman and L. Parkin, 'Atlantic Trading Estate, Barry', *Archaeol. Wales*, 26 (1986), 5.

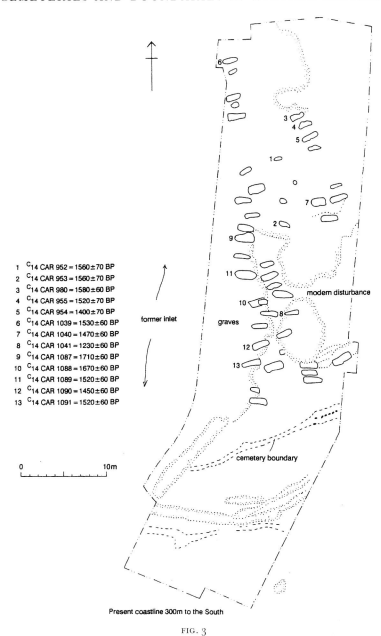

1 C_{14} CAR 952 = 1560±70 BP
2 C_{14} CAR 953 = 1560±70 BP
3 C_{14} CAR 980 = 1580±60 BP
4 C_{14} CAR 955 = 1520±70 BP
5 C_{14} CAR 954 = 1400±70 BP
6 C_{14} CAR 1039 = 1530±60 BP
7 C_{14} CAR 1040 = 1470±60 BP
8 C_{14} CAR 1041 = 1230±60 BP
9 C_{14} CAR 1087 = 1710±60 BP
10 C_{14} CAR 1088 = 1670±60 BP
11 C_{14} CAR 1089 = 1520±60 BP
12 C_{14} CAR 1090 = 1450±60 BP
13 C_{14} CAR 1091 = 1520±60 BP

former inlet

graves

modern disturbance

cemetery boundary

0   10m

Present coastline 300m to the South

FIG. 3
Atlantic Trading Estate, Barry (Vale of Glamorgan). The marked cemetery
boundary may well be no more than a revetment between the cemetery and the
dunes (after Newman, op. cit. in note 50).

earliest burials appear to be of late Roman date (on the basis of C14 dating). The site
is separated from the sea and dunes to the south by a series of boundaries. The
northerly one is the former course of a sea-wall, and the most seaward one, apparently

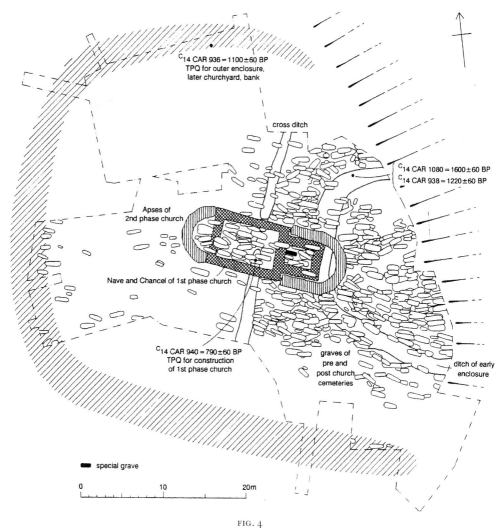

FIG. 4

Capel Maelog (Powys). Plan showing late date of enclosure around cemetery (after Britnell, op. cit. in note 23).

bolstered with a stone and masonry revetment, surely also fulfilled the same function. It is the boundary between these two sea-walls that has been called a cemetery boundary. However, there is no reason to believe that this too is anything other than a revetment marking the edge of the foreshore. There has been no evidence presented that ties this boundary chronologically to the period of cemetery use, and the site cannot be interpreted as an enclosed cemetery.

Excavations at the church site of Capel Maelog have uncovered an entire sequence of burials and enclosures on a hilltop site (Fig. 4).[51] A sub-rectangular ditch radiocarbon-dated from the sub-Roman to the early medieval period (A.D. 260–610,

[51] Britnell, op. cit. in note 23.

A.D. 670–970) defined the primary enclosure. These dates were both from charcoal in the ditch, found at different levels, implying a slow process of silting. The fill of the enclosure ditch contained a small quantity of Roman pottery, as well some glass fragments, dating from the 2nd to 4th centuries A.D. The precise function of this enclosure is uncertain; no structures were found, though only part of the interior was excavated, and much of this was damaged by later burials.

The primary burials of the medieval cemetery consisted of 14 graves, cut by the foundations of the first church. One of these graves cut the early enclosure indicating that it had silted up by the time burial began at the site. The site was not provided with an enclosure until around the 10th century (C14 date A.D. 776–1020), nor with a church until even later (A.D. 1044–1280). The chronology of burial, enclosure and church is a 'long' one. Although the site reflects Thomas's model for a developed cemetery, the development does not begin until the 10th century.

There are no indications from these few sites that enclosures, dedicated purely to burial, were in existence in the period c. A.D. 400–800, and they may indeed be much later. Unenclosed burial sites were clearly the norm, and continued to be so for a considerable time. The unenclosed burial site from Mawgan Porth (Cornwall), dated to the 10th/11th century, suggests that such sites could exist without enclosures much later than usually assumed.

RE-USE OF PREHISTORIC ENCLOSURES

The re-use of prehistoric enclosures by early medieval burial sites has frequently been noted. Yet again, however, the dating evidence is ambiguous, and even when there is good evidence for an early date it is far from certain as to whether the use of an enclosure should be seen as representing an overtly Christian enclosed site. Enclosure of burial sites should not be equated automatically with Christianity.

In Cornwall Romano-British and early medieval 'rounds' and hillforts were re-used as burial sites, yet none has produced evidence for re-use before A.D. 800.[52] Excavations on the church at St Dennis revealed a second rampart surrounding the known circular enclosure, suggesting the re-use of an Iron-age hillfort.[53] There was, however, no evidence for any early medieval activity within the enclosure, and Charles Thomas has suggested that the church was instead founded in the 11th century by the local landowners.[54] Equally extensive excavations at Merther Euny and St Buryan (both Cornwall), failed to reveal any evidence for an early medieval transition from domestic occupation to burial.[55]

There are other sites where there even appears to be an active disregard for earlier enclosures. At Arfryn, Bodedern (Anglesey), a complex sequence of ritual activity has been uncovered.[56] Early antiquarian reports suggest that Bronze-Age

[52] A. Preston-Jones, 'Decoding Cornish churchyards', 104–25 in Edwards and Lane, op. cit. in note 27, esp. 114.
[53] C. Thomas, 'The hillfort at St. Dennis', *Cornish Archaeol.*, 4 (1965) 31–5.
[54] Cited in Preston-Jones, op. cit. in note 52, 114.
[55] C. Thomas, 'Merther Euny, Wendron', *Cornish Archaeol.*, 6 (1968), 78–9; Preston-Jones, op. cit. in note 24.
[56] R. B. White, 'Excavations at Arfryn, Bodedern: long cist cemeteries and the origins of Christianity in Britain', *Trans. Anglesey Antiq. Soc. Field Club*, (1971–2), 19–51.

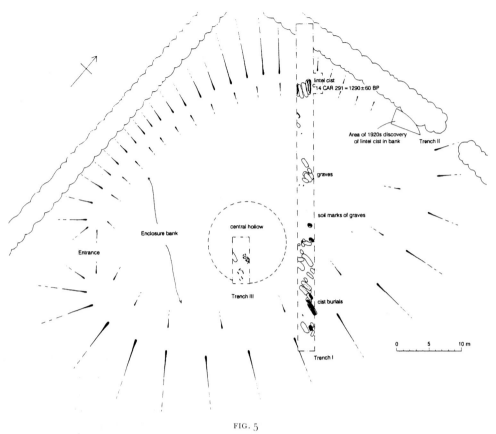

FIG. 5

Y Gaer, Bayvil (Pembrokeshire). A rare example of a well-dated early enclosed cemetery, re-using a prehistoric
(Iron Age) enclosure (after James, op. cit. in note 57).

urned burials were found on the site. There were then a number of unaccompanied
N.–S. graves and an enclosure surrounding the hilltop. There is no stratigraphic
relationship between these, and it is not clear which came first. However, there was
then a phase of W.–E. long-cist graves cutting both the N.–S. graves and the enclosure
ditch. One grave cut into the V-shaped ditch used a Class I stone as a lintel cover. The
excavator records that the ditch was deliberately backfilled and that W.–E. burials
were found on both sides of it. This seems to imply that with the advent of W.–E.
burial the pre-existing enclosure was actively ignored, a situation already seen at Capel
Maelog. It certainly does not seem to have retained any symbolic importance in the
early medieval period, and the lack of interest in an earlier enclosure has already been
seen at Capel Maelog.

One of the few sites where there is some early evidence for the re-use of prehistoric
enclosures for cemeteries is Y Gaer, Bayvil (Pembrokeshire), an Iron-Age enclosure
containing an early medieval cemetery (Fig. 5).[57] A C14 date from grave 4 of A.D.

[57] H. James, 'Excavations at Caer Bayvil, 1979', Archaeol. Cambrensis, 136 (1987), 51–76.

665 ± 60 (uncal.), stratigraphically one of the later burials in the cemetery, dates earlier than any enclosed cemetery discussed so far.

However there is no reason to assume in this instance that the presence of an enclosure was in any way specifically Christian. Situated in North Pembrokeshire the site was located in an area of strong Irish influence and immigration in the early medieval period, and we know from the presence of Ogham stones that some elements of Irish funerary practices had been introduced into the area. It is possible that the re-use of prehistoric enclosures was another such practice. In Ireland there is evidence for the use of enclosed burial areas in the later Iron Age. This is attested textually in the *Collecteana* of Tírechán from the Book of Armagh, dating to the later 7th century. In this work Tírechán makes several references to burial sites known as *ferta*. In one section of the work he describes the burial of Ethne and Fedelm, the daughters of King Lóiguire.

And the days of mourning for the king's daughter came to an end, and they buried them beside the wall of Clébach, and they made a round ditch after the manner of a *ferta* because this is what the heathen Irish used to do, but we call it *relic*.[58]

The word *fert* is frequently translated as 'burial mound',[59] but the passage from Tírechán makes it clear that it could also be an enclosure. This is also born out by other references. In *Coibnes uisci thairidne*, a 7th-century tract regulating matters relating to water-courses,[60] the phrase '*clad feirt*' is used, which is translated as 'the ditch-and-bank of a *fert*'.[61] Elsewhere in the same work the phrase '*maigen feirt*' is used, meaning 'the precinct of a *fert*'.[62] It is clear that a *fert* could be an enclosed burial site, and Tírechán is explicit that the *fert* could be structurally similar to a later enclosed Christian *relic*. Interestingly the *Coibnes uisci thairidne* distinguishes the ditch of a church from a ditch of a *fert*,[63] implying that the two were clearly seen as separate. This could be taken as an indicator of early enclosed Christian cemeteries, but it is not clear why the two should be so clearly distinguished if both the *fert* and the church enclosure were in ecclesiastical ownership, and a non-Christian origin for the *fert* makes more sense in this context.

There is also good archaeological evidence for such pre-Christian enclosed cemeteries in Ireland. At Lough Gur (Co. Limerick), a late Neolithic circular enclosure was found to contain a cemetery, with over 50 inhumations.[64] The general W.–E. alignment and lack of grave-goods would imply a predominantly Early Christian date, but beneath the main phase of burials was an earlier phase of inhumations aligned approximately N.–S., with the bodies in a partly crouched position, suggesting an Iron-Age date (Fig. 6).

---

[58] L. Bieler, *The Patrician Texts in the Book of Armagh* (Dublin, 1979).

[59] Thomas, op. cit. in note 4, 66–7; E. O'Brien, 'Pagan and Christian burial in Ireland during the first millennium AD: continuity and change', 130–7 in Edwards and Lane, op. cit. in note 27, esp. 133.

[60] D. Binchy, 'Coibnes uisci thairidne', *Ériu*, 17 (1955), 52–85; T. Charles-Edwards, *Early Irish and Welsh Kinship* (Oxford, 1993), 260, n. 2.

[61] Binchy, op. cit. in note 60, para.13.

[62] Ibid., para.11.

[63] Ibid., paras. 11, 13.

[64] E. Grogan and G. Eogan, 'Lough Gur excavations by Seán P. Ríordáin: further Neolithic and Beaker habitations on Knockadoon', *Proc. Royal Irish Acad.*, 87C (1987), 299–506, at 305.

FIG. 6

Circle J, Lough Gur (Co. Limerick). An early Christian cemetery overlaying an Iron Age burial site, both re-
using a neolithic enclosure (after Grogan and Eogan, op. cit. in note 64).

At Carbury Hill (Co. Kildare), there were two adjacent cemeteries which re-used circular enclosures.[65] Site A was a circular enclosure (85 ft diameter) marked by a bank and an internal ditch, with causeway entrances to the North-East and South-West. Originally an occupation site of Neolithic date, there were two later cremations accompanied by grave-goods of probable Iron-Age date[66]. Two hundred yards to the west of this lay site B, another earth-banked enclosure, also with an internal ditch. This too contained a number of burials: four cremations and fifteen inhumation burials. The cremations were unaccompanied, but one of the inhumations was accompanied

[65] G. F. Wilmot, 'Three burial sites at Carbury, Co. Kildare', *J. Royal Soc. Antiq. Ireland*, 68 (1938), 130–42.
[66] Ibid., 130–5.

by a pair of iron shears.[67] This juxtaposition of cremations and Iron-Age inhumation burials again shows a long-lived example of burial in circular banked and ditched enclosures.

A number of square enclosures were also used for burial in Ireland, for example at Knockea (Co. Limerick).[68] This square enclosure (c. 18 m × 18 m) was found to contain the remains of over 60 individuals. The form of the enclosure was very unusual: a square ditch with rounded corners was excavated, and the spoil used to built an internal bank, revetted on the inside with stone. A series of post-holes were also found around the central courtyard. There was no firm dating evidence, but the unusual shape and construction of the enclosure would suggest a very early medieval or Iron-age date, with the lack of early medieval material from the neighbouring settlement possibly suggesting the former. A structurally very similar burial enclosure is known from Relignaman (Omagh).[69]

Clearly the tradition of enclosed cemeteries re-using prehistoric enclosures was known in Ireland before the advent of Christianity, and may be expected to have influenced burial practice in areas under Irish influence, such as western Wales and Cornwall. Early enclosed cemeteries in Britain, when re-using prehistoric enclosures, need have no necessary link with Christianity, and merely reflect a pre-existing burial tradition from Ireland.

PLACE-NAME EVIDENCE FOR ENCLOSURES

One final source of information regarding the early enclosure of cemetery sites is place-name evidence. The Brittonic place-name element lann is commonly found in Wales,[70] Cornwall[71] and Brittany.[72] The word appears to have undergone a progression of meaning as follows: 'rough meadow' > 'small enclosed meadow' > 'enclosure' > 'churchyard, church, monastery'.[73] This clearly emphasizes the increasing importance of the enclosure in describing and defining ecclesiastical sites. However whilst the phonetic development of the word is reasonably well understood,[74] the chronology of the shifts in its semantic meaning is less certain. It is clear that the later form of the word has at least two meanings: one used to describe enclosures surrounding monasteries and by extension the monastery itself, and the other extended to mean any enclosed cemetery. These two meanings reflect the two different forms of early enclosure discussed above, the monastic *vallum* and the cemetery enclosure. To

---

[67] Ibid., 135–40.
[68] M. J. O'Kelly, 'Knockea, Co. Limerick', 72–101 in E. Rynne, (ed.), *North Munster Studies* (Limerick, 1967).
[69] A. Hamlin and C. Foley, 'A women's graveyard at Carrickmore, Co. Tyrone, and the separate burial of women', *Ulster J. Archaeol.*, 46 (1983), 41–6.
[70] T. Roberts, 'Welsh ecclesiastical place-names and archaeology', 41–4 in Edwards and Lane, op. cit. in note 27.
[71] O. J. Padel, 'Cornish names of parish churches', *Cornish Stud.*, 2 (1976–7), 4–5, 15–27; O. J. Padel, *Cornish Place-name Elements* (English Place Names Society Vol. LVI/LVII, Nottingham, 1977).
[72] G. Bernier, *Les Chretientes Bretonnes Continentales Depuis Les Origines Jusqu'au IXeme Siècle* (Rennes, 1982), 98–9.
[73] Thomas, op. cit. in note 27, 311.
[74] Ibid., 101.

confuse matters further the word was also used as part of place-names for dependent estates of ecclesiastical sites, even if there were no actual church present.[75]

Charles Thomas has suggested that in Rhigyfarch's *Life of St David* the reference to Paulinus' monastic school in *insula Wincdilantquendi* can be understood as describing a monastic site known as *lantquendi*, at a 'deserted place' (*in insula*), supplemented by the undefined descriptive noun-phrase *Wincdi*.[76] He suggests that this name was copied from a pre-600 source (Rhigyfarch's work dates to the 11th century). However whilst Rhigyfarch claimed to be using 'the oldest manuscripts in the land . . . written in the archaic fashions of the elders' there is no external reason to believe that these sources date so early.[77] Indeed, this claim to be using early sources may be partly rhetorical, perhaps reflecting Nennius's claim to be using writings 'of the Irish and the English and out of the traditions of our elders'.[78] Thomas lays particular importance on the early date of the name suggesting that 'It traps the word [*lan*] like a butterfly in the flight from British (Gaulish, Romano-Celtic) *landa* ("Vindolanda") through the fifth-century(?) apocope as *land* into sixth-century -*lant*- (written), /land/ (spoken), and then *lann* through assimilation of -*nd* to -*nn*, probably by the end of the sixth century (*LHEB* 511-13[79])'.[80] This, he suggests, means that as the *Wincdilantquendi* includes the element with a terminal -*t* the name must belong to the end of the 6th century at the latest. However in a charter of 834 from Brittany, Louis the Pious grants the estate of Langon '*in eodem pago locellum qui nominatur Lant-dego*',[81] a gift confirmed by Charles the Bald, using the name *landegon* in A.D. 850.[82] In both cases the -*nd* and -*nt* remain unassimilated, and Jackson notes that *landa* occurs as a common noun in Latin texts in the Cartulary of Redon.[83] The unassimilated -*nd*- is also found in the 11th-century Cornish *Life of St Petroc*, where Padstow is recorded under the name *Landwethinoch*.[84] Clearly in some cases place-names could retain the unassimilated *nd/nt* until at least the 9th or 10th century, and it is difficult to see the place-name *Wincdilantquendi* as a fossil of the 6th century without external evidence. Even if the name is taken from an early source there is no reason to believe that *lan* was being used in the sense of monastic site rather than one of its earlier meanings of a piece of land, particularly considering the unusual structure of the place-name, with the descriptive prefix.

Names incorporating *lan* are also found in land grants in the Llandaff charters.[85] Davies has claimed that some of these charters are very early, some possibly dating to

[75] W. Davies, *Wales in the Early Middle Ages* (Leicester, 1982), 145.

[76] Thomas op. cit. in note 27, 100–1.

[77] Rhigyfarch's *Life of David: the basic mid twelfth-century Latin text*, ed. and trans. J. W. James (Cardiff, 1967).

[78] Nennius, *British History and the Welsh Annals*, ed. and trans. J. Morris (London, 1980), 1.

[79] K. H. Jackson, *Language and History in Early Britain* (Edinburgh, 1953).

[80] Thomas, op. cit. in note 27, 111, n.36.

[81] A. de la Borderie, *Chronologie du Cartulaire de Redon* (Rennes, 1901), 220–1.

[82] Ibid., 208.

[83] Jackson, op. cit. in note 79, 508.

[84] P. Grosjean (ed.), 'Vies et miracles de S. Petroc' *Analecta Bollandiana*, 74 (1956), 131–88, 470–96.

[85] W. Davies, *An Early Welsh Microcosm: Studies in the Llandaff Charters* (London, 1971); W. Davies, *Llandaff Charters* (Cardiff, 1979)

the late 6th and 7th centuries.[86] However this early dating is not universally accepted,[87] and Dark has demonstrated a high level of corruption in the charters.[88] It is thus difficult to uncritically accept the charters as a source for pre-8th-century place-names. Nonetheless it is noticeable that sites which at a later date had *lan* names were often originally called *podum* in the 7th and 8th centuries,[89] though there are no examples of this process happening in reverse. This may suggest that *lan* names are chronologically later than *podum* names, and thus that many *lan* names may belong to a secondary stratum of ecclesiastical toponymy within the body of charters. Equally there is no evidence that at the period of the writing of the Llandaff charters, *lan* was used specifically to mean enclosed cemeteries, and was instead seemingly used in a more general sense to indicate a monastic site or its dependent estates.

The most thorough examination of these place-names has been Padel's examination of *lan* names in Cornwall.[90] He argues that, unlike the element *eglws*, names in *lan* were probably not being formed beyond the 11th century, though it is noticeable that none of the fifty known parish-church names in *lan* are attested before the 10th century. The exact meaning of the word in Cornwall is not clear; the earliest known examples of *lan* sites, such as *Landwithan* recorded in a 9th-century charter of Kenstec, Bishop of Cornwall,[91] are all likely to be monastic sites rather than simple cemeteries. *Landwithan* is identified by Finberg as Launceston and four neighbouring parishes, indicating the kind of substantial estate one would expect to find associated with a monastery, rather than attached to a simple burial site.[92] The church at *Lannaled* recorded in the incomplete, mid-10th-century *Missa propria Germani episcopi* is probably St Germans, a church with episcopal status,[93] again not a simple cemetery site. The first clear evidence that the word is used to mean cemetery only comes in 14th-century glosses to the Gotha *Life of St Petroc*.[94]

As we have seen, *lan* names are also known from Brittany. Less work has been done on Breton place-names, but *lan* could certainly be used as an indicator of ecclesiastical status. Wrmonoc's late 9th-century *Vita Pauli Aureliani* states 'Iste est locus qui nunc monasterium, sive vulgato nomine Lanna Pauli. . . dicitur'.[95] However it could also have the more general meaning of 'estate' or a piece of open or common land (*lande*),[96] and Padel notes that the religious toponymy of Brittany is distinct from Wales and Cornwall.[97] Even allowing for this there is no evidence for early *lan* names. The earliest I have been able to find is Langon, recorded as belonging to the machtiern Anau *de*

[86] The charters in her First Sequence are dated from the late 6th century, Davies 1979, op. cit. in note 85, 17.

[87] K. Dark, *Civitas to Kingdom* (Leicester, 1994), 140–8; P. Sims-Williams, 'Review of Wendy Davies *The Llandaff Charters*', *J. Ecclesiastical Hist.*, 33 (1982), 124–9.

[88] Dark, op. cit. in note 87.

[89] Davies 1979, op. cit. in note 85, 123–5.

[90] Padel 1976–7, op. cit. in note 71.

[91] D. Hooke (ed.), *Pre-Conquest Charter-Bounds of Devon and Cornwall* (Woodbridge, 1994), 18; P. H. Sawyer, *Anglo-Saxon Charters: an Annotated List and Bibliography* (London, 1968), S.1296.

[92] H. P. R. Finberg, *The Early Charters of Devon and Cornwall* (Leicester, 1963).

[93] L. Olson, *Early Monasteries in Cornwall* (Woodbridge, 1989), 60–6.

[94] Padel 1976–7, op. cit. in note 71.

[95] C. Cuissard (ed.), 'Vie de saint paul de léon en bretagne', *Rev. Céltique*, 5 (1881–2), 413–60.

[96] P. Gaillou and M. Jones, *The Bretons* (Oxford, 1991).

[97] Padel 1976–7, op. cit. in note 71.

landegon in A.D. 801.[98] Clearly in Brittany *lan* was used to describe a monastic site *in toto*, and not specifically a burial ground.

The *lan* place-names are noticeable for their relatively restricted distribution, and are concentrated in Wales, Cornwall and Brittany, with a few outliers, such as Landican (Cheshire),[99] Street, just to the south of Glastonbury (Somerset), recorded in an early charter as *Lantokai* in the Glastonbury Cartulary[100] and the monastic site of Sherbourne (Dorset), recorded as *Lanprobus*.[101] However it is unknown in other parts of Britain that were certainly Christian before the arrival of St Augustine, and in Ireland the nearest parallel seems to be *cell*, which although indicating a Christian site does not carry the connotations of an enclosure.[102] Although a number of names apparently containing the *lan* element are known from Cumbria and southern Scotland, including Lanercost (Cumbria) and Lanark (South Lanarkshire), they instead include the place-name element *-llanerch* meaning 'forest glade'.[103] In Yorkshire, Northumbria, the Midlands and southern Scotland, all areas of pre-Augustinian Christianity, *lan* names are unknown. Instead early Christian sites seem to be known by the name *eccles*,[104] and, in some areas, *both/bod*, originally meaning simply a residence, but in Wales and particularly southern Scotland developing a strong ecclesiastical resonance.[105] The pattern of *lan* place-names strongly complements the pattern of Anglo-Saxon occupation in the 8th century, whereas other names indicative of Christianity such as *eglws* and *bod/both* are found in areas occupied by both the Anglo-Saxons and the British. This would suggest that *lan* names only became common in British territories after the 8th century (Fig. 7).

There is relatively little evidence to suggest the widespread use of *lan* as a place-name element with specifically Christian connotations much before the 8th century, though admittedly, as with so many place-name elements, this may partly reflect the relative paucity of earlier written sources. More importantly though there is no early evidence to suggest that *lan* meant anything other than a monastic site, rather than having the more specific meaning of 'enclosed cemetery' until the 10th century at least.

CONCLUSIONS

The evidence for a pre-8th-century tradition of enclosed Christian cemeteries is sadly lacking. What little evidence there is for early cemetery enclosures places them in the 8th to 10th century, but no earlier, and cemeteries could well remain unenclosed as late as the 11th century. Place-name evidence suggests that the element *lan*, meaning

[98] P. Guigon, *Les Eglises du Haut Moyen Age en Bretagne* (St Malo, 1997).
[99] M. Gelling, 'Paganism and Christianity in the Wirral', *J. English Place-Name Soc.*, 25 (1992–3), 11.
[100] Padel, 1976–7, op. cit in note 71, 25.
[101] K. Barker, 'Sherborne in Dorset: an early ecclesiastical settlement and its estate', *Anglo-Saxon Stud. Archaeol. Hist.*, 3 (1984), 1–33.
[102] C. Thomas, 'Cellular meanings, monastic beginnings', *Emania*, 13 (1995), 51–68.
[103] C. Phythian-Adams, *Land of the Cumbrians: A Study in British Provincial Origins AD 400–1120* (Aldershot, 1996), 74, 82; W. Nicolaisen, *Scottish Place-Names: Their Study and Significance* (London, 1976), 164.
[104] K. Cameron, 'Eccles in English place-names', 87–92 in M. W. Barley and R. P. C. Hanson (eds.), *Christianity in Britain 300–700* (Leicester, 1968).
[105] S. Taylor, 'Place-names and the early Church in eastern Scotland', 93–110 in Crawford, op. cit. in note 22.

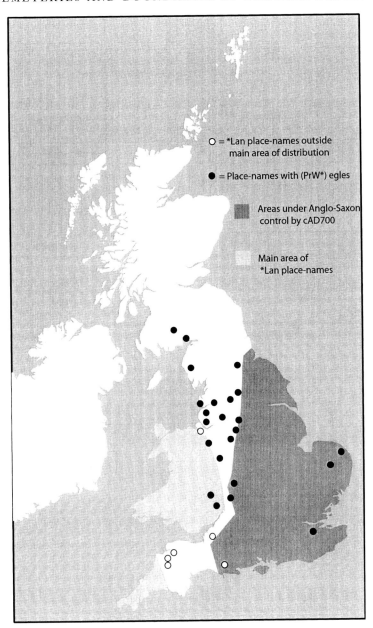

FIG. 7
Distribution of *lan* and *egles* place-names.

'enclosure' was primarily used to describe ecclesiastical sites, with only a later extension to mean specifically 'enclosed cemetery'.

Until the 8th century most cemeteries were as likely to be located on re-used prehistoric barrows, along important trackways or situated in conspicuous landscape locations as to be sited on ecclesiastical sites. The church seems to have made relatively little effort to involve itself in the burial of the majority of the population. Written evidence from Ireland suggests that monastic sites were only obliged to provide burial rites for their own monks and lay clients, and there is no indication that funeral rites were seen as a pastoral responsibility, owed to the whole community. The choice in cemetery location in general owed more to secular concerns than to ecclesiastical dogma. Irish documentary evidence demonstrates clearly the roles that burial sites played in disputes about land-tenure, and it was such factors which played a more important part in the placement of burials in the landscape.

The growth of cemetery enclosures from the 8th century onwards occurred in tandem with other developments in funerary ritual. Cemeteries stopped re-using prehistoric monuments, and the use of Class I inscribed stones, emphasizing status and lineage, ceased. All the evidence suggests the church had an increased interest in controlling burial in the community. The population were united together within the walls of the cemetery; the decline of Class I stones and the rise of the more anonymous Class II cross-inscribed stones, as well as the decline of secular focal graves, indicates an attempt by the church to down-play secular roles in death, and instead assert the primacy of the church. There appears to have been a move to replace one model of Christian kinship (which offered the choice between the secular kinship enjoyed by lay people and a sacred kinship, following a secular model, open to monks and monastic clients) with a wider all-encompassing concept of Christian kinship applying to both the secular and ecclesiastical segments of society. This can perhaps be recognized in the *Collectio canonum Hibernensis* which, although it recognized that people may want to be buried on their traditional ancestral burial sites, tried to encourage people to be buried at ecclesiastical sites.

The changes in funerary behaviour in the 8th century reflect wider changes in the church's attitude to death. These changes centre around a shifting conception of the destination of the soul following death — instead of a simple journey to heaven, there was a growing belief in the state of purgatory, as a transitional stage from death to heaven. One consequence of this development was the need to aid and maintain the soul after death; the story was not over and the living needed to continue to intervene in the affairs of the dead to ensure a satisfactory entry into heaven. For the first time in Christian thinking there was a continued active relationship between the living and the dead; a relationship which had previously been limited to the intercessory role of the saints. This belief in purgatory partly developed out of new attitudes towards penance, with new penitential practices arising in Ireland and England in the belief that sins not atoned for in life would have to be atoned for in death. Once in purgatory the dead were powerless to atone themselves and thus needed succour from the living, usually the surviving family, both natural and spiritual.[106] This is reflected in the development of the votive mass (*missa specialis*).[107]

The driving force for these changes may well have come from Ireland, via Anglo-Saxon England. Although the earliest Irish penitentials may have been influenced by

---

[106] F. Paxton, *The Christianisation of Death* (London, 1990), 68.
[107] B. Effros, 'Beyond cemetery walls: early medieval funerary topography and Christian salvation', *Early Medieval Europe*, 6/1 (1997), 1–23, esp. 9–11.

the Romanized liturgy of Caesarius of Arles there were as a clear divergence from the practices common in mainland Europe; whereas continental healing practices emphasized the return of physical health, in Ireland there was a move towards the spiritualization of healing. The practice of anointing the sick soon developed into a preparation for death and eternal life, and became a rite of the dying not the sick.[108] Paxton has suggested that this distinction arose partially out of the 8th-century reform movement known as *Céli Dé* (the Culdees).[109] He has drawn attention to various *Céli Dé* texts which suggest that they saw contact with the dead as ostensibly polluting, based on the injunction in Leviticus to the sons of Aaron that they should not defile themselves by contact with the dead.[110] Although the *Céli Dé* reforms only really developed in the mid-8th century there are hints that a similar attitude to the dead already existed, and in one passage of Adomnan's *Life of St Columba* the saint shows a reluctance to be with a dying man.[111] He suggests that the Irish developed a healing rite that functioned as a rite for the dying to help priests avoid coming into contact with the dead. The pre-Christian tradition of enclosed cemeteries in Ireland, outlined above, may also indicate an indigenous belief in the need clearly to define burial sites to avoid pollution. Irish or western British influence has also been cautiously suggested by Helen Gittos in her work on rites of churchyard consecration,[112] first appearing in Anglo-Saxon England only in the 10th century. Dumville has noted the evidence for a Celtic contribution towards the 10th-century English ecclesiastical renewal, thereby providing a context for western British influence on English burial practices.[113]

The developments of new attitudes to death in the 8th and 9th centuries saw the introduction of other new modes of commemoration. There was a continued development of the various classes of votive masses, but also the mid-8th-century growth of confraternities of prayer for the dead. These institutions seem to have been known amongst Irish monks by the turn of the 8th century.[114] Such confraternities said mass for the dead, and it is apparent that names of individuals to be commemorated were circulated. These bodies appear to have said prayers both for ecclesiastics and lay people and one way in which the names of such individuals could be recorded was through the placement of their names in memorial books, either purpose-made *Liber memorialis* or as marginalia in gospel books. Columba removed the name of a man from Islay (Argyll and Bute), Feradach, from the book of life, for ordering the murder of an exile in his protection, and thus condemned him to damnation.[115] This increased emphasis on praying for the souls of the dead can be seen on Class III inscribed crosses, which record their erection for the good of the souls of the benefactors or one of their intentions.[116]

[108] Paxton, op. cit. in note 106, 80–3.
[109] Ibid., 84–7.
[110] Leviticus 21: 1–12
[111] Adamnán., *Life of St Columba*, ed. and trans. R. Sharpe (Oxford, 1995), III:8; see also Paxton, op. cit in note 106, n. 364.
[112] Gittos, this vol.
[113] D. N. Dumville, *Liturgy and the Ecclesiastical History of Anglo-Saxon England* (Woodbridge, 1992), 111–8.
[114] Paxton, op. cit. in note 106, 100.
[115] Adamnán, op. cit. in note 111, II: 23.
[116] Nash-Williams, op. cit. in note 1, nos. 125, 182, 220, 233.

The archaeological, historical and place-name evidence all suggest that the enclosed Christian cemetery did not develop in any meaningful sense until the 8th and 9th century when burial within some form of a defined and enclosed Christian cemetery first became expected. Although these western British churchyards are undoubtedly earlier than the first Anglo-Saxon churchyards, western Britain was not as precocious in its development of enclosed cemeteries as is often assumed. The myth of the early Christian enclosed cemetery must be laid to rest, and the growth of such sites re-assigned from the 5th and 6th century to the period of increased ecclesiastical intervention and innovation in funerary rites in the 8th to 10th centuries.

ACKNOWLEDGEMENTS

I would like to thank all those with whom I have discussed the ideas presented in this paper, both before, during and after the conference. I would also like to thank Christine Kyriacou, librarian of the York Archaeological Trust for her help. Thanks are also due to Sam Turner, Department of Archaeology, University of York, and Neil McLeod, School of Law, Murdoch University.

Remains of Pagan Saxondom? — The Study of Anglo-Saxon Cremation Rites

By HOWARD WILLIAMS

Time which antiquates Antiquities, and hath an art to make dust of all things, hath yet spared these minor Monuments.[1]

The study and interpretation of early medieval cremation graves has a long history. They were first illustrated and recorded by Sir Thomas Browne in his *Hydriotaphia* of 1658.[2] The cinerary urns discovered near Walsingham in Norfolk formed the basis for complex speculation concerning the significance of cremation and mortality in ancient societies. Working before the first secure dating of burials and material culture to the early medieval period by Douglas in the late 18th century, Browne was unsure of the antiquity of the urns and, from a modern perspective, his work is strongly coloured by the religious convictions of the time. Despite this, *Hydriotaphia* continues to hold an important place in the study of cremation in early medieval England because in many ways, it represents the only attempt to interpret cremation graves of an early medieval date *primarily* in terms of ancient attitudes and practices concerning mortality and the afterlife. In stark contrast, from the observations of the 19th-century scholar John Kemble to the present day, most discussions of cremation burials have taken a very different course. Rather than telling us about past practices and attitudes towards death, cinerary urns and their contents have been used to construct a history of Anglo-Saxon invasion and settlement. This paper seeks to chart the persistence of this perspective through two centuries of scholarship and attempts a critical assessment of the motives and assumptions behind it. Subsequently, a new theoretical basis is suggested, one that focuses on the mortuary context of the archaeological material, and the role of funerary rites in defining group identities through ritual performance and the social use of space and place. The aim is not to dismiss earlier researchers whose work has been invaluable for our understanding of early medieval cremation rites. However, a critical review of the theories and ideas used to explain cremation rites is an inevitable and essential starting point if we are to develop a better understanding of cremation and its context in early medieval Britain.

THE HISTORY OF ARCHAEOLOGICAL INTERPRETATIONS OF CREMATION RITES

Burial rites have long been central to archaeological interpretations of early Anglo-Saxon England and continue to be so. Recently, however, a number of writers

---

[1] T. Browne, *Hydriotaphia, Urn-Burial; with an account of some urns found at Brampton in Norfolk* (London, 1893 [1658]), 71.
[2] Browne, op. cit. in note 1; S. Piggott, 'Sir Thomas Browne and Antiquity', *Oxford J. Archaeol.*, 7/3 (1988), 257–69.

have described and critiqued the changing archaeological interpretations of this burial record. In particular, many scholars have challenged the identification of immigrants, ethnicity and religious beliefs from 'Anglo-Saxon' burials.[3] However, such discussions have largely by-passed the cremation rite, even though an understanding of cremation is crucial for any interpretation of communities in eastern and southern Britain during the 5th to 7th centuries A.D. Consequently, the vast majority of discussions of cremation have remained similar to those of the 19th and early 20th centuries.

This situation stands in stark contrast to the large amount of empirical research conducted on early Anglo-Saxon cremation rites, especially in the last thirty years. From the catalogues of Anglo-Saxon pottery completed by J. N. L. Myres, to the extensive excavations and publications of cemeteries, such as Spong Hill (Norfolk), Newark (Nottinghamshire) and Sancton (East Riding of Yorkshire), we now have a sizeable body of archaeological data that has broadened and deepened our knowledge of cremation rites.[4] Osteological studies in particular have provided new insights into the technological and ritual aspects of cremation.[5] In the next few years, it is hoped that work on important and so far unpublished cemeteries with large numbers of cremation burials will increase our knowledge still further. Cremation cemeteries at Cleatham and Elsham (both Lincolnshire), and the mixed-rite cemetery from Mucking (Essex), might be proposed as a special priority for research and funding.[6] However, if we are to assess these sites adequately, both the archaeological data and the theories by which we approach these sites must be critically reviewed.

[3] C. J. Arnold, *An Archaeology of the Early Anglo-Saxon Kingdoms* (London, 1997), 19–32; H. Hamerow, 'Migration theory and the Migration Period', 164–77 in B. Vyner (ed.), *Building on the Past* (London, 1994); H. Hamerow, 'Migration theory and the Anglo-Saxon "identity crisis"', 33–44 in J. Chapman and H. Hamerow (eds.), *Migrations and Invasions in Archaeological Explanation* (BAR Int. Ser., 664, Oxford, 1997); J. Hines, 'The Anglian migration in British historical research', *Stud. zur Sachsenforchung*, 11 (1998), 167–76; S. Lucy, 'Reinterpreting Anglo-Saxon cemeteries', 27–32 in G. De Boe and F. Verhaeghe (eds.), *Death and Burial in Medieval Europe* (Zellik, 1997); S. Lucy, *The Early Anglo-Saxon Cemeteries of East Yorkshire: An Analysis and Reinterpretation* (BAR Brit. Ser., 272, Oxford, 1998) 5–21; S. Lucy, 'The early Anglo-Saxon burial rite: moving towards a contextual understanding', 33–40 in M. Rundkvist (ed.), *Grave Matters: Eight Studies of First Millennium AD Burials in Crimea, England and Southern Scandinavia* (BAR Int. Ser., 781, Oxford, 1999); C. Scull, 'Migration theory and Early England: some contexts and dynamics of cultural change' *Stud. zur Sachsenforchung*, 11 (1998), 177–85. For one of the few articles to focus upon cremation rites and their ethnic interpretation, see: C. Hills, 'Who were the East Anglians?' 14–23 in J. Gardiner (ed.), *Flatlands and Wetlands: Current Themes in East Anglian Archaeology* (East Anglian Archaeol., 50, Norwich, 1993).

[4] C. Hills, *The Anglo-Saxon Cemetery at Spong Hill, North Elmham Part I: Catalogue of Cremations* (East Anglian Archaeol., 6, Gressenhall, 1977); C. Hills and K. Penn, *The Anglo-Saxon Cemetery at Spong Hill, North Elmham Part II: Catalogue of Cremations* (East Anglian Archaeol. 11, Gressenhall, 1981); C. Hills, K. Penn and R. Rickett, *The Anglo-Saxon Cemetery at Spong Hill, North Elmham Part IV: Catalogue of Cremations* (East Anglian Archaeol., 34, Gressenhall, 1987); C. Hills, K. Penn and R. Rickett, *The Anglo-Saxon Cemetery at Spong Hill, North Elmham. Part V: Catalogue of Cremations* (East Anglian Archaeol., 67, Gressenhall 1994); A. G. Kinsley, *The Anglo-Saxon Cemetery at Millgate, Newark-on-Trent, Nottinghamshire* (Nottingham, 1989); J. N. L. Myres and B. Green, *The Anglo-Saxon Cemeteries of Caistor-by-Norwich and Markshall* (London, 1973); J. N. L. Myres and W. H. Southern, *The Anglo-Saxon Cremation Cemetery at Sancton, East Yorkshire* (Hull, 1973); J. Timby, 'Sancton I Anglo-Saxon cemetery: excavations carried out between 1976 and 1980', *Archaeol. J.*, 150 (1993), 243–365.

[5] J. Bond, 'Burnt offerings: animal bone in Anglo-Saxon cremations', *World Archaeol.*, 28.1 (1996), 76–88; J. McKinley, *The Anglo-Saxon Cemetery at Spong Hill, North Elmham. Part VII: The Cremations* (East Anglian Archaeol. 69, Gressenhall, 1994).

[6] E.g. K. Leahy, 'Cleatham, North Lincolnshire, the "Kirton in Lindsey" Cemetery', *Medieval Archaeol.*, 42 (1998), 94–5.

How have cremation rites been interpreted? A systematic review of the literature suggests that interpretations revolve around a number of pervasive and ubiquitous terms. Since the mid-19th century, antiquarian and archaeological work has frequently stereotyped the rite as 'Germanic' (or the equivalent terms 'Anglo-Saxon', 'Saxon' and 'Teutonic'), 'Anglian', 'pagan' and 'early'. To some extent these terms act as useful and convenient labels that describe the cultural and chronological affiliations of the rite and its historical setting within pre-Christian northern European societies. It may, however, be argued that through their frequent and often uncritical use, these terms have taken on an interpretative life of their own. When applied to other categories of evidence such as inhumation rites, and artefact styles, the validity of such labels has been questioned, with many scholars regarding them as simplistic and to some extent misleading. Given this, it is surprising that there has been no attempt to assess their application to cremation rites. This may be explained in part by the compelling nature of these terms when viewed in combination: the ethnic, religious and chronological labels are mutually dependent and consequently self-perpetuating.[7] In order to reassess their validity, let us trace the use of these terms through the research of the last two centuries. This will demonstrate that such epithets are simply the product of particular traditions in archaeological scholarship originally derived from racial and nationalistic 19th-century history. They do not necessarily help our understanding of the social significance of cremation in early medieval Britain, nor do they sufficiently explain the patterns in the archaeological evidence. Indeed, the uncritical use of these terms may distract our attention from other, perhaps more productive lines of enquiry.

RACE, CULTURE AND ETHNICITY

The term most commonly applied to the cremation rite is 'Germanic'. Intermittently it has also received the cultural epithet 'Anglian'. John Kemble was the first to identify the close similarities between cremation burials from England and Germany. For instance, he compared a burial from Eye in Suffolk, illustrated in Akerman's *Remains of Pagan Saxondom*, with urns from Stade-on-the-Elbe (Figs. 1 and 2).[8] From such comparisons he inferred that the similarities in material culture, together with the practice of cremation in both regions, suggested shared Germanic cultural and racial affiliations: 'The bones are those of men whose tongue we speak, whose blood flows in our veins'.[9]

Kemble believed the graves were 'The Burnt Germans of the age of Iron'.[10] He set an enduring precedent by interpreting cremation burials as reflecting members of the Germanic race, defined by biology, language and custom, and historically attested by Gildas, Bede and others, to have migrated from Germany to England in the 5th century A.D. Other antiquarians subsequently elaborated upon this basic observation,

---

[7] This corresponds to the overall lack of critical enquiry into the history of Anglo-Saxon archaeology. See Lucy 1998, op. cit. in note 3, 5.

[8] J. Y. Akerman, *Remains of Pagan Saxondom* (London, 1855); J. M. Kemble, 'On mortuary urns found at Stade-on-the-Elbe, and other parts of North Germany, now in the Museum of the Historical Society of Hannover', *Archaeologia*, 36 (1856), 270–83; J. M. Kemble, *Horae Ferales* (London, 1863).

[9] J. M. Kemble, 'Burial and cremation', *Archaeol. J.*, 12 (1855), 309–37.

[10] Ibid., 317.

U R N S.

FIG. I

Kemble's illustration of prehistoric cinerary urns from Germany and England (after Kemble 1863, op. cit. in note 8).

FIG. 2

The urn from Eye in Suffolk illustrated in Akerman's *Remains of Pagan Saxondom* (after Akerman, op. cit. in note 8).

describing cremation as 'Germanic', 'Saxon' or 'Teutonic'. To these scholars it appeared that the cremation graves provided incontrovertible proof of the *adventus Saxonum*, and writers such as Kemble saw this evidence as more reliable than the confused historical sources.[11] The result of this combination of textual and archaeological sources was that the concept of large-scale Anglo-Saxon migration became raised to a new level of historical legitimacy. The Germanic affiliation of cremation graves found in England was accepted without question by all key commentators throughout the 19th century. During the 20th century, discussions of 'race' were replaced by a focus upon 'culture', and most recently 'ethnicity', but despite this, the 19th-century tags ascribed to cremation have remained unquestioned,[12] even by those researchers interested in identifying evidence for British survival in the burial data, settlements and material culture of the 5th to 7th centuries A.D.[13]

Kemble and his contemporaries were reluctant to go further in assigning any regional or tribal ascription to cremation rites. Following Tacitus, they regarded cremation as a common trait of all Germanic peoples and saw it as embodying a racial identity, not a specific tribal one. Indeed, the broadness and lack of specificity of the 'Germanic' label may explain its enduring attraction. This view was translated to England, with Akerman, Wylie and Kemble all noting the widespread presence of cremation in both 'Anglian' and 'Saxon' areas from Yorkshire to the Isle of Wight.[14] Even in 'Jutish' Kent where Bryan Faussett had mainly uncovered inhumations, occasional cremations were already recorded and recognized by the mid-19th century.[15] Occasionally it was suggested that cremation was specifically Anglian, but a pan-Germanic view of the rite was usually preferred. In the early 20th century, H. M. Chadwick, E. T. Leeds and J. N. L. Myres accepted this broad and cautious view of the cultural affiliations of the rite. However, at the same time these authors recognized that cremation was particularly common in 'Anglian' areas in the 5th and 6th centuries.[16] Leeds summarized this viewpoint:

It has often been stated that the Angles practised cremation, and this statement is perfectly true, but it is likely to breed a misconception . . . It would be more correct to say that cremation is commoner in Anglian districts than elsewhere, but that it exists side by side with burial by

---

[11] It would be unfair to stereotype Kemble's use of archaeological evidence as simply reflecting Bede's account. He states that: 'I am not disposed to lay great stress upon the historical value of a tradition nearly three hundred years old, recorded before the eighth century, and introduced merely incidentally by an ecclesiastical historian; but I am nevertheless prepared to admit that some great influx of Germans than usual, upon the eastern and southern coasts of England, took place about the middle of the fifth century of our era . . .' (Kemble 1855, op. cit. in note 9, 319).

[12] Akerman, op. cit. in note 8; H. M. Chadwick, *The Origins of the English Nation* (Cambridge, 1907); E. T. Leeds, *The Archaeology of the Anglo-Saxon Settlements* (Oxford, 1913); E. T. Leeds, *Early Anglo-Saxon Art and Archaeology* (Oxford, 1936), 38–40; J. N. L. Myres, 'Cremation and inhumation in Anglo-Saxon cemeteries' *Antiquity*, 16 (1942), 330–41; G. Rolleston, 'Researches and excavations carried on in an ancient cemetery at Frilford near Abingdon, Berks, in the years 1867–1868', *Archaeologia*, 42 (1869), 417–83; G. Rolleston, 'Further researches in an Anglo-Saxon cemetery at Frilford, with remarks on the northern limit of Anglo-Saxon cremation in England', *Archaeologia*, 45 (1870), 405–10; W. Wylie, 'The burning and burial of the dead', *Archaeologia*, 37 (1860), 455–78.

[13] Summarized by Lucy 1999, op. cit. in note 3.

[14] Kemble, op. cit. in note 9, 321–2.

[15] Ibid., 320–1; Wylie, op. cit in note 12, 473–4.

[16] Chadwick, op. cit in note 12; Leeds 1936, op. cit. in note 12; Myres, op. cit. in note 12.

inhumation, which is if anything the more usual rite. The two rites are found side by side in the same cemeteries.[17]

Culture-historical archaeology sought to identify more detailed relationships between archaeological evidence and the settlement of Germanic peoples. However, Anglian, Saxon and Jutish zones were identified primarily according to metalwork styles rather than burial rites, and the ubiquity of cremation made its attribution to particular tribal groups difficult.[18] Pottery styles also did not fully support culture zones because within the same cremation cemeteries the cinerary urns displayed a variety of continental influences. This suggested to Myres that the process of migration was more complex than Bede supposed, with 'Saxons', 'Frisians' and 'Angles' burying their dead in the same cemeteries.[19] However, even though Myres accepted the complexity and heterogeneity of populations using cremation cemeteries, he simultaneously followed Kemble's view that cremation was a common Teutonic or Germanic practice. It is of fundamental importance to recognize that despite the caution of Leeds and Myres in describing cremation as 'Anglian', they failed to produce any alternative explanation for the distribution of cremation rites and the occurrence of both rites in the same cemeteries. Cultural affiliations were the only frame of reference they used to describe the rite with Myres stating that 'the broad distinction between cremation as a Teutonic and barbarian rite and inhumation as the Roman and civilised rite in this period is universally recognised'.[20]

Yet, as noted, the discovery of large numbers of cremation burials in the East Midlands and East Anglia increasingly led to the additional ascription of cremation as 'Anglian' and inhumation as 'Saxon'.[21] Allied to this view, the large cremation cemeteries of eastern England were provided with a specific historical interpretation. The 'pure cremation' or 'folk' cemeteries of eastern England were thought to indicate 'free German' mercenaries (*foederati*) settled by late Roman administrators. Using this interpretation, the diverse origins of the pottery styles found in cremation cemeteries could be explained as evidence of numerous barbarian groups settling from many parts of Scandinavia and northern Germany. Even though few scholars would now accept Myres's early dating of certain urns to the 4th century A.D., or the specific application of the *foederati* term in a British context,[22] similar ideas have been extremely

[17] Leeds 1913, op. cit. in note 12, 74.
[18] N. Åberg, *The Anglo-Saxons in England* (Uppsala, 1926); C. Hills, 'The archaeology of Anglo-Saxon England in the pagan period: a review', *Anglo-Saxon England*, 8 (1979), 297–329; J. Hines, *The Scandinavian Character of Anglian England in the Pre-Viking Period* (BAR Brit. Ser., 124, Oxford, 1984); E. T. Leeds, 'The distribution of the Angles and Saxons archaeologically considered', *Archaeologia*, 91 (1945), 1–106; J. N. L. Myres, 'The Angles, the Saxons, and the Jutes', *Proc. Brit. Acad.*, 56 (1969), 145–74.
[19] J. N. L. Myres, 'Some English parallels to the Anglo-Saxon pottery of Holland and Belgium in the Migration Period', *L'Antiquité Classique*, 17 (1948), 453–72; J. N. L. Myres, 'Two Saxon urns from Ickwell Bury, Beds., and the Saxon penetration of the eastern Midlands', *Antiq. J.*, 39 (1959), 201–8; J. N. L. Myres, *Anglo-Saxon Pottery and the Settlement of England* (Oxford, 1969); Hills 1979, op. cit. in note 18; P. Sawyer, *Anglo-Saxon Lincolnshire* (Lincoln, 1999), 40.
[20] Myres, op. cit. in note 12, 334
[21] E. T. Leeds, 'The Early Saxon penetration of the Upper Thames area', *Antiq. J.*, 13 (1933), 229–51; Myres, op. cit. in note 12.
[22] S. C. Hawkes, 'The South-East after the Romans: the Saxon settlement', 78–95 in V. Maxfield (ed.), *The Saxon Shore* (Exeter, 1989); J. Hines, 'Philology, archaeology and the *adventus Saxonum vel Anglorum*', 18–36 in A. Bammesberger and A. Wollmann (eds.), *Britain 400–600: Language and History* (Heidelberg, 1990).

influential and have persisted into current scholarship. In more recent studies the same narrative is projected on to the evidence, but the administrators are regarded as sub-Roman British tyrants.[23] Simultaneously, the practice of cremation was deemed to reflect immigrants' diverse cultural origins, their Germanic purity, and the substantial scale of immigration. Furthermore, these were groups who were regarded as having little or no interaction with indigenous groups:[24] 'Cremation, wherever it occurs in massive numbers, is a clear sign of Anglo-Saxon settlement in sufficient density, or so well organised, as to be uninfluenced by the native culture of Romano-British society'.[25]

Increasingly, distribution maps were employed to define a discrete 'cremating' region in order to support these ideas.[26] For example, drawing upon an extensive gazetteer and a distribution map (Fig. 3), an important review of the 1960s stated that:

In the southern, Jutish and Saxon kingdoms, cremation seems to have been used only in the very earliest period, and even then probably alongside inhumation, which rapidly became the sole rite. In the Anglian areas, discounting Mid Anglia and Northumbria, cremation seems to have been universal at the beginning and was used for the whole of the period of pagan burials, although a drift towards inhumation was observable at the end.[27]

and that:

. . .there is some truth in the old dictum that Angles cremated, Saxons and Jutes inhumed. The only "pure cremation" cemeteries— (that is, those with no inhumation at all, or only a few of late date) — are in the Anglian areas, and particularly in East Anglia.[28]

These statements indicate an increasing optimism in respect of the possibility of ascribing regional, tribal and ethnic labels to the rite, a process which was supported by distribution maps.[29] Such views were extremely influential throughout the 1970s, 1980s and 1990s, with many texts confidently referring to an Anglian region of 'cremating peoples' (Fig. 4):[30] 'These were out-and-out barbarians, many from far beyond the zone of previous direct contact with the Roman Empire, who, even after they arrived in Britain, remained totally unromanized both in their burial customs and their material culture'.[31]

The 'New Archaeology' of the 1970s and the post-processual and interpretative archaeologies of the 1980s and 1990s brought with them more rigorous methodologies and explicit theoretical perspectives. They also introduced a more critical and cautious attitude towards defining archaeological 'cultures' from material culture, building

---

[23] E.g. Hills, op. cit. in note 18, 300; Myres 1969, op. cit. in note 19; J. N. L. Myres, *The English Settlements* (Oxford, 1986). For a review and critique, see Hines, op. cit. in note 22.
[24] See Hawkes, op. cit. in note 22; Hills, op. cit. in note 18.
[25] Myres 1986, op. cit. in note 23.
[26] Hawkes, op. cit. in note 22. N. Higham, *Rome, Britain and the Anglo-Saxons* (London, 1992); Leeds 1936, op. cit. in note 12; A. L. Meaney, *A Gazetteer of Early Anglo-Saxon Burial Sites* (Oxford, 1964).
[27] Meaney, op. cit. in note 26, 15.
[28] Ibid.
[29] L. Alcock, *Arthur's Britain* (London, 1971), 287; J. Campbell, 'The lost centuries: 400–600', 20–44 in J. Campbell (ed.), *The Anglo-Saxons* (London, 1982); Hawkes, op. cit. in note 22; Higham, op. cit. in note 26; L. Laing and J. Laing, *Anglo-Saxon England* (London, 1979); J. Morris, *The Age of Arthur* (London, 1973) 59, 107.
[30] Hawkes, op. cit. in note 22, 85.
[31] Ibid., 84.

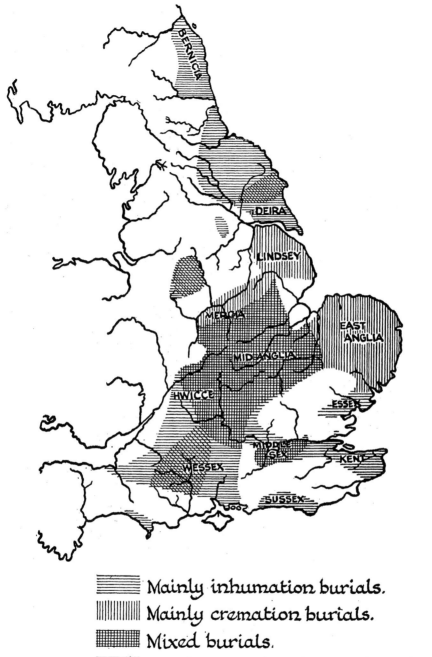

Mainly inhumation burials.

Mainly cremation burials.

Mixed burials.

Mainly secondary barrow burials.

FIG. 3

Meaney's distribution map of cremation, mixed-rite and inhumation rites (after Meaney, op. cit. in note 26).

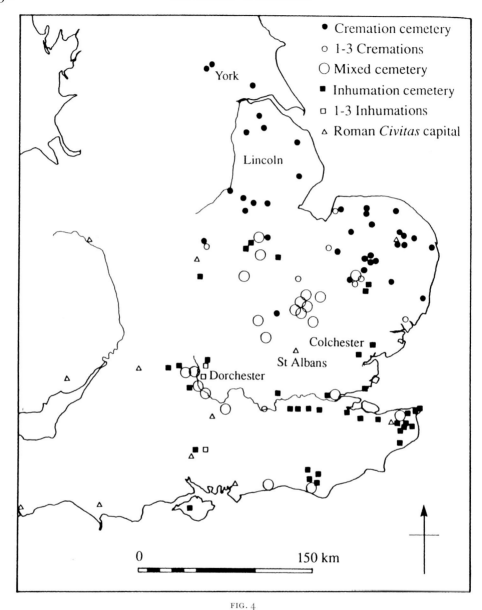

FIG. 4

Hawkes's distribution map of cremation, mixed-rite and inhumation rites (after Hawkes, op. cit. in note 22).

traditions and burial rites. These approaches percolated into Anglo-Saxon studies and brought novel methods and theories concerning the burial evidence, which overlapped and intermingled with more 'traditional' approaches. Nevertheless, while these paradigm shifts provided a change of emphasis, the labelling of cremation rites continued apace.[32] Leading proponents of a 'processual' view of the Roman-medieval transition downplayed the scale and significance of Anglo-Saxon immigration in the 5th century, yet adhered to the terminology of earlier scholars:

'Cremation has never been disputed as a Germanic burial rite, and one which is most common in eastern England; but it is found to some extent in all the Anglo-Saxon areas'.[33]

Even the minimal view of the size of Germanic immigration adopted by Higham does not prevent him from regarding cremation as indicating 'pure' and 'free' Germanic settlers.[34]

In recent years, discussions of migration and ethnicity have been in resurgence,[35] yet in marked contrast to the heated debates surrounding the cultural status of inhumation graves, interpretations surrounding cremation have remained fairly consistent. Cremation is perceived as unproblematic and easily explained using the terms defined by Kemble and other antiquarians. Perhaps the only partial exceptions to this situation have been qualifications suggested by the work of Julian Richards and Catherine Hills. In a detailed and quantitative survey, Richards has emphasized the internal diversity and regional variability of the cremation rite, while Hills has raised concerns about the traditional view of cremation rites when discussing the Spong Hill cemetery.[36] However, because detailed and thorough comparisons between Spong Hill and other continental cremation cemeteries show overwhelming similarities both in material culture and burial rite,[37] the traditional interpretations of those similarities are largely retained. With qualifications, migration is still perceived as the primary mechanism for the transmission of cremation rites to England, and the ethnic status of those buried in the graves remains the primary focus of interest. These perspectives can be traced back to the work of John Kemble.

[32] C. J. Arnold, *Roman Britain to Saxon England* (London, 1984); M. Faull, 'British survival in Anglo-Saxon Northumbria', 1–56 in L. Laing (ed.) *Studies in Celtic Survival* (BAR Brit. Ser., 37, Oxford, 1977).

[33] Arnold, op. cit. in note 32, 128.

[34] Higham, op. cit. in note 26, 17, fig. 6.4, 170–8; N. Higham, 'The Saxon conquests in Britain: literary evidence and the case for acculturation in the formation of Anglo-Saxon England', *Stud. zur Sachsenforschung*, 11 (1998), 135–44.

[35] Hamerow 1994, op. cit. in note 3; H. Härke, 'Archaeologists and migrations: a problem of attitude', *Current Anthropology*, 39 (1998), 19–45; J. Hines, 'The becoming of the English: identity, material culture and language in early Anglo-Saxon England', *Anglo-Saxon Stud. Archaeol. Hist.*, 7 (1994), 49–59; Scull, op. cit. in note 3.

[36] C. Hills, 'Did the people of Spong Hill come from Schleswig-Holstein?', *Stud. zur Sachsenforschung*, 11 (1998), 145–54; C. Hills, 'Spong Hill and the *adventus Saxonum*', 15–26 in C. E. Karkov, K. Wickham-Crowley and B. Young (eds.), *Spaces of the Living and the Dead: An Archaeological Dialogue* (Oxford, 1999); J. D. Richards, *The Significance of Form and Decoration of Anglo-Saxon Cremation Urns* (BAR Brit. Ser., 166, Oxford, 1987); J. D. Richards, 'Style and symbol: explaining variability in Anglo-Saxon cremation burials', 145–61 in S. T. Driscoll and M. R. Nieke (eds.), *Power and Politics in Early Medieval Britain and Ireland* (Edinburgh, 1988).

[37] M. Gebühr, 'Überlegungen zum archäologischen Nachweis von Wanderungen am Beispiel der Angelsächsischen landnahme in Britannien', *Archäol. Informationen*, 20.1 (1997), 11–24; M. Gebühr, 'Angulus desertus?', *Stud. zur Sachsenforschung*, 11 (1998), 43–86; M. Weber, 'Das Gräberfeld von Issendorf, Niedersachsen: Ausgangspunkt für Wanderungen nach Britannien?', *Stud. zur Sachsenforschung*, 11 (1998), 199–212.

PAGANISM AND CREMATION

The remarkable persistence of the ethnic interpretation of cremation can be explained by its association with another label, namely that cremation is 'pagan'. This view can be traced right back to the 'Brampton Urns' described by Sir Thomas Browne as representing 'Pagan vain-glories which thought the world might last forever'.[38] The idea that cremation indicates pagan belief was central to John Kemble's interpretation and he contrasted this with the Christian status of the inhumation rite: 'the occurrence of both modes in one cemetery has nothing at all to disturb us, or to throw doubt upon the one conclusion to which all other considerations lead; namely that the skeletons are those of Christians, — the urns, with ashes, those of Pagans'.[39]

While Kemble believed that few pagans would have been buried unburnt,[40] others realized that his scheme was inadequate. Rolleston accepted the contemporaneous date and 'Germanic' character of Anglo-Saxon inhumations and cremations, but differed from Kemble in regarding both cremation and inhumation as pagan. Despite this, for many, cremation still embodies the impact of paganism on England and it is often regarded as somehow 'more pagan' than inhumation or as the archetypal pagan practice:

'When we consider how distinctively Christianity opposed itself to the practice of cremation, every fresh discovery of these distinctively Anglo-Saxon urns shows us how thoroughly overrun our England was by the "heathen of the Northern sea" in the period which elapsed between the landings in it of Hengist and that of Augustine'.[41]

Since the 19th century, scholars have linked this view of cremation as 'pagan' and 'heathen' to an idea of cultural purity and the 'Germanic', barbarian and primitive nature of groups following the rite. Even though scholars today would accept the caveats and difficulties of ascribing religious labels to early medieval burial rites, the interpretation of cremation has largely escaped such discussions.[42] Pagan symbolism has been suggested to explain the provision of whetstones, iron miniature toilet implements, holed urns, runic pot decorations and the sacrifice of animals during cremation rites.[43] Scandinavian mythology has also provided inspiration for interpretations. For example, the freestyle decoration of a wolf and ship found on a fragment of biconical urn R9/10 from Caistor by Norwich (Norfolk) has been interpreted as a scene from Ragnarak depicting the giant wolf *Fenrir* and the boat *Naglfar* (Fig. 5).[44] Another perspective is to regard the cremation rite as reflecting the 'cult' of a particular pagan deity. By analogy with the attributes of gods described in later Scandinavian

[38] Browne, op. cit. in note 1, 74.
[39] Kemble, op. cit. in note 9, 332.
[40] Ibid., 325–6.
[41] Rolleston 1869, op. cit. in note 12; Rolleston 1870, op. cit. in note 12.
[42] E.g. R. Bruce-Mitford, 'The Sutton Hoo ship burial: some foreign connections', *Settimane di studio del Centro Italiano di Studi Sull'Alto Medioevo*, 32 (1986), 144–210; D. Wilson, *Anglo-Saxon Paganism* (London, 1992); J. Hines. 'Religion: the limits of knowledge', 375–410 in J. Hines (ed.) *The Anglo-Saxons from the Migration Period to the Eighth Century: An Ethnographic Perspective* (Woodbridge, 1997).
[43] T. C. Lethbridge, *A Cemetery at Lackford, Suffolk* (Cambridge, 1951); Myres and Green, op. cit. in note 4; M. Ravn, 'Theoretical and methodological approaches to Migration Period burials', 41–56 in M. Rundkvist (ed.), op cit. in note 3; N. Reynolds, 'The king's whetstone: a footnote', *Antiquity*, 54 (1980), 232–7; Wilson, op. cit. in note 42.
[44] Myres and Green, op. cit. in note 4, 118.

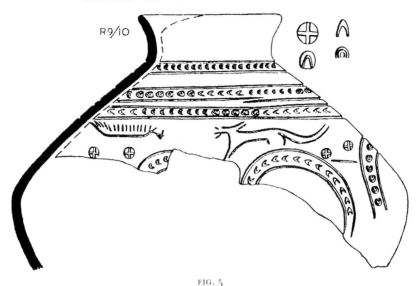

FIG. 5

Animal decoration on urns from Caistor-by-Norwich. (after Myres and Green, op. cit. in note 22).

written sources, it is considered that the Anglo-Saxon gods Woden, Thunor and Tiw are likely candidates to have been associated with the rite, especially as runes thought to be associated with Tiw have been identified on some cremation urns.[45]

Some comments have been ventured about the cremation process itself. It has been suggested that cremation functioned to release the spirit of the deceased, symbolized fertility and regeneration, and/or prevented the dead from harming the living.[46] Surprisingly, the possibility that cremation might facilitate transportation to a pagan afterlife is only occasionally broached.[47] Inspired by perspectives common in post-processual and symbolic archaeologies, Julian Richards has gone further in discussing the symbolism of the graves, but his interpretation is largely social (i.e. related to the roles of the deceased during life), rather than eschatological, cosmological or religious.[48]

There is one further influential idea that has been proposed concerning the pagan character of cremation. Rather than debating the symbolic and religious 'meaning' of cremation, Martin Carver has addressed the political and ideological context of the rite when used within the high-status barrow burial tradition of the late 6th and early 7th centuries. He has suggested that in combination with barrow building, ship burial,

[45] H. Ellis, *The Road to Hel* (Cambridge, 1943); H. Ellis-Davidson, *Gods and Myths of Northern Europe* (London, 1964) 83, 152; W. Filmer-Sankey, 'Snape Anglo-Saxon cemetery: the current state of knowledge', 39–51 in M. O. H. Carver (ed.) *The Age of Sutton Hoo* (Woodbridge, 1992); Reynolds, op. cit. in note 43; G. Owen, *Rites and Religions of the Anglo-Saxons* (New York, 1981), 79–95.

[46] Laing and Laing, op. cit. in note 29, 110; Meaney, op.cit in note 26, 16; B. Griffiths, *Aspects of Anglo-Saxon Magic* (Hockwold-cum-Wilton, 1996), 35–6; P. Stafford, *The East Midlands in the Early Middle Ages* (Leicester, 1985).

[47] R. I. Page, *Life in Anglo-Saxon England* (London, 1970), 34.

[48] J. D. Richards, 'Anglo-Saxon symbolism', 131–48 in Carver, op.cit. in note 45; Bond, op. cit. in note 5, 79.

and the conspicuous investment of wealthy and exotic material culture at the funeral, cremation may have formed part of a complex ritual statement on an international stage. At a time of hegemony or strong influence by the Christian kingdoms of Kent and Merovingian Gaul upon East Anglia, the remains of elaborate funerals from Sutton Hoo (Suffolk) and elsewhere may have had an important role as statements of ideological resistance.[49]

While many of these observations are invaluable, they all share some common features. Nowhere is the paganism of cremation explained as a coherent thesis; it is an assumed status for the rite based on later, continental sources. Furthermore, even if these sources do tell us that cremation was non-Christian in most contexts, there is no attempt to explain why it held pagan religious significance. The 'pagan' label is thought to be enough in itself. Consequently, interpretations share the implicit assumption derived from the work of Kemble, that cremation is inherently pagan and this religious label underpins and supports the Germanic cultural connotations of the rite.

CHRONOLOGY AND CREMATION

Let us now turn to the third element of the characterization of cremation rites: chronology. Once more we find the origins of modern interpretations in the work of Kemble. He stated 'I believe cremation to have been originally the universal rite of all Teutonic races, — as well as most others in the north of Europe, — and of by far the greatest number I can prove it to have so been'.[50]

In his earlier writings, E. T. Leeds's view was that 'cremation was unquestionably the older rite'.[51] He argued that the practice quickly waned in popularity in England as a result of practical difficulties and cultural interactions with native groups. He famously described a 'flight from cremation' at a very early date during the Anglo-Saxon settlement and, in his view, the occasional late cremation did not alter this fact.[52] In adopting this standpoint, he allowed many writers to regard cremation as a chronological marker, with the proportion of cremation burials at a site as a broad indication of how early the cemetery was established.[53] In other works, however, he took a different view and accepted that cremation rites were a 'persistent practice' and 'evidently continued to thrive practically down to the time when burial in the open country entirely ceased'.[54]

---

[49] M. O. H. Carver, 'Kingship and material culture in early Anglo-Saxon East Anglia', 141–59 in S. Bassett (ed.), *The Origins of Anglo-Saxon Kingdoms* (Leicester, 1989); M. O. H. Carver, 'Boat-burial in Britain: ancient custom or political signal?', 111–24 in O. Crumlin-Pedersen (ed.), *The Ship as Symbol in Prehistoric and Medieval Scandinavia* (Copenhagen, 1995); M. O. H. Carver, *Sutton Hoo: Burial Ground of Kings?* (Woodbridge, 1998), 134–6.
[50] Kemble, op. cit. in note 9, 323.
[51] Leeds, op. cit. in note 21, 234.
[52] Ibid.
[53] E. T. Leeds, 'An Anglo-Saxon cemetery at Wheatley, Oxfordshire', *Proc. Soc. Antiq. London*, 29 (1916), 48–65; J. Kirk, 'Anglo-Saxon cremation and inhumation in the Upper Thames Valley in pagan times', 123–31 in D. B. Harden (ed.), *Dark Age Britain* (London, 1956).
[54] Leeds 1913, op. cit. in note 12; Leeds 1936, op. cit. in note 12, 34–5; Leeds, op. cit. in note 21.

J. N. L. Myres also emphasized the longevity of cremation alongside inhumation and in an early article, disputed that cremation, mixed-rite and inhumation cemeteries should be attributed to different chronological phases. Yet for Myres, the *interpretative* importance of cremation graves lay in the ceramic urns and the early dating of some of them as evidence of Germanic settlement, rather than the longevity of the ritual practice.[55] Indeed, Myres was even willing to place the earliest cremation graves as far back as the 4th century, although his reasoning has since been seriously criticized. What were perceived to be 4th-century Germanic cremation burials are now either regarded as the continuation of early Roman cremation rites or the re-use of Roman vessels for 5th and 6th-century burials.[56]

Ceramic urns are notoriously difficult to date accurately, but many scholars have subsequently doubted that ceramics and metalwork from cremation graves can be securely assigned to before the mid-5th century.[57] Even so, the relatively early inception of large cremation cemeteries in the early or mid-5th century remains the orthodoxy, with many inhumation and mixed-rite cemeteries believed to begin later.[58] In turn, some accounts (although by no means all) have proposed that the reduced frequency of cremation in the Thames valley and further south reflects the later date at which these areas were settled from core areas in East Anglia.[59] In particular, the legacy of these arguments concerning the 'early' date of cremation has lead to the rite being caricatured as a 5th-century phenomenon with inhumation taking its place during the 6th century and 7th century.[60]

For Myres, Leeds and many others, then, both the early date of cremation and its persistence in eastern England provided strong evidence for the Germanic, pagan and conservative nature of those communities employing the rite. When ascribed to cremation graves, the term 'early' has taken on more than chronological significance. The phrase also seems to embody the cultural and religious character and conservatism of the cremation rite. This in turn is used to define cremation as evidence of early settlers from northern Germany and southern Scandinavia. Little attention is paid to the fact that cremation occurs contemporaneously with inhumation in many regions, often in the same cemeteries for many decades, and that it persisted into the 7th century.

[55] Compare Myres, op. cit. in note 12 with Myres, op. cit. in note 19; Myres, op. cit. in note 23.
[56] Hills, op. cit. in note 18; R. Philpott, *Burial Practices in Roman Britain* (BAR Brit. Ser., 219, 1991), 50–2; R. White, *Roman and Celtic Objects from Anglo-Saxon Graves* (BAR Brit. Ser., Oxford, 1991); V. I. Evison, *An Anglo-Saxon Cemetery at Alton, Hampshire* (Gloucester, 1988), 88.
[57] For recent reviews, see Hines, op. cit. in note 22; M. Welch, 'Relating Anglo-Saxon chronology to continental chronologies in the fifth century AD', 31–8 in U. von Freeden, U. Koch and A. Wieczorek (eds.), *Völker an Nord- und Ostsee und die Franken* (Bonn, 1999).
[58] H. W. Böhme, 'Das Ende der Römerherrschaft in Britannien und die anglesächsische Besiedlung Englands im 5. Jahrhundert', *Jahrbuch des Römisch-Germanischen Zentralmuseums Mainz*, 33.3 (1986), 469–574; Carver 1989, op. cit. in note 49; Hines, op. cit. in note 22; Myres 1969, op. cit. in note 19.
[59] Leeds, op. cit. in note 21, 238; Carver 1989, op. cit. in note 49.
[60] Böhme, op. cit. in note 58; Carver 1989, op. cit. in note 49; C. Hills, '*Beowulf* and archaeology', 311–24 in R. Bjork and J. Niles (eds.), *A Beowulf Handbook* (Exeter, 1997); Kirk, op. cit. in note 53; K. Leahy, 'The formation of the Anglo-Saxon kingdom of Lindsey', *Anglo-Saxon Stud. Archaeol. Hist.*, 10 (1999), 127–34; Sawyer, op. cit. in note 19, 40, 46; T. Williamson, *The Origins of Norfolk* (Manchester, 1993), 68.

THE ABSENCE OF INTERPRETATION

So far, this paper has suggested that cremation rites have been characterized in relation to three all-encompassing and self-perpetuating themes. However, the most common approach to cremation in the literature is one of description rather than interpretation.[61] Culture-historical studies were much more interested in the stylistic attributes of objects than the funerary contexts in which they were found.[62] Even in more recent studies, detailed analyses usually focus upon inhumation graves where the data are perceived to be of higher quality than in cremations.[63] Furthermore, as researchers have tried to move away from ethnic and religious labels when discussing burial rites there has been a tendency to disregard the potential importance of the mode of disposing of the dead. This attitude in itself has a long history which can be identified in antiquarian writings: 'To the heathen the two modes of sepulture were comparatively indifferent, and very slight reasons may have determined his choice of the one or the other'.[64]

According to E. T. Leeds, varying funerary practices reflected 'nothing more than local habit or some difference in origin'.[65] In summary, where cremation rites have not been categorized in terms of the three pervasive labels discussed above, the only alternative approaches have been to ignore interpretation altogether, or to regard the choice of disposal method as having limited importance.

A CRITIQUE OF TRADITIONAL PERSPECTIVES

These readings of cremation rites in early England can be traced from the antiquarian researches of the 19th century through culture-historical, processual and post-processual studies with a substantial degree of consistency both in detailed and specialist studies and more popular and synthetic accounts.[66] We must of course consider past studies within the historical context of their time, and the paradigms and academic traditions they employed. Indeed, we can perceive the interpretations as ideological products of the academic and social contexts in which they were written. However, the aim of this paper is not to blame individual scholars for the perspectives they have followed in the past, but instead, to chart the influence of the ideas generated in 19th-century research on the interpretation of cremation rites in subsequent academic generations. Without a critical awareness of the background to the interpretation of cremation rites, it is difficult to see how archaeologists can develop

[61] E.g. M. Welch, *Anglo-Saxon England* (London, 1992); Wilson, op. cit. in note 42.
[62] See recently, Hines, op. cit. in note 22; Hines, op. cit. in note 35.
[63] E.g. G. Fisher, 'Kingdom and community in early Anglo-Saxon eastern England', 147–66 in L. Beck (ed.), *Regional Approaches to Mortuary Analysis* (New York, 1995); J. Huggett, 'Social analysis of early Anglo-Saxon inhumation burials: archaeological methodologies', *J. European Archaeol.*, 4.3 (1996), 337–65; E.-J. Pader, *Symbolism, Social Relations and the Interpretation of Mortuary Remains* (BAR Int. Ser., 82, Oxford, 1982).
[64] Rolleston, op. cit. in note 12, 434.
[65] Leeds 1936, op. cit. in note 12, 32.
[66] Here I feel my argument follows that of Härke concerning interpretations of the weapon burial rite; that the readings of the evidence by 'traditionalist', 'new' and 'post-processual' archaeologists share many common features and can rest on misleading terminology (in his case study the phrase 'warrior graves'): H. Härke, ' "Warrior graves"? The background of the Anglo-Saxon weapon burial rite', *Past and Present*, 126 (1990); 22–43.

further understandings of the practice and introduce new ways of seeing the evidence. So, the purpose of the above has been to show how these terms have persisted and been uncritically accepted within many different schools of archaeological thought. It can be argued that in the course of their use, the terms 'Germanic', 'Anglian', 'pagan' and 'early' have become more than useful abbreviations for the character of the graves, becoming instead regarded as inalienable attributes of the rite. Consequently the terms themselves have come to embody implicit assumptions about the significance of burning the dead and the origins of those practising the rite. While archaeologists have become uncomfortable with these terms when applied to other categories of evidence, when considering cremation, they are rarely overtly criticized and sometimes staunchly defended.

In what ways then, are these terms misplaced? There is now a burgeoning literature discussing the nature of ancient migrations and the problems and possibilities of using archaeological evidence in their identification. There are also debates about the potential longevity, complexity and scale of immigration in the 5th and 6th centuries A.D.[67] Likewise, there are increasing concerns over viewing migration in isolation from a variety of other forms of cultural interaction and exchange across the North Sea at this time.[68] All these themes are commonplace in the recent archaeological literature.[69] Cremation was widespread across northern Germany and southern Scandinavian in the Roman Iron Age, and recent papers by Gebühr, Hills and Weber have convincingly identified close similarities between English and continental cremation rites.[70] However, the interpretation of these similarities needs further consideration. We are still not sure to what extent migration was important in the adoption of cremation in eastern and southern England as opposed to, or in combination with, other mechanisms of cultural transmission. This similarity equally does not explain the continued and changing uses of cremation from the 5th through to the 7th century within the English context. In the light of the above, terms such as 'Germanic' seem overly simplistic and may obscure a variety of complex social processes, cultural interactions, and population movements that we are only beginning to fully appreciate.

Concerning the parallel topic of culture and ethnicity, there is a wide range of anthropological, sociological and historical studies that lead us to question the traditional relationship between burial rites and ethnic groups in early medieval Britain.[71] These have been discussed in some detail elsewhere.[72] Many scholars perceive early medieval ethnic groupings to be relatively fluid (if not arbitrary), with their definition and expression dependant upon context and situation, and defined as much by symbolic and ideological criteria as by customs, language and physical

---

[67] Scull, op. cit. in note 3.
[68] Hines, op. cit. in note 18; Carver 1989, op. cit. in note 49; Hodges, op. cit. in note 32.
[69] Hamerow 1994, op. cit. in note 3; Hines, op. cit. in note 18; Hines, op. cit. in note 22.
[70] Hills 1998, op. cit. in note 36; Gebühr, op. cit. in note 37; Weber, op. cit. in note 37.
[71] Lucy 1999, op. cit. in note 3.
[72] Lucy 1998, op. cit. in note 3; Lucy 1999, op. cit. in note 3; see also H. Williams, 'Identities and cemeteries in Roman and Early Medieval Britain', 96–107 in P. Baker, C. Forcey, S. Jundi and R. Witcher (eds.), TRAC 98: Proceedings of the Eighth Annual Theoretical Roman Archaeology Conference, Leicester 1998 (Oxford, 1999).

differences.[73] Moreover, ethnic and group identities constituted through social and ritual practices are likely to be influential at a variety of social and regional levels and related to contemporary political arrangements.[74]

The particular role of funerals and cemeteries in relation to ethnic groups can also be re-appraised. Funerary rites can still be regarded as an important context for the expression of ethnic and political identities, yet we should not expect patterns in artefact distributions or burial rites to reflect group identities in a simplistic manner. We must consider the ideological roles of funerary practices in the construction, destruction and reproduction of social and ethnic identities. In other words, we should not simply regard mortuary practices as reflecting identities, but as being actively involved in their realization and transmission over time and space. When the discursive roles of mortuary practices are considered, it becomes evident that the material culture and modes of disposal employed may reflect aspirations, idealizations and (in some cases at least) conscious ideological programs, as much as the stable realities of past ethnic categories.[75] Consequently, the labels 'Germanic' and 'Anglian' may have little bearing on the actual character, complexity and fluidity of early medieval ethnic and social groups. While these labels are not completely invalid, they take the emphasis away from the active and formative role of mortuary practices in the process of ethnogenesis and the reproduction of group and community identity.

Alongside these theoretical points are some empirical ones. If cremation embodied ethnic identities, why do we find the rite over much of southern and eastern England, almost always in close proximity to contemporary inhumation rites? The reality of a defined 'cremating' region and an 'inhuming' region suggested by previous authors can be seriously questioned when we produce a distribution map of the frequency of both rites in all 5th and 6th-century cemeteries (Fig. 6).[76] This map was generated from a survey of all cemeteries with over ten graves where the relative proportions of cremation and inhumation are known with some degree of confidence. A glance at this map will demonstrate that the reality of any territorially exclusive region of cremation can be seriously questioned. Equally, in contrast to other distribution maps constructed in the past, it can be seen that mixed-rite cemeteries are found right across southern England and are not confined to the edges of those areas where cremation cemeteries are found. There are regional differences in the ways in which cremation is employed,

[73] E.g. P. Geary, 'Ethnic identity as a situational construct in the Early Middle Ages', 1–17 in E. Peters (ed.), *Folk Life in the Middle Ages* (Richmond, 1988).

[74] Ibid.

[75] Williams, op. cit. in note 72.

[76] The distribution maps presented here have been constructed from a sample of Anglo-Saxon cemeteries dated to the 5th or 6th centuries of at least ten graves. The definition of cemeteries is different from that usually used. 'Mixed-rite' cemeteries are defined as those sites with substantial numbers of both rites (15%–85% cremation). 'Inhumation' cemeteries are those with less than 15% cremation graves, 'cremation' cemeteries are those with over 85% cremation graves. In the North-East, a rare case of cremation being popular is at Hob Hill, Saltburn (North Yorkshire). In East Kent, Kemble noted early on that cremation was not completely absent, with only the poorly excavated cemetery at Westbere representing a possible mixed-rite cemetery; see R. F. Jessup, 'An Anglo-Saxon cemetery at Westbere, Kent', *Antiq. J.*, 26.3 (1946), 11–21. In Wiltshire and southern Hampshire, all the major cemetery excavations have produced little evidence of cremation rites. This stands in stark contrast to the neighbouring regions of the Upper Thames and northern Hampshire.

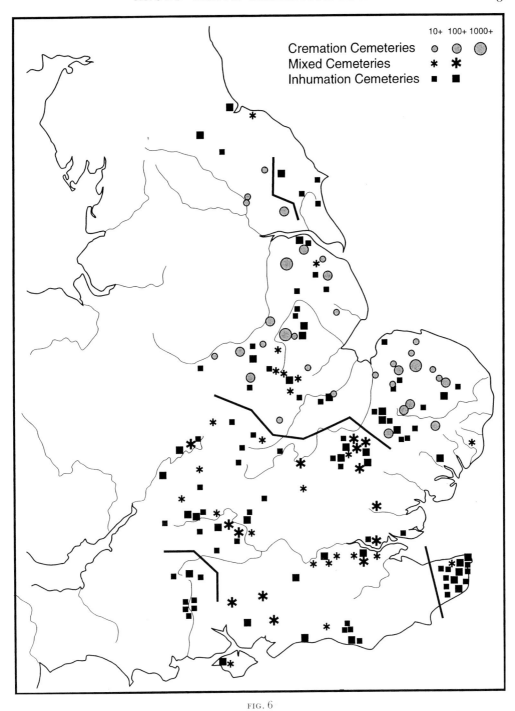

FIG. 6
A distribution map of cremation, mixed-rite and inhumation rites.

but this does not suggest that the use of cremation in itself defined a particular ethnic group.

The relationships between religious beliefs and mortuary practices have been debated in numerous contexts.[77] It is reasonable to assume that religious beliefs and practices had a central role in cremation rites, yet, such ideas have not so far been explored in any detail for early medieval Britain.[78] Firstly, as noted above, both inhumation and cremation are practised over much of early Anglo-Saxon England, and there is no reason to suppose that cremation in the late 5th and 6th centuries were any more 'pagan' or 'non-Christian' than contemporary inhumation rites. Furthermore, simply labelling the rite as pagan fails to focus attention on more specific lines of enquiry. For example, limited consideration has been given to the cultural and cosmological significance of fire as an agent of transformation on death,[79] nor has there been much discussion of the important roles of animal sacrifice in the funerary rite.[80] Further attention needs to be paid to the social and eschatological implications of post-cremation rites such as the motives for burying ashes in a communal cemetery.[81] In other words, the pagan label addresses the fact that cremation is taking place within a non-Christian and pre-Christian context, but it fails to deal with why and how cremation was pagan and what symbolic and religious significance the rite may have embodied. Indeed, as we have seen, most religious meanings inferred are isolated speculations concerning individual artefact types or exceptional pottery designs rather than a concern for the rite itself. So, as with the ethnic and cultural labels, the argument here is not that such labels are intrinsically 'wrong', but that they are simplistic, possibly misleading, and distract attention from a range of other potentially important and interesting questions.

Similarly objections can be put forward with regard to the chronological label. In terms of the available data, the oft-assumed 'early' date is misleading since, although cremation burials can sometimes be dated earlier than inhumation graves, in many cemeteries and regions, the rites were used contemporaneously over long periods. There is increasing evidence of cremation from secure 7th-century contexts, further emphasising the longevity of the rite.[82] It is also clear that a number of theoretical assumptions are implicit in the label 'early'. The term embodies a perception that cremation is somehow more pagan, more Germanic and more primitive than

---

[77] B. Young, 'The myth of the pagan cemetery', 61–86 in Karkov et al, op. cit. in note 36.

[78] H. Williams, 'The Burnt Germans of the Age of Iron': Early Anglo-Saxon Mortuary Practices and the Study of Cremation in Past Societies (unpublished PhD thesis, University of Reading, 2000); Wilson, op. cit. in note 42.

[79] P. Bachelard, The Psychoanalysis of Fire (London, 1964).

[80] Bond, op. cit. in note 5; P. Crabtree, 'The symbolic role of animals in Anglo-Saxon England: evidence from burials and cremations', 20–6 in K. Ryan and P. Crabtree (eds.), The Symbolic Role of Animals in Archaeology (Pennsylvania, 1995).

[81] E.g. M. M. Babu, 'Post-cremation-urn-burial of the Phayengs (Manipur): a study of mortuary behaviour', Eastern Anthropologist, 47.2 (1994), 157–71.

[82] K. Jarvis, Excavations in Christchurch 1969–1980 (Dorchester, 1973); T. C. Lethbridge, 'Anglo-Saxon burials at Soham', Proc. Cambridge. Antiq. Soc., 33 (1931), 152–63; T. Wilkinson, Archaeology and Environment in South Essex: Rescue Archaeology along the Grays By-Pass 1979–1980 (East Anglian Archaeol., 52, Chelmsford, 1988); K. R. Fennell, The Anglo-Saxon cemetery at Loveden Hill (Hough-on-the-Hill) Lincolnshire and its significance in relation to the Dark Age settlement of the East Midlands (unpublished PhD thesis, University of Nottingham, 1964).

inhumation. In this sense, it helps to perpetuate the ethnic and religious labels outlined above.

NEW PERSPECTIVES

If there are difficulties with these approaches, how can we move beyond simplistic labels towards a more adequate and sophisticated understanding of cremation rites? Unfortunately, a full discussion of potential new questions and approaches can only be fully explored elsewhere, but in this context, some basic observations can be made.[83] To some extent, this work has already begun with the research of Julian Richards and Mads Ravn whose emphasis is firmly on the social analysis of cremation graves, and mortuary variability within and between cemeteries.[84] Nevertheless, drawing on the work of Bourdieu and Giddens, we can also encourage the formation of a study focused on social practice and social reproduction rather than cultural categories.[85]

There is also a need to address the particular significance of funerary practices in the workings of society, the role of these rituals in constructing group identities and affinities as well as symbolising group differences.[86] In this regard, anthropological and sociological studies of mortuary practices provide a variety of valuable insights. It may be argued that the choice to cremate or inhume the dead was the most dramatic statement and distinction possible within the early medieval mortuary arena. In particular, we might wish to consider the significance of cremation as both a spectacle and a technology in defining social distinctions among the living through both observance and participation of the rites. In doing so, cremation also enhanced relationships between the living and the dead.[87] As a rite of passage fundamentally involved in the ritual transformation of the corpse, cremation and post-cremation rites serve to dissolve and reconstitute not only the identities of the deceased, but also those of the mourners.[88] As argued by Piers Vitebsky, Jonathan Parry and others, cremation and post-cremation rites in many societies are simultaneously social, cosmological and ontological events concerned with recreating the individual, society and the cosmos through performance.[89] If similar themes applied to the early medieval context, could the burning of the dead have been used by mourners as a deliberate ideological

[83] Williams, op. cit. in note 78.

[84] Richards 1987, op. cit. in note 36; Ravn, op. cit. in note 43.

[85] Lucy 1998, op. cit. in note 3; Lucy 1999, op. cit. in note 3.

[86] M. Parker Pearson, 'The powerful dead: relationships between the living and the dead', *Cambridge Archaeol. J.*, 3 (1993), 203–29; Williams, op. cit. in note 72.

[87] *Contra* Parker Pearson 1993, op. cit. in note 86, who sees cremation as 'distancing' the living from the dead in Iron-age Jutland.

[88] For rites of passage see M. Bloch and J. Parry, 'Introduction', 1–44 in M. Bloch and J. Parry (eds.), *Death and the Regeneration of Life* (Cambridge, 1982); R. Hertz, *Death and the Right Hand*, trans. R. Needham (New York, 1960); P. Metcalf and R. Huntingdon, *Celebrations of Death* (Cambridge, 1991).

[89] J. Parry, *Death in Benaras* (Cambridge, 1994); P. Vitebsky, *Dialogues with the Dead* (Cambridge, 1993). See also: K. Århem, 'Into the realm of the sacred: an interpretation of Khasi funerary ritual', 257–99 in S. Cederroth, C. Corlin and J. Lindström (eds.), *On the Meaning of Death: Essays on Mortuary Rituals and Eschatological Beliefs* (Uppsala, 1989); M. Hobart, 'The path of the soul', 5–28 in G. Milner (ed.), *Natural Symbols in South East Asia* (London, 1978); A. B. Hudson, 'Death ceremonies of the Padju Epat Ma'anyan Dayaks', *Sarawak Museum J.*, 13 (1966), 342–416; S. Kan, *Symbolic Immortality: The Tlingit Potlatch of the Nineteenth Century* (Washington, 1989).

statement of perceived group identity and origin myths as well as a powerful 'strategy of distinction'.[90]

Bearing these ideas in mind, let us briefly return to the large cremation cemeteries of eastern England, sites where cremation is the persistent and predominant burial rite for up to two centuries from the mid-5th century to the early-7th century A.D. (Fig. 7).[91] These cemeteries sometimes comprise several thousand graves representing the continued use of a site over long periods for the repeated burial of the dead of dispersed communities. In their size, early inception and the predominance of cremation, the cemeteries at Loveden Hill (Lincolnshire), Newark, Thurmaston (Leicestershire), Caistor-by-Norwich, Spong Hill and Lackford (Suffolk) contrast with neighbouring inhumation cemeteries. We can reasonably presume that these central places served as a focus for the assembly of large numbers of people for ritual practices.[92] Moreover, the burial of cinerary urns provided a special and distinctive form of mortuary space and a high spatial concentration of graves that would not be possible with inhumation rites. Each burial consisted of human remains, sometimes combined with cremated animal bones of a range of species including horses, sheep/goat, cattle, pigs and dogs that were slaughtered and apparently accompanying the dead on the pyre.[93] Pyre-goods were also retrieved and mingled with the human and animal bones buried in a ceramic urn. New burials were often placed in close spatial relationships to existing graves. Also, the cemeteries can be shown in some cases to deliberately focus upon prominent ancient monuments such as Bronze-age barrows (e.g. Pensthorpe (Norfolk) and Spong Hill), or occasionally overlooking the abandoned sites of Roman towns (e.g. Caistor-by-Norwich, Ancaster (Lincolnshire) and York).

At these sites, we can see the identity of the deceased person and their social group being defined by the mourners in at least two inter-related ways. Firstly, individuals were translated and physically reconstituted into a new state and identity through the ritual transformations of the cremation ceremony and subsequent burial. The mingling of the dead with the remains of sacrificed animals, artefacts and their inclusion in a ceramic urn, created a new 'social body' for the individual.[94] In a sizeable proportion of burials, more than one individual was buried in the same urn, and given that the urns are often placed in close spatial proximity and the landscape location of cemeteries, it appears as if space and place had an important role in creating identities in death.[95] This manner of burial created a distinctive community of the dead that slowly evolved and gained significance over time with the addition of new graves. In both these ways, through ritual transformation and the significance of place, cremation and post-cremation ceremonies created a specific forum within which individual and group identities were defined. While Julian Richards has emphasized the variability in urn forms and how they may represent the particular identities of individuals, the

[90] P. Bourdieu, *Distinction: A Social Critique of the Judgement of Taste* (London, 1984).
[91] Hills, op. cit. in note 4; McKinley, op. cit. in note 5.
[92] McKinley, op. cit. in note 5.
[93] Ibid.
[94] The idea that material culture employed in post-cremation rites can be regarded as a new 'body' for the deceased is widespread in many societies and is discussed in the anthropological literature. For example, see Babu, op. cit. in note 81.
[95] McKinley, op. cit. in note 5.

FIG. 7

Plan of the Spong Hill, Norfolk cremation cemetery (after McKinley, op. cit. in note 5).
Reproduced with kind permission of Norfolk Landscape Archaeology.

overall impression of the cemetery is one of relative uniformity. The individuality of specific urns and their contents would soon be forgotten and few wealthy artefacts were placed in the graves intact to signal the deceased's identity and group affiliation. Also, there are few signs of substantial grave-markers to identify individual graves. Instead of monuments and grave-goods, it was the process of transformation by fire, and the repeated use and growing significance of place, that in combination sustained links between communities and the dead. Distinctive conceptions of the dead person and community were defined and it is through these constructions that any ethnic and religious statements were expressed. Furthermore, the cremation and the cemetery space would have contrasted visibly with neighbouring communities who were practising inhumation as the predominant mortuary practice. This again would have asserted links between the use of cremation and people's sense of identity and social difference.

From such a perspective, traditional interpretations of cremation can be overturned. Instead of seeing cremation solely as evidence of Germanic immigration, we should be concerned with why this practice is followed at all in early medieval Britain. After all, if substantial groups were entering into Britain in the 5th and 6th centuries, then it is hard to believe that they would not have come into close contact with indigenous communities and been influenced by their rites.[96] Indeed this is one of the explanations for the increasing popularity of inhumation rites in the 6th century. Therefore, we need to address why certain groups retained cremation as an important social practice for so long, rather than seeing its presence as an inevitable consequence of Germanic immigration. It may be the conservatism of the rite, and the mythical and cultural statements it made about origins and community in a time of dramatic social and political change and its particular construction of a communal sacred place, that made it an enduring symbol of group identity. There are numerous anthropological analogies for the importance of funerary rites as the embodiment of group identities and links with the past and tradition for immigrant communities in the modern world undergoing rapid social change.[97] In other words, we may consider the use of cremation rites in 5th- and 6th-century eastern England as a powerful statement by individuals and groups of their ideological and political affiliations with parts of northern Europe. This may also explain why cremation rites endured to become such an integral part of high-status barrow burial rites in the early 7th century A.D.

Although there is not the room to explore the significance of these ideas further in this paper, it is hoped that these suggestions provide a basis for rethinking the way we study and interpret the significance of cremation in early medieval Britain. These themes may allow us to move beyond the narrow historical focus of John Kemble, and instead pursue the debate started by Sir Thomas Browne concerning the significance of cremation in ancient societies. Sociological and anthropological studies of cremation in communities from around the world can provide analogies and insights in this regard as discussed above, but inevitably it is only through the reappraisal of the archaeological evidence in the light of these theories that these ideas can be

---

96 The traditional interpretation rests on the view that 'cremating peoples' had little exposure to Roman culture. See Higham, op. cit. in note 26; Hawkes op. cit. in note 22.

97 Williams, op. cit. in note 78.

demonstrated further. Such a reassessment involves thinking of cremation as a social practice, rather than providing it with convenient labels or regarding it as a functional process. By doing so, we may provide a starting point for a more sophisticated view of early medieval cremation rites, moving beyond regarding cremation rites solely as the *Remains of Pagan Saxondom*.[98]

ACKNOWLEDGEMENTS

Many thanks to Bruce Eagles, Catherine Hills, Kevin Leahy, Aliki Pantos and David Petts for discussions and advice during research for this paper and for commenting on earlier drafts. Aliki Pantos must also be thanked individually for her special efforts in proofreading earlier drafts of this paper. However, all omissions and opinions remain my responsibility. Susan and Philip Williams provided constant support.

[98] Akerman, op. cit. in note 8.

Burial Practice in Early Medieval Eastern Britain: Constructing Local Identities, Deconstructing Ethnicity

By SAM LUCY

Until relatively recently, material culture — the structures, material remains and artefacts which are excavated by archaeologists— was assumed to be straightforward in nature. An excavated burial associated with, for example, a brooch decorated in a distinctive way, could confidently be linked to the 'archaeological culture' (in prehistoric archaeology) or the 'tribal group' (in proto-historic archaeology) with which that brooch-type was identified. This approach, commonly termed the culture-historical approach, was for many decades almost universally accepted by western European archaeologists.[1] As a result, archaeology as a discipline studied the history of 'cultures' or 'tribes' (the 'Beaker Folk or the 'Anglo-Saxons', for example), rather than the people wearing and using the material. The distribution of this material culture was assumed to represent the distribution of culture groups — groups whose members were often thought of as racially linked. The spread of that material from a neighbouring area was taken to represent the movement or expansion of that group, usually by the processes of invasion or migration.[2]

Such approaches have largely been rejected in Anglo-American prehistoric archaeology, which now places more emphasis on the internal dynamics which operate within societies. Changes in material culture are seen instead as reflecting more complex societal changes, rather than the simple replacement of one people by another, or the expansion of a group.[3] The brand of archaeology known as post-processual archaeology also recognizes that people actively use material culture, that there are generally many different types available, and that particular items are selected for use or display for particular reasons (although these may not be conscious or deliberate).[4]

Within early medieval archaeology, however, the view of material culture as straightforward is still deeply ingrained in many archaeologists' interpretations. A person buried with an 'Anglo-Saxon' brooch (i.e. a brooch which has typological and stylistic parallels in the Germanic or Scandinavian areas of the continent) is usually

[1] U. Veit, 'Ethnic concepts in German prehistory: a case study on the relationship between cultural identity and objectivity', 35–56 in S. Shennan (ed.), *Archaeological Approaches to Cultural Identity* (London, 1989).

[2] S. Jones, 'Discourses of identity in the interpretation of the past', 62–80 in P. Graves-Brown, S. Jones and C. Gamble (eds.) *Cultural Identity and Archaeology: The Construction of European Communities* (London, 1996).

[3] G. Clark, 'The invasion hypothesis in British archaeology', *Antiquity*, 40 (1966), 172–89; T. Champion, 'Theoretical archaeology in Britain', 129–60 in I. Hodder (ed.) *Archaeological Theory in Europe: The Last Three Decades* (London, 1991).

[4] J. Barrett, 'Contextual archaeology', *Antiquity*, 61 (1987), 468–73; I. Hodder, *The Meanings of Things: Material Culture and Symbolic Expression* (London, 1989).

assumed to be either a migrant, or the descendant of a migrant, from a particular continental region. In this paper this assumption, and the reasons behind it, will be addressed, before the archaeological evidence itself is turned to, with a case study on the inhumation cemeteries of the 5th to 7th century in the East Riding of Yorkshire. This case study aims to show how material culture and burial practices were actively used by the mourners to create and maintain local, rather than ethnic or racial, identities.

ARCHAEOLOGY AND IDENTITY

Anglo-Saxon archaeology has, in the past, been accused of being a 'hand-maiden' to history, providing material illustration of the events and processes highlighted by historians. Although in more recent years it has developed as a separate discipline, with its own material basis and methodologies, it can still be argued that it is, to some extent, in thrall of historical explanations for change. That this influence is especially strong for the 5th and 6th centuries is odd, as this is when the historical sources themselves are at their most fragmentary. The reasons for this are complex. It is certainly not the result of a simplistic acceptance of the historical sources, for even early archaeologists such as J. M. Kemble and E. T. Leeds had doubts as to their veracity.[5] Rather, it appears to be a deep-running influence, bound up with a whole series of aspects. These include how archaeologists interpret their material (which, although appearing straightforward, is actually reliant on a whole series of assumptions about the nature of that material); assumptions of what societies in the past were like, and how they operated; again, ideas which have complex histories.

The way that archaeologists classify material reflects to a certain extent on the role which they think it played in past society. Early medieval metalwork of the 5th and 6th centuries in Britain is commonly termed 'Anglian' or 'Saxon', according to its geographical distribution, and stylistic parallels with continental artefacts. The use of such classifications suggest that archaeologists assume that in the 5th century, and especially the 6th, the fact that a brooch-type was 'Anglian' or 'Saxon' would have been immediately apparent. This implies that archaeologists think that there were such large-scale, homogeneous tribal identities then in existence. This carries with it the further implications that everyone would have known to which of these identities they belonged, that they would have been aware of the significance of the different types of associated material culture and, moreover, that it was an identity which was fundamentally opposed to that of the Insular 'British'.

Discussing ethnicity in the present is a difficult area, and the problems are even worse when trying to talk about the past, when we are not even able to ask people how they view themselves in these terms. One of the main problems is that our notions of what ethnicity is, and how it operates, are very much bound up with nationalistic concerns. Inherent to these are various assumptions about the importance of kinship and blood relations, and a concern with identifying origins. From the mid-19th century there was a clear understanding that ethnic identity was something with which people

---

[5] J. M. Kemble, *The Saxons in England* (London, 1849), 3; E. T. Leeds, 'The distribution of the Angles and Saxons archaeologically considered', *Archaeologia*, 91 (1945), 1–106.

were born, that it was inherent and capable of exerting strong emotional ties. This view was reliant on theories about 'peoples' and 'races' which saw personal characteristics as inherited.[6] Although Darwinism was to show that humans could not have multiple origins, for we are all one species, they were still thought of as belonging to different ancestral stocks.[7] In addition, language and physical anthropology began to be equated with these groups, such that there arose the expectation that a 'Saxon' would speak a 'Germanic' language and be of a specific physical type. In the atmosphere of late 19th-century nationalism, where 'peoples' and 'nations' were supposed to coincide, there was an interest in tracing back the history and culture of such 'national' groups as far as possible.[8] The link between artefacts and these sorts of identities was thus made from the mid-19th century as a way of interpreting archaeological evidence so that it would fit in with historical debates, which were often framed around these concepts of 'races' and the origins of nations.

Although such 'racial' histories were largely rejected by academic circles in the first few decades of the 20th century (although they remain current in popular conceptions of the past), the idea of 'race' came to be replaced by that of 'culture'. In 1895 the German prehistorian Gustaf Kossinna put forward the idea that archaeology was capable of isolating cultural areas which could be identified with specific ethnic or national units and traced back into prehistory, later arguing that these areas corresponded unquestionably with the areas of particular tribes or peoples.[9] Although formalized in this way by Kossinna, and later by Childe,[10] a similar method had actually been used for decades by early historical archaeologists. As the documentary sources (often not as objective as one might assume) talked of the past as populated by distinct groups of people — the Saxons, Angles and Jutes, for example — it was easy to see the past in this light. Early archaeologists were thus expecting to be able to discern tribal differences in the material they excavated (most of which came from cemeteries), and it was natural for them to link the objects they discovered to the tribal differences which they thought the historical sources were telling them existed.

In addition, this has convincingly been argued to be the very model which early prehistorians like Childe and Kossinna took when they applied their theories to periods without historical sources.[11] Kossinna was thus partly basing his model on the movements of the post-Roman barbarians as they were described by early chroniclers. However, Goffart has argued that such 'great invasions' are a classic historian's explanatory device, a powerful way of explaining the divisions between epochs (which are themselves, of course, historical creations). He argues that this is clarity gained by hindsight, and represents a common theme among 8th-century historians, including

[6] L. P. Curtis, *Anglo-Saxons and Celts* (New York, 1968).

[7] S. Jones, *The Archaeology of Ethnicity* (London, 1997), 43.

[8] B. Olsen and Z. Kobyliński, 'Ethnicity in anthropological and archaeological research: a Norwegian-Polish perspective', *Archaeol. Polona*, 29 (1991), 5–27.

[9] J. Malina and Z. Vašiček, *Archaeology Yesterday and Today* (Cambridge 1990), 62; Veit, op. cit. in note 1, 37.

[10] G. Kossinna, *Der Herkunft der Germanen: zur Methode der Siedlungsarchäologie*, (Würzburg, 1911); V. G. Childe, 'Changing methods and aims in prehistory, Presidential Address for 1935', *Proc. Prehistoric Soc.*, 1 (1935), 1–15.

[11] D. Anthony, 'Migration in archaeology: the baby and the bathwater', *American Anthropologist*, 92 (1990), 895–914.

Bede, who saw the *adventus Saxonum* as a historical turning point. Tied up in these ideas are images of barbarians both as bringing about the fall of Rome, and as representing the dawn of modern civilization. The theme of 'barbarian invasions' is thus presented as violent encounters between groups whose collective identities were clearly grasped, thereby perpetuating the idea that these were self-conscious 'Germans' with a well-defined identity and culture.[12]

However, over fifteen years ago Patrick Geary pointed out the problems of using early medieval historical writings to investigate ethnicity in this period. He showed firstly the assumptions brought to bear by modern historians on these sources (such as that ethnicity would have been recognizable to others, that it would not change except over several generations, and that it was a source of friction within society), demonstrating how these have coloured our readings of the sources.[13] In addition, he, along with others, re-examined the contexts in which people or groups were ascribed 'ethnic' names in the documentary sources, drawing the conclusion that such groups as the Franks, the Burgundians and the Anglo-Saxons were as much historical creations as anything, and that the role of the church and its historians seems to have been a major factor in this process.[14] It has also been pointed out that many of those who are mentioned in early medieval sources are not described in these ethnic terms at all, and that perhaps an ethnic identity was important only for certain sections of the population, with such identities gaining their meaning through affiliation with elites.[15] We may well be seeing in our historical constructions 7th-, 8th- and 9th-century ideas about ethnic groups, rather than any reality from the 5th and 6th centuries.

Also recently has come the realization that ethnicity does not exist 'out there'; it is an aspect of personal identity which may become relevant in certain circumstances. If we talk of an 'ethnic group', we are talking about a number of people who have constructed (or had constructed for them) the idea that they belong together, and that they are different from others. While this is often framed in terms of shared origins, it is in fact far more flexible than is usually thought.[16] These doubts about the permanence of ethnicity and its importance for social relations have implications for the interpretation of early medieval funerary archaeology. It is still often framed in terms of certain assumptions such as, for example, that material culture, language, biology and ethnic identity can be simplistically equated. It is this equation which means that explanation of this period in Britain is always predicated on some version of the migration/invasion hypothesis (from mass migrations at one end of the scale to

---

[12] W. Goffart, 'The theme of "The Barbarian Invasions" in late Antique and modern historiography', 87–107 in E. Chrysos and A. Schwarcz (eds), *Das Reich und die Barbaren,*(Vienna, 1989).
[13] P. J. Geary, 'Ethnic identity as a situational construct in the early middle ages', *Mitteilungen der Anthropologischen Gesellschaft in Wien*, 113 (1983), 15–26.
[14] E. James, *The Franks* (Oxford, 1988); P. Amory, 'The meaning and purpose of ethnic terminology in the Burgundian Laws', *Early Medieval Europe*, 2 (1993), 1–28; P. Wormald, 'Bede, the *Bretwaldas* and the origins of the *Gens Anglorum*', 99–129 in P. Wormald (ed.), *Ideal and Reality in Frankish and Anglo-Saxon Society* (Oxford, 1983); W. Pohl, 'Ethnic names and identities in the British Isles: a comparative perspective', 7–40 in J. Hines (ed.), *The Anglo-Saxons from the Migration Period to the Eighth Century: An Ethnographic Perspective* (Woodbridge, 1997).
[15] P. Amory, 'Names, ethnic identity and community in fifth-and sixth-century Burgundy', *Viator*, 25 (1994), 1–30.
[16] F. Barth (ed.), *Ethnic Groups and Boundaries* (London, 1969); R. Jenkins, *Rethinking Ethnicity: Arguments and Explorations* (London, 1997); S. Jones, *The Archaeology of Ethnicity* (London, 1997).

Nicholas Higham's minimalist elite take-over at the other).[17] Even if such population movements can be demonstrated (in which DNA or bone isotope analysis may play a part in future), they are not the sole explanation for social and material change, although they may have provided some of the impetus for that change.

In previous accounts, Angles, Saxons and Britons have often been seen as the subjects of history; it is 'their' developments which archaeologists have tried to trace. This can be characterized as rather a 'top-down' approach to the past: archaeologists have started out with assumptions about what they were going to find (often based on Bede's tribal groupings), and have then looked for the evidence. They have thus been working back from the known entities of the 7th and 8th century, looking for their origins in the past. It is argued here that this is the wrong approach to take. Instead, it is the evidence of the 5th and 6th centuries which should be the starting point: what are these cemeteries evidence for?

ARTEFACTS AND CEMETERIES

In recent years, some archaeologists have been focusing on the active role that material culture plays in society, being used by people in their day-to-day lives to mediate relationships, convey information, and set up social expectations of the ways in which people should act. Through their use in specific contexts, this material culture can become imbued with meaning in the eyes of those who use them, and who watch them being used (in the same way that a uniform can convey authority or status).[18] The things that people use are the result of many separate choices, rather than being inevitable aspects of their society (i.e. their 'culture'). There will be, in any society, a range of such material to choose from, although this will of course be constrained by factors of production, trade, cost, and social attitudes.

It is in this context that we need to see the artefacts found through excavation of early Anglo-Saxon cemeteries, rather than regarding them as direct indicators of population movement. There is a further complication too, in that when we deal with cemetery evidence we are not looking at unconscious, everyday activities, but at intermittent and deliberate practices. The mourners are the active participants in burials, and such burials are the end result of many different culturally-situated decisions.[19] The early medieval inhumation rite was a selection of both practices (such as the orientation of the body, mode of deposition, location of grave goods and of the grave itself) and of items of material culture (the weapons, ornaments, dress fastenings and vessels, for example, which characterize the 5th- to 7th-century burials of eastern England). The mourners chose what to inter, where to place those items on and around the body, and then they chose where and how to bury that body. A person's identity cannot be simplistically 'read off' from the way in which they were buried, but their burial can shed light on the aspects of the deceased which the mourners thought important to emphasize through the use of material culture and other aspects of the

[17] N. Higham, *Rome, Britain and the Anglo-Saxons* (London, 1992).
[18] M. L. S. Sørensen, 'The construction of gender through appearance', 121–9 in D. Walde and N. Willows (eds.) *The Archaeology of Gender: Proceedings of the 22nd Chacmool Conference, Calgary* (Calgary, 1991).
[19] S. J. Lucy, *The Early Anglo-Saxon Cemeteries of East Yorkshire: An Analysis and Re-interpretation*, (BAR Brit. Ser., 272, Oxford, 1998).

ritual. The challenge to archaeology is how, then, to move from identifying the creation of that burial rite to being able to say anything about the society carrying out the burial.

One particular approach which can be useful in this respect is that known as 'an archaeology of practice' (ultimately based on the sociological and anthropological work of Anthony Giddens and Pierre Bourdieu).[20] Within this framework, societies are seen as being comprised solely of the actions, practices and beliefs of the people constituting them (thus societies change as those actions and practices change, while at the same time people's actions are to a certain extent determined by their own conception of appropriate behaviour within their society). This is a 'bottom-up' approach, which sees the everyday behaviour of people as important, as being what creates norms and values. Local communities can therefore be seen as the creators and maintainers of their society, which can be expected to be subtly different from neighbouring or subsequent communities. It is in this local patterning (in local burial rites, in this case) that evidence for the practices of a community will be seen.

From this perspective it is pointless to begin with a large body of data, culled from a wide geographical area, when investigating social practices; if similarities can be seen across such wide areas it is because local communities have chosen to adopt the same, or similar, ways of burying their dead. It is these choices which are of interest here. It is therefore only by starting with the most detailed level of analysis that the local patterns which combine to create the large-scale picture can be understood. It is important to look at who is buried with what, and how; at who is buried where, and at where those accumulations of burials are made, in order to understand the local picture, before looking on a grander scale of analysis to see broader similarities or changes over space and time. The work outlined here thus also takes a 'bottom-up' approach to the archaeological material. As the burial rite is created by the mourners, analysis of the funerary remains has to start at the level of the individual burial, which is taken to represent a single event, comprising a series of decisions. A cemetery is thus comprised of a number of these burials, or events, which take place over a span of years (often between 100 and 200 years in the case of many of these cemeteries).

The burial rite can be analysed, firstly, in terms of how different age and sex groups were treated; with which artefacts were they provided, where those artefacts were placed in the grave, how the body was positioned, and how the grave was physically constructed: its size, shape and orientation. The cemetery can also be taken as a unit of analysis: were different groups of people (of different ages, different sexes, those buried with different grave good types) distinguished in terms of their spatial location within the cemetery? Any such groupings may suggest the operation of long-term traditions which determined who was buried where. Any patterning within the data will indicate the localized burial practices made use of by the community creating the cemetery, and will thus throw light on how that society was constituted. This paper will now present a summary of the results from an analysis of early medieval inhumation cemeteries in eastern Yorkshire, and explore their significance for the creation and maintenance of local identities.

THE COMPLEXITY OF BURIAL PRACTICE

In order to analyse cemeteries by age and sex groups, the sites used for analysis must have independent sexing and aging (i.e. not making use of the grave goods). Within the East Riding of Yorkshire this limits analysis to the two extensive modern excavations at West Heslerton[21] and Sewerby.[22] At both these sites (Fig. 1) around half the burials (57.6 per cent at Sewerby and 44.6 per cent at Heslerton) did not contain either weaponry (i.e. a sword, spear or shield) or jewellery (defined as brooches, bead strings, pendants, sleeve-clasps or waist-ornaments such as girdle-hangers, latch-lifters or girdle-rings) buried with the body. If these burials have any grave goods they are those such as pottery or wooden vessels, buckles, a small number of beads, knives or animal bones. There are also many more burials with jewellery than those with weapons. It has been argued elsewhere that these burial assemblages represent something subtler than a simple gender distinction, due to the high proportion of 'ungendered' graves, and the large amount of variation within the assemblages themselves.[23]

Some of this variation can be seen in figures 2, 3 and 4, which show the different proportions, at these two sites, of jewellery, weapons and other burials which contain each artefact type. The weapon burials are extremely limited in their assemblage, whereas the jewellery burials draw on a wider range of artefacts (and differences can be seen between the two sites in terms of this variation). Looking at these differences in assemblage in detail highlights variations according to age (Figs. 5, 6 and 7). Some artefact-types seem to be restricted to certain age groups: at West Heslerton, for example, within the jewellery burials only those aged over 25 years old were found with penannular or square-headed brooches, or with tweezers. At the same site, burials under twelve years were not found with cruciform brooches, girdle-hangers or latch-lifters, but they were far more likely (in statistical terms) to be interred with pottery, small long brooches or a small number of beads. At Sewerby, a slightly different picture can be seen. Small long and square-headed brooches and dress pins were only found with burials over 25 years, while those aged under twelve years were not found with waist-ornaments, buckles or wooden vessels. Similar variations can be seen among the weapon burials at both sites. This assemblage seems largely restricted to burials over 25 years, especially when a shield or sword is included in the grave. Differences can also be seen between those burials with 'neutral' assemblages (non-weapon, non-jewellery, but some grave-goods): more varied assemblages are seen at West Heslerton, and again, at both sites various artefact types were restricted to certain age groups. At West Heslerton, tools and tweezers were only found with those over 25 years, while at Sewerby this is true for tweezers, wooden vessels and pottery.

---

[21] D. Powlesland, *West Heslerton: The Anglian Cemetery*, (forthcoming).
[22] S. Hirst, *An Anglo-Saxon Cemetery at Sewerby* (York, 1985).
[23] S. Lucy, 'Housewives, warriors and slaves? Sex and gender in Anglo-Saxon burials', 150–68 in J. Moore and E. Scott (eds.), *Invisible People and Processes* (Leicester, 1997).

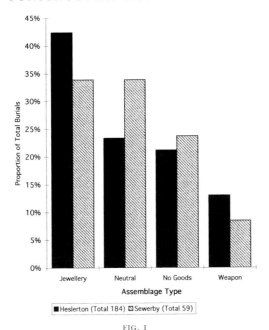

FIG. 1

Relative proportions of assemblage types at Sewerby and West Heslerton.

Thus the composition of grave good assemblages at these two sites seems to be partly determined by age.[24] However, the combinations of goods within each age group are different at the two sites. There was an active selection of grave goods for each burial, drawing from a much wider range of available material. Not all available material culture was deemed appropriate for inclusion as a grave good though — the rarity of tools within graves of this date illustrates this. The selection of appropriate grave goods was determined partly by age and gender (as far as it can be indicated by assemblage), but there is still more variation within these categories which suggests the role of other factors as well.

This patterning can be investigated further by looking at other aspects of the burial rite: the physical structure of the grave, the deposition of the body and the layout of the grave goods. Analysing these aspects by age, sex and assemblage also highlights some intriguing variations. Details of the physical grave structure were only available (like independent sexing and aging) for West Heslerton and Sewerby. Younger burials were generally found in smaller graves as might, perhaps, be expected. Differences in terms of sex and assemblage were noted, however. At West Heslerton, both male burials and burials with weapons had longer graves on average than female and jewellery burials, but the opposite was true at Sewerby. In addition, at West Heslerton the graves with the largest overall capacity (obtained by multiplying length, width and depth) were weapon burials aged between 35 and 45 years, whereas at Sewerby they were jewellery burials aged between 17 and 25 years. These findings indicate that

---

[24] And also by sex, though see Lucy, op. cit. in note 23, for a critique of sexing burials by assemblage.

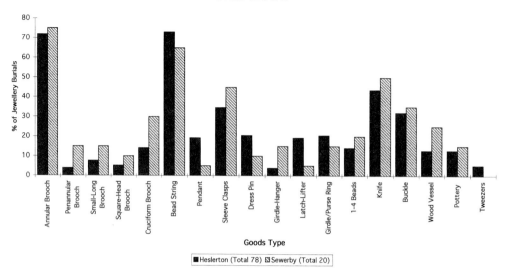

FIG. 2

Percentage of jewellery burials with goods type at Sewerby and West Heslerton.

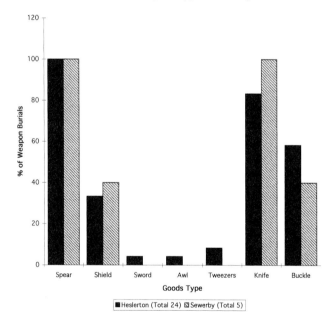

FIG. 3

Percentage of weapon burials with goods type at Sewerby and West
Heslerton.

differences between assemblages, and between the sexes, were articulated in different
ways at these two sites.

At both Sewerby and West Heslerton, there was a strong correlation between the
presence of weaponry or jewellery and the use of extended supine burial (i.e. the body

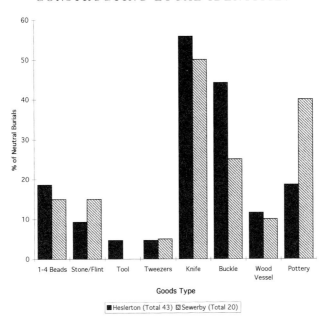

FIG. 4

Percentage of 'neutral' burials with goods type at Sewerby and West Heslerton.

Age Range	Annular Brooch	Penann. Brooch	Sml-Lng Brooch	Sq.-Head Brooch	Cruc. Brooch	Other Brooch	Bead String	Pendant	Sleeve Clasps	Dress Pin	Girdle-Hanger	Latch-Lifter	Girdle Ring	1-Apr Beads	Stone/ Flint	Tool	Tweezers	Knife	Buckle	Wood Vessel	Pottery
Sewerby																					
0-12 Years	■	░	░		░	░	■		░					░				░	░	░	░
12-25 Years	░		░		░		■				░			░				■	░		░
25+ Years	■	░	░	░	░	░	■		░					░				░	░	░	░
Heslerton																					
0-12 Years	░		░		░	░	░							░				░	░	░	░
12-25 Years	■		░		░	░	■		░					░				░	░		░
25+ Years	■		░		░	░	■		░					░	░			■	░	░	░

■ Found with 51% or more of age group ░ Found with 1-50% of age group ☐ Not found with age group

FIG. 5

Presence of goods type by age group in jewellery burials at Sewerby and West Heslerton.

laid on the back, with the legs straight). However, when similar analyses were carried out on other sites in the East Riding of Yorkshire with available data (Fig. 8), different conclusions were drawn. At Uncleby burial on the right side was correlated with weaponry and jewellery burial.[25] At Cheesecake Hill,[26] jewellery burials were always found placed on the left side (although this was not statistically significant due to the small number of burials available for analysis), and at Garton Station jewellery burials

[25] R. A. Smith, 'The excavation by Canon Greenwell F. S. A., in 1908, of an Anglo-Saxon cemetery at Uncleby, East Riding of Yorkshire', *Proc. Soc. Antiq. London.*, 24 (1912), 146–58.
[26] J. R. Mortimer, *Forty Years Researches in British and Saxon Burial Mounds of East Yorkshire* (London, 1905), 286–95.

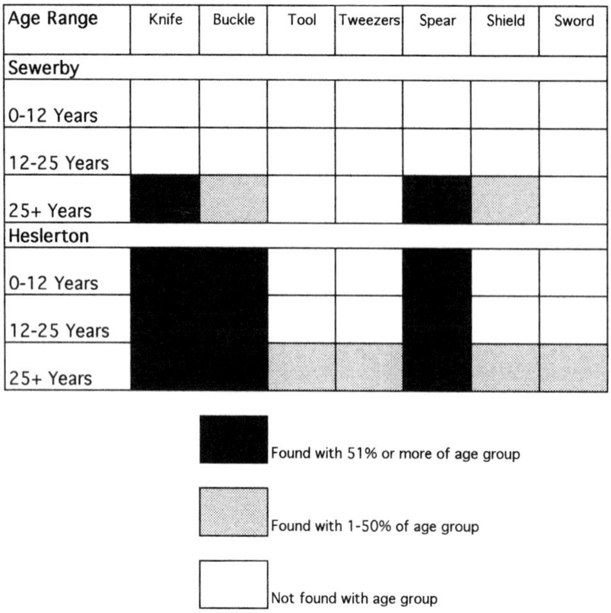

Age Range	Knife	Buckle	Tool	Tweezers	Spear	Shield	Sword
Sewerby							
0-12 Years							
12-25 Years							
25+ Years	■	▦			■	▦	
Heslerton							
0-12 Years	■				■		
12-25 Years	■				■		
25+ Years	■	▦	▦	▦	■	▦	▦

■ Found with 51% or more of age group

▦ Found with 1-50% of age group

☐ Not found with age group

FIG. 6

Presence of goods type by age group in weapon burials at Sewerby and West Heslerton.

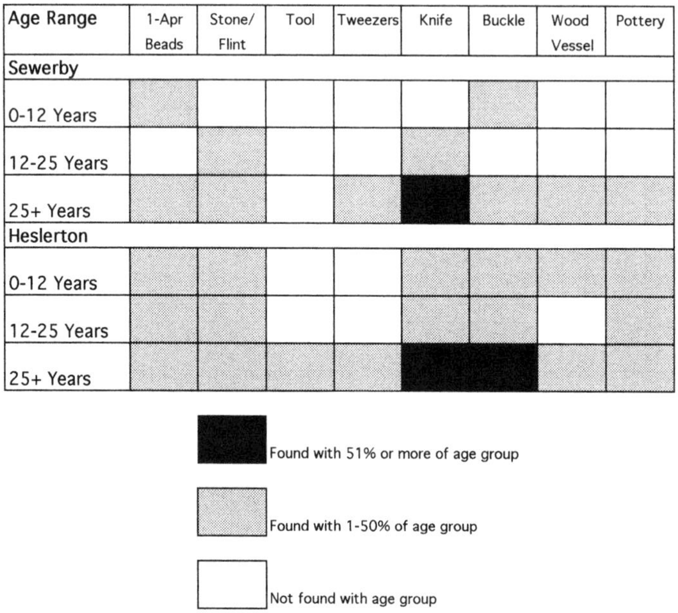

Age Range	1-Apr Beads	Stone/Flint	Tool	Tweezers	Knife	Buckle	Wood Vessel	Pottery
Sewerby								
0-12 Years	▦					▦		
12-25 Years		▦			▦			
25+ Years	▦	▦		▦	■	▦	▦	
Heslerton								
0-12 Years	▦	▦			▦	▦		
12-25 Years	▦	▦			▦	▦		
25+ Years	▦	▦	▦	▦	■	▦	▦	

■ Found with 51% or more of age group

▦ Found with 1-50% of age group

☐ Not found with age group

FIG. 7

Presence of goods type by age group in 'neutral' burials at Sewerby and Heslerton.

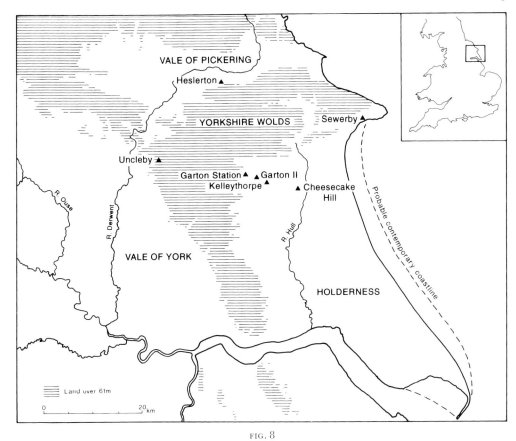

FIG. 8

Map showing location of early medieval cemeteries in the East Riding of Yorkshire (Yvonne Beadnell, after Hirst, op. cit. in note 11).

tended to be buried on the right side.[27] In contrast, weapon burials at this last site, and also at Kelleythorpe,[28] were more likely to be supine. Garton II does not show such distinctions.[29] There may well be some chronological differences here, as Uncleby, Garton Station and the analysed burials at Garton II can be shown to be later 6th- or 7th-century in date. However, there still remain differences between the contemporary 5th- to 6th-century sites at Sewerby, West Heslerton, Kelleythorpe and Cheesecake Hill.

There were also distinctions visible in the flexure of burials (i.e. the angle of the legs to the trunk; crouched burial is where the legs are at less than 90 degrees to the body). Elsewhere it has been shown that in this area crouched burial is a marked feature of later 6th- and 7th-century burial rites.[30] Nevertheless, it was still used in both

[27] I. Stead, *Iron Age Cemeteries in East Yorkshire* (London, 1991); British Museum records (unpublished).
[28] Mortimer, op. cit. in note 26, 271–83.
[29] Mortimer, op. cit. in note 26, 247–57. Only the western half of the cemetery was included in the analysis.
[30] Lucy, op. cit. in note 19.

the earlier and later cemeteries to distinguish between certain groups. At both Sewerby and Kelleythorpe there was a correlation between crouched burial and neutral assemblages, whereas at Garton Station jewellery burials were more likely to be found in this position. At Uncleby assemblage was clearly a determining factor for flexure: weapon burials were more likely to be contracted, burials without goods to be extended, and jewellery and neutral burials to be crouched. At West Heslerton, the use of this rite seemed to be dependent, not on assemblage, but on age: there was a strong correlation of crouched burial with those aged under twelve years.

At West Heslerton assemblage seemed to have a stronger relationship with orientation of the burial: jewellery burials tended to have heads to the West, neutral burials to North or North-West, while weapon burials tended to have the heads to South-West. Age also appeared to play a role in this, as burials under twelve years were more likely to have the heads to the South, while those over 25 years were more likely to have them to the West. A different picture was seen at Sewerby, where jewellery burials tended to have the heads to South or South-West, while weapon burials tended to have them towards the North-West. At Kelleythorpe, jewellery burials were more likely to have the heads to the South, but as the burials at this site were focused around a Bronze-age barrow, and the vast majority had their heads pointing to the centre of the barrow, this suggests that the real correlation here is of jewellery burials with interment in the northern part of the barrow.

Variations within the locations of grave goods also contributed to the complexity of the burial rite observed. Broad chronological differences in costume were noted between the two different phases represented by West Heslerton, Sewerby, Cheesecake Hill and Kelleythorpe on the one hand and Garton Station, Uncleby and Garton II on the other. In the earlier phase the jewellery costume seems to have been the typical 'Anglian' one,[31] which comprised the wearing of a 'peplos' type of gown often attached by two brooches at the shoulder,[32] along with waist-ornaments in many cases and also sleeve-clasps. At Garton II, Garton Station and Uncleby, however, only a few girdle-hangers and purse-rings are recorded, and most annular brooches (virtually the only brooch-type now found) are found singly on one shoulder (or on the chest in the case of Garton Station), suggesting a chronological factor, along with some local variation in this costume. There are similar changes within the weapon assemblages, with spears being the most common type at the earlier sites, being replaced by swords or seaxes at the later ones (though no weapon burials at all were found at Garton II).

Within these broad divisions, however, there were some subtler differences in furnishing, again suggesting variations between social groups. At West Heslerton and Cheesecake Hill there is a strong correlation of pottery vessels placed by the heads of jewellery burials, whereas this is not true at Sewerby or Kelleythorpe. The later sites of Garton Station and Garton II have a tendency for wooden vessels or boxes to be placed by the feet. This is also a feature at West Heslerton, although here it seems to have been more structured by age: wooden vessels by the waist or feet are more often found with burials under 25 years, whereas older burials were more likely to have them placed by the head.

---

[31] Hirst, op. cit. in note 22, 46.
[32] G. Owen-Crocker, *Dress in Anglo-Saxon England* (Manchester, 1986), 28–9.

The location of the burial within the cemetery is also something which seems to be structured in various ways. It has been noted elsewhere that there is a strong pattern in eastern Yorkshire, and indeed across the whole of Britain, of early medieval cemeteries using prehistoric monuments such as round barrows and linear earthworks as a focus.[33] Looking at a more detailed level, it is noticeable that those earthworks structure where individual burials are located and West Heslerton serves as a good example of this. The cemetery was situated in an area of prehistoric earthworks, including a neolithic hengiform enclosure, a Bronze-age barrow cemetery and an Iron-age pit alignment.[34] Those under twelve years old were more likely to be buried within the areas covered by barrows or encompassed by enclosure ditches, and the prone burials, although not numerous, were more likely to be found within those ditches themselves than elsewhere. Over the cemetery as a whole there seemed to be concentrations of burials, with a particular cluster of young burials around the barrow 2BA130. In the southern half of the cemetery, where bone preservation was better, female burials, young burials and burials that were flexed or crouched were more likely to be buried in the barrows or ditches, or within the enclosures, whereas weapon burials, and also extended burials were more likely to be found in other areas.

Thus, by examining in detail various aspects of the burial rite at these seven cemeteries in the East Riding of Yorkshire, it can be seen that there were two major 'ways' of burying people, which seem to be chronologically distinct. The earlier phase involved less structured orientation, a tendency to extended or flexed burials which were supine or on one side, and the inclusion of certain types of grave goods. The later phase had far more rigid structuring of orientation, and a tendency for crouched or flexed burial on one side. These later burials also had different types of jewellery and weapon assemblages. Burials belonging to the earlier phase tended to be positioned according to the age of the corpse or its assemblage, but this does not hold true for the later phase.

Within these broad divisions, however, substantial differences can be seen between contemporary sites, and between burials with different cultural assemblages, or of different age groups at the same site. These differences seem to have no logic to them, but must be inferred to be the 'way of doing' within each community when it buried its dead. These differences would have been meaningful to those communities, although the meanings of individual aspects of the rite may well have changed over time. We can only try to imagine what those differences would have signified. What can be said, however, is that the very fact of difference, between age groups and between those with different assemblages, indicates that those groups of people were thought differently of by the people that were burying them.

The analysis of the spatial layout of these cemeteries has also produced some interesting results. There is substantial evidence at some sites of spatial clustering according to age, sex or assemblage. This suggests either that memories of previous interments were drawn upon in making decisions about where and how to position later burials, or that more general ideas about appropriate places of burial were in

---

[33] Lucy, op. cit. in note 19; H. Williams, 'Monuments and the past in early Anglo-Saxon England', *World Archaeology*, 30 (1998), 90–108.
[34] Powlesland, op. cit. in note 21.

operation. Many of these cemeteries can also be seen to be highly structured by prehistoric earthworks, but in varying ways.

DISCUSSION

Even from the relatively small area of the East Riding of Yorkshire, it can be seen that the cemeteries represent a complex body of data. When this is analysed in a contextual way, taking into account chronological variations, patterning is evident on various different levels: at the level of the individual cemetery, groupings of people are differentiated — either spatially, through depositional similarities, or through use of material culture. With the archaeological evidence available, it is only possible to compare such variations against age, sex and assemblage. There may, however, be other groupings which are not so readily apparent. It is possible that some of these, such as family groupings, may become available through the use of DNA analysis.

On a wider level, regional differences are apparent in burial practices: the low percentage of weapon burials compared with other areas in the 5th and 6th centuries and the high rate of crouched burial in the 7th century, for example. On an even broader level, these burials made use of similar items of material culture to those which were found over quite a large part of eastern Britain in the 5th and 6th centuries (the 'Anglian' culture), including square-headed brooches, cruciform brooches and a variety of pottery forms. In the 7th century the items included with burials were those which were found over most of the country at that time, such as silver pendants, thread-boxes and seaxes.[35] In the past, archaeologists have concentrated solely on these regional distributions of artefacts as indicating identity. However, sometimes even these do not quite make sense: why, when in the 7th century there are historically attested political groupings — the kingdoms — is it at this point that the material culture becomes homogeneous?[36] In concentrating solely on the artefacts themselves, archaeologists have ignored all the other indicators of how people of the 5th to 7th centuries saw themselves and others — indications which archaeologists are now limited largely to seeing expressed through burial rites.

Perhaps in the 5th and 6th centuries it was differences between groups of people within communities, and the differences in how neighbouring communities did things, which were important? In the past, archaeologists have only concentrated on regional distributions of material culture, and thus seem to have assumed that this *was* how cultural identities were expressed (and that these were ethnic identities). However, if the creation of identities of any form arise out of the initial formation and maintenance of local differences, then this view must be rejected. It is possible that it is archaeologists themselves who have created the appearance of these 'ethnic' groupings in the 5th and 6th centuries; that the people living then were stressing more local identities, but drawing on, and deliberately selecting, various elements of the repertoire of material culture (which are thought of as being 'Anglo-Saxon') that would have been generally

---

[35] H. Geake, *The Use of Grave Goods in Conversion-Period England, c.600–c.850*, (BAR Brit. Ser., 261, Oxford, 1997).
[36] H. Geake, 'Invisible kingdoms: the use of grave-goods in seventh-century England', *Anglo-Saxon Stud. Archaeol. Hist.*, 10 (1999), 203–15.

available, but combining and placing them in different ways. Perhaps it was how the material culture was used that was important, rather than the fact that it was? Perhaps archaeologists, by ignoring, or not seeing, the local variations, have imposed on the 5th- and 6th-century communities a uniformity which was never there?

ACKNOWLEDGEMENTS

This paper has benefited from the comments offered by the participants at the Burial in Early Medieval Britain conference. I am grateful to Dominic Powlesland for providing me with the West Heslerton data in advance of publication, and to Yvonne Beadnell, University of Durham, for her assistance with the illustrations.

Lies, Damned Lies, and a *Curriculum Vitae*: Reflections on Statistics and the Populations of Early Anglo-Saxon Inhumation Cemeteries

By JOHN HINES

The title under which the preliminary version of this paper was read at the London conference was 'Cemetery and community: reflections and suggestions from the Barrington project'. In its own way that title encapsulated the way in which early Anglo-Saxon cemetery analysis is habitually conceived of and approached in terms of a series of collective nouns or plurals. The paper that now follows here, however, is in fact a plea for the conscious introduction of a degree of *individualism* into this important branch of British archaeology. This does not just mean recognition of personal individuality as a factor in early Anglo-Saxon life, but also of the individuality — the distinctness — of separate communities. The argument for this is based upon the presentation and evaluation of what purport to be a range of facts about certain early Anglo-Saxon cemeteries. These, it can be shown, are data which *may* be interpretable in terms of the detection and even measurement of such individuality between different burying communities, *if* certain acknowledged doubts about their factual status can be overcome.

A key factor in the formulation of these ideas has necessarily been the author's personal involvement in Cambridgeshire Archaeology's Edix Hill project, directed by Tim Malim. The cemetery known as Barrington A on Edix Hill, in the parish of Orwell (Cambridgeshire), discovered and part-excavated in the mid-19th century, was rediscovered by a responsible metal-detector user, Chris Montague, in 1987, and further excavated (still not completely) from 1987–91. With the benefit of funding from South Cambridgeshire District Council, Cambridgeshire County Council and English Heritage, it was possible to undertake three seasons' worth of extensive excavation (1989–91), and the subsequent post-excavation work, in time to have a book-length report published within ten years of the first season of excavation.[1] These are no mere formal and empty acknowledgements, for there are practical lessons as important as any others for the future of Anglo-Saxon cemetery archaeology to be learned from the, of course never perfect, but still exemplary organization, teamwork, and co-operation between public bodies and individuals that characterized this enterprise. At the project design stage, it was clear that Edix Hill offered exciting prospects for up-to-date cemetery analysis, especially analysis using a range of 'scientific' approaches, based on both the computer and the laboratory. This range included technical analyses in respect of the material and craftworking techniques of

---

[1] T. Malim and J. Hines, *The Anglo-Saxon Cemetery at Edix Hill (Barrington A), Cambridgeshire* (CBA Res. Rep., 112, York, 1998).

the substantial quantity of artefacts from the site; detailed osteological analysis of the well-preserved human skeletal material; and correspondence analysis — a computer-based mathematical method, which allows for the multidimensional exploration of patterns of relationship in terms of the association between variables (which can be both cultural and biological).[2] In several cases the range of study was able to go beyond Edix Hill (both the recent and the 19th-century finds) to other Cambridgeshire cemeteries, as well as to the well-known set of four recently excavated inhumation sites from Norfolk and Suffolk (Bergh Apton, Morningthorpe, Spong Hill and Westgarth Gardens). Amongst the conspicuous features of Edix Hill are two examples of the rare rite of bed burial, which, one could reasonably assume, implies some relatively high status for the deceased buried in this way.[3]

The date range of the Edix Hill cemetery appears to be *c.* A.D. 500 to 650. A reliable estimate of the approximate span of time during which burial took place is, of course, very important in assessing the probable size and therefore social structure of the buried and burying community. This date range covers the major cultural watershed within early Anglo-Saxon archaeology which I continue to call that between the Migration Period and the Final Phase. It was hoped, therefore, to gain more insight into the nature of this particular shift in material-cultural practices. We cannot claim that within the bounds of this project alone startling advances in knowledge were made, although the existing view was made clearer, in respect of the Cambridge region at least. In this area, we still appear to have an abrupt boundary between the two phases. There is a handful of ambiguous, and possibly transitional, grave assemblages, but no substantial transitional phase between the two. The change thus seems to have been sudden and thorough, in its material expression at least.[4]

The transition from the Migration Period to the Final Phase is a material-cultural change involving not only the types of grave-goods buried but also their distribution. In the Final Phase, the provision of grave-goods becomes far less frequent with female burials than it was in the earlier phase — to the degree that we actually have to presume that virtually all the unfurnished and very sparsely furnished women's graves excavated at Edix Hill belong to the period of the Final Phase.[5] This also, therefore, seems to imply greater social differentiation amongst women at the point of burial in the later phase. There may also be *more* investment of grave-goods in men's graves of the Final Phase than in contemporary women's graves, a reversal of the situation characteristic of the Migration Period.[6] The limits to our ability to date men's and women's graves, in any way whatsoever let alone in terms of equal confidence for both sexes, are a significant problem here, but it is nonetheless the case that very few men's graves at Edix Hill can be definitely assigned to the Migration Period, while eight

[2] Ibid., 284, and refs.
[3] Ibid. 261–8; G. Speake, *A Saxon Bed-Burial on Swallowcliff Down* (English Heritage Archaeol. Rep., 10, London, 1989).
[4] Malim and Hines, op. cit. in note 1, 279–91; J. Hines, 'Angelsächsische Chronologie: Probleme und Aussichten', 19–30 in U. von Freeden, U. Koch and A. Wieczorek (eds.), *Völker an Nord- und Ostsee und die Franken* (Bonn, 1999); id., 'The sixth-century transition in Anglian England: an analysis of female graves from Cambridgeshire', 65–79 in J. Hines, K. Høilund Nielsen and F. Siegmund (eds.), *The Pace of Change: Studies in Early-Medieval Chronology* (Oxford, 1999).
[5] Malim and Hines, op. cit. in note 1, 301–3, 317–8.
[6] Ibid., 287–9 and p. 298, tab. 8.5.

contained diagnostically Final-phase artefacts (compared with six women's graves of that phase datable on the basis of their grave-goods). Preliminary assessment of the very recently excavated inhumation cemetery of approximately the same date-range at Eriswell (USAF Lakenheath, Suffolk), similarly indicates that diagnostically furnished Final-phase male graves outnumber their female counterparts by 2:1, while Migration-period furnished female graves are far more numerous than both of these categories.[7]

The pattern encountered at Edix Hill and Eriswell in the Final Phase is, however, remarkably different from that at the Final-phase cemetery of Melbourn (Cambridgeshire), only 4 or 5 km south of Edix Hill.[8] At that site there appears to have been a much lower proportion of unfurnished graves altogether, at most 8 burials out of 31, and there is no significant difference between the sexes. The ostensible shift in emphasis between the genders at Edix Hill from the Migration Period to the Final Phase indicates that the increasing hierarchicization amongst the women's graves is not simply a matter of extending general social stratification: if that were implicit in this evidence, relations between men would appear to have moved in the opposite direction, to greater levelling in the later phase. In light of the similarity between Edix Hill and Eriswell noted here, it will be interesting to see if future research can tell us whether the differences between Edix Hill and Melbourn are in any way typical as a contrast between the Final-phase features of cemeteries founded in the Migration Period and characteristics of cemeteries that only came into being in the Final Phase, of which there are several examples in Cambridgeshire, Bedfordshire and Hertfordshire.[9]

The method used for the chronological investigations was correspondence analysis: a technique that has produced enviable results with contemporary furnished graves on the Continent and in Scandinavia.[10] It did not work so well for us — not in chronological terms at least. This was because it revealed another, intriguing phenomenon.[11] The existence of alternative material-cultural clusters within relatively small, contemporary communities was already known, in the form, for instance, of surprising contrasts in association between contemporary women's dress accessories:

[7] My thanks to Sue Anderson of Suffolk County Council (Archaeology department) for access to the finds and records of this important site, and permission to refer to it here.

[8] D. M. Wilson, 'The initial excavation of an Anglo-Saxon cemetery at Melbourn, Cambridgeshire', *Proc. Cambridge Antiq. Soc.*, 49 (1956), 29–41; Malim and Hines, op. cit. in note 1, 322–3.

[9] Malim and Hines, op. cit. in note 1, 323–5. Further excavations at Melbourn took place in the first half of 2000, after this paper had been completed and submitted. Preliminary reports indicate that the number of excavated and recorded burials from the site has now been tripled, but it is not confirmed that these are from a single cemetery with those excavated in the early 1950s. There is also no information available at the time of writing this supplementary note (June 2000) on the prevalence of grave-furnishing among the newly-excavated graves, although it would appear that most of the graves confirm the Final-phase predominance reported by Wilson (op. cit. in note 8). At least one grave with a great square-headed brooch, however, now indicates late Migration-period burial at this site.

[10] K. Høilund Nielsen, 'Zur Chronologie der jüngeren germanischen Eisenzeit auf Bornholm: Untersuchungen zu Schmuckgarnituren', *Acta Archaeol.*, 57 (1986), 47–86; L. Jørgensen and A. Nørgaard Jørgensen, *Nørre Sandegård Vest: A Cemetery from the 6th-8th Centuries on Bornholm* (Copenhagen, 1997), esp. 24–39; F. Siegmund, *Merowingerzeit am Niederrhein* (Cologne, 1998); J. Hines *et al.* (eds.), op. cit. in note 4, *passim*.

[11] Malim and Hines, op. cit. in note 1, 313–17; J. Hines, op. cit. in J. Hines *et al.* (eds.), op. cit. in note 4, esp. 68–72.

for instance cruciform and small long brooches on the one hand and square-headed and saucer brooches on the other.[12] The correspondence analysis suggested a considerably stronger and deeper patterning, which could be generalized as a pattern of four concurrent but contrastive female 'costume groups' (defined by their metal jewellery). Although, to some degree, distinctive cultural origins can be associated with these costume groups — such as the well-known Saxon origins of the saucer brooch characteristic of what we have called costume group A — this clustering and separation should only be conceptualized as identifiable tendencies within the material, not as a set of transmitted cultural traditions. In fact, as the two graphs in figures 1 and 2 imply, the distance or separation between the most diagnostic artefact-types — for instance the cruciform brooches — is greater than that between individual graves, where in the larger number of examples more hybrids, mergers and transitional assemblages occur. In other words, the costume groups represent abstract parameters within and between which individuals arrange their behaviour. As yet, we do not know what these assemblages represent —how they may have signalled individual identity and associations if they did so at all. There is not just more research, but really more data that are needed here.

At Edix Hill, we tried to look at these costume groups in relation to a pattern of possible family groups of burials that could tentatively be discerned within the cemetery.[13] There were two principal forms of evidence that could be used to postulate kinship, be that in the natural form of consanguinity (close genetic relationship through a common progenitor) or in the culturally created form of marriage or adoption. One of these was special collocation of burials, such as a double burial within a single grave, which it is not unreasonable to suggest may reflect a relationship between the deceased in life. The other was heritable anatomical features or genetic dispositions observable in the skeletal evidence (epigenetic traits). The latter in particular — principally in the form of metopic sutures, Wormian bones, possibly spondylolysis, and an abnormal vertebral count – showed an interesting pattern in that men sharing such distinctive features tended to be buried close together in the cemetery, and women to be markedly more dispersed (Figs 3–4). If we postulate family areas within a cemetery— as has also been done at Berinsfield (Oxfordshire)[14] —then this pattern is noticeably consistent with a system of female exogamy, which would mean that women disperse amongst families within a wider community rather than men. This hypothesis is actually neither confirmed nor refuted by the distribution of epigenetic traits at Berinsfield,[15] where the situation is obscured by a generally higher prevalence of such diagnostic features, suggesting that this was an intrinsically more closely genetically inter-related community. Returning to our female costume groups at Edix Hill, there is a marked diversity of range within one particularly distinct cluster of graves (Fig. 5), which again would agree with a hypothesis that the range of dress accessories reflects an identity related to preceding origins, rather than immediate circumstances, within society.

[12] J. Hines, *A New Corpus of Anglo-Saxon Great Square-Headed Brooches* (London, 1997), 236–50.
[13] Malim and Hines, op. cit. in note 1, 303–13 and 316–7.
[14] A. Boyle, A. Dodd, D. Miles and A. Mudd, *Two Oxfordshire Anglo-Saxon Cemeteries: Berinsfield and Didcot* (Oxford, 1995), 117–8 and 133–7.
[15] *Contra* Boyle *et al.*, op. cit. in note 14, 133.

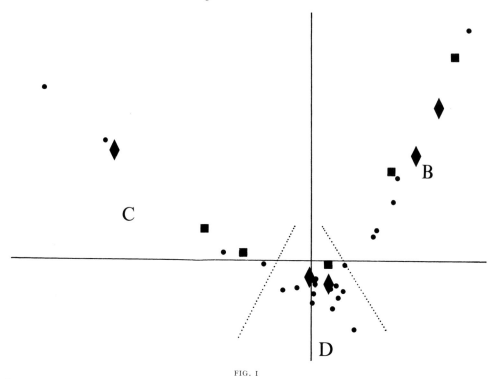

FIG. I

Correspondence analysis of grave groups from Cambridgeshire and East Anglia (after Malim and Hines, op.cit. in note 1, fig. 8.8ii): artefact-types. Rhombuses: cruciform brooch-types; squares: small long brooch-types; dots: other artefact-types. The postulated costume groups B, C and D marked.

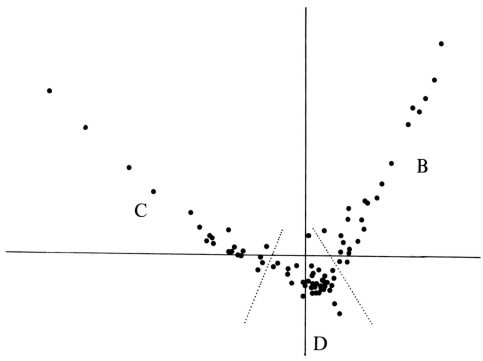

FIG. 2

Correspondence analysis of grave groups from Cambridgeshire and East Anglia (after Malim and Hines, op.cit. in note 1, fig. 8.8i): grave groups. The postulated costume groups B, C and D marked.

FIG. 3

Edix Hill, Cambridgeshire. Graves excavated 1989–91. Male burials with shared, possibly genetically inherited features.

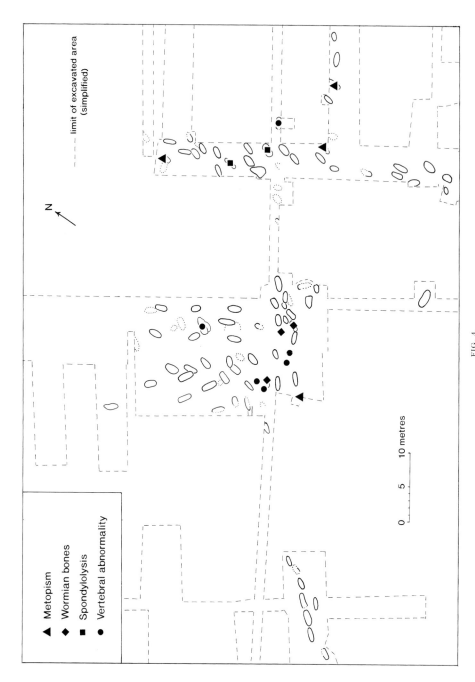

FIG. 4

Edix Hill, Cambridgeshire. Graves excavated 1989–91. Female burials with shared, possibly genetically inherited features.

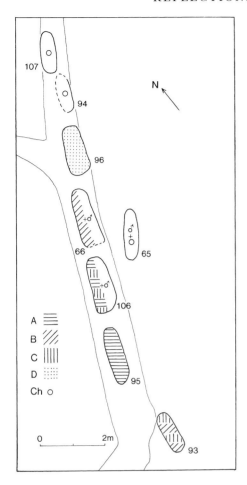

FIG. 5

Edix Hill, Cambridgeshire. Discreet group of burials found following the line of an Iron-age ditch to the South-West of the site (Trench XII). Costume group associations (A–D) of the female graves marked by shading. Ch = child's grave.

It also proved valuable to explore the correlation between the distribution of grave-goods and the osteological data. A particularly clear pattern emerged with the male burials. Men buried with two items of weaponry — the remaining parts, at least, of a shield, and a spear — were consistently those who were identified as having died in what should otherwise have been the prime of adult life: mostly 18–35 years old at death; none over 45. Correspondingly there was a very clear association of single items of weaponry with younger or older males.[16] The age: grave furnishing distribution is statistically significant by the standard χ^2 test — but, more meaningfully, is simply an observable fact in respect of a reasonably high proportion ($c.$ 33 to 50 per cent) of this community:[17] a proportion that is actually increased if we surmise, as suggested above, that this pattern relates disproportionately to the Final Phase at Edix Hill. We know, however, that it is not the whole picture in this case, because two sword graves were unearthed at this site in the 19th century, and we do not have any details of their

[16] Malim and Hines, op. cit. in note 1, 296–301.
[17] Ibid., 227–8 and 292–3.

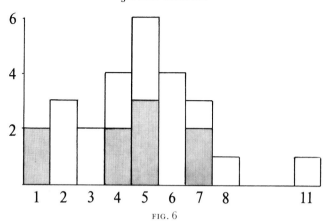

FIG. 6

Edix Hill, Cambridgeshire. Comparative distribution of NIAC scores (horizontal axis) in the burials of women aged under 25 and 25 or over at death respectively. The younger group shaded. Vertical axis = number of burials recorded.

occupants. For the Final-phase men of Edix Hill, nonetheless, status as implied by burial was directly correlated with age at death. It thus seems to have been the case that status in the living community changed with age, and could be both gained and lost.

It is far less clear that the same situation holds amongst the women of this community, although, as already noted, we have a more substantial view of how women were treated within society within a different phase from that of men: women's graves are easily recognizable from the Migration Period, and those seemingly datable to the Final Phase are much fewer. If, however, we look at the variety of identified artefacts in the graves of women aged under 25 at death against those of the 25-and-over age group from the Migration Period (Fig. 6), there is a distinct difference in the median and the upper range of the charts which could, tentatively, be suggested to be consistent with a higher range of status being available to older women, particularly in the 25–35 age bracket.[18] The occupants of the two bed burials, however, were aged 17–25 in the more richly furnished case, and 25–35 in the other.

Turning to focus, then, on the natural rather than the social or cultural profile of the community represented at Edix Hill, we seem to get a very clear view of death-rates and life-expectancy for the two sexes (Fig. 7). The death-rate of pre-teen (and generally unsexable) children is 23.13 per cent, a figure presumably depressed by much lower than expected observable infant mortality:[19] as usual (for whatever reason) very young children dying are substantially under-represented in the burial record. There is then a noticeable difference between the sexes, with around 36 per cent of socially adult women (i.e. teenage girls and women of presumably marriageable age) identified as dying in each of the age bands between 12–25 and 25–35, and thus only 28 per cent found to have reached an age higher than 35; in comparison, over 36 per

[18] Malim and Hines, op. cit. in note 1, 301–3 and 317–8. In the burials of women aged up to 25 at death, the mean NIAC (Number of Identified Artefacts count) per grave is 4.33, the median score 4 and the mode 5. For the group aged 25 or more at death, the mean NIAC is 5, the median 6 and the mode 6.
[19] C. Duhig, 'The human skeletal material', 154–99 in Malim and Hines, op. cit. in note 1, 160–1.

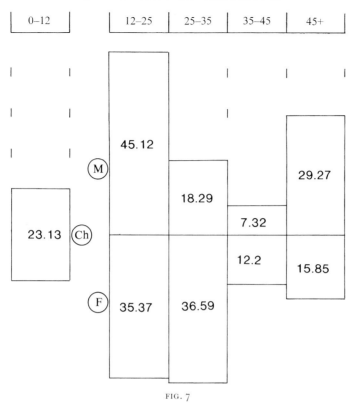

| 0–12 | | 12–25 | 25–35 | 35–45 | 45+ |

FIG. 7

Proportional distribution of ages at death for children (aged 0–12 at death, unsexed), and sexable individuals in the age bands 12–25, 25–35 and 45+ at Edix Hill. Mortality rates given as percentages: for children, as percentage of all aged and/or sexed skeletons; for adults (aged 12+ at death), as percentage of all skeletons of the same sex.

cent of the teenage and older men studied appear to have lived beyond 35, and, more significantly, nearly 30 per cent to have survived beyond 45, about twice the female figure. This sort of lower average female life expectancy has been paralleled elsewhere, and where we encounter it, it is easy to invoke the stresses of childbearing and -rearing as an explanation.[20]

In this case, if we test the figures for statistical significance, the probability that the differences represent random sampling variability within the Edix Hill population proves to be about 10 per cent. In this context, however, we should again bear it in mind that this is not a proportionately small sample from which we are trying to infer the age-structure of a community several times larger, let alone of the early Anglo-Saxon population generally: rather the figures are the observable distribution in what we estimate to be somewhere between one-third and one-half of the deceased buried in this cemetery. The uncertainties must not, of course, be waved aside, but we have to form our perceptions on the data we actually have — and these suggest for the living

[20] H. Härke, 'Early Anglo-Saxon social structure', 125–70 in J. Hines (ed.), *The Anglo-Saxons from the Migration Period to the Eighth Century: An Ethnographic Perspective* (Woodbridge, 1997), 135.

Barrington A community a set of old folk, potential 'elders', in which men would outnumber women by 2:1; although, conversely, it is possible that women who survived into 'old age' could have lived particularly long: two of those at Edix Hill had estimated ages of c. 55 at death, and one over 60.[21] This raises all sorts of fascinating possibilities in the modelling of social relationships: of men outliving wives of about the same age; older men taking younger second wives; this providing a source of potentially powerful young widows, who might compete for status amongst the women with the elderly; and so on.

Recent years, however, have seen the publication of several other Anglo-Saxon cemeteries of approximately the same date-range as Edix Hill (beginning of the 6th to the mid-7th century) with equally good osteological data. The Edix Hill data can be compared with these to see if the demographic profile is consistent. In fact the results are extraordinarily varied. The total comparative sample collected here involved 926 aged and sexed skeletons (Table 1).[22] The child mortality rate (up to and including 12 years of age) in the whole sample is 31.75 per cent of this set, and 27.37 per cent of all aged or sexed skeletons. One can then see a generally decreasing proportion dying in the succeeding age bands of ten to a dozen years each (Fig. 8). But the most surprising feature of all is that amongst the 632 aged and sexed adults, the reported death-rates of males and females are very similar indeed; certainly the differences bear no statistical significance. We do not see here a lower average life-expectancy for women of any great magnitude. (Things are just marginally different over 35.) Put simply, if Edix Hill has a majority of older men, there are other sites where the osteological analysis implies that there was a proportionately higher female survival rate and thus plausibly a majority of older women — for instance Castledyke (North Lincolnshire), where 56.3 per cent of the women are identified as having lived to over 35 as opposed to 48.8 per cent of the men, or Empingham II (Rutland) where 47.8 per cent of the women would appear to have lived beyond the age of 25 against only 35.1 per cent of the men.

The parameters of this whole set of data allow us an imaginative insight into early Anglo-Saxon communal and individual life. According to this, death was an ever-present possibility. Generally, in each age-bracket of ten to a dozen years at least one

[21] Malim and Hines, op. cit. in note 1, tab. 8.3, cf. tab. 8.4 (men).

[22] For the purposes of this study, the sample has been confined to published osteological reports only. Alton, Hampshire: V. I. Evison, *An Anglo-Saxon Cemetery at Alton, Hampshire* (Gloucester, 1988). Analysis by R. Powers and D. R. Brothwell; Berinsfield, Oxfordshire: A. Boyle *et al.*, op. cit. in note 14. Analysis by M. Harman; Castledyke, Lincolnshire: G. Drinkall and M. Foreman, *The Anglo-Saxon Cemetery at Castledyke South, Barton-on-Humber* (Sheffield, 1998). Analysis by A. Boylston, R. Wiggins and C. Roberts; Empingham II, Rutland, Leicestershire: J. R. Timby, *The Anglo-Saxon Cemetery at Empingham II, Rutland* (Oxford, 1996). Analysis by S. Mays; Great Chesterford, Essex: V. I. Evison, *An Anglo-Saxon Cemetery at Great Chesterford, Essex* (CBA Res. Rep., 91, London, 1994). Analysis by T. Waldron; Lechlade, Gloucestershire: A. Boyle, D. Jennings, D. Miles and S. Palmer, *The Anglo-Saxon Cemetery at Butler's Field, Lechlade, Gloucestershire. Vol. 1: Prehistoric and Roman Activity and Anglo-Saxon Grave Catalogue* (Oxford, 1998). Analysis by M. Harman; Mill Hill, Kent: K. Parfitt and B. Brugmann, *The Anglo-Saxon Cemetery on Mill Hill, Deal, Kent* (Soc. Medieval Archaeol. Mon., 14, London, 1997). Analysis by T. Anderson and J. Andrews; Watchfield, Oxfordshire: C. Scull, 'Excavation and survey at Watchfield, Oxfordshire, 1983–92', *Archaeol. J.*, 149 (1992), 124–281. Analysis by M. Harman. Where the age estimated for a skeleton covers two adjacent age-bands, scores of 0.5 have been entered in each category, following the practice in the Edix Hill report: Malim and Hines, op. cit. in note 1, 292–3 and tab. 8.5. In a small number of cases osteologically unsexed skeletons have been classified as male or female on the basis of clear association with unambiguous grave-goods. I consider it unnecessary here to provide exhaustive lists of the age and sex attributions made for all individual burials.

TABLE 1

DISTRIBUTION OF AGE AT DEATH IN A SAMPLE OF PUBLISHED ANGLO-SAXON CEMETERIES: ABSOLUTE FIGURES AND PERCENTAGES.

Site		Total skeletons	Total aged	0–12	Male 12–25	Male 25–35	Male 35–45	Male 45+	Male adult	Female 12–25	Female 25–35	Female 35–45	Female 45+	Female adult	All adults 12–25	All adults 25–35	All adults 35–45	All adults 45+
Alton	% Total aged	39	37	11	2.5	3.5	2	4	2	6	2	0	5	0	9.5	5.5	2	9
	% Sex			29.73	20.83	29.17	16.67	33.33		46.15	15.38		38.46		25.68	14.86	5.41	24.32
Berinsfield	% Total aged	101	88	30	6	11	5	5	4	13	4	3	5	9	25	15	8	10
	% Sex			34.09	22.22	40.74	18.52	18.52		52	16	12	20		28.41	17.05	9.09	11.36
Castledyke	% Total aged	168	149	23	8	13	7	13	10	19	12	21	19	9	36	26	29	36
	% Sex			15.44	19.51	31.71	17.07	31.71		27.76	16.9	29.57	26.76		24.16	17.45	19.46	23.49
Edix Hill	% Total aged	146	134	31	18.5	7.5	3	12	8	14.5	15	5	6.5	4	41.5	23	18	20.5
	% Sex			23.13	45.12	18.29	7.32	29.27		35.37	36.59	12.2	15.85		39.07	17.16	13.43	15.3
Empingham II	% Total aged	145	135	35	39.5	10.5	5	1	7	15	15.5	5.5	2	4	59.5	27	10.5	3
	% Sex			25.93	64.89	22.34	10.64	2.13		52.08	32.29	11.46	4.17		44.07	20	7.78	2.22
Great Chesterford	% Total aged	165	159	82	7	8	8	8	5	10	10	17	6	1	17	20	26	14
	% Sex			51.57	22.57	25.81	25.81	25.81		23.26	23.26	39.53	13.95		10.69	112.58	16.35	8.81
Lechlade	% Total aged	199	190	61	12	6	8	13	4	28	27	16	18	4	41	33	24	31
	% Sex			32.11	30.77	15.38	20.51	33.33		31.46	30.33	17.98	20.22		21.58	17.37	12.63	16.32
Mill Hill	% Total aged	72	70	12	6	3	6	4	1	11.5	3.5	2.5	2.5	1	26.5	9.5	12.5	9.5
	% Sex			17.14	31.58	15.79	31.58	21.05		50	15.22	10.87	23.91		37.86	13.57	17.86	13.57
Watchfield	% Total aged	39	32	9	5	2	4	1	3	4	2	3	1	4	10	4	7	2
	% Sex			28.12	41.67	17.67	33.33	8.33		40	20	30	10		31.25	12.5	21.88	6.25
TOTALS	% Total aged	1074	994	294	95.5	64.5	48	61	44	131	91	73	68	36	266	163	137	134
	% Sex			29.58	35.5	23.98	17.84	22.68		36.09	25.07	20.11	18.73		26.76	16.4	13.78	13.48

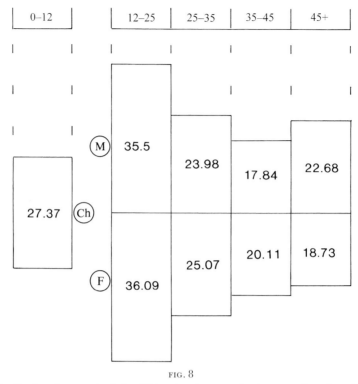

FIG. 8

Proportional distribution of ages at death for children (aged 0–12 at death, unsexed), and sexable individuals in
the age bands 12–25, 25–35 and 45+ in the full sample of cemeteries referred to. Mortality rates given as
percentages: for children, as percentage of all aged and/or sexed skeletons; for adults (aged 12+ at death), as
percentage of all skeletons of the same sex.

individual in three would perish, but whatever age one was up to one's mid-thirties one had a 60 per cent or more chance — or level of hope — of surviving into the next age-bracket. Only over 35 does death within the next decade become a fractionally more than even probability; and what the limits and distribution of longevity were beyond 45 we do not know. More than one in eight of those surviving infancy, and nearly one in five of those reaching adulthood, could expect to pass 45.

To model a 'normal', living community on this basis would require us to have a figure for the average rate of reproduction. If, as it appears, about one individual in three died before the age of sexual maturity, we can assume that each adult needed to have (as father or mother) at least three children on average for society to be maintained numerically. General population growth would imply a higher birth rate. As yet, our chronological understanding is not good enough for us to identify changes in community size through the early Anglo-Saxon Period of the 5th to 8th centuries.

The communities we can observe in buried form vary dramatically from the normal parameters implied by these aggregated figures. The χ^2 test shows that the skewed distribution of male death ages at Edix Hill is significantly different from the overall parameter at slightly above the 80 per cent level. In other words, what we encounter at Edix Hill is what we could expect to encounter in about one cemetery in five of this size. More striking is the fact that the female survival rates over the age of 35 at Castledyke and even at Great Chesterford (Essex) differ from the norm with more than 95 per cent statistical significance, although this pales by comparison with the extraordinarily high death-rate for men under 25 reported from Empingham II, which differs with significance at the 99 per cent level. Empingham II indeed has an abnormally high death-rate for both sexes below the age of 35. What is more, the excavation of the Empingham II cemetery seems to have been close to total.[23] The applicability of these statistical measures of the significance of the difference between individual sites and the aggregated norm is not that they allow extrapolated quantitative hypotheses to be built on the figures from individual sites, but rather that they form a rigorous measure of the variance between sites — to put it simply, they quantify just how different, and how unpredictable, separate communities were.

The crucial question is, of course, whether these startling contrasts between sites are nothing more than a reflection of the intrinsic inaccuracy of osteological aging methods. If that is the case, we should ask our human-bone specialists not to waste their time and ours estimating age at death in the future. It is important, of course, to recognize the fact that some difference between sites will be due to variation in the methods used to determine this figure. There has been tension and debate in the relevant scientific field lately, in particular with potentially serious charges that a set of criteria developed by the Workshop of European Anthropologists some twenty years ago had been substantially discredited when tested out on known-age individuals from the 18th- and 19th-century Spitalfields cemetery from London.[24] In assessing the impact of the Spitalfields experience on these data, however, it is important to recognize firstly that the inaccuracies of the 'complex method' used there can be described as 'systematic' rather than random errors, and secondly that there was no significant discrepancy between the sexes in this respect.[25] The age of individuals dying under 40 tended to be over-estimated, that of individuals dying over 70 under-estimated. The situation is further complicated for our purposes by the fact that the methods used for aging skeletons are not always adequately declared in the relevant reports on Anglo-Saxon cemeteries. Nonetheless it appears that the figures we have compared here should be relatively consistent with each other insofar as dental wear is evidently at least one of the primary criteria for assessing adult age, together with, in certain cases, some or all of assessment of pubic symphysis casts, auricular surface changes, and cranial suture closure. Dental development is also primary for distinguishing children, amongst whom closer age estimates based on other aspects of bone development do not concern us here.

It does not appear proper to draw the pessimistic conclusion from the Spitalfields investigations that all of the figures that have been reported on the age-structure of

[23] Timby, op. cit. in note 21, esp. 15–16.
[24] Workshop of European Anthropologists, 'Recommendations for age and sex diagnoses of skeletons', *J. Human Evolution*, 9 (1980), 517–49; T. Molleson and M. Cox, *The Spitalfields Project. Vol. 2: The Anthropology* (CBA Res. Rep., 86, York, 1993), 167–79; review of the latter by J. Rose, *International J. Osteoarchaeology*, 5 (1995), 97–9.
[25] Corinne Duhig (pers. comm.) notes that there is systematic inaccuracy in all aging methods, reflecting the influence of the reference sample on interpretations made. See J.-P. Bocquet-Appel and C. Masset, 'Farewell to paleodemography', *J. Human Evolution*, 11 (1982), 321–33.

Anglo-Saxon cemetery populations are illusory and meaningless. We do have to recognize, however, that they are estimates with a specifiable degree of uncertainty, not hard numerical facts.[26] Most specifically, the Spitalfields experience would suggest that the profiles discussed here are likely to be skewed towards older ages. If this is so, then the most extreme divergence we have, of an exceptionally low mean age of death at Empingham II, may be less untypical than it at present appears. We can also note that there is no discernible correlation between different methods used for aging and particular demographic patterns claimed for the cemeteries concerned as a result. Equally we should note that, while some cemeteries in the sample — particularly Alton (Hampshire) and Watchfield (Oxfordshire) — are too small for us to be willing to look for statistical significance in the age and sex distributions there, in no case is there any reason to suspect that the figures for a cemetery have been significantly distorted by the excavation of only some partial and unrepresentative segment of the site.

As Anglo-Saxon archaeologists, we have looked, very properly, for what is typical in early Anglo-Saxon cemeteries. In other words we have sought the general; we have sought out that which is shared between them: we have tried to find universal truths and facts about early Anglo-Saxon society. This has been and remains a necessary and valid research goal. But we cannot dismiss that which is inconsistent as wayward, erratic and haphazard; we cannot, in fact, dismiss inconsistency itself as a fact of early Anglo-Saxon social life.[27] The broader implications of this can probably be explored *ad infinitum*, but one vital point must be that, insofar as early Anglo-Saxon culture was functional, it would have to have taken account of both the fixed parameters and the unpredictabilities of Anglo-Saxon life.

ACKNOWLEDGEMENTS

I am deeply grateful to Corinne Duhig for her guidance on the issues concerning the status and interpretation of osteological data involved here. Responsibility for the views expressed in this article must, of course, remain entirely mine. For the first half of the title, my thanks to someone with wit and imagination far brighter than my own.

[26] Thus Bocquet-Appel and Masset, op. cit. in note 25, 325: 'What do we see? Under a 0.9 correlation level, it is impossible to estimate without a considerable risk of error both the individual age of a skeleton and the death structure to which it belongs. However, we are often told that rough age indicators and rough methods tend to give rough demographic results. This is a fallacy . . . we find nothing at all.'

[27] Cf. Bocquet-Appel and Masset, op. cit. in note 25, 332: 'Limited as it is, the information they [age indicators] give is valuable . . . It could not possibly be uninteresting to see most skeletons from one graveyard gather in the youngest age class, or in the oldest — provided that the age determination be without bias.'

Multiple Burials, Multiple Meanings? Interpreting the Early Anglo-Saxon Multiple Interment

By NICK STOODLEY

Considering that cemetery archaeology has again become fashionable, it is surprising that a detailed study of the early Anglo-Saxon multiple burial rite, where two or more people were buried in the same inhumation grave, has not yet been undertaken. The most recent general survey is by Wilson, who concentrates mostly on the unusual examples,[1] something which seems to be true of research generally. It is those that display unusual, or sinister, practices, which draw all the attention and are often interpreted in ritualistic terms. The most famous example is from Sewerby (East Riding of Yorkshire), though less spectacular cases still attract a modest degree of discussion.[2] The other more mundane, but more numerous, examples have generated little in the way of academic debate; simplistic or seemingly obvious interpretations of these have sufficed.

The main thrust of this paper is therefore directed at the other, less noted, examples. This study has two major aims: it will firstly assess the evidence for the construction and organization of the multiple burial, before looking at the possible causes which resulted in the interment of two or more individuals in the same grave.

THE SAMPLE

For the purpose of this study a database of multiple burials was compiled.[3] A brief examination of Table 1 clearly shows that most early Anglo-Saxon cemeteries within this sample have produced multiple burials. Thirteen (22 per cent) did not, although in the case of eight of these, it is estimated that only a small proportion of the cemetery was recovered by archaeological excavation. More interesting are those burial grounds that have been completely or almost completely excavated, but have not produced any examples, such as the unusual site at Bargates (Dorset).[4] From the high proportion of

---

[1] D. Wilson, *Anglo-Saxon Paganism* (London, 1992), 71–7.

[2] S. Hirst, *An Anglo-Saxon Inhumation Cemetery at Sewerby, East Yorkshire* (York, 1985), 38–45; S. J. Sherlock and M. Welch, *An Anglo-Saxon Cemetery at Norton, Cleveland* CBA Res. Rep., 82, London, 1992), 23–6

[3] This was produced by querying a large database of early Anglo-Saxon burials, initially constructed for the author's doctoral research (for a description of the original sample see: N. Stoodley, *The Spindle and the Spear: a Critical Enquiry into the Construction and Meaning of Gender in the Early Anglo-Saxon Burial Rite* (BAR Brit. Ser., 288, Oxford, 1999), 11–5). Since completing the research in 1997, other cemeteries have been added. The resulting database of 245 multiple burials, from 59 cemeteries, includes cemeteries from almost all the areas of England which have produced early Anglo-Saxon material culture (Tab. 1). Although the study does not involve an analysis of cremation burials and therefore does not provide an overall survey, it does claim to be broadly representative of those communities that practised the inhumation burial rite.

[4] K. Jarvis, *Excavations in Christchurch, 1969–1980* (Dorchester, 1983).

TABLE 1
CEMETERIES IN THE SAMPLE AND NUMBER OF MULTIPLE BURIALS BY SITE

Cemetery	Region	# Burials	# Multiples	Proportion
Ford	Wiltshire	2	0	0.00
Ports Down II	Hampshire	2	0	0.00
Broadway Hill	Worcestershire	8	0	0.00
Winterbourne Gunner	Hampshire	10	0	0.00
Leighton Buzzard II	Bedfordshire	19	0	0.00
Dinton	Buckinghamshire	20	0	0.00
Bargates	Dorset	30	0	0.00
Little Eriswll	Suffolk	33	0	0.00
Droxford	Hampshire	41	0	0.00
Stretton-on-Fosse II	Warwickshire	46	0	0.00
Lyminge II	Kent	64	0	0.00
Orpington	Kent	64	0	0.00
Leighton Buzzard III	Bedfordshire	68	0	0.00
Worlaby	Humberside	11	1	9.09
Meonstoke	Hampshire	17	1	5.88
Watchfield	Oxfordshire	31	1	3.23
Snell's Corner	Hampshire	34	1	2.94
Holborough	Kent	40	1	2.50
St Albans	Hertfordshire	41	1	2.44
Spong Hill	Norfolk	58	1	1.72
Alton	Hampshire	60	1	1.67
Holywell Row	Suffolk	101	1	0.99
Swaffam	Norfolk	19	2	10.53
Collingbourne Ducis	Hampshire	36	2	5.56
Winnall II	Hampshire	47	2	4.26
Dunstable	Bedfordshire	49	2	4.08
Bergh Apton	Norfolk	65	2	3.08
Andover	Hampshire	71	2	2.82
Pewsey	Wiltshire	105	2	1.90
Beckford B	Hereford & Worcester	107	2	1.87
Great Chesterford	Essex	164	2	1.22
Bekesbourne II	Kent	40	3	7.50
Long Wittenham I	Oxfordshire	196	3	1.53
Charlton Plantation	Hampshire	46	4	8.70
Fonaby	Lincolnshire	54	4	7.41
Sewerby	East Yorkshire	57	4	7.02
Westgarth Gardens	Suffolk	66	4	6.06
Brighthampton	Oxfordshire	69	4	5.80
Deal	Kent	80	4	5.00
Bidford-on-Avon	Warwickshire	191	4	2.09
Petersfinger	Wiltshire	71	5	7.04
Berinsfield	Oxfordshire	105	5	4.76
Alfriston	East Sussex	180	5	2.78
Ports Down I	Hampshire	28	6	21.43
Worthy Park	Hampshire	105	6	5.71
Broadstairs I	Kent	113	6	5.51
Apple Down I	West Sussex	116	6	5.17
Norton	Cleveland	117	6	5.13
Castle Dyke	Humberside	227	6	2.64
Harnham Hill	Wiltshire	79	7	8.86
Nassington	Northamptonshire	65	8	12.31
Abingdon	Oxfordshire	128	8	6.25
Wakerley I	Northamptonshire	88	13	14.77
Bedhampton	Hampshire	90	13	14.44
Empingham II	Rutland	149	14	9.40
Dover, Buckland	Kent	416	16	3.85
Sarre	Kent	294	17	5.78
Polhill	Kent	130	18	13.85
Edix Hill	Cambridgeshire	148	19	12.84

weapon burials, it seems to have had a strong martial/masculine association, which sets it apart from the majority of communal-type cemeteries.[5] This may explain the lack of multiple burials here. At Stretton-on-Fosse II (Warwickshire) (as yet unpublished) the cemetery was associated with two Romano-British cemeteries (Stretton-on-Fosse I and III), and continuity of population from the Roman to the Anglo-Saxon period is suggested by burial rites, genetic links and methods of textile production.[6] It is impossible to say whether the survival of a Romano-British population had any bearing on the decision not to use multiple burials, but as this is the only completely excavated community-type cemetery to have none, it is certainly the exception. It can therefore be claimed that the practice of interring two or more individuals in a single grave was a widespread phenomenon. However, in all these cases, they only make up a small proportion of the total number of burials: this ranges from under one per cent at Holywell Row (Suffolk) to just over 20 per cent at Ports Down I (Hampshire).[7] On the basis of this sample, the dominant rite throughout early Anglo-Saxon period was clearly that of single burial.

Practical factors, which may have had a bearing on whether multiple burial was used, have been sought. Its incidence bears little relation to geological features of the cemetery, such as subsoil (which might impede ease of grave-digging),[8] while an examination of whether the rite was linked to the available space in a cemetery did not give a consistent result. In some cemeteries which record a high proportion of multiples, for example Empingham II (Rutland) and Edix Hill (Cambridgeshire), space was limited and this may have influenced the decision to place several corpses together, but in others this certainly was not a factor.[9] It must be concluded that there is no simple explanation that can account for the decision to employ multiple burial.

From the sample of 46 cemeteries which have produced multiple burials, the average number of bodies in multiple burials is 5.4 per cent per site. However, these figures are only tentative, and probably do not reflect the true picture with any accuracy. The example of Dover Buckland (Kent) serves to illustrate this.[10] An analysis of this Kentish site based on the excavations in the early 1950s by Vera Evison would give only a single example, yet excavations in 1994, on the remainder of the cemetery produced a further 244 graves, of which fifteen were multiple interments. Without having a whole cemetery available for study, the number of multiples cannot be taken as a genuine indicator of the extent of this practice in a particular community. However, in reality very few sites are totally recovered, therefore we are forced to work with insufficient data.

[5] For more detail, see N. Stoodley, 'Burial rites, gender and the creation of kingdoms: the evidence from seventh-century Wessex', *Anglo-Saxon Stud. Archaeol. Hist.*, 10 (1999), 101–9.

[6] H. Härke, pers. comm.

[7] T. C. Lethbridge, *Recent Excavations in Anglo-Saxon Cemeteries in Cambridgeshire and Suffolk* (Cambridge, 1931); A. Corney, P. Ashbee, V. I. Evison and D. Brothwell, 'A prehistoric and Anglo-Saxon burial ground, Ports Down, Portsmouth', *Proc. Hampshire Field Club Archaeol. Soc.*, 24 (1969), 20–41.

[8] Stoodley, op. cit. in note 3, 54.

[9] J. R. Timby, *The Anglo-Saxon Cemetery at Empingham II, Rutland* (Oxford, 1996); T. Malim and J. Hines, *The Anglo-Saxon Cemetery at Edix Hill (Barrington A), Cambridgeshire* (CBA Res. Rep., 112, London, 1998).

[10] The excavations from the 1950s are published in V. I. Evison, *Dover: The Buckland Anglo-Saxon Cemetery* (London, 1987). The excavations from 1994 are currently at the post-excavation stage. Brief descriptions can be found in K. Parfitt, 'Buckland Anglo-Saxon cemetery, Dover: an interim report', *Archaeol. Cantiana*, 114 (1994), 454–56; K Parfitt, 'The Buckland Saxon Cemetery', *Current Archaeol.*, 144 (1995), 459–64.

TABLE 2
FREQUENCY OF MULTIPLE BURIAL BY DATE

	Early	Late	Long-Lasting
Average number of multiples	4.83	9.58	4.79
Number of cemeteries	29	8	9

An examination of multiple burial by region revealed little variation. Anglian regions generally had a higher incidence, especially the East Midlands where the relatively high numbers recorded at Empingham II and Wakerley I (Northampton-shire) placed this region at the top of the table.[11] At the bottom were East and West Sussex and the West Midlands. However, the figures are never large enough to suggest that the act of placing more than one burial in a grave was a particularly common, or uncommon, regional practice. A chronological analysis was more productive (Table 2). The results show that the practice increased in the 7th century, and this trend seems to have continued through the middle Saxon period as well. At Bedhampton (Hampshire), for example, a site where the majority of burials took place in the 7th and 8th centuries, a relatively high fourteen per cent were in shared graves.[12]

DEFINITIONS

Multiple burials can be divided into two principal groups: contemporary and consecutive types.[13] As the name suggests, contemporary multiple burials contain two or more individuals interred at the same time. This type was more common than the consecutive multiple, which saw the grave being reopened, at some time after the first burial, to allow a second or third interment. In the sample, 173 (70.6 per cent) involved burial contemporaneously and of these 154 (89.0 per cent) were double burials; seventeen were triples, one was a quadruple (Empingham II grave 119), and one contained five burials (Bedhampton grave 68).[14]

Only 58 (23.7 per cent) graves produced evidence to show that they had been reopened to allow another burial to be added. On closer inspection, under half of the cemeteries in the sample have evidence for this type of burial. The great majority of these have only one or two instances, and these are easily outnumbered by contemporary multiples. For example, Empingham II has thirteen contemporary, but only one consecutive, and Norton (Stockton-on-Tees) has five contemporary and one consecutive. The few exceptions to this are of considerable interest, for example, Abingdon I (Oxfordshire), with a ratio of five consecutive to two contemporary burials, while at Ports Down I (Hampshire), only six consecutive multiples were identified.[15] The relatively small cemetery of Ports Down I is intriguing: it seems to have been

---

[11] Timby, op. cit. in note 9; B. Adams and D. Jackson, 'The Anglo-Saxon cemetery at Wakerley, Northamptonshire', *Northamptonshire Archaeol.*, 22 (1990), 69–178.
[12] D. Runkin, pers. comm.
[13] Fourteen of the burials within the sample were of unknown type.
[14] In addition, a quadruple weapon burial was excavated at South Tidworth (Hampshire) in 1992. The publication of this burial is in preparation. The burial was not included in the sample because it seems to have been an isolated grave, and trial trenching around the grave failed to produce any more interments.
[15] E. T. Leeds and D. B. Harden, *The Anglo-Saxon Cemetery at Abingdon, Berkshire* (Oxford, 1936).

established at some point in the 7th century on a chalk ridge overlooking Portsmouth Harbour, with an earlier Bronze-age barrow as a focus. It has an uncharacteristically high number of males, suggesting a different social organization.[16]

GRAVE CONSTRUCTION

An analysis was undertaken to examine whether graves containing multiple burials differed in their constructional methods from those having only single interments. This was deemed to be an important question because it is natural to assume that, out of practical necessity, a grave dug for two or more individuals would be larger than a grave intended for a single person. As consecutive burial resulted in a later burial reusing a grave originally intended for one, the decision was taken to limit the analysis solely to contemporary multiples. The analysis was also confined to graves which only contained adults, or an adult and a sub-adult, as the inclusion of two sub-adults may only have had a limited effect on the size of the cut (although, as will be seen, pairings of sub-adults are extremely rare).

Overall, the graves with multiple burials are larger (Table 3). The greatest difference in size was noted in regard to the width of the pit. This is not that surprising, as the inclusion of multiple interments should have necessitated a wider, but not necessarily longer or deeper, grave. However, the average difference is just over 20 cm which is not that great, and certainly not wide enough to account for the extra width necessary to accommodate two fully grown adults extended side by side. In view of this, an analysis of the positions in which individuals were laid was undertaken. The majority of individuals were placed extended side by side in the grave (Table 4), while a variety of other positions were noted, and it is significant that the most popular of these also had at least one individual extended. For a single burial, an extended position was the most frequent position, and it seems clear that this practice applied equally to multiple interments, even if it resulted in a cramped grave.[17] Overall, although the evidence suggests that larger graves were dug, in most cases the resulting pit was only just big enough to accommodate the occupants. Certainly, with regard to size, a multiple burial did not attract a significantly greater amount of labour. An inspection of individual examples serves to demonstrate that space within the grave was at a premium. For example, at Castledyke (North Lincolnshire), grave 68 contained an adult male and a sub-adult, the latter crammed against the grave wall.[18] Exceptions are found, however. At Charlton Plantation (Wiltshire), two adult males (burials 59 and 60) were laid out extended in this roomy grave.[19]

This apparent unwillingness on the part of the grave digger/funeral party to construct graves of adequate width may explain the presence of contemporary 'stacked' multiples. In this situation the burials are not placed side by side, but on top of each other. Perhaps, as a way to accommodate the burials, this was considered more

---

[16] Stoodley, op. cit. in note 5, 102.
[17] Stoodley, op. cit. in note 3, 55.
[18] G. Drinkall and M. Foreman, *The Anglo-Saxon Cemetery at Castledyke South, Barton-on-Humber* (Sheffield, 1998).
[19] S. M. Davies, 'The excavation of an Anglo-Saxon cemetery (and some prehistoric pits) at Charlton Plantation, near Downton', *Wiltshire Archaeol. Nat. Hist. Mag.*, 79 (1985), 109–54.

TABLE 3
COMPARISON OF DIMENSIONS BETWEEN GRAVES WITH SINGLE BURIALS AND GRAVES WITH
MULTIPLE BURIALS

	Graves with multiple burials		Graves with single burials	
	Sample	Average cm.	Sample	Average cm.
Length	52	197.43	198	191.5
Width	53	98.17	207	77.13
Depth	58	46.31	240	44.03

TABLE 4
POSITIONS OF INDIVIDUALS IN MULTIPLE BURIALS

Position	Number	%
All extended	43	60.56
Extended and half turned	6	8.45
Extended and on side	6	8.45
Extended and crouched	3	4.23
Extended and prone	1	1.41
Both crouched	2	2.82
Crouched and half turned	1	1.41
Crouched and prone	1	1.41
Both on side	1	1.41
Both prone	1	1.41
Prone and half turned	1	1.41
Others	5	7.04
	71	100.00

agreeable than digging a wide grave. Most of the focus has been directed at those exhibiting 'ritual' overtones, and usually consist of the upper individual being placed face down over the lower extended supine burial. The most well-known example is to be found at Sewerby (burials 41 and 49), which has generated a variety of different interpretations, though other examples are known.[20] Recently the excavations at Dover Buckland produced a grave (263) containing a prone burial over an extended female. A small number of cases do exist where both burials are in extended supine positions, with neither displaying any ritual or sinister connotations. The depths of these contemporary graves are no deeper on average than those occupied by a single burial, thus resulting in the upper interment lying close to the surface and vulnerable to grave robbing and disturbance by animals. To deter this, a small barrow could have been erected, but this would have involved extra labour, and would have cancelled out the effort saved in using a single-width grave. Thus the stacked contemporary would probably not have been an acceptable alternative, and their scarceness in the sample reflects this.

One exception does exist: Dover Buckland, where in 1994 excavation produced no less than twelve contemporary stacked burials, of which one (grave 249) held three burials. Only three were of the side by side variety. An analysis by depth revealed that the graves containing stacked burials were no deeper than the single graves. Interestingly, two were surrounded by ring-ditches, which suggests the prior existence of a small barrow affording the occupants some protection.[21]

---

[20] For a discussion of the Sewerby burial and other examples see Hirst, op. cit. in note 2, 38–45.
[21] K. Parfitt, pers. comm.

The assumption that multiple burials did not attract any great expenditure of labour conflicts with the evidence from grave structures. Evidence of associated structures from early Anglo-Saxon burials is rare. It is difficult to know how common they originally were, because much of the evidence, particularly for wooden and external structures, may not have survived, or been recognized in earlier excavations. Admittedly, most of the samples are small, but proportionally the presence of multiple interments did not interfere with the decision to embellish the grave with additional features. Most noteworthy are coffins, the most popular type of structure, which are actually more numerous within graves that contain more than one individual. Four of the burials in the sample contained an adult and a sub-adult, and in three of the cases it is clear that the younger individual was placed over the adult with the coffin giving protection to both. There does not seem to be any evidence for large coffins, which would serve to protect two individuals lying side by side. Where multiples involving adults have produced evidence for coffins, they seem to have only protected one individual. For example, in grave 33 at Castledyke, of an adult male and female, it was the former who benefited. As mentioned above, barrows could also protect multiple burials, though on the available evidence this was a very rare practice. Dover Buckland is the only site to have produced more than one example (see above).

Difficulties are posed by an analysis of consecutive multiple burials. A large proportion of these burials are not recorded in enough detail, while almost a third of the sample of 58 consecutive burials had resulted in the later burial(s) seriously disturbing the primary interment. In many cases only fragmentary skeletal remains were seen, scattered throughout the fill of the secondary interment. The worrying implication of this is that many similar examples may have been overlooked. In a number of cases the remains of the primary burial(s) were moved, usually to the edges of the grave, in order to accommodate secondary interments. For example, at Bedhampton both graves 48 and 49 produced evidence to show that the primary burials were scattered around the sides (Fig. 1). A similar situation occurred at the neighbouring cemetery of Ports Down I. In grave 9, the pit was re-used on two occasions and in each case the earlier occupants were moved aside. The fact that graves were being re-used with so little respect being shown to the earlier occupant raises some important questions regarding cemetery organization, the implications of which will be returned to.

A grave dug for one corpse would not normally have been large enough to comfortably fit two. If the burial party wished to re-use an earlier grave there would have been little choice except to disturb the primary burial. However, as some examples show, later interments could be placed above without any damage occurring to the primary burial. Incidences of stacked consecutive burials account for fourteen (24.0 per cent) graves in the sub-sample. These burials may suggest that more respect was being shown to the earlier occupant. However, in many cases the latest burials were close to the surface, and in several instances plough damage had resulted in serious disturbance. It is entirely possible that in some circumstances the latest burials may have been completely removed, thus leaving a seemingly single inhumation. Again, our sample of burials may be misleadingly small.

By far the rarest type of consecutive multiples was for the later individual to be placed alongside the earlier one: 8.6 per cent (n = 5). The most interesting case is from

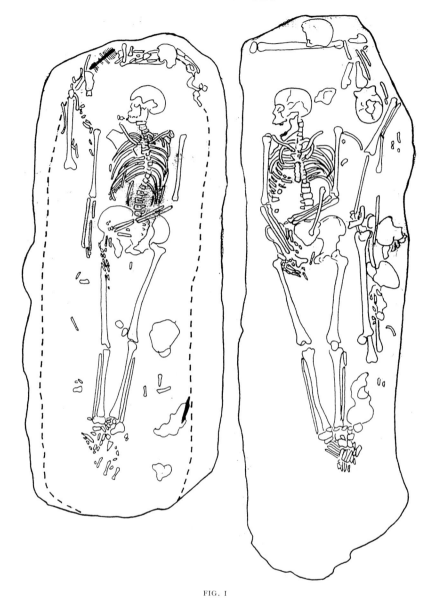

FIG. I

Bedhampton graves 48 and 49: two graves that were reused which resulted in
disturbance to the primary interments.

Mill Hill, Deal (Kent). The primary interments in grave 105 are of an adult male and
female buried at the same time. A careful examination, however, seems to suggest that
the grave was reopened for the addition of a child. Evidence for this is given by the
position of the two adults and the fact that some grave goods seem to have been

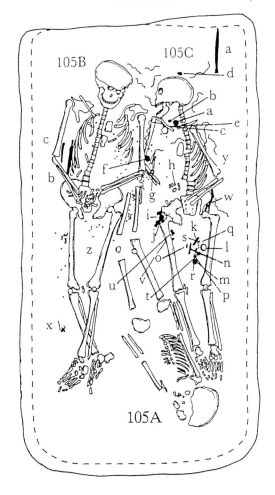

FIG. 2

Deal grave 105: an example of a grave, containing a double contemporary burial (B and C), which was later reopened for the burial of A (after Parfitt and Brugmann 1997, fig. 76).

disturbed (Fig. 2).[22] A different and unusual case was found at Meonstoke (Hampshire).[23] Grave 13 belongs to a double interment of two sub-adults. Originally a single grave, it was enlarged both in length and width to allow the addition of the second sub-adult, who was placed at a greater depth than the primary burial.

Structures are rarely associated with consecutive multiples, whatever their form. This is possibly because any structures belonging to the primary burial were destroyed by later interments. In fact, out of the nine consecutive burials to produce evidence for structures, these belonged to the primary depositions in only two cases. Edix Hill provides us with grave 18, where the earliest burial belonged to an adult female who was placed on a bed. Less spectacular is the pair of sub-adults from Meonstoke mentioned above. The earliest of these had a complete Roman tile placed at the foot

[22] K. Parfitt and B. Brugmann, *The Anglo-Saxon Cemetery on Mill Hill, Deal, Kent* (London, 1997), 28.
[23] N. Stoodley and M. Stedman, 'Excavations at Shavards Farm, Meonstoke: the Anglo-Saxon cemetery', *Proc. Hampshire Fld. Club Archaeol. Soc.*, 56 (2001), 129–59.

end of the grave. Although grave structures are rare, it is pertinent that four burials had associated post-holes. At Apple Down (West Sussex), grave 99 was a large, S.–N. burial, which was enclosed by a four-post structure.[24] The adult male had totally destroyed an earlier infant burial. In addition, a female of over 45 years had been laid at the foot end of this grave, but aligned E.-W., with the head at the E. end. A similar case was discovered at Castledyke where grave 167, an adult female, had a single post-hole along both the long sides of the grave, a further one at the foot end, whilst another possible post-hole was in a central position.[25] All four examples are secondary interments, which may suggest that the positions were being marked for still more depositions. Alternatively, we may be able to explain it chronologically. Three of the four burials are all dated to the 7th century. The exception is Edix Hill grave 10 (A), which lacked grave goods, and is therefore undatable by conventional typological methods, but which overlay an adolescent with 6th-century grave-goods. The occurrence of post-holes, and other external grave structures, mainly in 7th-century graves was noted in the early 1970s by Hogarth.[26]

SEX AND AGE COMBINATIONS

An examination of the combinations in contemporary multiples demonstrates a great degree of variety: in fact almost all possible age and sex pairings are represented in the sample (Table 5). On closer inspection, however, it can be seen that two major groups dominate the sample: combinations of adults and those of adults and sub-adults. It is very rare for two or more sub-adults of any age to be combined. This lack of paired sub-adults has also been noted in individual cemeteries, for example at Edix Hill.[27] Looking first at the adult-only combinations, which made up just under a third of the total sample, it was slightly more common for adults of the opposite sex to be interred together. These are not, however, accurate statistics because the sex of one or more of the individuals in 26 burials could not be determined. With regard to the age associations of these pairs no clear patterning emerged. Of the eleven pairs with an anthropologically determined age, four were of a similar age, for example at Wakerley I, where burials 50 and 51 were both around 30 years old. Pairs could also be separated by a large margin, such as at Castledyke (grave 33), which consisted of a female of around 21 years and a male of over 40 years. Slightly more single-sex multiple burials contained females, but this is not a large enough difference to be significant, although it is noted that these are spread over a greater number of cemeteries than the male examples. Only two sites can boast single-sex multiples of both sexes: Charlton Plantation and Dover Buckland.

Combinations consisting of adults and sub-adults are more numerous (57.3 per cent). The age of a sub-adult seems to have played an important role: the younger a person, the more likely they were to be placed with an adult. Although sub-adults were placed with both sexes, overall they were more likely to be interred with a female. Not

[24] A. Down and M. Welch, *Chichester Excavations 7: Apple Down and the Mardens* (Chichester, 1990).
[25] Drinkall and Foreman, op. cit. in note 18, 213.
[26] A. C. Hogarth, 'Structural features in Anglo-Saxon graves.' *Archaeol. J.*, 130 (1973), 104–19.
[27] Malim and Hines, op. cit. in note 9, 312.

TABLE 5
COMBINATIONS IN CONTEMPORARY MULTIPLE BURIALS. NOTE:
ONLY INCLUDES SEXED AND AGED BURIALS

Combination	number	%
Male and male	8	7.27
Male and female	19	17.27
Male and infant	1	1.01
Male and child	17	15.45
Male and adolescent	10	9.09
Female and female	9	8.18
Female and infant	12	12.12
Female and child	22	20.00
Female and adolescent	1	1.01
Child and child	6	6.06
Child and adolescent	3	3.03
Infant and child	1	1.01
Infant and adolescent	1	1.01

only are these combinations distributed over a wider number of cemeteries than the contemporary male variety (M14: F19), but more sites have produced multiples that only involve females and sub-adults (M7: F12), demonstrating that the pairing of females and younger individuals was a more established practice.

An analysis of the age associations of the adults was undertaken, but it seems that the age of the adult was not a significant determining factor in the decision concerning with whom to place a sub-adult. However, if we compare the age relationships between pairs, with the sex of the adult, a distinct pattern is found (Table 5). A clear tendency to pair a male with an older sub-adult and a female with a younger one is observed. In this sample, only one infant was laid to rest with a male adult, and only one adolescent was laid to rest with a female adult. Thus combinations of adults and sub-adults were governed by clear age-related constraints.

A similar analysis was conducted for consecutive multiples, which resulted in some constrasting findings (Table 6). The same two groups are still dominant, but adult/sub-adult combinations now constitute a smaller group. Insufficient evidence exists to permit an analysis of the age relationships of the adult pairings. In contrast to the contemporary sample, there are over twice as many pairings of males as there are females, though the small sample casts serious doubt on the reliability of this finding. Over a third of the graves consisted of males and females, but there was no sex-specific pattern to the sequence of burial.

The age relationships of consecutive multiples also contradict the findings from the contemporary group. To begin with, males were more likely to be found in a grave that also contained a sub-adult. Also, the age-based limitations that were placed on the pairings of adults and sub-adults in the contemporary group do not apply here. Most notable are the associations between adult females and adolescents, and the total dearth of combined infant and female burials. Sub-adults are numerous in the group of stacked burials, which is in contrast to the group generally: for example at Collingbourne Ducis (Wiltshire), an adult male was placed on top of a possible male sub-adult of about sixteen years.[28] In contrast to contemporary multiples, consecutive

[28] C. J. Gingell, 'The excavation of an early Anglo-Saxon cemetery at Collingbourne Ducis, Wilts', *Wiltshire Archaeol. Nat. Hist. Mag.*, 70/71 (1975–76), 61–98.

TABLE 6
COMBINATIONS IN CONSECUTIVE MULTIPLE BURIALS.
NOTE: ONLY INCLUDES SEXED AND AGED BURIALS

Combination	number	%
Male and male	5	12.5
Male and female	14	35.0
Male and infant	2	5.0
Male and child	5	12.5
Male and adolescent	3	7.5
Female and female	2	5.0
Female and infant	0	0.0
Female and child	4	10.0
Female and adolescent	4	10.0
Child and child	2	5.0
Child and adolescent	0	0.0
Infant and child	1	2.5
Infant and adolescent	0	0.0

burials do not display any clear structure. Choosing a pre-existing grave for a burial was seemingly a random process. From the dearth of sub-adults, the only consideration taken into account was the size of the grave-pit.

DISCUSSION AND INTERPRETATION

Now that the practical aspects concerning multiple burial have been surveyed it is time to consider the purpose and function of these burials. Consecutive multiples are the easiest type to understand and have to be treated as a separate class, characterized by the re-use of an earlier grave pit. In carrying out this act, the burial party/grave digger seldom showed any due care and attention to the earlier occupant. Either the primary burial was totally destroyed, or the remains were unceremoniously moved to the edges of the grave in order to admit the later burial. In spite of this, the intention was not to deliberately disturb the primary interments. That almost a quarter of the burials are stacked without any damage occurring to the primary interment, suggests that earlier burials were only disturbed when they were encountered accidentally. However, when this did occur, it did not prevent the burial being carried out and only in exceptional circumstances does the evidence show that the damage inflicted had been rectified. In conjunction with the lack of any clear structure governing the deposition of consecutive burials, this suggests that an association did not exist between the occupants. This view would explain why all the burials at the non-community-type cemetery of Ports Down I were of this variety.

Thus it is false to interpret these as family plots. In some cases this is confirmed by the fact that a substantial period of time had passed before the grave was reopened, for example Edix Hill grave 66. It seems that in these cases we are simply dealing with the re-use of graves, which on the basis of their relative rarity was not an established practice. The possibility of a single grave taking family members cannot be dismissed entirely, however. Examples of a grave being reopened and a secondary burial carefully being added, for example at Mill Hill, Deal (grave 105), may be proof of the practice, though such situations are extremely rare. This does not have to mean that there was a general disregard of one's descendants. Rather, other means were available. The use of household plots, which have been identified in certain cemeteries, probably sufficed.[29]

Contemporary multiple burials display more structure and accordingly have more to contribute to our understanding of mortuary practice. The fact that two or more individuals were interred together, when the great majority in any cemetery population were granted single burial, is evidence for contemporaneity of death, but also suggests that a relationship may have existed which demanded a joint burial. But what was the nature of the relationship(s)? The analysis revealed that burials consisting of adults only and of adult and sub-adults dominate the sample. The most recent contribution is by Wilson and is largely concerned with the stacked variety, which he feels may have religious or ritual significance. The more usual side-by-side variety he suggests are '. . . members of the same family buried in a communal grave', although he presents no evidence to support this idea. He invokes the same reason for the occurrence of stacked burials that do not exhibit any unusual features, again without any supporting evidence.[30] Elsewhere, interpretation has mainly been confined to excavation reports, and again the practice is explained in a similar manner. Combinations of adult females and sub-adults are usually interpreted as mother and child, while pairings that involve adult males and females are routinely viewed as husband and wife.[31] In some cases, we may indeed be correct to view them in this way. However, for both explanations we have to assume that the deaths would have occurred sufficiently close enough together to permit a joint burial. In addition, it has been reported that infants and children have occasionally been buried with unrelated women.[32] In view of these cautionary remarks, it is argued that the usual generalizations cannot be taken uncritically to explain the choices that resulted in multiple burial. Nor do they adequately explain the variety of different multiple burials, or the differences in treatment, that the above analysis has revealed. To arrive at a more thorough understanding of the underlying reasons, a detailed analysis of the data, both archaeological and skeletal, is necessary.

Without a doubt there was a tendency to place members of the opposite sex together, which on the surface could be taken to indicate partners related by marriage. Although it is unlikely that both partners will have died sufficiently close enough in time to permit joint burial, this cannot be ruled out entirely. It may actually find support in the fact that pairings of adult males and females are spread thinly between individual cemeteries. It is even more likely when it is considered that most early cemeteries witnessed the burial of three or four generations. Of the fourteen sites with this evidence, only two produced more than one burial of a male and female adult (Norton and Polhill (Kent)). Contemporary death could result from disease, acts of violence or accidents. If both burials were to produce such evidence this would

[29] H. Härke, 'Warrior graves? The background of the Anglo-Saxon weapon burial rite', *Past and Present*, 126 (1990), 41–2; Stoodley, op. cit. in note 3, 131–5.
[30] Wilson, op. cit. in note 1, 71–7.
[31] For mother and child interpretations see Malim and Hines, op. cit. in note 9, 312–3; for marriage partners see Drinkall and Foreman, op. cit. in note 18, 334.
[32] S. Anderson, 'The human skeletal remains from Burgh Castle', in M. J. Darling and D. Gurney (eds.), *Caistor-on-Sea Excavations by Charles Green, 1951–5* (*East Anglian Archaeol.*, 60, Gressenhall, 1993), 267; S. Crawford, 'When do Anglo-Saxon children count?', *J. Theoretical. Archaeol.*, 2 (1991), 17–24.

strengthen the case, but it still would not give decisive proof. Unrelated individuals could have died at the same time for any of the above reasons and have been interred together for the sake of convenience. However, none of the multiple burials have produced evidence of trauma, wounding or infection which might suggest that both individuals had met an untimely end, though there are plenty of causes of death that do not leave any skeletal evidence.

The enquiry can be taken further, however. If the couples involved were of roughly the same age, this would add some weight to the marriage hypothesis. However, this is problematical because so little is known in general about marriage in the early period, let alone the age at which it took place. It is not unreasonable though, to assume that both partners in a marriage would be of a similar age, and that it would be unlikely for there to be more than ten years separating them, especially when the low average age of death is considered.[33] From the eleven multiple burials for which an age determination was available for both adults, only five were of a similar age. Most noteworthy are the pair in Edix Hill (grave 106), which are only separated by around two years (male 18 years, female 19–20). In contrast, there are two cases in which the male, and two in which the female, is considerably older. For example, at Dunstable (Bedfordshire) the female was around twenty years older than the male in grave B3/4.[34]

Thus an analysis of age has weakened the marriage argument. There are of course other possible relationships and it is conceivable that these burials might have belonged to siblings. Genetic associations between the burials would aid such an interpretation. However, it is only fairly recently that skeletal material has been analysed for epigenetic or non-metric traits which can possibly assist in the identification of biological relationships. An analysis of these burials against the incidence of epigenetic traits found no evidence to suggest that individuals who were associated through inclusion together in a grave shared a family relationship.

An examination of burial wealth and other aspects of the rite revealed further complications. Many of the multiple burials do not have what we would term a 'normal' burial rite, that is an alignment and deposition similar to that exhibited by the majority of single inhumations at the same site. For example, at Blacknall Field, Pewsey (Wiltshire), the male was in a crouched position next to the female (burials 12/13), while in Polhill grave 108, the two adults had opposing alignments, and although the male was supine, the female had been placed on her side.[35] Even in Edix Hill, grave 106, whose occupants were laid side by side and facing each other, which could be taken to reflect their closeness in life, the grave has a rare, for this site, WSW. alignment. One grave at Norton (joint burial 98/99) involved a lower prone female overlain by a crouched male. Both burials had very few objects and their grave was placed on the western extremities of the cemetery. A similar example was found at Andover (Hampshire): grave 2/2A consisted of a middle-aged male without any

[33] M. Marlow, 'The human remains', in Sherlock and Welch, op. cit. in note 2, 112.
[34] C. L. Matthews, 'The Anglo-Saxon cemetery at Marina Drive, Dunstable', *Bedfordshire Archaeol. J.*, 1 (1962), 25–47.
[35] The cemetery at Blacknall Field, Pewsey is as yet unpublished; B. Philp, 'Site 24. The Anglo-Saxon Cemetery at Polhill, Dunton Green', 168–86 in B. Philp (ed.), *Excavations in West Kent 1960–1970* (Dover, 1973).

artefacts overlying a mature female who was accompanied by a single disc brooch.[36] Significantly, the grave was placed in an isolated position right on the cemetery's southern edge.

These burials seem to have been marked out, not only by the multiple burial, but also by other aspects of the rite. Intriguingly though, the decision to bury individuals together did not seem to interfere with the deposition of grave goods. Only one male and female, in different graves, were without any goods and the average number of types of grave goods (M2.8: F4.0) is only slightly down on the average for single burials (M3.1: F4.9). This finding is underlined by the types of artefact that have been recovered from multiple burials. In addition to the common grave goods, such as knives, spears and beads, rarer items, such as imports, or items involving precious metals and considerable time and effort in their construction, have been recovered. For example, the female in Wakerley I (grave 50) had a bucket and a copper-alloy vessel, while the male in Buckland (grave 96) was accompanied by a sword and shield.

When the burials are examined closely, we discover a range of different assemblages. The two assemblages which have traditionally characterized the early Anglo-Saxon burial rite are both represented. Over half of the males and females had weapons and jewellery respectively. These separate assemblages were instrumental in signalling the gender-identity and stage in the lifecycle of the individual, which it has also been argued, was bound up with household and community status.[37]

The analysis revealed that a modest proportion of contemporary multiples involved individuals of the same sex. Scholarship has generally shied away from an interpretation of these. We could suggest that these were the graves of partners — and we would not be the first. Vera Evison suggested that homosexuality may explain the pairing of two sword-bearing adults in Dover Buckland 96.[38] However, this is an unusual burial, because individual B is judged on skeletal evidence to be female. The situation is far from straightforward, not least because there are various other reasons why two males, and also two females, may be buried together: the most obvious being siblings (though yet again the evidence from epigenetic traits has cautioned against such an interpretation). Adoptive relationships may offer a further explanation.[39]

Individuals of the same sex who experienced concomitant death may have been related through lifestyle/profession, religion or even ethnicity. The latter two are difficult to prove, but the former may be discernible from skeletal evidence. For example, in the quadruple burial from South Tidworth (Hampshire), all four adult males with weapons may have died in battle, although only one was found to have evidence of trauma which may have resulted in death.[40] Aside from this example, evidence for violent death, or even for a stressful lifestyle, for the individuals in any type of multiple burial is rare.

---

[36] A. M. Cook and M. W. Dacre, *Excavations at Portway, Andover 1973–1975* (Oxford, 1985).
[37] For a discussion of the early Anglo-Saxon lifecycle see N. Stoodley, 'From the cradle to the grave: age organisation and the early Anglo-Saxon burial rite', *World Archaeol.*, 31.3 (2000) 456–72; Sherlock and Welch, op. cit. in note 2, 102, suggest that it was the heads of the households that received the greatest burial wealth. This involved both a male and a female with weapons and jewellery respectively, in addition to status symbols such as buckets.
[38] V. I. Evison, op. cit. in note 10, 126.
[39] J. Hines, pers. comm.
[40] For details see note 14.

Single-sex multiples also include some graves that are set apart by other aspects of their rite. At Empingham, a quadruple burial (31) of three males and a young child was excavated: two weaponless males flanked the central one with weapons. In addition, the grave was sited in a separate cluster of weapon burials, clearly separated from the main body of the cemetery. It does seem that this group of individuals had a special status in this community, and the status of the weapon-bearing male in grave 31 was further underlined by his central position. Holywell Row (grave 3) yielded a stacked double of two males, in which the upper body had been laid prone over a half-turned male. This is paralleled in the female group by the aforementioned Sewerby (burials 41/49), which consisted of a lower coffined female overlain by a prone female, who appears to have been held in the grave by a stone on her back. An observation that has been made on a number of occasions, is that the prone woman was not impoverished; rather her assemblage, which included a pair of annular brooches, and a necklace of amber and glass beads, is typical of many found with 6th-century women in Anglian areas.[41] This is generally true of same sex multiples and serves to underline the similarities that these and male/female multiples have in common. Moreover an analysis of their burial wealth and gender-identities produced similar findings to that observed in the former group. From the latest excavations at Buckland comes grave 391, which contained two adult females. Burial B was exceptionally wealthy and was accompanied with, amongst other things, a bucket, a crystal ball, gold threads, five brooches and three pendants (one each of gold, silver and crystal).

Turning now to the issue of paired adults and sub-adults, these constitute the largest group of contemporary multiple burials and it is usually assumed that they are of parents and their offspring. Subjectively a parent-and-child relationship seems understandable, especially when the positions of the burials in the female and infant group are studied. In five of the twelve cases there is a direct spatial relationship between the female and the infant. Most notable is Empingham II (grave 49), in which the infant was placed in the crook of the female's right arm. It is easy to believe that these are mother and baby, the two dying during childbirth or shortly after. However, when the ages of the infants are examined, it is observed that very few are of the right age: about nine foetal months. The only ones that satisfy the criteria are Apple Down (grave 175 B) and Worthy Park (Hampshire) (grave 26).[42] The latter is almost certainly an example of a woman who died during childbirth, as the legs of the foetus were found in the woman's pelvic girdle. For older infants, both could have died from another cause, such as infection following a successful delivery.[43] But yet again there is no way of definitely proving the relationship.

There are other complications. The analysis of the age associations of adults and sub-adults yielded a very intriguing pattern in the fact that infants were restricted to females. Thus the burial options for an infant were limited; but at the same time, infants are the least likely of all age groups to receive burial in a single grave. The lack of a female with whom to bury an infant may go someway towards explaining their

[41] Wilson, op. cit. in note 1, 74.
[42] S. C. Hawkes, forthcoming, *The Anglo-Saxon Cemetery in Worthy Park, Kinsworthy, near Winchester.*
[43] C. Duhig, 'The human skeletal material', in Malim and Hines, op. cit. in note 9, 197.

scarcity in early Anglo-Saxon cemeteries.[44] But it may also suggest that the grave of any available female was considered an appropriate last resting-place. This may have been necessary, not only in terms of convenience, but also to maintain the strict age-related associations evidenced in multiple burials. The implications are important, possibly demonstrating how a young person's tutelage shifted between the sexes. This also has implications for our understanding of gender roles in the early Anglo-Saxon period, in particular how they may have fluctuated between children of different ages.

Several of the infant/female multiples also display unusual features. For example, the head of the female in Edix Hill (grave 84) was resting on top of the infant; an infant at Norton (burial 116) was thought to have been laid prone by the side of a female. The situation regarding adults and children is less clear. Children were interred with both males and females, and many were laid alongside the adult, again inviting a parent/child interpretation. But yet again a number exhibit unusual features which mark them out. In some of the burials, one or both of the individuals were laid on their side. This may have been to accommodate them, but an analysis of the grave dimensions suggests that this was not necessary in every case. Most notable in this respect is the triple burial at King Harry Lane, St Albans (Hertfordshire) that contained an adult, adolescent and child, all on their sides, in a grave that was almost 1.50 m wide.[45] At Empingham, grave 113 consisted of a young male adult and child. The child was under the adult's legs and both were prone. Finally, at Apple Down, grave 41, a child of twelve years and a female were both crouched and facing each other.

Other similarities that the adult/sub-adult group shares with the adult-only group are related to the burial assemblages. Yet again the analysis revealed that a range of different goods were present, including weapons and jewellery. Research into the age associations of various grave goods has identified an association between women who have jewellery, but who also have girdle items (keys and girdle-hangers), and burial with sub-adults. Interestingly, the results show that these died younger than the women without girdle items, and it was argued that girdle items reflect a role associated with children.[46] Only a relatively small proportion of adult women in any one cemetery had these items. In some sites it works out as one per generation.[47] The implication is that the children buried with these women may not have belonged to them, rather they could have been under their care, supervision or instruction.

This study has shown that the multiple burial rite was complex and multidimensional. No simple explanation can account for the sheer variety of treatment evidenced. However, a number of trends have been identified that offer an insight into the decisions that went into placing a select few together in a grave. The discovery that many of these graves have unusual features, which sets them apart from the rest of the cemetery population is important. To understand why these individuals were being

---

[44] S. Crawford, 'Children, death and the afterlife in Anglo-Saxon England', *Anglo-Saxon Stud. Archaeol. Hist.*, 6 (1993), 83–91.
[45] B. M. Ager, 'The Anglo-Saxon cemetery', 219–39 in I. M. Stead and V. Rigby, *Verulamium: the King Harry Lane Site* (English Heritage Archaeol. Rep., 12, London, 1989).
[46] Stoodley, op. cit. in note 37.
[47] Stoodley, op. cit. in note 3, 133.

marked out necessitates a consideration of these communities in life. Early Anglo-Saxon settlements were relatively small scale, usually amounting to no more than a small group of buildings.[48] In these communities it must have been comparatively rare for two people to die at the same time, and for the occurrence of simultaneous deaths to exceed this rate was even rarer. The implications of simultaneous deaths, and the negative consequences this may have held for these small, agriculturally self-sufficient, units were far-reaching. It has been argued that the disruption caused by a death may have been one of the reasons behind the accompanied rite in the first place.[49] Two or more simultaneous deaths would have caused even greater disruption. This, it is argued, provoked a number of ritual responses in an attempt to stem any more deaths: a multiple burial containing the recent dead, and various practices that differed to the norm. Moreover, in some cemeteries multiple burials were placed on the outskirts of the burial ground, most notably at Bidford-on-Avon (Warwickshire), where the four multiples, which incidentally includes two triples, were all located on the eastern edge.[50] The majority of multiple burials were accorded unusual features, because multiple deaths were relatively unusual. The increase in multiple burials in the 7th century may have been a result of an enlarging population and a rise in the numbers of simultaneous deaths.

This explains the range of individuals of different status. If burial wealth can be taken as an indicator of an individual's position in a social hierarchy, then it is clear that people from throughout society were chosen. Also, on the basis of this evidence, it did not result in a loss of status for that individual. A multiple burial was not just for those who were unable to attract the energy that was involved in the construction of a single grave. Inclusion in multiple burial did not result from something that individual did, or that happened to that individual, in life. For example, it is unlikely that these burials belonged to criminals. In this regard it is important that none of the individuals have produced evidence for decapitations, amputations or tied limbs, although burial 25B, of an adult female, at Mill Hill, Deal produced evidence of trepanation. Moreover, although there is some evidence pertaining to disabilities or disfigurations, it is not abundant and we certainly do not encounter paired individuals with this evidence. These are not people who were perceived as different in life. Rather, their only 'fault' was to be unlucky enough to die at the same time as another member of the community.

Analysis has revealed that deposition in a multiple burial was not a random process, however. Certain rules governed which combinations were appropriate. The strictest rules were age-related. It was very rare for sub-adults to be paired, which is surprising since mortality among the youngest members of a community would have been high. In all probability there should have been more contemporary child deaths

---

[48] H. Härke, 'Early Anglo-Saxon social structure', 125–70 in J. Hines (ed.), *The Anglo-Saxons from the Migration Period to the Eighth Century: An Ethnographic Perspective* (Woodbridge, 1997), at p. 138.
[49] G. Halsall, 'Female status and power in early Merovingian central Austrasia: the burial evidence', *Early Medieval Europe*, 5 (1996), 1–24.
[50] J. Humphreys, J. W. Ryland, E. A. B. Barnard, F. C. Wellstood and T. G. Barnett, 'An Anglo-Saxon cemetery at Bidford-on-Avon, Warwickshire', *Archaeologia*, 73 (1923), 89–116; J. Humphreys, J. W. Ryland, E. A. B. Barnard, F. C. Wellstood and T. G. Barnett, 'An Anglo-Saxon cemetery at Bidford-on-Avon, Warwickshire: second report on the excavations', *Archaeologia*, 74 (1924), 271–88.

than adult ones. The fact that children were almost always placed with an adult may indicate that the responsibilities, and security, provided by older members of the community were believed to extend into the realm of the dead. The evidence suggests something more intricate than a simple parent-child relationship. In fact the sex-specific age-related patterns argue against interpreting these burials purely in familial terms, and gives credence to the idea that multiple burials consisted of unrelated members of the community.

CONCLUSION

Most early Anglo-Saxon cemeteries produce examples of multiple burials, although they are always in a minority. Multiples consisting of two individuals are by far the most common; graves containing more burials are extremely rare. This has to be a simple reflection of the mortality patterns of these rural agriculturally based settlements. Simultaneous deaths were rare, but when they did occur they caused anxiety and induced a reaction that was aimed at stopping any further deaths. These responses are totally believable, especially when the superstitious character of these people is considered. These burials should now be recognized as belonging to a distinctive class of burial, not simply the final resting-places of family members, but neither do they deserve to be classified as deviant burials. Rather, the multiple burial rite can now be placed alongside the use of amulets as a method of dealing with situations which were out of the control of these communities.[51]

In concluding this paper some suggestions for future research can be made. The exciting prospects offered by DNA analysis may help us to understand more about the relationships of the individuals which archaeology can not provide. From a methodological perspective we need to be extra vigilant when it comes to the excavation and recording of multiple burials. The precise location of any grave goods, grave structures and the positions of the burials are essential so that scholars in the future will have more reliable material to work with. However, despite the limitations, this study has contributed to our understanding of both the practical and ideological aspects surrounding the multiple burial rite, in addition to commenting on aspects of social organization, especially attitudes to the youngest members of society.

ACKNOWLEDGEMENTS

I would like to thank the following people for their help and assistance. Dr Heinrich Härke (Reading), for allowing me to use his database of early Anglo-Saxon male and sub-adult burials to which the female, and any other outstanding, burials were added for the purpose of my doctoral research, and for drawing my attention to the South Tidworth quadruple burial. David Rudkin (Chichester), generously allowed me access to the Bedhampton archive and granted permission to reproduce the plans of graves 48 and 49 ahead of publication. Keith Parfitt (Canterbury), kindly provided details about the Dover Buckland multiple burials. I would also like to acknowledge the following people for information about unpublished sites: S. Anderson, Bury St Edmunds; K. Annable, Devizes; K. Ainsworth and G. Denford, Winchester; W. J. Ford, Alnwick; D. Miles, London; P. Robinson, Devizes; R. A. Rutland, Leicester; J. Timby, Stroud; L. Webster, London; P. Wise, Warwick.

[51] A. L. Meaney, *Anglo-Saxon Amulets and Curing Stones* (BAR Brit. Ser., 96, Oxford, 1980).

Cross-Channel Contacts between Anglo-Saxon England and Merovingian Francia

By MARTIN WELCH

This paper provides an introduction to an Anglo-French research project designed to investigate the nature of cross-Channel contacts between lowland Britain and Gaul in the Early Medieval period.[1] The presence of Frankish objects in Kent, but also elsewhere in Anglo-Saxon England, has been an important aspect of the archaeology of the Early Medieval period in Britain. These can be dress-fittings, such as brooches and buckles; weapons, such as the *fauchard* from Buckland II, Dover (Kent); and vessels such as the imported wheel-thrown Merovingian pottery.[2] The issue of whether Frankish warleaders played a significant role in the 5th-century settlement of southern England has been debated at length,[3] though in some cases at least we might be looking at Saxon warriors who had acquired Frankish weaponry and dress-fittings.[4] Frankish dress-fittings, including radiate-headed bow brooches, cloisonné disc brooches and bird brooches, are a particular feature of some of the richer female

[1] This project has been developed from a joint agreement for academic co-operation between the Musée des Antiquités Nationale (MAN) at Saint-Germain-en-Laye, near Paris and the Institute of Archaeology at University College London (UCL). This provides for academic staff and students from UCL and Paris I (Sorbonne), through its association with archaeologists based at MAN, to become involved in a series of joint projects. To date, these cover aspects of prehistoric, protohistoric and now also early medieval archaeology. Additionally, in the case of the Early Medieval period, some staff in the Department of Medieval and Modern Europe at the British Museum in London have indicated their wish to contribute actively to this research project. It is proposed that individual French students from Paris will undertake surveys and preliminary assessments of Frankish material, whether recovered from excavated sites or as stray finds, including metal-detector finds, in Britain. London students will be able to do the same for identifiable Anglo-Saxon material in France and in either case the students will be working under the supervision of academic staff from both MAN and UCL. Scientific analysis of samples taken from pottery and other artefacts can be carried out by London-based students and analysis of human skeletal material from relevant cemetery contexts can take place in both countries, though it is important that agreement is reached by the human biologists involved on the use of a standard methodology to permit direct comparison of results. A synthesis of the results will be developed from the catalogues and preliminary conclusions drawn by the students in their individual dissertations and project reports and this will be undertaken by the international team of project supervisors and will be published jointly. Fortuitously, there are already research students, one each from Paris and London, working towards dissertations which can contribute to this project. The Paris-based Masters research involves a comparative study of weapon graves in southern England and north-eastern France in the Merovingian period (by Axel Kerep supervised by Patrick Périn). The London doctoral research is on Anglo-Saxon trade, with particular reference to Thanet and the Wantsum Channel in Kent. This has an active fieldwork component, now with two seasons' work to locate the former ports at Fordwich, Sarre and Sandwich on the Stour/Wantsum Channel waterways (Stuart Brooks supervised by Martin Welch and Gustav Milne).

[2] V. I. Evison, *Wheel-Thrown Pottery in Anglo-Saxon Graves* (London, 1979).

[3] E.g. V. I. Evison, *The Fifth-Century Invasions South of the Thames* (London, 1965); V. I. Evison, 'Distribution maps and England in the first two phases', 126–67 in V. I. Evison (ed.), *Angles, Saxons and Jutes* (Oxford, 1981); S. C. Hawkes, 'The early Saxon period', 77–81 in G. Briggs, J. Cook and T. Rowley (eds.), *The Archaeology of the Oxford Region* (Oxford, 1986).

[4] M. Welch, *Early Anglo-Saxon Sussex* (BAR Brit. Ser., 112, Oxford, 1983), 172 and 222–3.

graves in Kent attributable to the 6th century and have recently been reassessed by a German archaeologist for the Mill Hill, Deal (Kent) cemetery report.[5] The fact that characteristically Frankish brooches are found in the 'wrong positions' in relationship to the corpse and the strange absence of ear-rings implies that those women who had acquired such brooches were not Frankish migrants, but local people who had been given these dress-fittings and then adapted them as best they could to their own traditional costumes.

The Chessell Down cemetery on the Isle of Wight excavated in the mid-19th century also has a Frankish and Kentish character.[6] It has been seen as a Kentish colony which relates to Bede's description of Wight and the mainland opposite as a *natio iutarum* sharing a Jutish origin with the province of Kent.[7] Equivalent cemeteries with a marked Kentish character do not occur in Hampshire on the mainland, however, though some Kentish and even a few Frankish items are found at sites in Hampshire and also in the neighbouring counties of Wiltshire and West Sussex.[8] Indeed, occasional finds of Frankish imports are recorded from most regions of southern England and are even found across eastern England as far north as Norton (Stockton-on-Tees) near the east coast.[9] Such links continue on beyond the 6th century into the 7th century, with finds such as the imported inlaid iron belt sets from Updown, Eastry (Kent),[10] and an inlaid iron loop from a buckle recovered from amongst the demolition debris of a documented royal villa at Yeavering (Northumberland).[11]

Our awareness of the presence of Frankish objects in Anglo-Saxon burials goes back well into the 19th century and has led to extensive debate in the literature during the 20th century. The contribution of Anglo-Saxon objects to the repertoire of finds in Frankish cemeteries did not attract quite as much attention until rather more recently. There is however, the notable exception of Delamain's publications of Kentish material from the Merovingian row-grave cemetery at Herpes (Dép. Charente), in south-western France.[12] Rescue excavations of French cemeteries datable to the Late Roman and Early Medieval periods from the 1960s onwards did draw attention to the presence of Anglo-Saxon material in northern France. Some of these sites were located in the north-east region closest to Kent, e.g. the cemeteries at Nouvion-en-Ponthieu and Vron,[13] but many others occurred in western Normandy, especially around Caen

[5] K. Parfitt and B. Brugmann, *The Anglo-Saxon Cemetery on Mill Hill, Deal, Kent* (Leeds, 1997).
[6] C. J. Arnold, *The Anglo-Saxon Cemeteries of the Isle of Wight* (London, 1982).
[7] *Bede's Ecclesiastical History of the English People*, ed. and trans. B. Colgrave and R. A. B. Mynors (Oxford, 1969), I.15.
[8] E.g. M. Welch, 'Anglo-Saxon Hampshire', 35–9 in D. A. Hinton and M. Hughes (eds.), *Archaeology in Hampshire: A Framework for the Future* (Winchester, 1996).
[9] S. J. Sherlock and M. Welch, *An Anglo-Saxon Cemetery at Norton, Cleveland* (CBA Res. Rep., 82, London, 1992).
[10] S. C. Hawkes, 'Recent finds of inlaid buckles and belt-plates from seventh century Kent', *Anglo-Saxon Stud. Archaeol. Hist.*, 2 (1982), 49–70.
[11] M. Welch, 'The dating and significance of the inlaid buckle loop from Yeavering', *Anglo-Saxon Stud. Archaeol. Hist.*, 3 (1984), 77–8.
[12] C. Haith, 'Un nouveau regard sur le cimetière d'Herpes (Charente)', *Revue Archéol. Picardie*, 3–4 (1988), 71–80.
[13] D. Piton, *La Nécropole de Nouvion-en-Ponthieu* (Berck-sur-Mer, 1985); C. Seillier, *Le Cimetière de Vron* (forthcoming).

(Calvados), but also in the Cherbourg peninsula (Cotentin), more or less opposite the Isle of Wight, e.g. Réville, Frénouville, Giberville and Saint-Martin-de-Fontenay.[14]

Their excavation and publication drew attention to the existence of a small, but significant, corpus of Anglo-Saxon material from much older findspots and excavations in these two regions,[15] which were a theme of at least one special exhibition.[16] These finds included a quoit brooch from Bénouville[17] and, in combination with the recent excavated finds, these have been assessed in surveys by international scholars.[18] In such studies, their significance has often been considered in terms of a possible relationship to documented references to 'Saxons' settled around the trading emporium of Quentovic (near Étaples on the Canche) in the Pas-de-Calais region[19] and around Bayeux in western Normandy.[20] A reference by Procopius to Angles migrating on an annual basis from Britain (*Brittia*) to be settled on deserted continental territories by Frankish kings has also been argued to be relevant here.[21] On the other hand, other historical sources also refer to the presence of Saxons based in the lower reaches of the Loire valley during the 5th century, for whom there is no recorded archaeological trace.

Diplomatic relations and trade networks have been seen as providing a context for active exchange, which might be reflected in the material culture of funerary practice. The marriage of Æthelberht, a Kentish prince (and later king) to Bertha daughter of King Charibert of Paris (561–567) has certainly encouraged such thoughts. After all, it was this marriage alliance between a member of the pagan Kentish royal dynasty and a rather unimportant Merovingian Christian princess which provided the context for Gregory, Bishop of Rome, to send a mission led by Augustine to the Anglo-Saxon kingdoms in 597. Of course, this mission bypassed the Gallic Church authorities and the Merovingian kings, though Frankish clerics did become increasingly involved as the mission moved on from Kent to attempt the conversion of the ruling class in each Anglo-Saxon kingdom through most of the 7th century. The roles of Agilbert and Leutherius in the mission to the West Saxon kingdom suggests that Dagobert I (623/29–638/39) may have taken an interest in influencing events in southern England.[22]

---

[14] F. Scuvée, *Le Cimetière Barbare de Réville (Manche), VIe-VIIe Siècle, Fouilles 1959–1966* (Caen, 1973); C. Pilet, *La Nécropole de Frénouville* (BAR Int. Ser., 83, Oxford, 1980); C. Pilet, J. Lemiere and A. Alduc-Le Bagousse, *La Nécropole de Giberville* (Caen, 1981); C. Pilet and A. Alduc-Le Bagousse, *La Nécropole de Saint-Martin-de-Fontenay, Calvados* (Paris, 1994).

[15] E.g. G. Bellanger and C. Seillier, *Répertoires des cimetières mérovingian du Pas-de-Calais* (Arras, 1982).

[16] For a catalogue, see *Le Nord de la France de Théodose à Charles Martel* (Lille, 1983).

[17] Evison 1981, op. cit. in note 3, 133–4, fig. 3.

[18] H. Vierck, 'Zum Fernverkehr über See im 6. Jahrhundert angesichts angelsächsischer Fibelsätze in Thüringen. Eine Problemskizze', 355–95 in K. Hauck (ed.), *Goldbrakteaten aus Sievern* (Munich, 1970), fig. 52; C. Lorren, 'Des Saxons en Basse Normandie au VIe siècle? À propos de quelques découvertes archéologiques funéraires faites récemment dans la basse vallée de l'Orme', *Stud. zur Sachsenforschung*, 2 (1980), 231–59; M. Welch, 'Contacts across the Channel between the fifth and seventh centuries: a review of the archaeological evidence', *Stud. zur Sachsenforschung*, 7 (1991), 261–9.

[19] M. Rouche, 'Les Saxons et les origines de Quentovic', *Revue du Nord*, 59 (1977), 457–78.

[20] Gregory of Tours, *The History of the Franks*, trans. L. Thorpe (Harmondsworth, 1974), V.26 and X.9.

[21] Procopius, *History of the Wars*, ed. H. B. Dewing (London, 1914–40), VIII.20, 8–10; I. Wood, 'Franken und Angelsachsen', 341–5 in A. Wieczorek, P. Périn, K. von Welck and W. Menghin (eds.), *Die Franken Wegbereiter Europas* (Mannheim, 1996), at p. 341.

[22] I. Wood, 'The Channel from the 4th to the 7th centuries', 93–7 in S. McGrail (ed.), *Maritime Celts, Frisians and Saxons* (CBA Res. Rep., 71, London, 1990).

In a letter to the Emperor Justinian, Theudebert I (533–547) claimed overlordship over the Saxons and Jutes and, according to Procopius, a Frankish king sent some Angles as part of a diplomatic mission to Constantinople to demonstrate this fact.[23] It is far from clear what form that overlordship took or how effective it proved in practice, though it seems to have been exercised by other Merovingian rulers during the 6th and 7th centuries. The *Pactus Legis Salicae* provides for the recovery of Frankish slaves who escaped overseas, but in practice real influence was probably limited to the southern English kingdoms. Nevertheless, we lack detailed evidence for what these Frankish claims to overlordship amounted to in reality.[24]

Archaeology can make some contribution here, for the concentration of luxury imported goods, such as glass and metal vessels, rock crystal balls and beads, garnets, amethysts and cowrie shells in east Kent during the 6th to 7th centuries seems too marked to be accidental.[25] For the 6th century, such imports can also be found on the Isle of Wight, notably at Chessell Down. Not surprisingly, it has been proposed that the Kentish kingdom enjoyed the equivalent of 'favoured nation' status in the eyes of Merovingian rulers, effectively being granted a monopoly on international trade with the Frankish kingdoms up until the early 7th century.[26]

During the 7th century there seem to be creations of new riverine and estuarine trading centres around the coast of England, with at least one port for each major kingdom to provide their rulers with access to international trade. Ipswich (Suffolk) was developed as such a trading place for the East Anglian kings, York (*Eoforwic*) for the Deirans, London (*Lundenwic*) for the East Saxons and subsequently the Mercians, with finally Southampton (*Hamwic*) created by the West Saxons, perhaps by Ine *c*. A.D. 700 as a replacement for the role previously played by the Isle of Wight.[27] Their main counterparts in the 7th to 9th centuries were Quentovic on the Canche and Dorestad in the Rhine delta, but doubtless other Frankish and Frisian centres were involved.[28]

The dating of the Anglo-Saxon finds from sites in northern France and also at Herpes (near Cognac in south-western France) is derived from the decorated metalwork and is remarkably consistent. It can be argued that we should ignore earlier or even contemporary continental Saxon or Scandinavian metalwork in these cemeteries, as this might reflect direct settlement in Gaul by migrants from northern Germany or southern Scandinavia. Such Germanic migrants could have bypassed Britain and the fact that similar metal fittings appear in Anglo-Saxon graves need not be significant.[29] Examples would be the applied saucer or disc brooches of Böhme's Muids type found at Muids (Eure) and Sigy-en-Bray (Seine-Maritime),[30] or the

---

[23] Wood, op. cit. in note 21, 341–2.

[24] I. Wood, *The Merovingian North Sea* (Alingsås, 1983); Wood, op. cit. in note 21; Wood, op. cit. in note 22.

[25] J. Huggett, 'Imported grave-goods and the early Anglo-Saxon economy', *Medieval Archaeol.*, 32 (1988), 63–96.

[26] E.g. S. C. Hawkes, 'Anglo-Saxon Kent c. 425–725', 64–78 in P. E. Leach (ed.), *Archaeology in Kent to AD 1500* (CBA Res. Rep., 48, London, 1982).

[27] R. Hodges, *Dark Age Economics: the Origins of Towns and Trade AD 600–1000* (London, 1982); Welch, op. cit. in note 18.

[28] S. Lebecq, 'Franken und Friesen', 338–40 in A. Wieczorek, P. Périn, K. von Welck and W. Menghin (eds.), *Die Franken Wegbereiter Europas* (Mannheim, 1996), Abb. 278.

[29] Welch, op. cit. in note 18, 263.

[30] H. W. Böhme, *Germanische Grabfunde des 4. bis 5. Jahrhunderts zwischen unterer Elbe und Loire* (Munich, 1974), Karte 7.

Scandinavian gold bracteates from Hérouvillette (Calvados) graves 11 and 39.[31] If, instead, we limit consideration to object types which seem to be manufactured in southern Britain, then the dating seems to belong to a tightly-defined period, approximately from the end of the 5th century to the middle of the 6th century.[32]

Brooches of specifically Anglo-Saxon manufacture take the form of great square-headed brooches, Kentish small square-headed brooches, Kentish jewelled disc brooches and jewelled equal-arm brooches, small bow brooches of 'Bifrons' type, button brooches, applied saucer brooches and disc brooches. In addition, there is some reason to believe that quoit brooches and some belt-fittings decorated in the Insular Quoit Brooch Style may have crossed the Channel at much the same time as these Anglo-Saxon brooches.[33] Such dress-fittings might represent gifts to local women either by men who were crossing the Channel on a regular basis or by immigrants from southern England who chose to settle in France. It is thus not surprising that skeletal studies at Frénouville suggest that the wearers of Anglo-Saxon brooches were local people and not migrants of either Saxon or Frankish origin.[34] Although such brooches are female dress-fittings, the presence of a sword pommel with an attached ring of Kentish type at Grenay (Pas-de-Calais) provides potential evidence for an adult male presence of some status.[35] It suggests the possibility of settlement of men whose social standing permitted them to own a prestige weapon or, at the very least, implies gift exchange across the Channel involving such individuals.

Handmade pottery vessels from at least seven sites in north-eastern France and two others in Calvados (western Normandy) provide a rather stronger argument for believing that people travelled to and settled in these regions, as opposed to seeing these items as trinkets acquired by trade. Not that trade in handmade pottery is out of the question, as a recent paper considering Anglo-Saxon pottery containing a distinctive (granodiorite) filler in eastern England makes clear.[36] On the other hand, the dominance through the Early Medieval period of wheel-thrown, well-fired pottery produced using Roman commercial technology in northern Gaul is well documented in both cemetery and settlement archaeology. By contrast, wheel-thrown pottery completely disappears from the archaeology of eastern Britain with the end of the Roman period and, with the exception of one piece of Argonne ware from Chessell Down,[37] the first imports of Merovingian pottery in Kentish contexts occur no later than the late 6th to early 7th centuries.[38] Of course, handmade pottery belonging to northern German ceramic traditions is not unique to Anglo-Saxon England. It may be that the few items involved could have been produced by migrants from Belgium, the Netherlands or north-western Germany arriving in northern France between the 5th

---

[31] J. Decaens, 'Un nouveau cimetière du haut moyen-âge en Normandie, Hérouvillette (Calvados)', *Archéol. Mediévale*, 1 (1971), 1–125, figs. 11, 28.
[32] Welch, op. cit. in note 18, 263–7.
[33] Welch, op. cit. in note 18, 265.
[34] Pilet *et al.* 1994, op. cit. in note 14, 58–9.
[35] V. I. Evison, 'A sword pommel with ring-knob at Grenay, Pas-de-Calais', *Septentrion*, 9 (1979), 37–9.
[36] D. Williams and A. Vince, 'The characterization and interpretation of early to middle Saxon granite tempered pottery in England', *Medieval Archaeol.*, 41 (1997), 214–20.
[37] Evison, op. cit. in note 5, 26, fig. 98; J. N. L. Myres, *Anglo-Saxon Pottery and the Settlement of England* (Oxford, 1969), 92.
[38] Evison, op. cit. in note 2.

and 6th centuries. Nevertheless, its presence strongly suggests local manufacture by settlers in their new homes, whether those settlers came from across the Channel or from further east along the North Sea coastlands.

Until this pottery is subjected to scientific analysis, we can do little more than note general similarities to handmade pottery in other regions. Fabric analysis of pottery can draw on well-established techniques for identifying both clay sources and the filler materials used to strengthen the potting clay. It will be possible to devise a programme of sampling all the handmade pottery in museum collections for thin-section analysis using the facilities at the UCL Institute's laboratories in order to establish whether they were the products of the immediate region in which they were deposited. Surveys of local clay sources in each region in collaboration with geologists and pottery find specialists for each region should permit us to establish whether these handmade pots are likely to be local products. If any of these pots appears not to be a local product, then we need to consider those alternative regions which might provide a suitable source for their raw materials. The key problem here is that the geology of both northern France and southern England are very closely related, the Channel cutting across the chalklands and chalk-ringed basins which characterize both regions. Occasionally we get a distinctive geological feature which enables us to pinpoint the origin of some pottery. This occurred in the case of vessels demonstrably made in Armorica (including the Cherbourg peninsula) during the pre-Roman Iron Age, which were excavated at Hengistbury Head (Dorset).[39] All too often, however, we can expect to face a situation in which we cannot be certain whether particular vessels were produced in southern England or northern France. While we need not be too negative at the outset of the project, we should be realistic about these methodological problems, but there may be technical solutions and, until we attempt such analysis, we cannot state that it has no chance of success.

The other aspect which will demand systematic study under expert supervision is a thorough re-examination of the skeletal evidence, wherever it remains available for further study. This should take in as many of the possible burial sites which have produced Anglo-Saxon material in France and Frankish material in England. Those graves which contain 'foreign' dress-fittings may well belong to the 'local' population, acquiring these items as gifts, possibly through marriage. Nevertheless, there is a good chance that other individuals buried in the same cemetery might represent an immigrant element. Consistency of approach is the key issue here and it will be crucial that all the researchers work to a common methodology. New approaches are emerging continually in the study of ancient human populations from skeletal material. For example, the potential of foot bones to reveal what appear to be genetically-based differences has been argued for the Early Anglo-Saxon cemetery at Lechlade (Gloucestershire) and seems to be applicable to other sites in southern Britain for both prehistoric and protohistoric remains, as well as those of historical periods.[40] While it may prove to be the case that we cannot convincingly detect immigrants from the

[39] B. Cunliffe, *Hengistbury Head, Dorset. Vol. I: the Prehistoric and Roman Settlement 3500 BC–AD 500* (Oxford, 1987), 310–16, ills. 219 and 223.
[40] P. Jackson, 'Footloose in archaeology', *Current Archaeol.*, 144 (1995), 466–70. In a blind test, Phyllis Jackson successfully differentiated Iron-age, Romano-British and Anglo-Saxon skeletal material from Cambridgeshire sites (C. Duhig, pers. comm.).

skeletal evidence, unless we are prepared to study this material on a multiple-site, large-sample basis, we cannot rule out the possibility that such evidence exists.

An oddity of the present distribution of Anglo-Saxon material in Merovingian Frankish cemeteries is the presence of so many sites in the Pas-de-Calais and Picardy regions between Boulogne and the valley of the Somme, matched by another concentration around Caen and the Cherbourg peninsula and lastly the isolated row-grave cemetery of Herpes in the Saintonge. The wine trade between the Saintonge region and England in the Angevin period, represented by finds of classic Saintonge painted jugs in London, Southampton and other English ports, suggests the possibility of a bulk trade in wine and related products as an explanation for the presence of 6th-century Kentish metalwork at Herpes. Until such time as further Merovingian period row-grave cemeteries are excavated in the Saintonge to modern standards and further discoveries made in them of Anglo-Saxon artefacts as parts of assemblages, we cannot take such a tentative suggestion much further.

Indeed in the case of Herpes, doubts have been expressed about the provenance of many of the finds attributed in museum inventories to that site.[41] This is because the Delamain collection was sold through auction houses and dispersed to many museums and collections, including the British Museum, the Metropolitan Museum in New York and also to Berlin. The loss of the Herpes material from Berlin during the Second World War does not help, of course. Nevertheless, careful analysis of the published record does suggest that some of the more extreme criticisms of the Herpes material can be answered,[42] although it is equally clear that not every single item attributed to Herpes necessarily originated from Delamain's excavations there.[43]

If the wine trade is a possible explanation for the Kentish finds at Herpes, are trading relations the explanation also for their presence in western Normandy and in north-eastern France? The fact that these two regions are exactly opposite the Jutish kingdoms of Hampshire and Wight in the West and East Kent in the East is suggestive. Modern ferries cross the waters between Portsmouth and Oustrehem near Caen and again between Dover, Folkestone and Calais (together with the Channel Tunnel). We also have a modern ferry service between Newhaven and Dieppe, while Rouen was an important medieval port on the Seine. The question therefore arises, why do we not find 6th-century Anglo-Saxon artefacts in Merovingian-period sites in Upper Normandy (the modern départements of Eure and Seine-Maritime)? Until recently there had been relatively little work on Merovingian burial sites in the region between the Seine and the Somme. The only approach available to the present author in the 1980s was to look through the finds in the museum at Rouen from the published excavations by the Abbé Cochet at Envermeu and Londiniéres. A couple of disc brooches which

---

[41] E.g. E. James, *The Merovingian Archaeology of South-West Gaul* (BAR Int. Ser., 25, Oxford, 1977); H. Ament, 'Franken und Romanen im Merowingerreich als archäologisches Forschungproblem', *Bonner Jahrb.*, 178 (1978), 377–94.

[42] Haith, op. cit. in note 12.

[43] B. Ager, 'Recent re-discoveries in the continental early medieval collections of the British Museum', 139–44 in G. De Boe and F. Verhaege (eds.), *Method and Theory in Historical Archaeology, Vol. 10* (Zellik, 1997). I am grateful to Mrs Cathy Haith (British Museum) for her observations on this tantalizing body of material, which could benefit from further research into the documentary sources held in the relevant museums.

might be Anglo-Saxon were illustrated by the author,[44] but these hardly provide a convincing basis for arguing that the Anglo-Saxon contacts were evenly distributed along the coastline in the 6th century between Armorica (Bretagne) and the Pas-de-Calais region.

A number of rescue excavations of early medieval cemeteries in the eastern part of Seine-Maritime département at Haudricourt, Villy-le-Bas, Fallencourt, Criel-sur-Mer and Longroy between 1987 and 1992 have provided a fresh sample of data (Fig. 1).[45] The only distinctively Anglo-Saxon material recovered, however, was a pair of button brooches from Criel-sur-Mer. Allowing for the fact that ancient grave robbing is a marked feature of these cemeteries, this new sample suggests that the relative frequency with which Anglo-Saxon finds are revealed in such sites in western (Lower) Normandy or between Boulogne-sur-Mer and the Somme valley will not be repeated in the territory between the two, i.e. eastern (Upper) Normandy. The fact that three seasons of complete excavation of the Longroy cemetery did not produce a single Anglo-Saxon artefact is valuable negative evidence, which must be taken seriously. It suggests that the established distribution patterns represent a genuine picture which we must investigate further.

The recent excavations at Haudricourt have revealed another feature which links its community to those in southern England and in the Netherlands and Germany east of the Rhine. The two small square post-based structures on the southern edge of the excavated area are probably not parts of domestic buildings belonging to an associated settlement.[46] Instead, they can be paralleled at sites such as Apple Down, Compton (West Sussex) and Alton (Hampshire) by five-post structures in which the outer post-holes can be linked by shallow trenches.[47] These have been interpreted as timber funerary structures associated with cremation burial practices.[48] Similar structures are known, for example, from the later Roman Iron-age site at Looveen (Drenthe, Netherlands) and from 7th- to 8th-century contexts at Oldendorf (Niedersachsen, Germany).[49] Although the excavators of Haudricourt detected no trace of cremations in association with the two structures, this was also the case for the majority of those excavated at Apple Down. Cremation in a late Roman or Merovingian-period context in northern France seems to imply a burial practice introduced by immigrants, in this case probably Germanic and possibly Anglo-Saxon immigrants.

Finally, mention must be made of the rescue excavation in advance of motorway construction of the early medieval cemetery at La Calotterie above the valley of the Canche.[50] This belongs firmly in the north-east block of sites and some of the finds

---

[44] Welch, op. cit. in note 18, 265, pl. 1.3.

[45] E. Mantel and M.-L. Merleau, 'Aperçu des connaisances archéologiques récentes sur les cimetières en Seine-Maritime', 233–50 in *La Datation des Structures et des Objets du Haut Moyen Age, Méthods et Résultats: Actes des XVème Journées Internationales d'Archéologie Mérovingienne* (Rouen, 1988).

[46] Mantel and Merleau, op. cit. in note 45, fig. 2.

[47] A. Down and M. Welch, *Chichester Excavations 7: Apple Down and the Mardens* (Chichester, 1990); V. I. Evison, *An Anglo-Saxon Cemetery at Alton, Hampshire* (Gloucester, 1988).

[48] M. Welch, *The English Heritage Book of Anglo-Saxon England* (London, 1992), 66, fig. 47.

[49] W. A. van Es, 'Wijster: a native village beyond the imperial frontier, 150–425 A.D.', *Palaeohistoria*, 11 (1967); F. Laux, 'Der Reihengräberfriedhof in Oldendorf, Samtgemeinde Amelinghausen, Kr. Lüneburg, Niedersachsen', *Hammaburg*, N.F. 5 (1980), 91–147.

[50] G. Blancquaert and Y. Desfossés, 'La nécropole gauloise à incinération de la Calotterie "La Fontaine aux Linottes" (Pas-de-Calais)', *Revue Archéol. Picardie*, 1–2 (1998), 135–69.

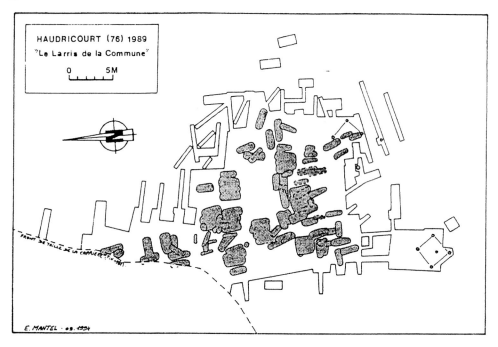

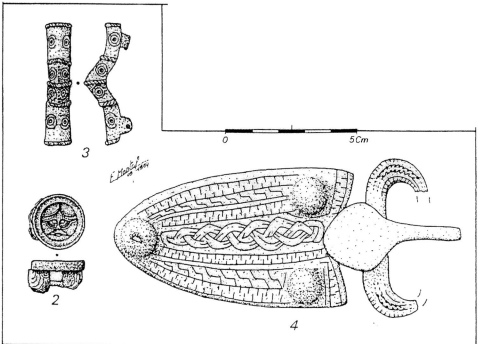

FIG. I

Plan of the 1989 rescue excavation of part of the Merovingian-period cemetery at Haudricourt
(Seine-Maritime) including two four-post structures and a button brooch (2) and two other objects excavated at
Criel-sur-Mer (Seine-Maritime) (after E. Mantel).

suggest Anglo-Saxon influence, if not actual presence. A high proportion of well-equipped weapon assemblages are a feature of this cemetery, which immediately differentiates it from the normal pattern of weapon burial in contemporary cemeteries within this region.[51] The post-excavation programme of finds conservation will take at least five years,[52] but it is clear already that London-based archaeologists can make a contribution to the analysis of this cemetery by the excavators and their academic archaeological advisors.

To sum up, the complete excavation of the cemetery at Longroy and the full publication of this and other cemeteries excavated by Etienne Mantel over the last dozen years in the Dép. Seine-Maritime, taken together with the analysis and eventual publication of the cemetery at La Calotterie (Pas-de-Calais), will provide a wealth of new data with which to assess the extent of Anglo-Saxon influence in northern France. This will be accompanied by new surveys to draw in both the new and old finds of Anglo-Saxon material in France. Isolated and currently unpublished finds of button brooches are recorded deep inland in Picardy,[53] for example, and these must be mapped and assessed. Fabric analysis and full recording of the handmade pottery and a detailed reassessment of the skeletal populations are further strands of a co-operative research programme. On the English side of the Channel, fresh surveys of continental material will be welcome and these can be related to the current post-excavation analysis of Kentish cemeteries at Buckland II, Dover, and St. Peter's Tip, Broadstairs, by the British Museum and of Updown, Eastry by the author (on behalf of the late Mrs Sonia Hawkes).

We will then have a firmer basis for developing models to explain the nature of the cross-Channel connections represented in the material culture from both settlements and cemeteries. Are we observing the policing of a trade monopoly relationship between the Frankish kingdoms and Kent? Was the South Saxon kingdom (modern Sussex between Eastbourne and the Hampshire border) really excluded from cross-Channel trade in the 6th and 7th centuries?[54] Can we even be sure that trade provided the key element here? Tourism as represented by modern ferry day-trips seems improbable, but fishing rights in the Channel cannot be omitted from our analysis. Immigration and emigration can be two sides of the same coin, but clearly we need to ignore modern state boundaries and accept that the Channel, like most motorways, links considerably more than it divides. The ability to examine the evidence from both coasts should prove illuminating here.

[51] P. Périn, pers. comm.
[52] D. Piton, pers. comm.
[53] D. Bayard, pers. comm.
[54] Welch, op. cit. in note 4, 259–60; Welch, op. cit. in note 18, 267–8.

Reflections on the Meanings of Monumental Barrows in Anglo-Saxon England[1]

By MARTIN CARVER

Barrows, or burial mounds, constitute some of the most prominent of Anglo-Saxon memorials. But the Anglo-Saxons did not build barrows always and everywhere, and nor were they the only barrow-builders of the early medieval period. The barrow is, therefore, an attribute of Anglo-Saxon culture, but does not define it. Early 'Anglo-Saxon culture', referring to the behaviour of people occupying southern and eastern Britain between the 5th and the 8th centuries, sometimes included the erection of burial mounds, just as it sometimes included the erection of churches and monasteries. Barrow-building is an activity which was undoubtedly important to the early medieval period, but it was undertaken unevenly in time and space. This leaves us with a problem: what did the barrow-builders intend? When and why did people become barrow-builders? What forces provoked these monuments?

A study of these questions became particularly pressing on the completion of the recent research campaign at the Anglo-Saxon cemetery of Sutton Hoo (Suffolk), where eleven burial mounds have now been excavated.[2] Mound 1, excavated in 1939, covered a ship which lay in a trench below ground-level[3] and is well known because, unlike the majority of burial mounds (in England as elsewhere), it had escaped the grave-robbers. Mound 2 had also contained a ship, but in this case it lay on the Anglo-Saxon ground surface, and a chamber-grave lay beneath it, in the manner of the ship burial enacted at Haithabu/Hedeby some 200 years later.[4] Mounds 3, 4, 5, 6, 7 and 18 had contained cremations, the majority of which had been wrapped in cloth and placed in a bronze bowl. Mound 14 contained a burial, probably of a woman, in a chamber-grave. Mound 17 covered the burial of a young man and his horse, this being the only barrow other than Mound 1 to have escaped successful robbing. Three other graves were modestly furnished and one at least had once been covered by a small mound. All three were probably children or adolescents. Around Mound 5 were sixteen unfurnished graves, mainly of young men, many of whom had been hanged or beheaded, and these are interpreted as executions. A similar group of 23 graves lay on

---

[1] A version of this paper was originally published as 'Uberlegungen zur Bedeutung angel-sächsischer Grabhügel', 259–68 in A. Wesse (ed.), *Studien zur Archäologie des Ostseeraums von der Eisenzeit zum Mittelalter: Festschrift fur Michael Müller-Wille* (Neumünster, 1998).

[2] M. O. H. Carver, 'The Anglo-Saxon cemetery at Sutton Hoo: an interim report', 343–71 in M. O. H. Carver (ed.), *The Age of Sutton Hoo* (Woodbridge, 1992); idem. (ed.), *Bulletins of the Sutton Hoo Research Committee, 1–8, 1983–93* (Woodbridge, 1993), vol. 8, 18–19; idem, *Sutton Hoo: Burial Ground of Kings?* (London, 1998).

[3] R. L. S. Bruce-Mitford, *The Sutton Hoo Ship-Burial* (London, 1975–83, 3 vols.).

[4] M. Müller-Wille, *Das Bootkammergrab von Haithabu* (Berichte über die Ausgrabung in Haithabu, 8, Neumünster, 1976).

the eastern edge of the cemetery. The radiocarbon dates of these execution burials, and of a wooden post attributed to a gallows, show that they began in the 8th century and continued into the 11th century.[5]

A first interpretation of the new discoveries has suggested that the Sutton Hoo cemetery was inaugurated in the late 6th to early 7th century as a separate burial ground for the pagan elite, and lasted barely one hundred years.[6] Mound 5 was probably the first mound to be built, and the rite of cremation found there was continued in Mounds 6, 7, 3 and 4, which formed a N.–S. alignment and were probably built in that order. The horse-burial (Mound 17) and the female chamber-grave (Mound 14) were added to the West and East of this main line of barrows. In a later phase, ships were included in the two monumental barrows: the ship above the chamber in Mound 2 and the chamber in the ship under Mound 1. One of the execution burials around Mound 5 may have been contemporary with the construction of the mound, but was more plausibly a later addition. Some of the burials in the eastern group may also have belonged to the same generation as the subjects of furnished burial in the barrow cemetery, since they have produced radiocarbon dates in the 7th century. But most of the execution burials can be assigned by radiocarbon dating to the 8th to 11th century and are seen as the response of the Christian authorities to deviation from the new order.[7] The Sutton Hoo barrows are interpreted as the monuments of 'status-seeking parvenus', the creation of new leaders and their heirs attempting to achieve kingship without Christianity, enacting an extravagant series of Scandinavian-style burials in order to oppose the imperialism of the Christian Franks, proclaiming the rhetoric of independence and individual enterprise in a 'theatre of death'.[8]

Important reflections on the thinking behind the use of burial mounds have been offered by Shephard for Anglo-Saxon England[9] and by Bradley for the broader theatre of prehistoric Britain.[10] These and later studies have emphasized that the location and distribution and date of appearance of the monuments have as much to say about their message as the grave furnishings. In Britain, burial mounds were constructed extensively during the Bronze Age, spasmodically and marginally in the Iron Age (mainly in eastern Yorkshire) and very rarely in the Roman period (the Bartlow Hills (Essex) being the best known example). The first post-Roman mounds, appearing from the 5th century, are small and appear as clusters of ring-ditches or as groups of small mounds. They are found in Pictland and Wales as well as Anglo-Saxon England, or

---

[5] Carver 1998, op. cit. in note 2.

[6] Ibid. In April 2000, a group of 6th-century burials, some surrounded by ditches which may indicate mounds, was excavated in advance of the building of the new Sutton Hoo Visitor Centre some 500 m to the North of Mound 1. These burials most probably belong to middle-ranking predecessors of the Sutton Hoo community.

[7] Carver 1998, op. cit. in note 2, 143.

[8] M. O. H. Carver, 'Sutton Hoo in context', *Settimane di Studio del Centro Italiano di Studi sull'Alto Medioevo*, 32 (1986), 77–117, at 108; Carver 1992, op. cit. in note 2, 365.

[9] J. Shephard, *Anglo-Saxon Barrows of the Later 6th and 7th Centuries AD* (unpublished PhD thesis, University of Cambridge, 1979); see J. Shephard, 'The social identity of the individual in isolated barrows and barrow cemeteries in Anglo-Saxon England', 47–80 in B. Burnham and J. Kingsbury (eds.), *Space, Hierarchy and Society* (BAR Int. Ser., 59, Oxford, 1979) for a summary.

[10] Carver, op. cit. in note 8; see R. Bradley, *Altering the Earth* (Edinburgh, 1994) for his most recent analysis and discussion of the meaning of prehistoric monuments.

the area of south-eastern Britain. Large 'monumental' mounds, which Shephard calls 'isolated barrows', appear in Anglo-Saxon England in the early 7th century. Shephard comments: 'The distribution of the barrow cemeteries [in Anglo-Saxon areas] is confined to the south-east of England, especially Kent and Sussex', while the isolated barrows 'are virtually absent from the areas of the south-east in which the barrow cemeteries are found'.[11] In the areas of Viking occupation, the barrow returns briefly in the 9th century, but not in numbers comparable to those in Scandinavia.[12] The distributions of the monuments as we deduce them today are not, of course, complete; a scraped-up earthen mound can be an impressive memorial but disappears completely under quarrying or the plough. Nevertheless, England's is a relatively well-explored archaeology, and future alterations to Shephard's map are likely to be in emphasis rather than substance. We can therefore assume that the pattern we have is worth studying: the Anglo-Saxon barrow cemeteries with their large numbers of small mounds begin in the 6th century and are clustered in the South-East. Large isolated 'monumental' barrows begin in the early 7th century and are sparsely distributed over the English settlement area, with local concentrations in Wessex and the Peak District. Sutton Hoo represents a hybrid, but the monumentality of the mounds is probably more significant than the fact that they are grouped in a cemetery.

The distribution of monumental burial mounds in central, northern and eastern Europe is also uneven.[13] There are notable clusters along the fjords of western Norway, on the Oslo fjord, in the Swedish Mälaren area and along the Rhine. In the Slavic areas to the East, the burial mounds appear to be smaller, more numerous, more widely distributed and later in date than in the West; but there are monumental groups too, for example in the region of Kiev.[14] The dating of all these monuments has yet to be systematically achieved, and where the dates differ, the context and thus the meaning of the burials will differ too. Impressionistically, it can be observed that the use of early medieval barrows in the North Sea area appears to follow a curious trajectory. They appear, for example, in north Frankia and south-western Norway in the 5th century, England in the early 7th century and in Swedish Uppland in the later 7th century.[15]

Searching for meaning in the Anglo-Saxon material, we should first review some common assumptions. It is accepted that the Anglo-Saxons knew what prehistoric burial mounds were, and often re-used them to bury their own dead. Their knowledge may have extended to the way prehistoric barrows were used, socially and politically, in which case this too may have been imitated to suit the context of 7th-century

---

[11] Shephard, op. cit. in note 9, summarized on a map in Carver, op. cit. in note 8, fig. 5. For Pictish barrow groups, see S. Foster, 'The state of Pictland in the seventh century', 217–34 in M. O. H. Carver (ed.), *The Age of Sutton Hoo* (Woodbridge, 1992); idem., *Picts, Gaels and Scots* (Edinburgh, 1996), 75.

[12] J. D. Richards, *Viking Age England* (London, 1991).

[13] M. Müller-Wille, 'Monumentale Grabhügel der Völkerwanderungszeit in Mittel- und Nordeuropa: Bestand und Deutung', 1–20 in W. Paravicini (ed.), *Mare Balticum: Beiträge zur Geschichte des Ostseeraums in Mittelalter und Neuzeit: Festschrift zum 65. Geburtstag von Erich Hoffmann* (Kieler Historische Stud., 36, Sigmaringen, 1992), Abb. 6, 7, 9.

[14] M. Lutovsky, 'Between Sutton Hoo and Chernaya Mogila: barrows in eastern and western early medieval Europe', *Antiquity*, 70 (1996), 671–6.

[15] M. O. H. Carver, 'Ideology and allegiance in East Anglia', 173–82 in R. Farrell and C. Neuman de Vegvar (eds.), *Sutton Hoo: Fifty Years After* (Oxford, Ohio, 1992), at p. 179.

England. This burial rite, and all others, may have reflected a b
although it will also have had a conscious message for the livir
location and maintenance of power. The adoption of barrow buria'
a change in the relations of power, and of social organization, refl
newly-formed upper class to promote its rank. Another assur
making of specific memorials by specific ethnic groups. Althoug!.
hardly supports the idea of an immigrant 6th- or 7th-century 'mouna ᵖ..
continental Europe burials are often considered to be a means of promoting identity,
and ethnic identity in particular. We have long been encouraged to accept ethnic
migration as a cause of change, and must examine this premise. We have long been
encouraged too, to accredit powerful individuals with both building mounds and being
commemorated by them; the historical records, sparse though they be, have
accustomed us to attribute events and change to successful warriors, those major
players on the Dark-age stage who were the movers and shakers of their day.

As is concluded below, these different explanations need not, in fact, be considered
as exclusive of each other; but it might be as well to attempt a brief evaluation of each
in turn, grouping them as four 'models' entitled, for the sake of brevity and
convenience, the 'dynastic', the 'ethnic', the 'social' and the 'ideological' explanations.
The purpose here is not to offer a general explanation for all barrows, but to review
some of the possibilities in the hope of attributing a meaning to those excavated at
Sutton Hoo.

'DYNASTIC' EXPLANATIONS

Medieval history, as reported in documents and seen in the monumental legacy
of castles and abbeys, leaves us with an abiding impression of the hunger for power of
individual families, a hunger which those families made every effort to institutionalize.
For some eminent historians, such individual power-broking determined much of the
development of the Anglo-Saxon period.[16] No one now suggests that this represents
the whole story of society, and nothing could be more unfashionable than to credit
historical events, change or invention to an individual; but it would be equally foolish
to decide that the individual was never the cause of anything. Nor is it really sufficient
here to say that the actions of individuals were only ephemeral within a broader *longue
durée*. If particular families are to be credited with the monumental mounds, their
creations resulted in a permanent change to the vocabulary of the landscape. In other
words, they created part of the *longue durée* themselves, much as their deeds did when
fossilized in heroic literature.

The temptation to accredit the mounds to heroes is even more understandable
given the small number of individuals involved: the Ynglingas are named for the
Norwegian mounds and those of Uppland[17] and the Wuffingas (from Uppland) for
East Anglia.[18] The new monumental mounds constructed at Lejre (Denmark) at the
beginning of the 6th century have been seen as the result of a shift of dynastic power to

[16] E.g. F. M. Stenton, *Anglo-Saxon England* (Oxford, 1971).
[17] Müller-Wille, op. cit in note 13.
[18] Bruce-Mitford, op. cit. in note 3, 1975, 488–577.

at place.[19] It would only take a little imagination to extrapolate these points of contact into a network of aristocratic families responsible for producing all the monumental mounds from the 4th to the 8th century, and indeed into the Viking period, in lands which fell in turn under the control of members of their dynasty.

Such a network of mound-building, kingdom-forming aristocrats need not, therefore, be complete fantasy. However, whether it could be said to offer a sufficient explanation for monumental mounds is more a matter for faith than science. Archaeological evidence for the identity of these or any other individuals is generally unspecific and can rarely be safely attributed to graves or rituals. The Anglo-Saxon genealogies, in which historical figures claim descent from Woden or Caesar, demonstrate a mode of thinking and self-representation that would surely be reflected in other media too. This must apply particularly to the monumental burial mound, which has a reasonable claim to be the principal panegyric of a non-literate age. If burial mounds are official poems, they have all offical poetry's faults: exaggeration, allusion, delusion. When burial mounds were used by individual families, they meant just what those families wished them to mean, neither more nor less. Such a code may be very difficult to crack.

TERRITORY AND ETHNICITY

The problems of using burials to indicate identity are still more severe when the identity is that of a whole people. Here too, we cannot disregard the fact, evident and credible in documentary sources, that groups of people were given names and were said to move in large numbers during a period often termed the 'Migration Period'. But in modern prehistoric studies, explanations of change due to popular movement have been questioned, and the dearly held idea that finds, particularly grave-goods, are indications of ethnicity is, in Britain, extremely unfashionable and often challenged.[20] The problem for archaeological scholarship of the Early Middle Ages is that the equation between cemeteries and ethnic groups is widely accepted on the Continent and used as the basis for writing historical geography. The distribution maps of brooches and burial practices which provide the staple data-set of central and eastern Europe are, it is fair to say, largely interpreted as due to the migrations and settlement of social entities.[21] Other explanations, which adapt current non-diffusionary models from prehistory, oblige us to believe that a whole people suddenly decided to adopt an exotic burial rite. The reduction of this argument to absurdity

[19] L. Hedeager, 'Kingdoms, ethnicity and material culture: Denmark in a European perspective', 279–300 in M. O. H. Carver (ed.), *The Age of Sutton Hoo* (Woodbridge, 1992), 294.
[20] E.g. V. G. Childe, 'Changing methods and aims in prehistory. Presidential address for 1935', *Proc. Prehistoric Soc.*, 1 (1935), 1–15, at 4; C. Renfrew and P. Bahn, *Archaeology: Theories, Methods and Practice* (London, 1991), 371; D. Harris, 'Pathways to world prehistory. Presidential address for 1994', *Proc. Prehistoric Soc.*, 60 (1994), 1–13, at 10.
[21] See, for example, V. V. Syedov, *Vostochnye Slavyanye v VI–XIII vv* (Moscow, 1982).

requires us to accept that 5th-century Britons at a given moment assumed an 'Anglo-Saxon' persona en masse, without however offering any satisfactory explanation as to why they did so.[22]

It would clearly be very contrived to dismiss all records of early medieval migration as baseless propaganda. The Roman *hospitalitas* system which caused large numbers of Germanic mercenaries, with or without families, to be moved from part of the late Empire or its periphery to another, is unlikely to be complete fiction.[23] It would certainly have resulted in a new settlement area for people who had every chance of remembering where they came from. That such popular movements continued for the next few hundred years in Europe, in numbers large and small, is not incredible. The problem comes in associating these movements with territorial claims, and using material culture to do it – a problem which began in the Migration Period and continues to this day, as Europeans and the United Nations have been only too painfully aware.

Among the attributes of early medieval cemeteries, the burial mound is among the least specific, and unlike brooches or weapons, commands few claims to be seen as the property of a particular people. They are found all over the Germanic areas, but also in areas designated as 'Slavic'[24] or 'Celtic'.[25] The burial mound was therefore an option to be adopted, and it could be adopted in particular places and at particular times, without any ethnic imperative. The mounds have no easy equation with territories or ethnic zones, however designated. The arrival of the burial mound is therefore far more likely to signal social or political change than a demographic movement.

SOCIAL EXPLANATIONS

Is the prime mover for the construction of monumental mounds a change which occurred within society? The argument here depends on the idea that, at a given stage in its formation, a community may become more hierarchical, that is, increase the rank and resources of the few at the expense of the many. It has then to be argued that this increased social stratification is reflected in burial practice, for example by the increased value and reduced distribution of grave-goods. Burial mounds, in this reading, are signs of increased status for some individuals, presumably at the expense of others. From the changes in the distribution of grave-goods, and the adoption of large burial mounds, it has been suggested that Anglo-Saxon society in the 6th to 7th century experienced just such a change, the rise of an aristocratic class presaging the creation of kings.[26]

---

[22] For example S. Lucy, 'Early Medieval burials in East Yorkshire: reconsidering the evidence', 11–18 in H. Geake and J. Kenny (eds), *Early Deira: Archaeological Studies of the East Riding in the Fourth to Ninth Centuries AD* (Oxford, 2000), 16.
[23] E. A. Thompson, *Romans and Barbarians: the Decline of the Western Empire* (Wisconsin, 1982).
[24] Syedov, op. cit. in note 21.
[25] Foster, op. cit. in note 11.
[26] C. J. Arnold, 'Wealth and social structure: matter of life and death', 81–142 in P. A. Rahtz, T. M. Dickinson and L. Watts (eds.), *Anglo-Saxon Cemeteries 1979* (BAR Brit. Ser., 82, Oxford, 1980).

An objection to this argument is that it does not always take account of the investments, other than burial, available to a community. Social stratification may be present but expressed in other forms of investment, for example in the building of churches, towns or palaces.[27] A univalent relationship between society and burial would imply that when burial mounds and grave-goods were discontinued in 8th century England, the community must have returned to some egalitarian mode of life. In fact, burial need not be chosen to represent society at all. Hedeager shows that the presence of secure kingship in 7th-century Jutland was heralded not by burial mounds, but by settlement form, place-names, writing and a new symbolic language.[28] In early Anglo-Saxon England, settlements, as well as cemeteries, became more 'ranked' in the late 6th to early 7th century, so it remains possible that Anglo-Saxon society did actually experience a major social change around A.D. 600.[29] The variation of investment in grave-goods which is then seen does not have to reflect the real variation in available wealth, otherwise the hierarchy would indeed appear extreme, the haves having everything and the have-nots nothing. The use of grave-goods in 6th- to 8th-century England may have reflected not the wealth, but the taxation status of the individual concerned. Use of grave-goods implies that the burial party was free of tax obligations and was free to demonstrate the status of the commemorated person; absence of grave-goods in the same period mean that a duty was payable. This explains the coincidence between the cessation of furnished burial of lesser rank and the onset of kingship. A 'king' can be defined as a leader who can tax; the new subjects signal the transference of their allegiance from their 'folk' to the king by paying tax rather than burying grave-goods.[30]

If social change was responsible for barrow-building, and if such change resulted in the claiming of territory, it is still necessary to ask what caused the social change in the first place. Some blame the climate, with stratification resulting from competition for reduced resources.[31] But an increase in social stratification has also been seen as resulting from an *increase* in resources through diplomatic priming, the wooing of the periphery by the core.[32] Whether any of these factors was, on its own, an imperative for change, rather than an incidental excuse to justify political action, is less certain.

The advent of burial mounds also altered the geography of the land, both for the contemporaries and those who came after. For contemporaries, they may have served to indicate inherited local territory.[33] There have also been a number of attempts to show that the position of the monumental mounds imply hinterlands which their occupants had dominated.[34] Arnold used 'central place theory' to try to discover the territories to which the monumental mounds of England might refer, although without

[27] Carver, op. cit. in note 8, 98; M. O. H. Carver, *Arguments in Stone* (Oxford, 1993), 61.
[28] Hedeager, op. cit. in note 19, 287.
[29] M. O. H. Carver, 'Kingship and material culture in early Anglo-Saxon East Anglia', 141–58 in S. Bassett (ed.), *The Origins of Anglo-Saxon Kingdoms* (Leicester, 1989).
[30] Carver, op. cit. in note 8, 96; Carver, op. cit. in note 29; Carver, op. cit. in note 15.
[31] C. J. Arnold, 'Stress as a stimulus for socio-economic change: Anglo-Saxon England in the seventh century', 124–31 in C. Renfrew and S. Shennan (eds.), *Ranking, Resource and Exchange* (Cambridge, 1982).
[32] B. Myhre, 'Chieftains' graves and chiefdom territories in South Norway in the Migration Period', *Stud. zur Sachsenforschung*, 6 (1987), 169–97.
[33] Shephard, op. cit. in note 9; Carver, op. cit. in note 8, 90.
[34] Summarized in Müller-Wille, op. cit. in note 13, 13.

convincing equations with known territories such as those of the Heptarchy.[35]
Cautions, similar to those necessary when determining an increase in social stratification, can be expressed about using the mounds in this way, since they might not have
been in any sense either the principal investment of a community, or central to its
territory. In south-western Norway, however, Myhre's analysis achieved a satisfying
equivalence between monuments and territories, using a range of different elements,
each of which could indicate 'centralization' of power: burials, hill-forts and 'ship-
sheds'. The territories deduced for 5th- to 6th-century Norway were given additional
credibility from their coincidence with later documented land divisions.[36]

For Anglo-Saxon England many of the monumental mounds are not central to
any kingdoms that are documented. Naturally, it is possible that they represent
different, earlier, territorial claims which did not endure; or that other, larger, burial
mounds more central to the kingdoms or sub-kingdoms of the Heptarchy await
discovery. More probably, the relationship between monumental burial grounds and
territory was not one of centrality. If Sutton Hoo represents the 'royal' burial ground
of East Anglia, it lies at the edge of it (and also at the edge of the neighbouring kingdom
to the South). The reason for this may simply be that the land-based geography that
we now use was of less significance to the Anglo-Saxons than a sea-based geography.[37]
In this case, the Sutton Hoo mounds would lie right at the front gate of East Anglia,
albeit on a minor river constituting one of the kingdom's trickier entrances. However,
the siting of the major groups becomes still more interesting when ideological
explanations are pursued (see below). In this case the locations of monumental mounds
not only indicate forgotten highways, but the frontiers where highways cross from
regions of one political colour to another. Sutton Hoo then becomes the gateway of
the first landfall from Essex or from Kent, the Christian kingdom. A similar argument
could be advanced for the barrows of the Peak District which, far from belonging to
the local *Pēcsǣte*, may be the monuments of the pagan kings of Mercia, constructed in
confrontation to a newly Christian Northumbria.

IDEOLOGICAL EXPLANATIONS

It was always to be hoped that the great achievements of processual archaeology
inaugurated in the 1960s would provide explanations for social change which would
apply to and satisfy any scientific study of the past. However, through the experiences
of the last century, and those of contemporaries of different cultures, we have become
more conscious of the tendency of people to delude themselves, each other and their
successors in human communication of every kind. Not only the written documents,
but also the archaeological monuments, are distorted by extravagant claims and
wishful thinking which blurs the reality or nudges it beyond our reach. The
monumental burial mound must have been a favoured medium for such deception.
Here is a major investment which celebrates an individual and provides a permanent

[35] Arnold, op. cit. in note 32, fig. 1; C. J. Arnold, *An Archaeology of the Early Anglo-Saxon Kingdoms* (London,
1988), 66–7.
[36] Myhre, op. cit. in note 32.
[37] M. O. H. Carver, 'Pre-Viking traffic in the North Sea', 117–25 in S. McGrail (ed.), *Maritime Celts,
Frisians and Saxons* (CBA Res. Rep., 71, London, 1990).

message for the living. Such a monument could hardly provide a more attractive opportunity for signalling what one wishes were true. This is the province of ideology, and its practical expression, politics.

In the ideological type of explanation, mound-burial is seen as being adopted for political reasons and having a political meaning. It has to be assumed that the meaning was known to contemporaries, at whom it was largely directed. There may or may not have been a devotional meaning too, in our sense of the religious; but that is not really under discussion here. The ritual and the belief system, it is suggested, are products of the ideology, and not the other way round. The meaning of the burial mound need not have been the same each time, but will have depended on the context in which it was erected.[38]

In the case of the Anglo-Saxon mounds, I have suggested that they were erected in response to the activities of the Christian Merovingian Empire; that is, the monumental mounds were employed in late 6th- to early 7th-century England as symbols of pagan autonomy in confrontation, even defiance, of the predatory attentions of Christianity.[39] The first signs of such confrontation were in Kent, where the ideological 'front-line' lay in the 6th century, and there the barrow-building reaction was small-scale but widespread. Later, in the 7th century, mounds were used in the rest of England, in more majestic isolation, as the flagships of the unconverted. At the same time, the political stand of non-Christian England was reinforced by a brief flirtation with ship burial.[40] At Sutton Hoo, in particular, the use of cremation, burial mounds, ships and the subjection of imperial by heroic ideas in grave-goods are seen as deliberate allusions to the enterprise politics of Scandinavia, as opposed to the imperial programme of Latin Europe.[41]

Van de Noort has extended this idea to western Europe as a whole;[42] but it is more difficult to argue a specifically Christian confrontation from the date and distribution of the Scandinavian[43] and Slavic barrows.[44] Christianity was hardly a threat to the builders of Vendel, although Merovingian elements have been detected there.[45] The context of the barrows of the Svear and the Oslo fjord should be different, and the imperatives and explanations should be different too. The barrows of the Slavic areas provide a different context again; but all these should be discoverable. Although no Christians may have been involved, it is reasonable to assume that barrow-builders were suffering some political stress, even if we cannot identify what it was. Discussing the monumental Högom mounds, built in Medelpad on the central Baltic coast of Sweden in A.D. 450-550, Ramqvist comments that the time of their

[38] Carver, op. cit. in note 8, 101; for 'contextuality' see I. Hodder, *Theory and Practice in Archaeology* (London, 1992) for a convenient summary.
[39] Carver 1986, op. cit. in note 8, 99; 1989, op. cit. in note 29, 158; 1992, op. cit. in note 15.
[40] M. O. H. Carver, 'Boat burial in Britain: ancient custom or political symbol?', 111–23 in O. Crumlin-Pedersen (ed.), *The Ship as Symbol in Prehistoric and Medieval Scandinavia* (Copenhagen, 1995).
[41] Carver, op. cit. in note 15.
[42] R. van de Noort, 'The context of early medieval barrows in western Europe', *Antiquity*, 67 (1993), 66–73.
[43] Müller-Wille, op. cit. in note 13, Abb. 6, 7.
[44] Syedov, op. cit. in note 21; Lutovsky, op. cit. in note 14; see also Foster, op. cit. in note 11 for Pictish mounds. These modify the map in van de Noort, op. cit. in note 42.
[45] J. P. Lamm and H.-Å. Nordström (eds.), *Vendel Period Studies* (Stockholm, 1983).

construction was 'a period of crisis for central Norrland society, when this petty kingdom was faced by difficult conflicts primarily with the Mälaren valley'.[46]

Similar conclusions had already been reached by Lotte Hedeager in her multi-faceted model for the emergence of a Danish state, in which the role of barrows, or the lack of barrows, is particularly revealing.[47] The monumental mound may be a signal of the establishment of a new elite,[48] but the need for such a signal diminishes once the new authority feels secure.[49] The absence of rich burial in late Roman Iron-age Jutland can even be used to reinforce the impression of a stable kingship, which is otherwise detectable from place-names and settlement patterns,[50] as well as the demonstration that Jutland/Skåne was the origin centre for innovation in Germanic animal art of the Merovingian period.[51] Insecurity may return with the predatory agenda of a neighbour, resulting in a new investment of monumental burial: 'Both Christianity and paganism were political tools, and these [rich] graves also belong to areas in which the two religions were in conflict: the Frankish Rhineland and Southern England'.[52] In the areas thought to be remote from the Christian threat, such as the polities implied by mounds at Gamla Uppsala, in Gotland or in southern Norway, the predatory agents are the (pre-Viking) Danes.[53]

In his recent study of Merovingian Metz, Guy Halsall also emphasizes the political role adopted by burial in certain historical contexts.[54] In the 6th century, the Frankish cemetery was an important theatre of 'competitive discourse', in which burial and costume were used to signal social status, as opposed to investment in monumental architecture.[55] Among the people of Frankia, ethnicity was a construct, and burial may have reflected taxation status: 'The adoption of Frankish ethnic identity, the acquisition of Frankish status, would be a valuable strategy, especially if it brought with it at least partial tax exemption. It is not difficult to see why Frankish identity should have become almost universal by c. 600'.[56] In some parts of the Frankish area (such as the Alamannic), analogies with the sequence of burial practice in Anglo-Saxon England are strong: 'a removal of aristocratic graves away from the community cemetery in the early seventh century often associated with extreme displays of prestige: exceptionally lavish funerary displays, horse-burials and the construction of barrows and even churches'.[57] But, 'by the mid seventh century, the funerary furnishings have become

---

[46] P. H. Ramqvist, *Högom I: The Excavations 1949–1984* (Stockholm, 1992), 225.
[47] Hedeager, op. cit. in note 19; L. Hedeager, *Iron-Age Societies: From Tribe to State in Northern Europe 500 BC to AD 700* (Oxford, 1992).
[48] Hedeager 1992, op. cit. in note 47, 253.
[49] Ibid., 246, 250.
[50] Hedeager, op. cit. in note 19, 291; Hedeager, op. cit. in note 47, 246, 250.
[51] Hedeager, op. cit. in note 19, 293.
[52] Ibid., 294.
[53] Ibid., 294–5.
[54] G. Halsall, *Settlement and Social Organisation: the Merovingian Region of Metz* (Cambridge, 1995).
[55] Ibid., 253, 261.
[56] Ibid., 258.
[57] Ibid., 260.

low key and standardized, while the emphasis on investment is moving to above-ground monuments such as grave-markers and decorated sarcophagus lids'.[58] In the 8th century the focus of social display returns to the dwelling-place.[59]

The barrow may have been a type of monumental statement that was well understood in 7th-century Frankia, but it was by no means universally adopted even by those who could afford to do so. The adoption of the barrow may be explained by social change and a change in the location of the theatre of discourse into the cemetery, where families paraded their status and ideology. But that does not explain the Rhineland distribution, which is predominantly marginal to the main Frankish area. It must be supposed that here, as in England, the barrow signalled allegiance to a political viewpoint that was under threat and which eventually failed or was superseded.

CONCLUSION

It would seem that we are on the threshold of an exciting period in the study of burial mounds. If the use of mounds could be analysed within their local archaeological context, while allowing their adoption to be largely interpreted as an ideological signal, it should be possible to write a new type of political history for early Europe which depends for its arguments not on migration, ethnicity or the individual, but upon that most human of preoccupations: the battle of ideas.

As for Sutton Hoo, the battle of ideas in 7th-century Europe was surely its principal inspiration and prime mover, but I do not deny that the other explanations can have some validity too. The structure of society does seem to have changed in eastern England during the 6th century, if the adoption of burial mounds, together with nucleated settlement and palace sites, can be interpreted as witnesses of that change. The product of the process was a new kind of kingship, in which the claiming and naming, and taxing, of territory was a natural concomitant. Although the actual derivation of the population was likely to have been very complicated, an assumed 'ethnicity' was part of the same nation-building project as the claiming of territory. We can even give some credence to the role of the individual in the Sutton Hoo cemetery. The burials are most certainly celebrations of individuals; there is every reason to suppose that they had names and that these were remembered as epitomes of the success or failure of the politics of their reigns. Although archaeology can do little to confirm it, they may be the names of the members of the Wuffing dynasty that have otherwise come down to us.

The people of Sutton Hoo used the burial mound as an instrument in their adoption of kingship and designation of territory in the early 7th century. They did it then, because they were under provocation from their politically acquisitive neighbours, that is Merovingian France and her newly acquired puppet kingdom, Kent. In defiant reaction, the East Angles invested in a pagan kingship, symbolically recognizable to the opposition, by emphasising their alliance with the politics and ideology of

---

[58] Ibid., 271; see now H. Geake, *The Use of Grave-Goods in Conversion-Period England, c. 600–c. 850* (BAR Brit. Ser., 261, Oxford, 1997) for the comparable process in England.
[59] Halsall, op. cit. in note 54, 277.

the North. They developed a special pagan royal apparatus, inventing where they could not emulate, and incorporating cremation, burial mounds, ship-burial, the ritual killing of horses and a specially-designed 'sceptre' which referred to Germanic, Celtic and Byzantine symbolism. This spirited experiment soon failed and the newly-created kingdom passed into the political embrace of Christian Europe, its former burial ground of kings now a *gulag* for the disposal of dissidents. But the ideology that East Anglia had momentarily championed was to re-appear intermittently over the next 1400 years, and is not wholly unfamiliar in England even now.

ACKNOWLEDGEMENTS

I am most grateful to Tania Dickinson, Helen Geake, Madeleine Hummler and Sam Lucy for their comments on an earlier draft of this paper.

Persistent Problems in the Study of Conversion-Period Burials in England

By HELEN GEAKE

This paper will examine four difficult problems in the study of 7th- and early 8th-century burial practice, which are fundamental to our understanding of this critical period, and may have wider implications. These problems can be summarized as the paucity of early 7th-century burials; the apparent desertion of the Isle of Wight; the enigma of the disappearing men; and some problems surrounding the interpretation of early church-related burial. Although the paper puts forward a number of possible theories, it does not necessarily seek to solve the problems, but rather to highlight them as worthy of further research. For the sake of euphony, it will refer to the date-range involved as the Conversion Period; this term has the advantage of distinguishing it from the immediately preceding Migration Period, and at the same time avoids unnecessary arguments about absolute chronology.

WHERE ARE ALL THE EARLY 7TH-CENTURY BURIALS?

The first problem to be confronted is the relative invisibility of early 7th-century burial. My doctoral research on Conversion-period burials began with the collection of all furnished burials with grave-goods that had previously been dated to the 7th to early 9th century, following scholars such as Leeds, Lethbridge, Hyslop, Meaney and Hawkes, Shephard, and Evison.[1] Analysis of the results showed that, as expected, there were widespread changes between the Migration-period grave-good assemblage and the Conversion-period assemblage, and that this appeared to date from c. 600.[2]

But there were very few artefact-types that could be dated specifically to the *early* 7th century, or to the later 6th/early 7th. Examples included garnet-inlaid disc brooches, bracteates bearing Style II decoration, buckles with triangular plates, buckles with shield-shaped plates on their pins, 'Coptic' bronze vessels, shoe buckles, Dickinson Group 3 and Group 6 shield-bosses, one type of seax, and some types of glass vessels; these types tended to be unisex or male-linked, and tended to have

---

[1] E. T. Leeds, *Early Anglo-Saxon Art and Archaeology* (Oxford, 1936); id., 'The distribution of the Angles and Saxons archaeologically considered', *Archaeologia*, 91 (1945), 1–106; T. C. Lethbridge, *Recent Excavations in Anglo-Saxon Cemeteries in Cambridgeshire and Suffolk* (Cambridge, 1931); id., *A Cemetery at Shudy Camps, Cambridgeshire: Report of the Excavation of a Cemetery of the Christian Anglo-Saxon Period in 1933* (Cambridge, 1936); M. Hyslop, 'Two Anglo-Saxon cemeteries at Chamberlain's Barn, Leighton Buzzard, Bedfordshire', *Archaeol. J.*, 120 (1963), 161–200; A. L. Meaney and S. C. Hawkes, *Two Anglo-Saxon Cemeteries at Winnall* (London, 1970); J. Shephard, *Anglo-Saxon Barrows of the Later Sixth and Seventh Centuries AD* (unpublished PhD thesis, University of Cambridge, 1979); V. I. Evison, *Dover: Buckland Anglo-Saxon Cemetery* (London, 1987).

[2] H. Geake, *The Use of Grave-Goods in Conversion-Period England, c. 600–c. 850* (BAR Brit. Ser., 261, Oxford, 1997), esp. p. 8 and p. 11.

distributions concentrated in Kent. Much more common were items such as necklaces made up of small glass beads and silver rings, cabochon pendants, iron-bound buckets and so on, which could not be dated more closely than to the Conversion period in general.[3]

This seems an odd pattern to those used to the cemetery archaeology of the preceding century. Fashions change fast but steadily in the 5th and 6th centuries, and Susan Hirst has suggested two possible mechanisms. Perhaps Migration-period women put their brooches back in the melting pot every ten years or so; alternatively a woman could have obtained her brooches at a standard age and worn the same brooches all her life.[4] Either would fit the observed pattern in the Migration Period; fashions change fast, and graves rarely appear to contain grave-goods of widely varying date. But in the 7th century the situation alters, and most of the objects in use in the Conversion period— particularly women's dress accessories —cannot be more closely dated than to the entire period of the 7th and early 8th century.

A salutary example is grave 93 at the Boss Hall cemetery on the edge of Ipswich (Suffolk). A woman was buried in this grave with a knife at the waist and a leather pouch at the neck. In the leather pouch were all the other grave-goods, and these included an iron chatelaine; a silver toilet set; silver wire rings; cabochon pendants; silver beads; gold disc pendants; glass beads and string; a composite disc brooch with the surface almost entirely covered in garnets; and two coins. One was a pierced gold solidus of Sigebert III, who was king of the Franks from 634 to 656. The other was a Series B sceatt dated to c. 690.[5] If the people burying this woman had decided not to put the sceatt in, we would still have had a firm coin-date for this grave, and it would have probably been put at soon after 656. This would have been unproblematic; but it is also unproblematic to date the burial to the 690s or even 700. Adding forty years or so to the date of the burial does not make the woman look old-fashioned.

There are some possible reasons for the comparative invisibility of early 7th-century burials. One is that the production and burial of coins begins in the second half of the 7th century. Mark Whyman has argued that the cessation of Roman coin production is skewing our dates for late Romano-British pottery[6] and, in the same way, the start of Anglo-Saxon coin production may be skewing the dates for early 7th-century grave-goods. If there is a coin in the grave, it is most likely to be a pale gold thrymsa or a sceatt and to date to after about 660 at the earliest; thus the grave-goods will also be dated to c. 660 or later. Earlier object-types, which do not occur in conjunction with coins, may at the later end of their chronological range occur in conjunction with other objects which *can* be linked to coins — thus resulting in their dating either spuriously to c. 660 or later, or just to the 7th/early 8th century as a whole. Under this explanation, the reason for the concentrations in Kent is that here the incidence of earlier Frankish coins is much higher, so although the skewing effect

[3] Geake, op. cit. in note 2, table 6.1.
[4] S. M. Hirst, *An Anglo-Saxon Inhumation Cemetery at Sewerby, East Yorkshire* (York, 1985), 95.
[5] L. Webster and J. Backhouse (eds.), *The Making of England: Anglo-Saxon Art and Culture AD 600–900* (London, 1991), 51–3.
[6] M. C. Whyman, 'Invisible people? Material culture in 'Dark Age' Yorkshire', 61–8 in M. O. H. Carver (ed.), *In Search of Cult* (Woodbridge, 1993), at p. 64.

of the coins still exists, it does not result in such a late date. This possible explanation can be summarized as 'we've got the object dates wrong'.

Another putative reason is much more simple; that fashions just *did not* change. It is possible that the basic fashion of one or more short necklaces with rings, beads and various pendants began in the early 7th century and continued in use throughout the Conversion Period, overlaid with more chronologically specific types only later in the century.

One final possible theory is much harder to prove. There are hints that early 7th century burial might be characterized by its oddness, by its peculiarities, and by its uncertainties, rather than its own distinctive character. To briefly state the case, in the 6th century most women were buried in a Germanic style of costume which includes markers of their chosen 'ethnic' group, whether Anglian, Saxon or Kentish. Around the year 600, something happened to change this, and to considerably lessen the signals that are sent out by women's graves. If we can assume that the burial costume was similar to the costume of the living, we can say that women who had been advertising a Germanic descent group in their clothing suddenly stop. It is as if they all got up one morning and just couldn't think what to wear. They seem almost to have lost confidence in the old costume.

There seems, then, to be some sort of crisis in burial in the early 7th century. The old order has passed away, and there is great uncertainty about what should be done now; people try all sorts of tactics, some of which seem to work, and are then more widely used, and others which do not and which always remain uncommon. These experiments include ship burial, cremations in bronze bowls, bed burial and, if documentary sources are to be believed, burial in the vicinity of churches.[7] This solution could be summarized as 'they don't make a coherent group'.

The high-precision radiocarbon dates and statistical techniques that are now being applied to furnished graves of the late 6th to early 8th century should substantiate or disprove these three possible solutions to the problem.[8] The next problem to be looked at is closely related and may help to shed light on early 7th-century burial in general.

THE APPARENT DESERTION OF THE ISLE OF WIGHT

The Isle of Wight was the last kingdom of England to be converted to Christianity, soon after the kingdom of the South Saxons, both in the 680s.[9] Interestingly, Sussex has very few Conversion-period cemeteries, and those that have been identified have very few diagnostic grave-goods. But the Isle of Wight is even more badly off; I have

[7] For cremation in bronze bowls, see T. M. Dickinson and G. Speake, 'The seventh-century cremation burial at Asthall barrow, Oxfordshire: a reassessment', 95–130 in M. O. H. Carver (ed.), *The Age of Sutton Hoo* (Woodbridge, 1992). For bed burials, see T. Malim and J. Hines, *The Anglo-Saxon Cemetery at Edix Hill (Barrington A), Cambridgeshire* (CBA Res. Rep., 112, York, 1998), 261–8 and G. Speake, *A Saxon Bed Burial on Swallowcliffe Down* (London, 1989).

[8] C. Scull and A. Bayliss, 'Radiocarbon dating and Anglo-Saxon graves', 39–50 in U. von Freeden, U. Koch and A. Wieczorek (eds), *Völker an Nord- und Ostsee und die Franken* (Bonn, 1999), at p. 50.

[9] *Bede's Ecclesiastical History of the English People*, ed. and trans. B. Colgrave and R. A. B. Mynors, (Oxford, 1969), IV.16 (for the Isle of Wight) and IV.13 (for the South Saxons).

managed to identify precisely one solitary Conversion-period burial on the island among all its well-furnished and well-researched cemeteries.[10]

What is causing this dearth of burials on such a well-populated island? Of course, the last place to adopt a new ideology might be expected to look old-fashioned in terms of its material culture for longer. There is no evidence, however, that the Isle of Wight continued to use a Migration-period-type assemblage longer than any other part of England. There is no evidence for the next hypothesis either, but it makes an interesting byway to explore.

During the early 7th century, some people — or everyone, in the Isle of Wight and Sussex — may have begun to dispose of their dead in an unrecognizable way. As areas changed their ideology to Christianity, they perhaps began to use a distinctive assemblage of grave-goods and then few or no grave-goods at all. Sussex and the Isle of Wight, however, could have converted too late to be able to catch up with the distinctive grave-goods; they could have gone straight to the few or no grave-goods stage.

This hypothesis has two possible ramifications. It could be that this unrecognizable disposal was something exotic —like burial at sea or in rivers, or excarnation. If so, it might fit in quite well with the other sorts of exotica that I mentioned before as perhaps being used by funeral organizers in the early 7th century. Or, it could be that the unrecognizable disposal was simply unfurnished isolated burial. If so, we should perhaps re-think our ideas on what constituted pagan and Christian practice in the early 7th century; pagan kingdoms seem to be using unfurnished graves, but Christian kingdoms seem to be using furnished ones! At this point I may be pushing the evidence too far, and so we shall move on to the next persistent problem.

THE CASE OF THE DISAPPEARING MEN

In the early 7th century, many of the graves outside Kent which are easily recognizable are the richly furnished graves of men. These are the familiar ones of Taplow (Buckinghamshire), Broomfield (Essex), and of course Mounds 1, 2 and 17 at Sutton Hoo (Suffolk); other examples are Coombe Bissett, also known as Salisbury Race Course (Wiltshire), and Caenby (Lincolnshire).[11]

As the 7th century goes on, one of the most noticeable things is the increase in the visibility of women: as already remarked, the few grave-good-types datable to the early 7th century are most often either unisex or male-linked. The increase in the visibility of women occurs at all levels, from the most poorly to the most richly furnished graves. Famous examples of richly furnished women's graves include Desborough (Northamptonshire), Swallowcliffe Down and Roundway Down (both Wiltshire), Galley Low (Derbyshire), and Hawnby (North Yorkshire).[12] These graves are not as

---

[10] C. J. Arnold, *The Anglo-Saxon Cemeteries of the Isle of Wight* (London, 1982), 109; id., 'The Anglo-Saxon cemeteries of the Isle of Wight: an appraisal of 19th-century excavation data', 163–75 in E. Southworth (ed.), *Anglo-Saxon Cemeteries: A Reappraisal* (Stroud, 1990), at pp. 174–5; K. Ulmschneider, 'Archaeology, history and the Isle of Wight in the middle Saxon period', *Medieval Archaeol.*, 43 (1999), 19–44; H. Geake, 'When were hanging bowls deposited in Anglo-Saxon graves?', *Medieval Archaeol.*, 43 (1999), 1–18.

[11] Summaries and bibliographies for these sites can be found in Geake, op. cit. in note 2.

[12] Summaries and bibliographies for these sites can be found in Geake, op. cit. in note 2.

staggeringly rich as, for example, Mound 1 at Sutton Hoo, but the women are fairly well provided for nevertheless. Poorly and moderately furnished men's graves continue to be recognizable alongside, but oddly the rich male graves of the early 7th century do not continue into the later part of the century. Benty Grange, it has been suggested, should date to the second half of the 7th century on the grounds of the Christian symbolism of the cross appliqués from the helmet and cups,[13] but similar Christian symbolism can be found in the earlier 7th-century Sutton Hoo Mound 1. Undoubtedly later graves, such as Lowbury (West Berkshire) and Ford (Wiltshire), dated by their tall Group 7 shield-bosses to the later 7th or early 8th century, are not so conspicuously wealthy.

Why should this be? Where are the relatives of *Mister* Swallowcliffe Down planning to bury him, when they have just put his wife's body into a richly furnished barrow? Wherever he goes, he disappears from the archaeological record. The most likely possibility is that he is buried in the vicinity of a church, without anything in the actual grave to betray his status. But if he is going to be buried near a church, why is a barrow chosen for his wife?

There are a number of possibilities. Perhaps it was in some way easier for a man to be buried in a church-related cemetery, and so therefore furnished female graves could have become more important in the signalling of a family's status at a time of bereavement. We have, however, no support from written sources to suggest that men had differential access to churchyard burial; there are plenty of instances of women (albeit those who are in holy orders) being buried in church cemeteries as a matter of course.

A more subtle reading could be that the opportunities for improving one's social standing through the administration and patronage of the Church may have been less easy for women —there may have been a glass ceiling which is not evident in the written sources — and therefore these women could have begun to use rich grave assemblages for this purpose. The major hurdle to a theory like this is that of course a marvellous grave assemblage is actually no good to the woman *herself* now, as she is dead; and if the family needs the status, why can it not derive it from her husband's activities with the Church? It could be argued that, in the Migration Period, complex signalling appears to be done more through female graves than through male graves, but as we have seen, in the early 7th century that role appears to have been extended to men.

Any other theory of the type that is hard to disprove, such as the idea that these well-furnished female graves were those of unmarried women, has of course to have a chronological element which can explain the change in the burial wealth of women over the course of the 7th century.

In fact, I find it hard to believe that the menfolk of these later 7th-century women were buried in the vicinity of churches, and to explain why we must turn to the most knotty of the persistent problems.

---

[13] R. L. S. Bruce-Mitford, *Aspects of Anglo-Saxon Archaeology* (London, 1974), 242.

THE RELATIONSHIP BETWEEN CHURCH-RELATED AND
NON-CHURCH BURIAL PRACTICE

This problem is less easy to summarize briefly. In the Frankish areas of continental Europe, churches and churchyards have in many cases been found to contain furnished burials. Some are very famous, as in the case of the so-called 'Arnegunde' grave (number 49) at St-Denis in Paris, and the rich graves under Cologne Cathedral.[14] These furnished burials occur within church-related cemeteries through one of two mechanisms: firstly, the church could be placed within an earlier cemetery containing furnished burials, and secondly, burials which took place in and around churches could continue to contain extremely rich furnishings.

In newly converted 7th-century England, however, the situation is different, and our problem is why. Burials in church-related cemeteries, almost without exception, never contain grave-goods. This means that the church-related cemetery was *not* placed on the same site as earlier Anglo-Saxon burials with grave-goods, and that the new cemeteries did *not* receive burials with grave-goods. Churchyard burial and burial with grave-goods were simply incompatible, and that is why it seems unlikely (though not of course impossible) that the menfolk of families who buried their women in richly furnished graves were buried in or around churches.

This is not to say that *Christianity* and burial with grave-goods were incompatible. A good illustration of this is one of the most beautiful pieces of Anglo-Saxon jewellery ever found, the Desborough necklace. It is a very short necklace made up of eight gold and garnet cabochon pendants of different shapes, one larger than the rest; nine gold 'bulla' pendants; and nineteen gold beads. In the centre is a gold and garnet cross.[15]

It is of course possible to argue that we will never know whether the woman buried wearing the Desborough necklace was personally a Christian or a pagan, and that we can never prove that she had even heard of the Christian Church. But the central cross has clearly been added to an existing necklace, pushing the centrepiece of the large gold and garnet pendant out of the way and destroying the symmetry of the piece. It seems therefore likely that the Church had touched her life in one way or another, and she may very well have accepted its structures and authority. But she was buried in an ordinary cemetery with other furnished graves, not in a churchyard,[16] and moreover she was not buried in the same *manner* as those buried around churches.

The full range of burial sites in Conversion-period England can be roughly sorted into three categories. The first, and by far the most numerous, is the cemetery with a number of well-furnished, easily datable graves, and quite a few unfurnished graves. This type is often called the 'Final-phase' cemetery, and around 300 are known from

---

[14] J. Werner, 'Frankish royal tombs in the cathedrals of Cologne and St-Denis', *Antiquity*, 38 (1964), 201–16; P. Périn 'Pour une révision de la datation de la tombe d'Arégonde, épouse de Clotaire Ier, découverte en 1959 dans la basilique de Saint-Denis', *Archéol. Mediévale*, 21 (1991), 21–50.

[15] Webster and Backhouse, op. cit. in note 5, 28–9.

[16] Geake, op. cit. in note 2, 171.

England.[17] The well-furnished graves in these cemeteries continue to be deposited right up to the very end of furnished burial, around 720 or 730.[18]

The second category of cemetery could be called the 'churchyard type'; that with very few grave-goods— perhaps a single pin or a knife in one grave only — or none at all. We know about many fewer of these, perhaps under fifty, as they are of course harder to date securely. Most are around a known church, as these are more easily identified and dated. In some cases, the excavated area has been too small to be certain if a church was present or not; in a few, it seems likely that the cemetery was never associated with a church (see below).

The third type of cemetery is the rarest, and could be described as intermediate between the other two; the cemetery which, although largely of 'churchyard type', does have a few well-furnished burials. It could include a conventional 'Final-phase' cemetery which goes on to develop into an unfurnished 'churchyard-type' cemetery, but should ignore stray finds of early Anglo-Saxon date in churchyards, as well as sites with the occasional knife. Four examples serve to illustrate those which might possibly come into this category.

The first, and the most improbable, is Taplow. This rich early 7th-century burial was found underneath a mound standing within the churchyard in 1882, but it remains the only part of the churchyard to have been excavated and the relationship between the mound, the other burials and the church is unclear.[19]

The second possible example, and again a rather unlikely one, is St Paul-in-the-Bail in Lincoln (Lincolnshire). A rectangular building with an eastern apse was excavated within the Roman forum at Lincoln, on the site of the medieval church of St Paul-in-the-Bail. From its shape, and the surrounding unfurnished graves, it is thought to have been a church. Radiocarbon dates from the graves suggest that the apsidal building was built between the 4th and 7th centuries A.D., and was replaced in the 7th or 8th century by an overlying single-celled rectangular building on a slightly different alignment.[20] A grave-shaped pit was found just inside the east end of the 'nave' of the apsidal building, beneath where the altar might have been if it had indeed been a church, and central to the single-celled building; it was not stratigraphically related to either. The possible grave was stone-lined, but otherwise empty; under part of the stone lining a hanging bowl was found. If the pit is a grave, the hanging bowl dates it to after c. 600.[21] The excavator suggested that the bowl may have been deliberately

---

[17] A. Boddington, 'Models of settlement, burial and worship: the final phase reviewed', 177–99 in E. Southworth (ed.), op. cit. in note 10; Geake, op. cit. in note 2, 23.

[18] Geake, op. cit. in note 2, 125. Note, however, that Ipswich Buttermarket grave 38 has recently been re-numbered to 4152 and radiocarbon-dated to c. 600–660; see C. Scull and A. Bayliss, 'Dating burials of the seventh and eighth centuries; a case study from Ipswich, Suffolk', 80–8 in J. Hines, K. Høilund Nielsen and F. Siegmund (eds.), *The Pace of Change: Studies in Early-Medieval Chronology* (Oxford, 1999), at p. 86 and Table 5.1.

[19] D. Stocker and D. Went, 'The evidence of a pre-Viking church adjacent to the Anglo-Saxon barrow at Taplow, Buckinghamshire', *Archaeol. J.*, 152 (1995), 441–54.

[20] M. J. Jones, 'St Paul in the Bail, Lincoln: Britain in Europe?', 325–47 in K. Painter (ed.), *Churches Built in Ancient Times: Recent Studies in Early Christian Archaeology* (London, 1994).

[21] Geake, op. cit. in note 10.

concealed within the grave and the body subsequently translated, and that those who exhumed the body may have been unaware of its existence.[22]

The problems with citing St Paul-in-the-Bail as an exception to the rule are various; the uncertainty as to whether the pit was a grave; the uncertainty over whether either building was a church; the complete lack of stratigraphic link between the buildings and the grave; and the fact that post-excavation work is continuing.[23]

The third example of a church-related grave including grave-goods is the famous grave of St Cuthbert. Cuthbert died in 687 and was buried within the church on Lindisfarne (Northumberland) immediately. In 698 he was translated into an above-ground shrine; Bede says that the monks took some of the vestments in which Cuthbert had been buried out of the tomb, and replaced them with new ones.[24] When the coffin was re-opened in 1827 Cuthbert was wearing a gold and garnet pectoral cross dating to the 7th century, and the grave also contained a comb and a portable altar. It is just possible that all these objects, even the pectoral cross, could have been added in 698 when Cuthbert was given this extremely unusual re-burial. But what is odd is that Bede happily states that Cuthbert was clothed (in vestments) at his original burial. This time, however, the problem with the grave of St Cuthbert disproving the rule of unfurnished burial in the vicinity of churches is that his was clearly such an exceptional case.

The fourth example, and the least problematic one, is Eccles (Kent). The cemetery was discovered during the excavation of a Roman villa over a number of years in the 1960s and 1970s. It has not yet been fully published. The cemetery seems to have been in use for some time, as there were many intercutting graves. Among those thought to be the earliest were five with grave-goods numerous and interesting enough to be exhibited at the Society of Antiquaries. Nineteen other graves were furnished, out of a total of about 200, but doubts have been expressed as to whether they are all of Anglo-Saxon date. Among the many postholes, at least one timber structure might plausibly be identified. It may be significant that this exception is in Kent, an atypical county that has of course exceptionally strong links with Francia.[25]

On the whole, therefore, it can be said that the 'Final-phase' cemeteries and the 'churchyard-type' cemeteries are mutually exclusive — and yet can exist at the same time within a few miles of each other. Burials were still being added to the 'Final-phase' cemetery of Winnall II (Hampshire) after burial had commenced in the churchyard of Winchester Old Minster only a mile away; the possible monastic sites of

[22] B. J. Gilmour, 'The Anglo-Saxon church at St Paul-in-the-Bail, Lincoln', *Medieval Archaeol.*, 23 (1979), 214–7.

[23] Jones, op. cit. in note 20. I am indebted to M. J. Jones for discussing the St Paul-in-the-Bail site with me.

[24] J. Campbell, *The Anglo-Saxons* (Oxford, 1982), 80–1; Bede, op. cit. in note 9, IV.30.

[25] A. P. Detsicas, 'Excavations at Eccles', *Archaeol. Cantiana*, 86 (1971), 25–34; 87 (1972), 101–10; 88 (1973), 73–80; 89 (1974), 119–34; 91 (1975), 41–5; 92 (1976), 157–63; A. P. Detsicas and S. C. Hawkes, 'Finds from the Anglo-Saxon cemetery at Eccles, Kent', *Antiq. J.*, 53 (1973), 281–6; R. Shaw, 'The Anglo-Saxon cemetery at Eccles: a preliminary report', *Archaeol. Cantiana*, 114 (1994), 165–88; N. Brooks, 'Canterbury, Rome and the construction of English identity', forthcoming in J. M. H. Smith (ed.), *Early Medieval Rome and the Christian West: Essays Presented to D. A. Bullough* (Leiden, 2000). I am indebted to Professor Brooks for sending me the text of his article in advance of publication. For other ecclesiastical anomalies in Kent, see T. Bell, 'Churches on Roman buildings: Christian associations and Roman masonry in Anglo-Saxon England', *Medieval Archaeol.*, 42 (1998), 1–18.

Caister-on-Sea and Burgh Castle (both Norfolk) are contemporary with the rich burials found while building the Norwich Southern Bypass at Harford Farm (Norfolk), 25 or so miles away; and Repton (Derbyshire) was being used at the same time as the remarkably wealthy series of mound-burials again only 25 miles away.[26]

At this point it must be stressed that, in examining the nature of English church-related burials in the Conversion Period, I am extrapolating from relatively few examples. Obviously an unfurnished grave is hard to date, and an early grave in a medieval churchyard is very vulnerable to disturbance from later grave digging. Most of the known graves come from the small number that have been radiocarbon-dated — none with a high-precision date — and many have come from churchyards later abandoned, and so perhaps atypical.

The observed pattern, however, is surprisingly strong. There is not merely a tendency to have fewer grave-goods and more unfurnished graves in churchyards; there is a very strong and consistent avoidance of the grave-good habit. And this is at a time when contemporary cemeteries outside churchyards —cemeteries which have been legitimately interpreted by many as the burying-places of Christians — contain some of the richest and rarest grave-goods of the entire Anglo-Saxon period. It seems, therefore, that some people who have access to great wealth decide to commemorate their dead with grave-goods, and some with churches, and that the two never mix. So what is causing this pattern in England, and why is it so different from the situation in Francia?

POSSIBLE EXPLANATIONS

CHRONOLOGY

One of the first explanations that can spring to mind when faced with the difference between English and Continental burial rite is that it stems from a difference in date. But unfortunately this is not the case. 7th-century burials with grave-goods are being added to churchyard cemeteries in western Continental Europe at the same time as the English churches appear to be excluding them (e.g. St-Denis in Paris, and St Severin in Cologne).[27]

RE-USE OF OLDER CEMETERIES

The difference in grave-good deposition between England and the Continent also seems *not* to be due to a difference in the re-use of older cemeteries. Frankish churches can be found on the sites of earlier cemeteries, in some cases including grave-goods

[26] For Winchester Old Minster see M. Biddle, 'Archaeology, architecture and the cult of saints', 1–31 in L. A. S. Butler and R. K. Morris (eds), *The Anglo-Saxon Church* (CBA Res. Rep., 60, London, 1986), at p. 16; M. J. Darling, *Caister-on-Sea: Excavations by Charles Green, 1951–55* (*East Anglian Archaeol.*, 60, Gressenhall, 1993); S. Johnson, *Burgh Castle: Excavations by Charles Green, 1958–61* (*East Anglian Archaeol.*, 20, Gressenhall, 1983). For Harford Farm, see K. Penn, *Norwich Southern Bypass, Part II: Anglo-Saxon Cemetery at Harford Farm, Caistor St Edmund* (*East Anglian Archaeol.*, 92, Dereham, 2000). For Repton, see Geake op. cit. in note 2, 149.
[27] F. Naumann-Steckner, 'Death on the Rhine: changing burial customs in Cologne, 3rd–7th century', 143–79 in L. Webster and M. Brown (eds), *The Transformation of the Roman World, AD 400–900* (London, 1997), at p. 175.

(e.g. St-Brice, Tournai).[28] English churches have not been found to be built over furnished burials, but they do seem in some cases to have been built over unfurnished burials. Not only do we know of many church excavations where the earliest evidence for activity on the site is unfurnished burials,[29] but there also seem to be a number of small cemeteries of unfurnished burials which never developed into churchyards. Roche Court Down III (Wiltshire) is a possible example, and perhaps Sedgeford (Norfolk).[30] Tyler Bell draws attention to a few Anglo-Saxon churches or churchyards over the sites of Roman mausolea.[31] But even if English churchyards were always *de novo* foundations around a church, this would not account for the fact that Frankish churches can then receive furnished burials and English churches cannot.

SETTLEMENT CONTEXT

A further possibility might be that the English and Frankish churchyard burials are located in different types of settlement context. Frankish churchyard burials with grave-goods tend to be found in urban areas, such as Paris and Cologne. If 7th-century churchyard burials do not occur in urban areas in England, then it may be that the Continental phenomenon is intimately connected in some way with urban life and the effect that this has on social structures. Unfortunately for this explanation, however, we do find conventionally English churchyard burials of this date in towns, both in old Roman towns, such as Winchester, and in newly created towns, such as Southampton. In general, those churchyard-type cemeteries that we have been able to recognize tend to be within contemporary settlements, whereas Migration-period and 'Final-phase' cemeteries tend to be outside areas of settlement. This difference may be crucial, and the study of the landscape context of Anglo-Saxon cemeteries deserves more attention. It is not yet clear whether exceptions to the rule, such as the newly excavated settlement and cemetery at Carlton Colville (Suffolk), are exceptional in any other way.[32]

CHURCH REGULATIONS

Another explanation might be that there was a difference in the organization of the Church in England, or in its interest in burial. We might expect the English Church to have specifically forbidden the continuing use of ancient cemeteries, or the use of grave-goods. But on the contrary, English scholars, notably Richard Morris, have emphasized the lack of interest that the early English Church appears to have shown in burial; there is just as little legislation on the subject as there is on the Continent.[33]

---

[28] A. Dierkens and P. Périn, 'Death and burial in Gaul and Germania, 4th–8th century', 79–95 in L. Webster and M. Brown (eds.), op. cit. in note 26, at p. 86.

[29] R. K. Morris, *Churches in the Landscape* (London, 1989), 152.

[30] A. L. Meaney, *A Gazetteer of Early Anglo-Saxon Burial Sites* (London, 1964), 181 and 273; Geake, op. cit. in note 2, 170; N. Faulkner (ed.), 'Sedgeford Historical and Archaeological Research Project 1996: first interim report', *Norfolk Archaeol.*, 62 (1997), 532–5; A. Cox, J. Fox and G. Thomas, 'Sedgeford Historical and Archaeological Research Project: 1997 interim report', *Norfolk Archaeol.*, 63 (1998), 172–7; E. Biddulph, 'Sedgeford Historical and Archaeological Research Project: third interim report (1998)', *Norfolk Archaeol.*, 64 (1999), 351–2.

[31] Bell, op. cit. in note 25.

[32] R. Mortimer and J. Tipper, 'Excavation of an early-middle Saxon settlement at Bloodmoor Hill, Carlton Colville, Suffolk', *Lowestoft Archaeol. Local Hist. Soc. Annual Rep.*, 31 (1998–9).

[33] R. K. Morris, *The Church in British Archaeology* (CBA Res. Rep., 47, London, 1983), 50.

The grave of St Cuthbert is also a stumbling block to this argument, which on the whole seems to have little to recommend it.

SOCIAL MEANINGS OF GRAVE-GOODS AND CEMETERY LOCATIONS

Those who used particular sorts of early medieval grave-goods were doing a number of things with them. They were advertising their wealth, status and power (in a way that might suggest to us that they were not very secure in that wealth, status and power). But it is generally believed that they were also, by choosing from a range of *equally desirable* items, advertising the sort of person that the deceased was, and the sort of group that they belonged to — perhaps a social group, or a geographical or religious group, and so on. For example, I have suggested that the grave-goods used in the Conversion period had a strong classical flavour to them, and that they were used to advertise membership of a group of people who allied themselves with Roman-style politics — that is, politics that required kings, laws and taxation.[34]

Membership of certain groups — such as the Christian Church— could of course be a very powerful political tool. The role of the church in fostering kingship was crucial, as was the role of the kings in promoting the church; to be a Christian was to ally yourself not only with spiritual power but also with secular power.[35]

It may be that in England the very location of the grave— the churchyard — was enough advertisement of the group that a Christian belonged to, and there was consequently no need for the deposition of grave-goods. In fact, almost simultaneously, the wealth of kings and the aristocracy seems to have been advertised in ways rather different to rich burial deposits — in building churches, endowing them with treasures, and producing manuscripts and sculpture.

This explanation is superficially very attractive, but has two problems. Firstly, the most obvious interpretation of the observed pattern is that grave-goods were actively unwelcome, not just unnecessary. Secondly, it does not explain why this logical sequence of events did not apparently occur in the rest of Europe.

CONCLUSION

At the end of this discussion, what have we found out? None of the problems have been solved, but we do perhaps have a clearer idea of where we should be looking. The first two problems relate to the archaeological invisibility of unfurnished burial, a problem that arises at times in nearly every period of history and prehistory before the widespread construction of churches in the 10th and 11th centuries. This is a substantial area of ignorance within archaeology yet could be easily studied, with the certainty of interesting results; it is odd that, in the half-century since the discovery of radiocarbon dating, no multi-period research project has addressed it.

---

[34] Geake, op. cit. in note 2, 132–6.
[35] J. M. Wallace-Hadrill, *Early Medieval History* (Oxford, 1975), 181–2; J. Nelson, 'Inauguration rituals', 50–71 in P. H. Sawyer and I. N. Wood (eds.), *Early Medieval Kingship* (Leeds, 1977); A. Angenendt, 'The conversion of the Anglo-Saxons considered against the background of the early medieval mission', *Settimane di Studio del Centro Italiano di Studi sull'Alto Medioevo*, 32 (1986), 747–81.

The second two problems concern high-status burial both away from and close to a church, and both need to be examined in a European context. This paper can do no more than outline the problems, but when they are looked at in detail the explanations may come to us more readily.

The Case of the Missing Vikings: Scandinavian Burial in the Danelaw

By JULIAN D. RICHARDS

Where are the Vikings? For the period A.D. 400–600 there are tens of thousands of known Early Anglo-Saxon burials: vast folk cremation cemeteries, each one containing hundreds or even thousands of burial urns; huge inhumation cemeteries with whole armies of make-believe warriors; barrows and kings.

What do we have for the next major invasion of England? Another place-name transformation certainly, but of the mortal remains of the people themselves, only a handful of unimpressive accompanied burials. For the period A.D. 800–1000 there are less than 25 known burial sites which have been described as Scandinavian, and the majority of these comprise single burials — a sword from the churchyard at Heysham (Lancashire), for example; a ring-headed pin from Brigham (Cumbria), and at Saffron Walden (Essex) a burial in a row of late Saxon graves which contained a knife and a necklace with silver pendants.[1] In Scandinavia by contrast we see a revival of ostentatious furnished burial rites in the 9th and 10th centuries as paganism came into contact with Christianity. This is the era of Oseberg and Gokstad, of stone settings, and of large numbers of warrior burials.[2]

Whilst this paucity of accompanied Scandinavian burials *has* been seen as a problem, archaeologists studying the Scandinavian settlement have not tended to question the identification of an intrusive population. Discussion of Viking burials in the Danelaw has rarely gone beyond the identification and dating of burials, usually on the basis of Scandinavian-style grave-goods. Scholars of the early Anglo-Saxon period are now inclined to adopt a more critical approach to their source material. Many have expressed concerns that the proportion of Anglo-Saxon to sub-Romano-British burials should not be taken at face value. In line with general trends in archaeological interpretation, burials have come to be seen as documents, which must be read. A Germanic weapon-burial rite is no longer regarded as identifying the occupant as someone who migrated from Angeln or Saxony; instead it is seen as making a statement about ethnicity, and could just as well be an ideological ploy

[1] See, for example, D. M. Wilson, 'Archaeological evidence for the Viking settlements and raids in England', *Frühmittelalterliche Stud.*, 2 (1968), 291–304; D. M. Wilson, 'The Scandinavians in England', 393–403 in D. M. Wilson (ed.), *The Archaeology of Anglo-Saxon England* (Cambridge, 1976); J. D. Richards, *Viking Age England* (London, 1991), 109–16.

[2] M. Müller-Wille, 'Boat-graves in northern Europe', *Int. J. Nautical Archaeol. and Underwater Exploration*, 3.2 (1974), 187–204; E. Roesdahl, *Viking Age Denmark*, (London, 1982), 164–76; A. Pedersen, 'Weapons and riding gear in burials —evidence of military and social rank in 10th century Denmark?', 123–35 in A. N. Jørgensen and B. L. Clausen (eds.), *Military Aspects of Scandinavian Society in a European Perspective, AD 1–1300* (*Stud. Archaeol. Hist.*, 2, Copenhagen, 1997).

adopted by a sub-Roman inhabitant of East Anglia reinventing himself as a New Age follower of Woden.[3]

It is my aim in this paper to suggest that arguments about the Scandinavian settlement based upon the shortage of pagan burials need to take account of these approaches. In short, the lack of Scandinavians may be just as much an illusion as the surplus of Pagan Anglo-Saxons. There are many unaccompanied 9th- and 10th-century burials from the Danelaw that have not been considered in discussions of Scandinavian settlement, since they do not contain diagnostic elements of Scandinavian burial practice, yet these might easily be burials of settlers. Similarly, whether it can be claimed that all examples of accompanied burials of the 9th and 10th centuries were those of Scandinavian settlers is debatable. As Guy Halsall suggests, we should not rule out the possibility that Scandinavian influence might temporarily encourage the revival of burial with grave-goods among the indigenous population.[4] In many cases there is nothing specifically Scandinavian about the objects involved.

In re-examining the burial evidence for the period 800–1000 we need to be aware that burial forms are actively manipulated and used as strategies of legitimation and negotiation. In a situation where well-established and well-matched cultures meet we should not expect to see one or other culture dominate, but we might expect to find evidence of assimilation and acculturation. Rather than searching for burial-types that can be matched in Scandinavia we should therefore be looking for the creation of new cultural identities.[5]

In this paper I will follow three separate, but related avenues. Firstly, I will sketch what evidence we have for Scandinavian-style burial in the Danelaw. Secondly, I will look at accompanied graveyard burials and consider the creation of new burial rites, most notably the use of hogback grave markers. Thirdly, in order to prove the rule I will look at the exception: the overtly pagan Viking burials of Repton (Derbyshire) and of the neighbouring cremation cemetery at Heath Wood, Ingleby, and consider why we should find Scandinavian cemeteries at these two sites, and why only there?

SCANDINAVIAN BURIALS IN THE DANELAW

There have been various attempts to catalogue and map the candidates for Scandinavian burials in England.[6] Presentations of burials as dots on a map have tended to ignore the fact that they represent at least two distinct trends. In north-western England and Cumbria there is a cluster of burials, sometimes under mounds and frequently with weapons. These burials should really be seen as part of a distribution of Norse burials in the areas bordering on the Irish Sea; they reflect a similar culture to that known from the Isle of Man where there is a relatively large

---

[3] For a discussion of the differences in approach to the Anglo–Saxon and Scandinavian settlements see S. Trafford, 'Ethnicity, migration theory and the historiography of the Scandinavian settlement of England', 17–39 in D. Hadley and J. D. Richards (eds.), *Cultures in Contact: Scandinavian Settlement in England in the Ninth and Tenth Centuries* (Turnhout, 2000).

[4] G. Halsall, 'The Viking presence in Britain? The burial evidence reconsidered', 259–76 in Hadley and Richards, op. cit. in note 3.

[5] See D. Hadley, this volume, for a discussion of other northern burial forms.

[6] Wilson 1968, op. cit. in note 1, 295; Wilson 1976, op. cit. in note 1, fig. 10.1; Richards, op. cit. in note 1, fig.71.

number of highly visible Norse burials.[7] A number of possible outliers to this group can be found spreading across the Pennines to the Viking Kingdom of York, where they become intermingled with less characteristically Hiberno-Norse burials.

By contrast, in lowland England there are very few strong candidates for Scandinavian burials. With the exception of the cemeteries at Repton and Heath Wood, Ingleby, to which I shall return, the rest of the Viking burial corpus comprises a handful of burials in church graveyards or other Christian cemeteries which have been singled out as unusual because they have been accompanied by artefacts.

This is not the place to provide a complete corpus but to illustrate the differences I shall consider some examples from each group, starting with the North-West. In the late 18th century a mound at Beacon Hill, Aspatria (Cumbria), was found to contain a stone cist or chamber, comprising six stones, within which was a skeleton. The finds were published in 1792 and although they have subsequently been lost we can be fairly certain that the grave contained a skeleton with a sword with a silver encrusted hilt and a spearhead with a decorated silver socket. In addition, an ordinary axe is illustrated and 'pieces of a shield' are referred to in the description of the find. More unusual is the presence of a gold buckle and a strap-end of Carolingian type, confirming the high status of the deceased, further underlined by an iron horse-bit and spur.[8]

At Hesket-in-the-Forest (Cumbria) a layer of charcoal, bones and ashes with several grave-goods was found in 1822 lying on a bed of sand under a cairn. All the burnt bones were of animals, which had been cremated as part of the burial rite; there was no trace of a human skeleton. The weapons had been deliberately damaged. The sword and spears were bent; the shield had been broken in two; the sword had been bent back twice on itself, by heating and hammering, so as to render it useless. Horse and weapons may also have been thrown on the cremation pyre as it was reported that the sword, shield boss and horse-bit were all burnt. There was also an axe head, a pair of spurs, a fine un-burnt comb with its protective comb case, a sickle and a whetstone.[9]

A third mound burial was also discovered in 1822 at Claughton Hall, Garstang (Lancashire) when a small sand mound was cut through in the course of road building. The objects comprised a pair of gilt copper-alloy oval brooches, apparently wrapped up back-to-back in cloth and encasing two beads and a molar tooth, a Carolingian silver mount re-used as a brooch, and various iron objects, including a sword, spear, axe and hammer. This may have been a double burial of male and female, but it is more likely that the burial was male and the brooches formed a ritual deposit of various amulets or keepsakes. There may have been a wooden chamber two or three feet below the surface but the finds also included a Bronze-age axe hammer and a pot containing a cremation, now lost, so the finds from Claughton may represent another Scandinavian cremation, or secondary usage of a prehistoric barrow.[10]

---

[7] For a summary of the Isle of Man burial evidence see Richards, op. cit. in note 6, 102–9.
[8] H. Rooke, 'Druidical and other British remains in Cumberland', *Archaeologia*, 10 (1792), 105–13; B. J. N. Edwards, *Vikings in North West England* (Lancaster, 1998), 8–10.
[9] C. Hodgson, 'An account of some antiquities found in a cairn, near Hesket-in-the-Forest in Cumberland', *Archaeol. Aeliana*, 1st Series, 2 (1832), 106–9; Edwards, op. cit. in note 8, 11–14.
[10] B. J. N. Edwards, 'The Claughton Viking burial', *Trans. Hist. Soc. Lancashire Cheshire*, 121 (1969), 109–16; Edwards op. cit. in note 8, 14–16.

A small number of other sites in the North-West have also been advanced as Scandinavian burials, but only that at Eaglesfield (Cumbria) is likely to have been a mound burial. A skeleton accompanied by a sword, a spearhead (described as a 'halberd'), and possibly a ring-headed cloak pin (described as a 'fibula') was found on the limestone crags in 1814.[11]

Outside Cumbria, Scandinavian barrow burials are extremely rare in England. At Cambois, Bedlington (Northumberland) three bodies were found in a cist-grave in a mound. One was a female, aged 45–60; the other two were males, the first in his twenties, and the second in his forties. The only grave-goods were an enamelled disc brooch and a bone comb.[12] Further south, a sword and spear buried with a skeleton in a natural hill at Camphill near Bedale (North Yorkshire) may represent the choice of a natural prominence for a burial to avoid erecting a mound.[13] There is an antiquarian report that in 1723 a skeleton, horse-bit and an iron knife with a bone handle were found in the middle of the top of Silbury Hill (Wiltshire) but the finds are now lost and this is impossible to date to the Viking Age.[14] Another possible Viking mound burial has been identified at Hook Norton (Oxfordshire), where skeletons were found associated with a late 9th-century coin hoard.[15]

Such individual burials represent a distinct tradition of Scandinavian pagan burial that is paralleled especially in Norway, and examples of which are also found in the Northern and Western Isles of Scotland, as well as the Isle of Man. This north-western group reflects uncontrolled isolated burial away from churchyards and outside the control of authority.[16] Such burials often seek to become part of the landscape, frequently by the use of mounds, which are generally interpreted as reflecting claims to land, and the evocation of ancient traditions.[17] There are other candidates for single burials that must also represent pagan Scandinavian practice, and may once have been marked by mounds or some other distinctive feature, although no structural evidence survives. Stirrups, shears, a horseshoe and a prick-spur were found in 1884 near Magdalen Bridge in Oxford. Originally thought to have been casual losses they have recently been reinterpreted as the remains of a Viking warrior and his horse, buried on an island in the Cherwell around A.D. 1000. The horseshoe and a third small

[11] J. D. Cowen, 'A Viking sword from Eaglesfield near Cockermouth', *Archaeol. Aeliana*, 4th Series, 26 (1948), 55–61; J. D. Cowen, 'Viking burials in Cumbria', *Trans. Cumberland Westmorland Antiq. Archaeol. Soc.*, New Series, 48 (1948), 73–6; J. D. Cowen, 'Viking burials in Cumbria — a supplement', *Trans. Cumberland Westmorland Antiq. Archaeol. Soc.*, New Series, 67 (1967), 31–4; Edwards, op. cit. in note 8, 19.

[12] M. L. Alexander, 'A 'Viking-age' grave from Cambois, Bedlington, Northumberland', *Medieval Archaeol.*, 31 (1987), 101–5.

[13] H. Shetelig, *Viking Antiquities in Great Britain and Ireland*, IV (Oslo, 1940), 15.

[14] I am grateful to A. Reynolds for further information about this find. A drawing of the horse-bit was published by Stukeley in 1723; it appears to be an 11th-century piece, a date which ties in with the date of A.D. 1010 provided by a coin of Æthelred associated with the erection of a timber palisade on top of the mound. There is no direct association, however, between the horse-bit and the burial.

[15] M. Biddle and J. Blair, 'The Hook Norton hoard of 1848: a Viking burial from Oxfordshire?', *Oxoniensia*, 52 (1987), 186–95.

[16] See H. Geake, H. Gittos and A. Reynolds, this volume, for a discussion of the development of controlled churchyard burial.

[17] See, for example R. Bradley, 'Time regained: the creation of continuity', *J. British Archaeol. Assoc.*, 140 (1987), 1–17; R. Bradley, *Altering the Earth* (Edinburgh, 1993); R. Bradley, *The Significance of Monuments* (London, 1998); H. Williams, 'Ancient landscapes and the dead: the reuse of prehistoric and Roman monuments as early Anglo-Saxon burial sites', *Medieval Archaeol.*, 41 (1997), 1–32.

stirrup are seen as later intrusive objects but two larger stirrups with brass overlay, the prick-spur and shears are each seen as consistent with a pattern of late 10th-century equestrian burials in Jutland. If so then this is one of the last furnished warrior burials known from England. The man may have belonged to one of the armies that raided the region in the 990s, or even to Svein Forkbeard's army which attacked Oxford in 1009 and 1013. It may be significant that the burial site is close to St Clement's, the possible site of a Cnut-period Danish 'garrison'.[18]

CHURCHYARD AND GRAVEYARD BURIAL

A second group of burials that has been identified as Scandinavian is represented by objects found in churchyards. Their interpretation is rather problematic. In the first place churchyards are inevitably heavily disturbed and the association between objects and a skeleton is rarely clear. Secondly, there is a tendency to categorize any accompanied grave as pagan and therefore Scandinavian, despite the lack of any documentary sources that would indicate that the Christian church prohibited the practice, and the fact that many of the objects are ostensibly Anglo-Saxon in style.[19] Thirdly, the clear physical juxtaposition between Scandinavian and Christian burials does not in any case necessarily indicate a causal link. The burials may be adjacent, as in the case at Repton where the burials are adjacent to the church, but not in the area of the monastic cemetery, which only later spread over it.[20] Or the burials may pre-date the use of the land by the Christian church, as may be the case at Kildale (North Yorkshire) where seven or eight E.–W. burials accompanied by swords and other weapons were observed when the floor of the church was removed in 1867.[21] Nonetheless, the accepted wisdom is still that 'the Vikings respected Christian burial grounds and used them for the disposal of their own dead'.[22] Thus the dearth of identifiable pagan burials is accounted for by the fact that, whether pagan or Christian, the incoming population rapidly adopted churchyard burial as the norm, with the conclusion that their burials are both rarely observed during archaeological investigation and in any case are indistinguishable from those of the native population.[23]

The fact that a number of weapons have been recovered from Cumbrian churchyards gives some support to the idea that whilst some pagan settlers in this area sought to legitimate claims to land through prominent mound burial, others chose to associate themselves with churchyard sites. It also indicates that there was a greater tendency to maintain the weapon-burial practice in churchyards in an area where

[18] J. Blair and B. E. Crawford, 'A Late-Viking burial at Magdalen Bridge, Oxford?', *Oxoniensia*, 62 (1997), 135–43.

[19] H. Geake, *The Use of Grave-Goods in Conversion-Period England, c. 600–c. 850* (BAR Brit. Ser., 261, Oxford, 1997), assesses the evidence for the continued use of grave-goods throughout the Middle Saxon period and Halsall, op. cit. in note 4, also questions whether accompanied burials post-850 need be pagan.

[20] M. Biddle and B. Kjølbye-Biddle, pers. comm.

[21] F. Elgee, *Early Man in North-East Yorkshire* (Gloucester, 1930), 220, fig. 67.

[22] D. M. Wilson, 'The Vikings' relationship with Christianity in northern England', *J. British Archaeol. Assoc.*, 3rd Series, 30 (1967), 37–46, at 37.

[23] J. Graham-Campbell, 'The Scandinavian Viking-age burials of England—some problems of interpretation', 379–82 in P. Rahtz, T. Dickinson and L. Watts (eds.), *Anglo-Saxon Cemeteries 1979* (BAR Brit. Ser., 82, Oxford, 1980).

weapon burial was more widely practised anyway. A sword, shield boss, iron bar and knife were found in the churchyard at Ormside (Cumbria) in 1898.[24] An elaborate silver bowl had been found at the same site at least 75 years later, and may represent a second grave, or earlier disturbance of an object from the same grave. Swords have also been found in the churchyard at Rampside (Lancashire) and near the vicarage at West Seaton, Workington (Cumbria).[25] The latter was bent and broken as if it had been ritually 'killed'. There is also a record of an iron spearhead being found, about 1800, in the same place as a fine hogback stone in the churchyard of St Peter's at Heysham.[26] When put alongside a female burial with a bone comb from the cemetery beside the adjacent chapel of St Patrick, it is suggestive of the presence of a number of accompanied burials.[27] Similarly, a ring-headed cloak pin recovered from the churchyard at Brigham (Cumbria) may have originated in a burial.[28] These burial rites were also maintained in the larger population centres and in the context of major ecclesiastical sites. A number of early 10th-century burials with grave-goods were revealed by excavations at Carlisle Cathedral in 1988.[29]

Like mound burial, churchyard weapon burial is also found across the Pennines in Yorkshire. As well as the possible Kildale finds mentioned above another male burial was found in Wensley churchyard (North Yorkshire). This grave was also oriented E.–W. and contained a sword, spear and knife, and an iron sickle.[30] Other than at Repton, however, the evidence for accompanied burial in the graveyards of the southern Danelaw is very slight, and there is often nothing distinctively Scandinavian about many of the candidate burials. In Essex, there are two examples of Anglo-Saxon cemeteries in which there are accompanied burials. At Saffron Walden (Essex) one burial in a row of late Saxon graves contained a knife and a necklace with silver pendants that had probably been manufactured in Scandinavia in the 10th century. A copper-alloy strap-end was also found on the site, and may have been disturbed from a second burial.[31] There is a mention of a man being found buried with a horse from the same cemetery. At Waltham Abbey (Essex) a middle Saxon cemetery with un-coffined burials also continued in use in the Viking period.[32] One grave contained a decorated copper-alloy plate of the late 10th or early 11th century.[33] At Sonning

[24] R. S. Ferguson, 'Various finds in Ormside churchyard', *Trans. Cumberland Westmorland Antiq. Archaeol. Soc.*, 1st Series, 15 (1898), 377–80; Edwards, op. cit. in note 8, 17–8.
[25] H. Gaythorpe, 'The Rampside sword; with notes on the church and churchyard of Rampside in Furness', *Trans. Cumberland Westmorland Antiq. Archaeol. Soc.*, 2nd Series, 10 (1910), 298–306; Edwards, op. cit. in note 8, 21–2.
[26] Edwards, op. cit. in note 8, 92.
[27] T. W. Potter and R. D. Andrews, 'Excavation and survey at St Patrick's Chapel and St Peter's Church, Heysham, Lancashire, 1977–8', *Antiq. J.*, 74 (1994), 55–134, at 122–4, 127.
[28] Cowen, 'Viking burials in Cumbria', op. cit. in note 11; Edwards, op. cit. in note 8, 20.
[29] D. Gaimster, S. Margeson and T. Barry, 'Medieval Britain and Ireland in 1988', *Medieval Archaeol.*, 33 (1989), 174.
[30] Lord Bolton, 'A sword of the Viking period and other objects found in Wensley churchyard, Yorkshire', *Proc. Soc. Antiq. London*, 2nd Series, 28 (1916), 228–30; F. and H. W. Elgee, *The Archaeology of Yorkshire* (London, 1933), 214, fig. 38.
[31] V. I. Evison, 'A Viking grave at Sonning, Berks', *Antiq. J.*, 49 (1969), 336–41, 343–4.
[32] P. J. Huggins, 'Excavation on the north side of Sun Street, Waltham Abbey, Essex, 1974–75: Saxon burials, precinct wall and south-east transept', *Essex Archaeol. Hist.*, 19 (1988), 117–53.
[33] P. J. Huggins, 'A note on a Viking-style plate from Waltham Abbey, Essex and its implications for a disputed Late-Viking building', *Archaeol. J.*, 141 (1984), 175–81.

(Reading) the skeletons of two young males were discovered in 1966 during gravel quarrying. They were buried with a sword, a ring-headed pin (perhaps suggesting a northern link), an Anglo-Saxon knife and six arrowheads.[34] At Santon Downham (Norfolk) an iron sword and pair of oval brooches were discovered in 1867.[35] They have been interpreted as representing a double burial of the late 9th century, but the brooches may represent an offering, like those at Claughton Hall. Burial 451 from Middle Harling (Norfolk) contained four knives, a copper alloy buckle with iron plate, an iron buckle, a whetstone, a copper-alloy earscoop, and an iron spur.[36] Finally, there are a seax and knife from Wicken Fen (Cambridgeshire), although the knife is thought to be Anglo-Saxon.[37]

Nonetheless, it is surely the case the Scandinavian settlers were using established cemeteries. Where there has been the opportunity for large-scale churchyard excavation then accompanied burials have sometimes been found, as at Repton, but such cases appear to be unusual. At Wharram Percy (East Riding of Yorkshire), where establishment of the nucleated village may date to the Scandinavian settlement, and Borre-style dress fittings have been recovered from the South Manor site, complete excavation of the church and associated cemetery has yielded no accompanied graves.[38] Radiocarbon dating of the skeletons, however, has identified that a large number date to the founding of the church, around the 10th century.[39]

Instead of seeking to identify Scandinavian burials in England we should be aware that where cultures are in contact new identities and new burial forms may result. One of the most interesting features of late Saxon burial is the sheer diversity of burial rites. At Caister-on-Sea (Norfolk) an extensive cemetery has been excavated containing 12 burials that included clench nails.[40] The cemetery is generally regarded as being middle Saxon, but some of the clench nail burials may be later. Developed Stamford ware was found in two graves, and a silver penny of Ecgbert of Wessex dated c. 830–5 in another. Six of the burials with clench nails were of males; four were of females; one was an adolescent, and the last was of a child, aged 3–4 years. At Caister, in almost all cases the nails were spread over the body; only in one case were the timbers used as a bier. It appears, therefore, that re-used, lapped planks, possibly derived from boats, were being employed as grave-covers or coffin lids. At St Peter's Church, Barton-on-Humber (North Lincolnshire), there were 16 graves with coffins of wood held together by clench nails; again these are seen as being boats, or parts of boats, used as coffins or covers.[41] Parts of old boats might have simply provided handy materials from which to construct coffins and biers in coastal and riverine regions, but

[34] Evison, op. cit. in note 31.
[35] Evison, op. cit. in note 31, 333; Shetelig, op. cit. in note 13, 12–3; S. Margeson, *The Vikings in Norfolk*, (Norwich, 1997), 15.
[36] Margeson, op. cit. in note 35, 16–7.
[37] Evison, op. cit. in note 31, 341.
[38] J. D. Richards, 'The Anglo-Saxon and Anglo-Scandinavian evidence', 195–200 in P. A. Stamper and R. A. Croft, *Wharram: A Study of Settlement on the Yorkshire Wolds, VIII. The South Manor Area Excavations* (York, 2000); A. R. Goodall and C. Paterson, 'Non-ferrous metal objects', 126–32 in Stamper and Croft, ibid.
[39] S. Wrathmell, pers. comm.
[40] K. Rodwell, 'Post-Roman burials', 245–55 in M. J. Darling and D. Gurney (eds.) *Caister-on-Sea: Excavations by Charles Green 1951–55* (East Anglian Archaeol., 60, Gressenhall, 1993).
[41] W. Rodwell and K. Rodwell, 'St Peter's Church, Barton-on-Humber: excavation and structural study, 1978–81', *Antiq. J.*, 62 (1982), 283–315, at 291.

this is really too mundane an explanation. Given the Scandinavian tradition of ship burial it is possible that the symbolism of the boats' timbers was significant, and that even those burials without grave-goods may be Scandinavian settlers, who may have accepted a Christian-style burial, but retained at least one element of their own customs. Similarly, at Thorpe-by-Norwich (Norfolk) at least two rows of clench nails were discovered with a burial beneath the former church.[42] A Viking-age silver pin was also found, although apparently not with the burial. At Heath Wood, I have suggested that some of the nails found in earlier excavations might also have derived from ship's planking.[43]

In York, capital of a Viking kingdom, many years of excavation have produced less than half-a-dozen burials that have been identified as Scandinavians. Four skeletons were found immediately to the North of the present church of St Mary Bishophill Junior.[44] The first was of an adult male with a St Peter's penny of *c.* 905–15 among his finger bones, a schist whetstone and a copper alloy buckle plate. The second, of indeterminate sex, had a silver arm ring on the upper left arm. Two young females were buried with them on the same alignment, but these were unaccompanied by grave-goods. At the neighbouring church of St Mary Bishophill Senior there was a further possible Scandinavian grave with a 10th-century strap-end and a piece of Scandinavian silver appliqué ornament has been identified from the same site, probably from another burial.[45]

On the other hand, a wide variety of burial rites has been identified in excavations of Viking Age deposits under the Minster.[46] A cemetery was established on the site of the Roman basilica, beneath the south transept of the present Minster, in the early 9th century. Its limits were apparently defined by the bases of the outer walls of the old Roman headquarters building, and a Roman road that continued in use as a routeway. The Anglo-Saxon church probably lay to the South-West. Over 100 burials have been excavated, with roughly equal numbers of males and females. Less than 10 per cent of the burials were in coffins. One was in a lidded stone coffin with a recess for the head; up to six may have been in wooden coffins constructed of planks, and four were buried in wooden domestic storage chests, comprising one adult female, two adult males, one with a coin of 841–8, and an adolescent with traces of gold thread from a fine costume. There were also seven cist-type graves, including the use of pillow stones, and one corpse laid on a bed of mortar. Two of the bodies appear to have been placed upon wooden biers, rather than in coffins. The first was an adult male lying between two rows of clench nails that held together the oak planks of a wool-caulked clinker construction. Pillow stones had been positioned to support the head. This grave was also exceptional in that it was aligned E.–W., unlike the others which followed the alignment of the Roman building. The second body laid on a bier was a child, aged

[42] Rodwell, op. cit. in note 40, 254.
[43] J. D. Richards with M. Jecock, L. Richmond and C. Tuck, 'The Viking barrow cemetery at Heath Wood, Ingleby, Derbyshire', *Medieval Archaeol.*, 39 (1995), 51–70.
[44] L. P. Wenham, R. A. Hall, C. M. Briden and D. A. Stocker, *St Mary Bishophill Junior and St Mary Castlegate* (The Archaeology of York, 8/2, London, 1987).
[45] R. A. Hall, 'A silver appliqué from St Mary Bishophill Senior, York', *Yorkshire Archaeol. J.*, 70 (1998), 61–6.
[46] B. Kjølbye-Biddle, 'Iron-bound coffins and coffin-fittings from the pre-Norman cemetery', 489–521 in D. Phillips and B. Heywood, *Excavations at York Minster, Vol. I*, ed. M. O. H. Carver (London, 1995).

4–6. The rest of the York burials were simply placed in holes in the grounds, generally in oval-shaped cuts, without coffins or shrouds.

Twelve of the York burials were, however, placed on a bed of charcoal. They included both coffined and un-coffined burials. In just one case the charcoal had been laid over the body; otherwise the body was laid on the charcoal. These were not the latest burials and this must be seen as a particular custom reserved for a subset of burials. Charcoal burials are known from other cathedral cemeteries, including Exeter, Hereford, Oxford and Worcester, and appear to range in date from the 9th to the 12th centuries. Charcoal may have served the practical function of soaking up fluids from a decaying corpse and avoiding unpleasant smells, but it seems to have been reserved for those of special status; perhaps it was thought to preserve the body from corruption. At Hereford all the burials inside the church were given a charcoal lining.[47]

Twelve of the York Minster burials were marked by recumbent carved stone slabs. A few had separate head- and/or foot-stones, including cut-down shafts, or fragments of earlier recumbent slabs. Most had a single recumbent slab decorated on the top only, including two of hogback form. Hogbacks are a particularly distinctive form of Anglo-Scandinavian sculpture that are known fairly widely throughout the British Isles, but which are concentrated in the Viking kingdom of York and may indeed be partially derived from the Minster burial forms. Other than at York Minster none has ever been found in direct association with a burial but they are widely believed to have functioned as burial markers.[48] Hogbacks are recumbent stone monuments, generally about 1.5 m (5 ft) in length. They are basically the shape of a bow-sided building with a ridged roof and curved side walls and are often decorated with architectural features such as shingle roofs, and stylized wattle walls. Over 50 hogbacks are also decorated with end-beasts. These are generally bear-like creatures, although wolves or dogs are also known; sometimes they are shown with two legs, sometimes with four; many are clearly muzzled. The distribution of hogbacks is mainly restricted to northern England and central Scotland, with a few outliers. They are especially concentrated in North Yorkshire and Cumbria, with none in the Isle of Man, and only single examples in Wales and Ireland. There are no hogbacks in the Danelaw areas of Lincolnshire and East Anglia and their distribution appears to be restricted to those areas that also have Hiberno-Norse and Norse place-names. Thus hogbacks appear to have developed in areas settled by the Hiberno-Norse. It is likely that hogbacks are a 10th-century phenomenon; Jim Lang suggested that most were carved within a 50-year period of 920–70.[49] Their origin has been much-debated as they have no clear ancestry, either in Britain or Scandinavia. Lang saw elements of the Irish house shrine; Stocker has suggested that the bear, possibly holding the monument and licking it as a newborn cub, may be a Christian symbol of re-birth.[50] Whatever their meaning, in considering Viking burials we must include the hogbacks, and indeed

[47] R. Shoesmith, *Hereford City Excavations, Vol 1: Excavations at Castle Green* (CBA Res. Rep., 36, London, 1980).
[48] The association of the Heysham hogback with the recovery of a spear and possibly sword has also been advanced as support for their function as burial markers: see Graham-Campbell, op. cit. in note 23.
[49] J. Lang, 'The hogback: a Viking colonial monument', *Anglo-Saxon Stud. Archaeol. Hist.*, 3 (1984), 83–176.
[50] D. Stocker, 'Monuments and merchants: irregularities in the distribution of stone sculpture in Lincolnshire and Yorkshire in the tenth century', 179–212 in Hadley and Richards, op. cit. in note 3.

the corpus of stone crosses erected over elite burials; both represent the invention of new forms of grave marker which is neither Anglo-Saxon nor Scandinavian, but instead reflects a new cultural identity, properly called Anglo-Scandinavian. Other new burial forms, such as the charcoal burial rite, or chest plank burials, should also be seen in the light of the creation of new identities.

THE EXCEPTION THAT PROVES THE RULE: REPTON AND INGLEBY

So far I have demonstrated that Scandinavian-style burials are rare in England; instead we have evidence for assimilation and the creation of new social identities expressed through new burial types. However, there are two exceptions in the East Midlands: the cemeteries at Repton and Heath Wood, Ingleby. At these two sites, only 4 km apart, there is a cremation cemetery of up to 60 mounds, an ossuary containing the partial remains of at least 249 individuals, and a number of overtly pagan inhumations buried adjacent to a Christian cemetery. In order to make sense of them it is necessary to examine the circumstances that make them exceptions, and thereby hopefully to throw more light on why such sites are not more common. It is suggested that the primary reason was the key role played by this area in the Scandinavian conquest of England. In Scandinavia and in Scandinavian colonies such as the Isle of Man we can see the use of a number of burial strategies to legitimate authority, including re-use and control of ancestral burial sites, prominent mound burial, cenotaph memorials, human and animal sacrifice, and the evocation of that most powerful Viking symbol, the ship, either though burial of a complete vessel, or the use of stone settings.[51] These are each themes that I propose were developed at Repton and Ingleby in the war against Mercia.

From A.D. 865 England was subject to escalating Viking raids by a highly mobile force led by Ivar the Boneless and his brother Halfdan. It is difficult to get a clear understanding of the size of this army, beyond the fact that the Anglo-Saxon Chroniclers considered it to be 'Great' (*micel*), and the fact that it regularly over-wintered in England. On the strength of its coherence over several years and on the basis of its recorded achievements, it has been suggested that it must have numbered some two to three thousand. After the conquest of Northumbria in 866, and East Anglia in 869, Alfred Smyth has suggested that the Great Army was reinforced by what the Anglo-Saxon Chronicle describes as the Summer Army, before it forced Wessex to make peace in 871.[52] The combined force was subsequently active in various parts of the extended kingdom of Mercia.

The Anglo-Saxon Chronicle records that in A.D. 873–4 the Viking Army went to Repton, near Derby, and 'took winter quarters there'. It was from this base that the

[51] E. Roesdahl, 'Prestige, display and monuments in Viking Age Scandinavia', 17–25 in H. Galieni (ed), *Les Mondes Normands (VIIIe–XIIe s.)* (Caen, 1989); E. Roesdahl, 'Landscape sculpture in Viking Age Denmark', *Aarhus Geoscience*, 7 (1997), 147–55; G. Bersu and D. M. Wilson, *Three Viking Graves in the Isle of Man* (London, 1966); J. D. Richards, 'Boundaries and cult centres: Viking burial in Derbyshire', forthcoming in R. A. Hall, J. Graham-Campbell, J. Jesch and D. Parsons (eds.), *Vikings and the Danelaw: Proceedings of the Thirteenth Viking Congress.*
[52] A. Smyth, *Scandinavian Kings in the British Isles 850–880* (Oxford, 1977), 240–2; also see S. Keynes, 'The Vikings in England, c.790–1016', 48–82 in P. Sawyer (ed.), *The Oxford Illustrated History of the Vikings* (Oxford, 1997), at pp. 54–5.

Vikings drove the Mercian king Burghred into exile in Rome, planting a puppet king Ceolwulf in his place. The significance of the choice of Repton is that this was probably a royal burial site, deep within the Mercian kingdom.[53] Its position on the River Trent would, moreover, make it a natural boundary. On a map of Scandinavian-type place-names Repton sits just on the frontier zone, between the area that was to follow Danish law and that which was to be part of Ælfred's Wessex.[54]

Repton appears to have been an important Anglo-Saxon royal and ecclesiastical centre from at least the 7th century. Excavations have revealed an early stone church with a sunken baptistry. This later became a crypt in which twisted columns evoke St Peter's grave in Rome. In the 8th century a two-celled sunken stone structure was built west of the church and appears to have functioned as a mausoleum of the royal Mercian house.[55]

The church sits on the edge of a cliff that marks the edge of the flood plain of the River Trent. In the 9th century it is likely that the course of the Trent would have taken it directly under the cliff. In A.D. 873 the Viking Army arrived at Repton. Excavations by Martin and Birthe Biddle have revealed that during the 9th century a massive D-shaped enclosure was constructed, utilising the Trent cliff as its long side. The enclosure comprised a substantial bank and V-shaped ditch, some 4 m deep.[56] The church tower was itself incorporated into the Vikings' defensive circuit and appears to have been used as a gatehouse, although the re-use of this fine Mercian stone structure was probably as much symbolic as it was functional. The royal mausoleum remained outside the defended enclosure although the Vikings made a number of burials around the E. end of the church, but away from the area of Christian burials.[57]

The earliest grave was of a man aged at least 35–40, who had been killed by a massive cut to the top of his left leg. He wore a necklace of two glass beads and a silver Thor's hammer amulet. By his side was a sword in a leather-bound wooden scabbard with a fleece lining, a folding knife, and a key. A wild boar's tusk and a jackdaw bone had been carefully placed between his thighs; the former may be seen as symbolically replacing that which had been cut off by the sword blow. A substantial post-hole at the eastern end of the grave suggests that the burial was marked by a wooden post. Other graves were accompanied by knives and weapons; it is likely that an axe found in the graveyard in 1922 also came from a grave. One burial was accompanied by five silver pennies and a gold finger ring, lying together beside the skull. The coins suggest a burial date in the 870s; it is likely that these were further burials of Viking warriors of the 'Great Army' which wintered at Repton in 873–4.[58]

It is the fate of the mausoleum, however, that has attracted most interest. The structure was first noted in 1726 when Dr Simon Degge recorded in his journal a visit to Repton and the story told to him by a labourer, Thomas Walker, aged 88. About 40 years earlier Walker had been clearing some ground when:

[53] P. Stafford, *The East Midlands in the Early Middle Ages* (Leicester, 1985), 107.
[54] Richards, op. cit. in note 1, fig. 17.
[55] M. Biddle and B. Kjølbye-Biddle, 'Repton and the Vikings', *Antiquity*, 66, (1992) 36–51, at p. 42.
[56] Biddle and Kjølbye-Biddle op. cit. in note 55, 40.
[57] Biddle and Kjølbye-Biddle, op. cit. in note 55, 40–2.
[58] Biddle and Kjølbye-Biddle, op. cit. in note 55, 48–50.

near the surface he met with an old Stone Wall, when clearing farther he found it to be a square Enclosure of Fifteen Foot . . . In this he found a Stone Coffin, and with Difficulty removing the Cover, saw a Skeleton of a Humane Body Nine Foot long, and round it lay One Hundred Humane Skeletons, with their Feet pointing to the Stone Coffin . . .[59]

Excavation by the Biddles in a mound in the vicarage garden at Repton has appeared to confirm this story and revealed that in fact the eastern compartment of the mausoleum had been re-used as a charnel house, after it had been levelled and a layer of clean sand deposited. The central burial did not survive, but the deposit contained many objects that may originally have accompanied it, including a sword and axe, fragments of gold and silver objects and a small group of coins deposited some time after A.D. 871. Analysis of the main burial deposit shows that 80 per cent were robust males in the age-range 15–45.[60]

There have been many interpretations of the identity of these skeletons, including that they are the slaughtered dead of the Anglo-Saxon monastery, a defeated Anglo-Saxon army, or the remains of the Viking Great Army, decimated over a harsh winter by starvation and influenza.[61] Analysis of the skeletal remains, however, has indicated that although the remains of at least 249 individuals are present very few of them are represented by complete skeletons. This is a very mixed collection of bones gathered together for reburial in a charnel house from many primary graves. One possibility might be that these are burials disturbed from the monastic churchyard when the great V-shaped ditch was dug through it. Another interpretation is that this is a war grave of the remains of warriors gathered together for communal burial because the bodies could not rest safely where they had been slain. The emphasis is certainly on a communal monument, as in the war cemeteries of more recent conflicts. In any case the choice of burial site cannot have been coincidental. By re-using the site of a Mercian royal tomb the Great Army were declaring their victory, and the legitimization of their control by invoking an indigenous ancestral burial place. The stone kerb and its cairn are a construct of the Scandinavian world; they have no Anglo-Saxon parallels. The mound was constructed on the crest of the hill; it would have been visible from the Trent, itself an important political boundary.

Radiocarbon dating of the bones, undertaken in the course of a television documentary about the site, also emphasizes the mixed nature of the bone assemblage. Whilst many of the dates are indeed consistent with burial in the late 9th century there is a second cluster of dates, much earlier.[62] It is quite feasible that these may be remnants of the original occupants of the mausoleum, or of the monastic cemetery. If this is the case, then what could be a more potent symbol of conquest and continuity? The bones of the ancestral leaders of Mercia, disturbed and mingled with those of their conquerors. The burial deposit bears witness to an overt act of desecration and sublimation.

---

[59] S. Degge, 'An account of an humane skeleton of an extraordinary size, found in a repository at Repton in Derby-shire'. *Philosophical Trans.*, 35 (1727–8), 363–5, quoted in M. Biddle, B. Kjolbye-Biddle, J. P. Northover, and H. Pagan, 'A parcel of pennies from a mass-burial associated with the Viking wintering at Repton in 873–4', 111–22 in M. A. S. Blackburn (ed.), *Anglo-Saxon Monetary History* (Leicester, 1986), at p. 112.

[60] Biddle and Kjolbye-Biddle, op. cit. in note 55, 45.

[61] Ibid.; BBC, *Evidence of Vikings*, BBC2 Timewatch, first broadcast 8 October 1995.

[62] BBC, op. cit. in note 61.

That is not the end of the story however, for nearby there is a second Viking cemetery at Heath Wood, Ingleby, some 4 km SE. of Repton. Heath Wood is the only known Scandinavian cremation cemetery in England. The site occupies rising ground on the south side of the Trent valley and today lies at the centre of a block of woodland known as Heath Wood, but in earlier times would have commanded impressive views northwards. Although not so immediately apparent on the skyline without its present spire, the Anglo-Saxon church at Repton would have been visible from the site. The cemetery originally comprised some 59 barrows. In total 20, or approximately one-third, of the mounds have been examined by excavation on three separate occasions.[63] In *Ten Years' Diggings* Thomas Bateman records that he opened five on 22 May 1855, and found that each covered the site of a funeral pyre, upon which calcined human bones remained as they had been left by fire.[64]

We have few details of Bateman's excavation but work in the 1940s and 50s confirmed the presence of cremation hearths, but also indicated that some of the mounds were cenotaphs.[65] Two mutilated swords were recovered, as well as the sacrificial remains of cremated animals, including ox, horse, sheep, pig and dog. Excavation of Mounds 50 and 56 in 1998–2000 has further demonstrated the presence both of human cremation and animal sacrifice, but has also thrown doubt on the existence of empty cenotaph mounds. Rather than the burial being represented by an *in situ* cremation deposit, Mound 56 contained a small off-centre deposit of burnt human bone, on the edge of the barrow, associated with a ring-headed pin. Thus although this was clearly a human burial the traces were so ephemeral they could easily have been missed in the earlier investigations. Mound 50 contained a large spread of charcoal and burnt bone at the base of the barrow, more typical of those burials previously reported. However, excavation has also demonstrated the deliberate dumping of a layer of clean sand, some 0.1 m thick, under the cremation deposit, paralleling the sand layer dumped beneath the Repton charnel deposit. The examination of the relationship of a number of mounds in the main cluster has also shown that these mounds were constructed on the same surface and that they are broadly contemporary. It is proposed that the cemetery was in use for a relatively brief period of time, and certainly no more than 20–30 years. Although cremation is rare in England there are cremation barrow cemeteries from northern Jutland and from Sweden.[66] I have suggested that the presence of iron nails might also represent fragments of ships planking used as biers, as possibly the case with Viking burials excavated under York Minster, and that these may represent a token form of ship burial.[67] The nails from some of the cremations are quite small and much more likely to be derived from fastenings such as shields. There are some nails however, such as

---

[63] Richards *et al.*, op. cit in note 43.

[64] T. Bateman, *Ten years' Diggings in Celtic and Saxon Grave Hills, in the Counties of Derby, Stafford, and York, from 1848 to 1858* (London, 1861), 92.

[65] C. Clarke, and W. Fraser, 1946, 'Excavation of pagan burial mounds: Ingleby, Derbyshire', *Derbyshire Archaeol. J.*, 66 (1946), 1–23; C. Clarke, W. Fraser and F. W. Munslow, 'Excavation of pagan burial mounds at Ingleby. Second report', *Derbyshire Archaeol. J.*, 69 (1949), 78–81; M. Posnansky, 'The pagan-Danish barrow cemetery at Heath Wood, Ingleby', *Derbyshire Archaeol. J.*, 76 (1956), 40–56.

[66] T. Ramskou, 'Viking-age cremation graves in Denmark. A survey', *Acta Archaeol.*, 21 (1950), 137–82; Anne-Sofie Graslund, pers. comm.

[67] Richards *et al.*, op. cit. in note 43, 62–5.

those from Mound 5 for example, which are of the clench-nail variety and may have been derived from sections of ship's planking. The 1950s excavation also revealed a section of a V-shaped ditch, similar to that examined as part of the Repton fortification.[68] This was rediscovered in 1998–2000, but was seen to be much smaller than that at Repton, and dating evidence now recovered suggests that it is a prehistoric field or territorial boundary rather than a later defensive feature.

A very definite commitment to paganism is demonstrated at Heath Wood by the performance of cremation rites and animal sacrifice in conjunction with mound burial and the laying out of stone kerbs. Rather than peaceful, permanent, stable settlement the barrow cemetery at Heath Wood seems to reflect instability and insecurity of some sort. In this way, the Heath Wood burials might represent a deliberate and physically imposing allusion to the pagan homeland of those who produced them: a statement of religious, political and military affiliation in unfamiliar and inhospitable surroundings. Animal sacrifice, cremation and mound burial convey a message of *Vikingness* as strong as any communication of ideological beliefs.

Whilst Repton and Heath Wood can therefore both be seen as active political statements, the relationship between them is likely to remain unclear for some time. It is intrinsically likely, nevertheless, that the populations buried at Heath Wood and Repton were somehow linked. The implementation of very similar techniques in the raising of grave mounds, the dumping of layers of sand, and the laying out of stone-settings, as well as geographical proximity, reinforce the similarities between the sites.

On the other hand, there are also clear differences: cremation versus inhumation; one in the middle of a Mercian royal and ecclesiastical complex; the other on an isolated hilltop. One explanation might be that the two cemeteries represent a division in the Viking camp, the first group preferring legitimation through association with the Mercian site; the other preferring traditional pagan values.

It might be significant that from Repton the army split into two bands, perhaps reflecting the two forces that had been combined. This was not simply spontaneous fragmentation because of numbers but the result of a specific agreement between Halfdan and Guthrum.[69] Halfdan's army was tired of war and returned to Northumbria where in A.D. 876 he and his men 'shared out the land of the Northumbrians, and they proceeded to plough and support themselves'. Guthrum, on the other hand, left Repton in A.D. 874 and marched on East Anglia and then Wessex.[70]

In Repton and its environs we can therefore witness the playing out of a major political drama in the 870s. This war-torn frontier zone acted as a stage first for the demonstration of the power of the Great Army, but then for an unfolding drama of dissent within its ranks. With its tradition of royal Mercian patronage and its prestige as a focus of pilgrimage, Repton would have provided the perfect location for a demonstration of new spiritual convictions combined with political and military subjugation. The Mercian landscape and even the royal church and mausoleum were appropriated by one section of the Great Army in order to legitimate their political

[68] Posnansky, op. cit. in note 65, 48–9.
[69] Smyth, op. cit. in note 52, 243.
[70] Ibid., 243–4.

control. However, on a side stage 4 km away a more traditional ideology of cremation, ship burial and sacrifice was being practised on the hilltop at Heath Wood.

SUMMARY

In summary, I have argued that the absence of Scandinavian burials in England is not a problem. It is not the result of recovery factors and archaeologists having missed them. Rather the issue needs to be problematized, borrowing from approaches now current for the early Anglo-Saxon period. We need to consider that the settlers may have conducted a variety of types of burial practice and commemoration of the dead. We need to look, for example, at burial forms such as charcoal and pillow stones such as those found at York Minster. We need to consider the creation of an Anglo-Scandinavian identity manifested through hogback tombs. We need to consider the nature of very special circumstances, such as Repton and Heath Wood, Ingleby, where Viking armies used burial as a propaganda weapon. The apparent lack of Scandinavian burials needs to be seen as part of an active process, leading sometimes to integration and sometimes to legitimation.

ACKNOWLEDGEMENTS

The current fieldwork at Heath Wood, reported in this paper, was undertaken with Scheduled Monument Consent from English Heritage, and the permission of the Church Commissioners and the Forestry Agency. It was sponsored by the Society of Antiquaries of London and the Department of Archaeology, University of York. The support of Repton School Enterprises is also gratefully acknowledged. The fieldwork was co-directed by the author and Marcus Jecock, of English Heritage. I am also pleased to acknowledge the encouragement of Martin Biddle and Birthe Kjølbye-Biddle, Richard Hall and James Graham Campbell for the current fieldwork at Heath Wood.

Lesley Abrams and Dawn Hadley each provided helpful comment on this paper and stimulating discussion; the remaining flaws are, of course, my own.

Burials, Boundaries and Charters in Anglo-Saxon England: A Reassessment

By ANDREW REYNOLDS

THE DEVELOPMENT OF A CONCEPT

Perhaps the earliest reference to an Anglo-Saxon burial site on a boundary was made by S. Shaw in his compendious *History and Antiquities of Staffordshire* published in two volumes in 1798 and 1801.[1] The context for Shaw's observation was a consideration of a charter of 1008 granting land at Rolleston in the county that describes '*þer ða þoefes licgan*' (where the thieves lie) as one of the boundary marks of the estate.[2] Later, Charles Perceval's communication of the Anglo-Saxon bounds of an estate at Fenstanton (Cambridgeshire) to the Society of Antiquaries of London in 1865, commented on the shire boundary location of the '*cwealmstow*', or 'killing place' named as a boundary mark.[3] Perceval also quoted an earlier comment by J. M. Kemble on the Fenstanton *cwealmstow*, noting how the place of execution was 'properly in the mark'.[4]

Subsequent to these observations, little attempt has been made to understand the relationship between boundary burial sites, both documented and excavated, and boundary hierarchies. Clearly, at least by the 10th century, boundaries can be ranked from simple enclosures around individual homesteads, to field and tithing boundaries, and then on up to estate, hundred and shire boundaries, with the physical limits of kingdoms at the very top of the scale.[5] Despite the fact that references to burial sites were known to exist in the corpus of charter bounds, few attempts have been made to explore the potential of such material since Kemble's list of 'heathen burials' and other similarly documented burial sites was published in 1857.[6]

Desmond Bonney's work on early Anglo-Saxon burials in relation to parish boundaries in Wiltshire provided the first explicit attempt to suggest that pagan communities buried their dead at the limits of their estates. Bonney's figure of 28.6 per cent of 'pagan' Anglo-Saxon burials on boundaries in Wiltshire is rather higher than that from the subsequent national analysis undertaken by Ann Goodier which provided a figure of 17.9 per cent, but Bonney's argument lay in the view that the existence of pagan burials on the boundaries of Anglo-Saxon estates and medieval parishes could

---

[1] S. Shaw, *The History and Antiquities of Staffordshire* (London, 1798–1801), Vol. 1, 28.
[2] P. H. Sawyer, *Anglo-Saxon Charters: An Annotated List and Bibliography* (London, 1968), no. 920.
[3] Ibid., no. 1562; C. S. Perceval, 'Remarks on an unpublished portion of a charter of King Ethelred, A.D. 1012 from the Textus Roffensis', *Proc. Soc. Antiq.*, (2nd series), 3 (1865), 47–50.
[4] J. M. Kemble, *The Saxons in England* (London, 1849), 47.
[5] A. Reynolds, *Later Anglo-Saxon England: Life and Landscape* (Stroud and Charleston SC, 1999), 65–110.
[6] J. M. Kemble, 'Notices of heathen interment in the Codex Diplomaticus', *Archaeol. J.*, 14 (1857), 119–39.

only mean that the latter existed by or during the early Anglo-Saxon period.[7] Bonney revisited the topic in a later article, where he incorporated references to 'heathen burial(s)' in the Wiltshire charters into his analysis in order to strengthen his claim.[8] He assumed that 'heathen burial(s)' referred to the memory of pagan Anglo-Saxon burials, a view that has been frequently restated by virtually all other commentators on the term, despite the broad definition of the word 'heathen' itself as 'a person who does not belong to a widely held religion', 'an unenlightened person; a person regarded as lacking culture or moral principles'.[9] In our case, it seems probable that the term refers to the perceived status of the burial site itself, denoting a clear distinction between consecrated and unconsecrated burial grounds, rather than a theological distinction relating to individual burials.

Donald Bullough has noted that 'heathen burials . . . seem to be predominantly barrows', based upon the small handful of *possible* associations between 'heathen burials' and tumuli, although G. B. Grundy was adamant that 'in no traceable instance are they associated with a tumulus of any kind' and the most recent study could only

[7] D. Bonney, 'Pagan Saxon burials and boundaries in Wiltshire', *Wiltshire Archaeol. Nat. Hist. Mag.*, 61 (1966), 25–30; A. Goodier, 'The formation of boundaries in Anglo-Saxon England: a statistical study', *Medieval Archaeol.*, 28 (1984), 1–20.

[8] D. Bonney, 'Early boundaries and estates in southern England', 72–82 in P. H. Sawyer (ed.), *Medieval Settlement: Continuity and Change* (London, 1976).

[9] For example, M. Gelling, *Signposts to the Past* (Chichester, 1988), 157; J. N. L. Myres, *The English Settlements* (Oxford, 1986), 38, n. 2; L. V. Grinsell, 'Barrows in the Anglo-Saxon land charters', *Antiq. J.*, 71 (1991), 51; D. Hooke, *The Landscape of Anglo-Saxon England* (Leicester, 1998), 99. Definition of 'heathen' taken from D. Thompson, *The Concise Oxford Dictionary* (Oxford, 1995), 627. The use of the term in the Anglo-Saxon period appears to have been virtually identical with the modern definition: see for example J. Roberts and C. Kay with L. Grundy, *A Thesaurus of Old English* (London, 1995), Vol. 2, 1041. Dr Audrey Meaney, however, has kindly contributed the following notes based on the linguistic aspects of the term as it appears in the charter bounds (numbers in brackets refer to the Appendix to this paper): 'The references to 'heathen (and other) burial-place(s)' are in stereotyped phrases governed by the prepositions *in* and *oþ*, both meaning 'as far as', *innan* 'into, within', and *wiþ*, 'up to' (in (59)) all of which take the accusative case, and *to*, 'to', *of*, 'from', and *on*, 'within' ((40), (60) and (71)–(74)), which all take the dative case (though in (18) it takes the accusative). *Byr(i)gels* is the usual noun combined with *hæþen*, and is normally masculine (but in (39) used as a neuter noun, and in (69) as a feminine) and is used in both singular and plural. In numbers (31), (41) and (62), the much more common feminine noun *byrgen*, also meaning 'burial-place' is used instead of *byrgels*. Evidently, then, there is some difference in usage between these two nouns, which research might establish. If the meaning of the phrase had been 'burial(s) or 'burial-place(s) of heathens', a genitive of the noun *hæþena* (masc) would have been used in the singular (*hæþenan*) or plural (*hæþenra*). But in 'heathen burial-place', *hæþen* is an always an adjective modifying the nouns, *byr(i)gels*, *byrgen* or *beorg*; its form is governed not only by its case and number, but also by the presence or absence of the definite article, by the gender of the noun modified, and by the local and contemporary forms of the language. The meaning of *hæþen* in this phrase is problematic. It is clear from the uses cited in the Venezky *Concordance* (see note 62 below) that when applied to humans *hæþen* always means 'heathen, pagan', in the religious sense, corresponding to late Latin *gentilis*, 'not Christian or Jewish'. It is not used in a general sense of 'barbarian' ((*pace* Roberts, note 43 below), except, perhaps, in the sense that barbarians *were* heathen, and heathens were barbarian) or for bad Christians, who may, however, be *compared* to heathens. The only adult heathens who were about in late Anglo-Saxon England were Vikings (or perhaps their unconverted descendants) who were in the north and east, not in the areas covered by the charter bounds. However, unbaptised children were regarded as heathen, and I think this gives a clue as to the meaning of *hæþen* in the phrase *se hæþena byrgels*. The burial-place was 'heathen' because it was unconsecrated, outside the burial-ground sanctified by being associated with the church. As such, it probably usually referred to places where criminals and other deviants such as suspected witches were buried, but I don't think one could definitively rule out its usage for pre-Christian burials, whether prehistoric, Roman or pagan English, if the later Anglo-Saxons had disturbed such burials — or even if they had assumed that a mound contained burials'.

identify three such possibilities.[10] More outlandish explanations have been offered. H. C. Brentnall suggested that a tradition, recorded at least by the 18th century, of 'heathen burials' in two fields at Seagry (Wiltshire) was best explained in relation to finds of prehistoric material, whereas T. R. Thompson proposed that the 'heathen burials' in an undated set of bounds for Little Hinton (Wiltshire) recorded the location of a fight.[11]

Fred Aldsworth, however, made a significant step forward in his discussion of the important early Anglo-Saxon cemetery at Droxford (Hampshire), published in 1979.[12] Aldsworth concluded by suggesting that 'heathen burial' sites referred to graves or cemeteries for capital offenders and others prohibited from Christian burial; the implications of this interpretation are explored further below.

Besides references to 'heathen burials', which are by far the most common burial sites encountered in the bounds, there is a small group of sites where the interment of a named individual is recorded and yet fewer instances of boundary marks termed simply 'burials'. Both of these latter categories of burial sites have eluded satisfactory explanation and Della Hooke has noted the need for a comprehensive study.[13] Within the series of boundary clauses there are references to places of judicial execution, described using a range of terms, usually descriptions of gallows. This latter material, while broadly relevant, will be dealt with elsewhere, partly due to limitations of space, but largely owing to the desire to deal only with boundary marks that refer explicitly to burials.

A further category of material (barrows) is left out of this study, partly because other scholars are currently working on it and partly because the only detailed analysis yet undertaken indicates that this material is not directly related to our discussion.[14] Bonney's various analyses, however, included secondary inhumations in barrows, a common form of inhumation in 7th-century Wessex and elsewhere.[15]

It is well known that Old English boundary clauses commonly refer to barrows denoted with personal names. Burial features recorded in the charter bounds, however, are, of course, not necessarily the same thing as places of burial contemporary with the documents that record them. Furthermore, Hooke has shown that the two commonest place-name elements used to signify a burial mound (*beorg* and *hlæw*) could in fact be applied to a range of landscape features ranging from minor barrows to natural hills or even mountains.[16] Kemble was the first to suggest that barrows with OE personal names attached to them were not long-remembered names made with reference to the

[10] G. B. Grundy, *Saxon Oxfordshire Charters and Ancient Highways* (Oxfordshire Record Series, 15, Oxford, 1933), 49; Grinsell, op. cit. in note 9, 51.

[11] H. C. Brentnall, 'Heathen burials', *Wiltshire Archaeol. Nat. Hist. Mag.*, 53 (1950), 373–4; T. R. Thompson, 'The early bounds of Wanborough and Little Hinton: an exercise in topography', *Wiltshire Archaeol. Nat. Hist. Mag.*, 57 (1959), 203–11.

[12] F. G. Aldsworth, 'Droxford Anglo-Saxon cemetery, Soberton, Hampshire', *Proc. Hampshire Field Club Archaeol. Soc.*, 35 (1979), 93–182, at 175–9.

[13] D. Hooke, 'Burial features in West Midlands charters', *J. Eng. Place-Name Soc.*, 13 (1981), 1–40, at 29.

[14] Hooke, op. cit. in note 13.

[15] For an insightful criticism of Bonney's data, see M. Welch, 'Rural settlement patterns in the Early and Middle Anglo-Saxon periods', *Landscape Hist.*, 7 (1985), 13–25. For a discussion and analysis of secondary barrow burial, see H. Williams, 'Ancient landscapes and the dead: the reuse of prehistoric and Roman monuments as early Anglo-Saxon burial sites', *Medieval Archaeol.*, 41 (1997), 1–32.

[16] Hooke, op. cit. in note 13, 2.

individual interred within, but rather that they record the names of the owners of
estates whose bounds incorporated the relevant feature.[17] This contention is borne out
in particular in the case of the Swallowcliffe Down (Wiltshire) high-status burial. The
Early Bronze-age barrow into which the interment was made is arguably recorded in
a set of bounds for Swallowcliffe dated 940, where the mound is referred to as *Posses
hlaew*.[18] As George Speake has noted, incorporating comments made by John Dodgson,
Poss is a male name whereas the Anglo-Saxon secondary burial was that of a woman
aged between about 18 and 24.[19] Elsewhere, Martin Welch has strongly argued that
the incorporation of barrows into estate boundaries merely reflects the practicalities of
land surveying in the later Anglo-Saxon period.[20] Such a pragmatic interpretation
seems best suited to the charter evidence, although a secondary interment in a Bronze-
age barrow in the churchyard at Ogbourne St Andrew (Wiltshire) can be dated to the
late 9th or 10th century on the basis of iron coffin fittings found with the burial.[21]
Furthermore, there is no observable correspondence between the explicitly described
'burials' of various types recorded in the bounds and barrows. This factor provides
further support for the view that barrows with associated personal names refer to
ownership and delineation of land and not to individual interments remembered in
local nomenclature.

   Overall, there has been no comprehensive attempt to explore the context and
meaning of the range of burial sites explicitly referenced in the charter bounds. This
paper attempts to define and interpret the available evidence and to place it within the
context of what is known from the burial archaeology of the period with reference to
further documentary sources including the laws.

THE NATURE OF THE CHARTER MATERIAL

   Anglo-Saxon charter bounds provide a dated corpus of references to burial sites,
many of which are frequently locatable in the modern landscape with varying degrees
of accuracy and confidence. Prior to the present writer's work much of the burial data
contained in boundary clauses remained either untapped, or continually related to the
pre-Christian scene. Little allowance was made for the possibility that burial sites
incorporated into boundary clauses could in fact be related to contemporary practice
rather than representing a distant memory of local toponyms orally transmitted for
centuries only to be preserved by accident by late Anglo-Saxon land surveyors. Now
that the fragmentation of large estates, especially during the 10th century, is accepted
as an historical process, the evidence from charter bounds can be reviewed afresh.

   The difficulties of working with Anglo-Saxon charters are manifold. The surviving
corpus reveals strong regional and chronological trends, but rather than viewing these
aspects as a negative feature, they probably have more to say about regional trends in
landscape history. The majority of charters with bounds are concentrated in southern

[17] Kemble, op. cit. in note 6, 128.
[18] Sawyer, op. cit. in note 2, no. 468.
[19] G. Speake, *A Saxon Bed Burial on Swallowcliffe Down* (English Heritage Archaeol. Rep. 10, London, 1989), 118–23.
[20] Welch, op. cit. in note 15, at 19 and 21.
[21] S. Semple, pers. comm.

and western England, whilst the most intense period of granting land by charter is observed during the middle decades of the 10th century.[22] Additional material has undoubtedly been lost by various means, although the general chronological picture of intensification in the granting of land is widely accepted.

The dating of individual documents is a frequently contentious issue. The production of forgeries, in order to lay false claim to a title, is known, but even largely authentic grants may have later material interpolated into them by copyists. For our purposes, however, the ground is rather safer, for grants rather than their boundary clauses were more likely to suffer at the hands of forgers.[23] Prior to the later 9th century, contemporary boundary clauses were generally written in Latin, whereas later bounds are normally in the vernacular, Old English. This latter aspect allows for the identification of later boundary clauses attached to early charters. Unless a clear objection is apparent, the dating of the bounds considered below follows that of the associated charter, although certain sets of bounds exist in isolation and therefore lack a precise date. Further comments on the authenticity of individual charters can be found in Sawyer's 1968 handlist.

THE CHARTER EVIDENCE: EXAMPLES AND TYPES

Burial sites apparently in use contemporaneously with the bounds that record them can be divided into three categories. The most straightforward category is the 'heathen burials'. The terminology applied to burial sites in this group, it is argued, is unambiguous and appropriately describes a widespread cemetery type specifically for the burial of social outcasts, principally execution victims. The second category comprises individual named burials; the third, probably Christian field cemeteries. The total number of references to burial sites in boundary clauses is 74, which represents 60 individual sites after duplication in successive bounds and those of adjoining estates are accounted for. This is an impressive total, especially when compared to the number of excavated burial sites of the later Anglo-Saxon period. References to burial sites in the appended handlist are given in brackets.

HEATHEN BURIALS

Altogether, there are a total of 51 references in boundary clauses to 'heathen burials', either in the singular or plural, which amount to 39 individual sites, with a strong concentration in central southern England (Fig. 1). It is argued that these sites purport to describe places of execution and burial of executed offenders and other social outcasts. Patrick Wormald, who has analysed the dating of charters where boundary clauses record 'heathen burials', has noted that the earliest reliable example is dated 903 (5).[24] The absence of concrete instances before this date further increases the likelihood of a contemporary late Anglo-Saxon context for these sites as opposed

---

[22] D. Hill, *An Atlas of Anglo-Saxon England* (Oxford, 1981), 21, fig. 35 and 26, fig. 36.
[23] D. Hooke, *Worcestershire Anglo-Saxon Charter Bounds*, (Woodbridge, 1990), 2–3; M. Costen, 'Settlement in Wessex in the tenth century; the charter evidence', 97–107 in M. Aston and C. Lewis (eds.), *The Medieval Landscape of Wessex* (Oxford, 1994), at p. 97.
[24] P. Wormald, *The Making of English Law: King Alfred to the Twelfth Century*, Vol. 2 (Oxford, forthcoming).

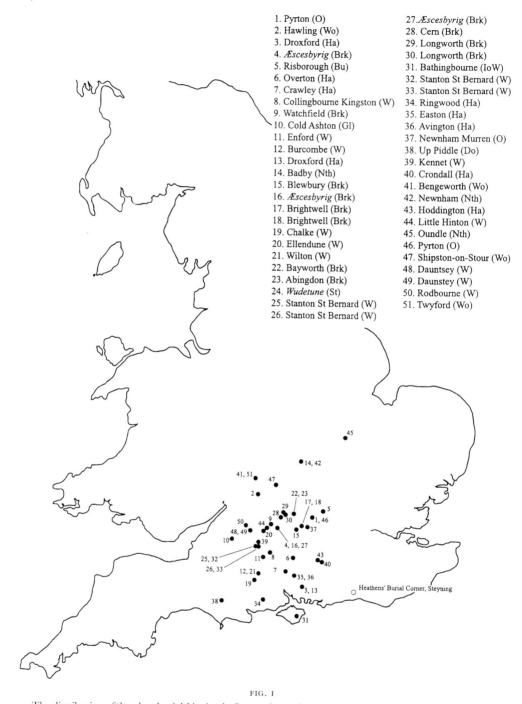

1. Pyrton (O)
2. Hawling (Wo)
3. Droxford (Ha)
4. *Æscesbyrig* (Brk)
5. Risborough (Bu)
6. Overton (Ha)
7. Crawley (Ha)
8. Collingbourne Kingston (W)
9. Watchfield (Brk)
10. Cold Ashton (Gl)
11. Enford (W)
12. Burcombe (W)
13. Droxford (Ha)
14. Badby (Nth)
15. Blewbury (Brk)
16. *Æscesbyrig* (Brk)
17. Brightwell (Brk)
18. Brightwell (Brk)
19. Chalke (W)
20. Ellendune (W)
21. Wilton (W)
22. Bayworth (Brk)
23. Abingdon (Brk)
24. *Wudetune* (St)
25. Stanton St Bernard (W)
26. Stanton St Bernard (W)

27. *Æscesbyrig* (Brk)
28. Cern (Brk)
29. Longworth (Brk)
30. Longworth (Brk)
31. Bathingbourne (IoW)
32. Stanton St Bernard (W)
33. Stanton St Bernard (W)
34. Ringwood (Ha)
35. Easton (Ha)
36. Avington (Ha)
37. Newnham Murren (O)
38. Up Piddle (Do)
39. Kennet (W)
40. Crondall (Ha)
41. Bengeworth (Wo)
42. Newnham (Nth)
43. Hoddington (Ha)
44. Little Hinton (W)
45. Oundle (Nth)
46. Pyrton (O)
47. Shipston-on-Stour (Wo)
48. Dauntsey (W)
49. Daunstey (W)
50. Rodbourne (W)
51. Twyford (Wo)

FIG. I

The distribution of 'heathen burials' in Anglo-Saxon charter bounds and the location of Heathens' Burial Corner, Steyning (West Sussex).

to the memory of pagan cemeteries, whereas the landscape context of the locatable examples (all but two) provides further confirmation of their special character. There is a small handful of modern place-names that could be derived from Old English 'heathen burials' with varying degrees of certainty.[25] Of particular importance is a recent small-scale excavation at Heathens' Burial Corner, Steyning (West Sussex) (Fig. 1) that has revealed two skeletons interred with heads to the SSE. and without objects. The earliest recorded forms of the Steyning 'heathen burials' date to 1279 and 1288,[26] and it seems most likely that the memory of the name has survived due to the site's proximity to important population centres at Steyning in the late Anglo-Saxon period and later at Bramber. Radiocarbon determinations from both skeletons (cal. A.D. 981–1025 and A.D. 981–1023 at 1 sigma and cal. A.D. 896–1155 and A.D. 897–1151 at 2 sigma) only serve to confirm the hypothesis presented here.[27] Additionally, the Steyning burials are situated on the boundary between Steyning and Bramber parishes beside a major early highway 500 m to the West of the boundary between Steyning and Burbeach hundreds.

Of the 37 locatable 'heathen burials', 23 lie on the boundaries of Domesday hundreds, with 14 upon estate boundaries, which are not also those of hundreds. The significance of this observation lies in the self-contained nature of the hundredal unit with regard to its judicial affairs. The physical limits of such territories provided a fitting repository for those who were precluded by law from burial in consecrated ground and of the twenty excavated execution cemeteries of the late Anglo-Saxon period all but one is located upon either a hundred or county boundary.[28] Closer analysis of the charter material, however, strengthens the view that hundred boundaries were preferred in the case of the 'heathen burials'. In Hampshire, for example, all seven instances are so located (Fig. 2). A smaller number of examples also conform to this pattern in Buckinghamshire (one out of one), Gloucestershire (two out of two) and Worcestershire (two out of two). In Berkshire the figure is five out of eight instances (Fig. 3), although the two distinct instances recorded in the bounds of Longworth (29) and (30), one on a hundred boundary, the other not, could feasibly represent a process of relocation due to reworking of hundred boundaries. In fact, the dynamics of hundred-boundary movement within the late Anglo-Saxon period is barely recognized. The 'heathen burials' now observed on mere estate boundaries may provide a means of approaching such a question, although this line of enquiry should not be pushed too far.

Further evidence to support the emergence of a clearly defined concept of social exclusion during the 10th century can be gained from the laws. The earliest clause in the laws to refer explicitly to exclusion from consecrated cemeteries is found in

---

[25] Gelling, op. cit. in note 9, 157.
[26] Ibid.
[27] I am indebted to Dr Sally White, Worthing Museum and Art Gallery, and Chris Tod, Steyning Museum, for providing information about the Steyning burials prior to their publication. The radiocarbon dates were obtained via the Scottish Universities Research and Reactor Centre, East Kilbride, and measured at the University of Arizona AMS facility, certificate nos. AA-38009 and AA-38010.
[28] A. Reynolds, *Anglo-Saxon Law in the Landscape* (unpublished PhD thesis, University of London, 1998), 175 and tab. 15.

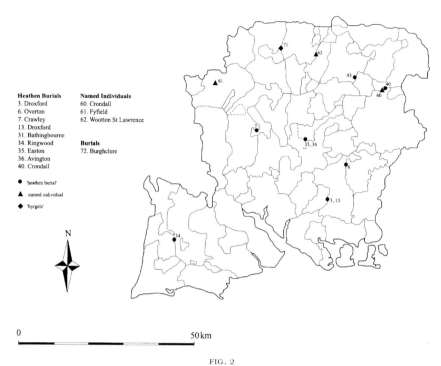

FIG. 2

The relationship between 'heathen burials' and hundred boundaries in Hampshire,
also showing other documented burial sites.

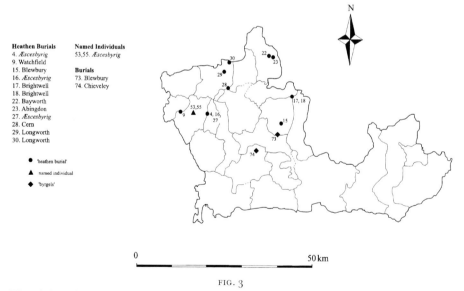

FIG. 3

The relationship between 'heathen burials' and hundred boundaries in Berkshire, also showing other
documented burial sites.

Athelstan's second code.[29] The fact that exclusion occurred in practice is clearly described in the preamble of two remarkable charters of 962 and 995.[30] The former document, regarding forfeiture of an estate at Sunbury (Greater London), concerns a certain Ecgferth who was drowned, for committing an unknown offence, and subsequently barred from burial in consecrated ground.[31] The latter charter relates to land at Ardley (Oxfordshire) and refers to a dispute about the fact that two brothers killed while defending a thief were illegally given Christian burial.[32] Widespread application of the concept of exclusion is confirmed by evidence from the north of England in the form of the early 11th century Law of the Northumbrian Priests.[33] The heathen burials can now be argued on the basis of clear locational characteristics and archaeological evidence to refer not to pagan burial grounds, but more likely to later Anglo-Saxon judicial execution cemeteries, fittingly described using appropriate contemporary terminology.

NAMED INDIVIDUALS

References to named individuals are limited to 12 examples recorded in 15 sets of bounds (Fig. 4). The distribution of examples is widespread with four from Wiltshire, three from Hampshire, two from Worcestershire and one each from Berkshire, Sussex and Surrey. Ten out of the twelve named individuals are of males, with two females (53)/(55) and (54), and all are referred to in the singular in their respective boundary clauses.[34] One particular example, in the bounds of Crondall (Hampshire) (60), clearly records contemporary knowledge of a named person. The clause in question runs '*swa on ðone hæðenan byrgels. ðonan west on ða mearce wær Ælfstan lið on hæðenan byrgels*' (so to the heathen burial. then west to the boundary where Ælfstan lies in a heathen burial). Kemble considered Ælfstan a Christian owing to the fact that the Anglo-Saxon boundary surveyors had distinguished him by name from the 'heathen burial' noted as the preceding boundary mark (40).[35] It might be more plausible to suggest either that Ælfstan was the latest addition to the 'heathen burial' site when the bounds were drawn up, or that he was a local notable whose interment in a cemetery for outcasts caused sufficient fuss for his name to become incorporated into its nomenclature. The specific wording of the boundary clause, however, notes that Ælfstan lies to the West of the aforementioned site, indicating a separate burial place described in no uncertain terms.

---

[29] A. J. Robertson, *The Laws of the Kings of England from Edmund to Henry I* (Cambridge, 1925), II Ath. 26: *Ond se ðe manað swerige, 7 hit him on open wurþe, ðæt he næfre eft aðwyrþe ne sy, ne binnon nanum gehalgodum lictune ne licge, þeah he forðfore, buton he hæbbe ðæs biscopes gewitnesse, ðe he on his scriftscire sy, þæt he hit swa gebet hæbbe, swa him his scrift scrife.* 'And if anyone swears a false oath and it becomes manifest he has done so, he shall never again have the right to swear an oath; and he shall not be buried in any consecrated burial ground when he dies, unless he has the testimony of the bishop, in whose diocese he is, that he has made such amends as his confessor has prescribed to him.'
[30] Sawyer, op. cit. in note 2, nos. 702 and 883.
[31] A. J. Robertson, *Anglo-Saxon Charters* (Cambridge, 1956), no. 44.
[32] D. Whitelock, *English Historical Documents. Volume I, c. 500–1042* (London, 1979), 571.
[33] Ibid., 475, cap. 62.
[34] All personal names were checked against W. G. Searle, *Onomasticon Anglo-Saxonicum: a List of Anglo-Saxon Proper Names from the time of Beda to that of King John* (Cambridge, 1897).
[35] Kemble, op. cit. in note 6, 125.

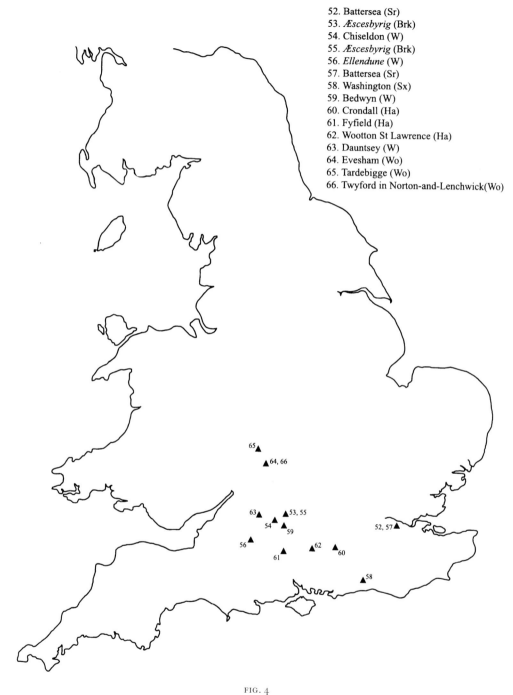

52. Battersea (Sr)
53. *Æscesbyrig* (Brk)
54. Chiseldon (W)
55. *Æscesbyrig* (Brk)
56. *Ellendune* (W)
57. Battersea (Sr)
58. Washington (Sx)
59. Bedwyn (W)
60. Crondall (Ha)
61. Fyfield (Ha)
62. Wootton St Lawrence (Ha)
63. Dauntsey (W)
64. Evesham (Wo)
65. Tardebigge (Wo)
66. Twyford in Norton-and-Lenchwick(Wo)

FIG. 4
The distribution of named individual burials in Anglo-Saxon charter bounds.

The remaining eleven examples are surely what the bounds purport to describe, burials of named individuals, broadly contemporary with the bounds that record them, or at the very least belonging to the Christian period. The great majority of the named individual burials are located beside major routes. With the exception of one unlocated burial (63), all examples are either beside or immediately adjacent to routeways (Fig. 5). Four sites lie beside Roman roads, (52)/(57, (54), (59) and (64)/(66), with (62) alongside a *herepað*. The remaining sites are associated with routeways of varying importance, but most are seemingly major highways.

If the status of Ælfstan is anything by which to judge it can be suggested that the named burials represent deviants, perhaps previous owners of the estates upon whose boundaries they lie. This contention is supported by the fact that, unlike the 'heathen burials', the named individuals lie on estate boundaries more frequently than on those also of hundredal status in the order of 8 to 4.

A possible context for such burials might be estate forfeiture as a result of the legal process. Perhaps the best known example of this procedure is recorded in a charter of 963 x 975[36] that describes the drowning of a woman, the so-called 'widow of Ailsworth', at (a) London Bridge (probably in Northamptonshire).[37] Such a scenario presents a plausible context for the naming of a particular location as a result of such a notable event. Indeed, the location of the Ailsworth widow's execution by a route of communication agrees well with the instances presented above. Similarly, the case of Ecgferth's drowning and estate forfeiture outlined previously provides another possible example. There is further contemporary documentary evidence to support the notion that individual burials of deviants were seen as a separate phenomenon. Ælfric, writing in the late 10th or early 11th century, notes how 'witches resort to crossroads, *and* (my emphasis) to heathen burial sites with their evil rites, and call upon the devil, and he arrives in the form of the person who lies buried there as if he had risen from death'.[38]

Archaeological evidence for individual boundary burial in the later Anglo-Saxon period is scarce, although an inhumation found in a wooden coffin with iron fittings on the boundary between the Domesday manors of Choulston and Figheldean (Wiltshire) may belong to this class.[39] The status indicated by the coffin with iron fittings contrasts with its liminal location, but the burial of a dispossessed thegn might leave exactly such a trace.

In essence, then, the named individuals buried in roadside locations might be seen as forerunners of the rather better known crossroads burials of the late medieval to early modern era.[40] Where recorded in the place-name record, the names of certain of these latter burials, often of suicides, present an identical form of evidence. The place-name Oram's Grave in the parish of Maddington (Wiltshire), for example, records the burial of a suicide at the crossroads there in 1849, although officially the

---

[36] Sawyer, op. cit. in note 2, no. 1377.
[37] D. Hill, 'London Bridge: a reasonable doubt?', *Trans. Lond. Middlesex Archaeol. Soc.*, 27 (1976), 303–5.
[38] B. Griffiths, *Aspects of Anglo-Saxon Magic* (Hockwold-cum-Wilton, 1996), 35. Dr Audrey Meaney (pers. comm.) translates this passage with minor differences to Griffiths' reading. Dr Meaney reads 'delusive magic' for 'evil rites', 'comes to them' instead of 'arrives' and 'arise' instead of 'had risen'.
[39] Bonney, op. cit. in note 8, 76–8 and fig. 7.9.
[40] C. Daniell, *Death and Burial in Medieval England* (London, 1997), 105–6.

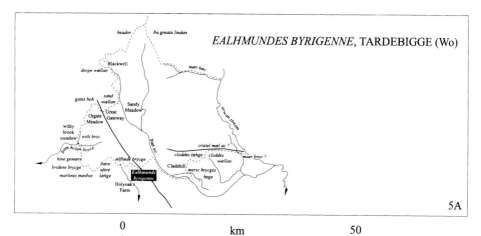

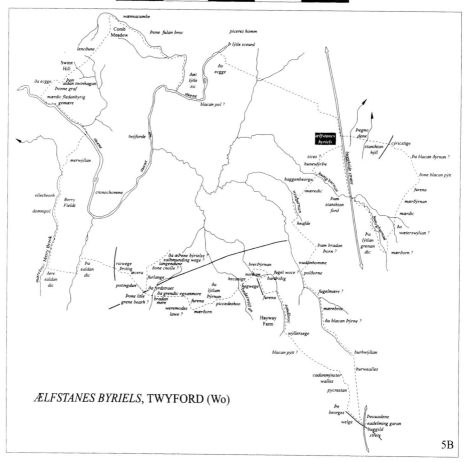

FIG. 5

The location of named individuals by major routes. (A) *ealhmundes byrigenne*, Tardebigge (Worcestershire) and (B) *ælfstanes byriels*, Twyford (Worcestershire). Redrawn from D. Hooke, op. cit. in note 23, 404 and 410–11. Handlist this paper, nos. 65 and 66.

practice was ended by a Parliamentary Act in 1823.[41] Until now, the earliest suggested example of a documented crossroads burial is dated 1510, being that of Robert Browner, superior of Butley Priory in Suffolk, who hanged himself on account of fiscal incompetence.[42]

MISCELLANEOUS BURIALS AND BURIAL SITES

Two burial locations are known using the term *lic*, meaning 'body, dead body' (Fig. 6).[43] The place 'where the thieves lie' in the Rolleston (Staffordshire) bounds (67) considered earlier, surely represents a site of judicial execution and burial. The second example is rather less straightforward. The bounds of Witney (Oxfordshire) (68), dated 1044, record where the *cnihtas licgað* (where the lads lie) along a stretch of the estate boundary that is also that of the hundred. Excavations at Shakenoak Farm, close to the boundary in question, revealed a series of human burials cut into the upper layers inside the ruins of a Roman villa.[44] Margaret Gelling has suggested a link between the *cnihtas* recorded in the boundary clause and the excavated burials, four of which showed signs of injury,[45] although the site is some 200 m from the boundary itself. Patrick Wormald has further observed that an earlier set of bounds for the same parcel of land do not record the presence of the *cnihtas* there in 969.[46] In the light of the slab-lined treatment of one of the villa burials and their significant distance from the boundary itself, it seems just as likely that the Shakenoak interments are unrelated to those in the boundary clause and perhaps relate to a late pagan phenomenon as recently noted by John Blair.[47] In a post-969 context, the Witney *cnihtas* are best seen as execution burials on the hundred boundary itself.

The interpretation of boundary marks termed simply '*byrgels(as)*' is limited by the paucity of examples (six sites) (Fig. 6), but some suggestions can be advanced. Examples are widespread with two from Wiltshire, two from Berkshire and one each from Hampshire and Sussex. The location of four out of the six instances is known, with (73) located along a ridgeway, (74) at a confluence of major routes, and the other two sites (70) and (72) located on open downland. Sites (72), (73) and (74) lie on the boundaries of hundreds, whilst (70) lies upon an estate boundary.

In the first instance, it appears that a range of burial sites is being described in the charters. The best indication of this aspect is provided by the successive sets of bounds for Stanton St Bernard (Wiltshire). The earliest set, of 903, records 'burials' (69), whereas they had become 'heathen' by the time the second of three sets of bounds had

[41] J. E. B. Gover, A. Mawer and F. M. Stenton, *The Place-Names of Wiltshire* (English Place-Name Society, Cambridge, 1939), 234; R. Halliday, 'Criminal graves and rural crossroads', *British Archaeol.* (June 1997), 6.

[42] Halliday, op. cit. in note 41.

[43] J. Roberts and C. Kay with L. Grundy, *A Thesaurus of Old English* (London, 1995), Vol. 2, 1139.

[44] A. C. C. Brodribb, A. R. Hands and D. R. Walker, *Excavations at Shakenoak Farm, Near Wilcote, Oxfordshire. Part IV: Site C* (Privately printed, 1973), 34–5 and fig. 17.

[45] M. Gelling, 'The place-name evidence', 134–40 in A. C. C. Brodribb, A. R. Hands and D. R. Walker (eds.), *Excavations at Shakenoak Farm, Near Wilcote, Oxfordshire. Part III: Site F* (Privately printed, 1972).

[46] Wormald, op. cit. in note 24.

[47] J. Blair, *Anglo-Saxon Oxfordshire* (Stroud, 1994), 32–3 discusses the Shakenoak villa burials and notes mid- to late 6th-century and 7th-century parallels at Barton Court Farm and Great Tew (both in Oxfordshire) respectively.

○ **Lic**

    67. Rolleston (St)
    68. Witney (O)

◆ **Burial**

    69. Preston (Sx)
    70. Stanton St Bernard (W)
    71. East Overton (W)
    72. Burghclere (Ha)
    73. Blewbury (Brk)
    74. Chieveley (Brk)

FIG. 6

The distribution of *lic* and *byrgels* in Anglo-Saxon charter bounds.

been drawn up in 957 (25). Either the status of the burial site changed between 903 and 957 or the language of recording had become more specific. It seems unlikely that a community cemetery would be adopted for burying deviants, and there are no excavated examples, but perhaps the carving up of the Pewsey Vale, much of it into *bocland*, during the 10th century resulted in the incorporation of a field cemetery into a boundary and thus into a liminal location. Why a similar process cannot be observed in the remainder of the material is interesting, but the Stanton St Bernard example could equally reflect an intimately local response to changing landscape structure during the late Anglo-Saxon period.

The remaining sites are possibly field cemeteries, perhaps with middle Anglo-Saxon origins. Their positioning within the landscape of the later Anglo-Saxon period might suggest that they are relics of an earlier pattern of settlement, incorporated into boundary clauses during landscape reorganization and the origins and growth of the local manorial system in England. Michael Costen has recently shown that settlements could be found on the boundaries of Anglo-Saxon estates through his study of settlement and agricultural terms in the Wessex charters. Whilst shepherds and certain other estate workers were likely to require seasonal or occasional accommodation away from principal settlements, it seems unlikely that such loci would attract, let alone require, a burial plot. A probable sheepfold and associated occupation debris excavated on the parish boundary of Easton (Hampshire) gives a likely impression of the kind of settlement involved.[48]

What is clear is that none of the burial sites of this class became churchyard cemeteries and they are seemingly unconnected to the religious geography of the post-Conquest period. It is possible, or even probable, that such field cemeteries continued in use until a parish church and cemetery was established. John Blair has recently defined an archaeological dimension to burial in field cemeteries in the middle Anglo-Saxon period, having drawn attention to a growing corpus of sites, containing small groups of W.–E. aligned burials not associated with structures or cemetery boundaries of any kind.[49] Occasional finds include small iron knives, but dress fittings are not found indicating preparation for burial, perhaps in a shroud. These burial grounds appear to span the 7th to 9th centuries, although cemeteries of this type at Milton Keynes, with at least 100 burials, and Shepperton Green (Greater London), adjacent to a contemporary settlement, are certainly in use to a later date and support the hypothesis that such cemeteries continued until the building of a parish church.[50]

In a comparative discussion of field cemeteries in medieval Ireland and England, Susan Leigh Fry has collated a body of documentary evidence which indicates that field cemeteries were a feature of both places into the late Middle Ages.[51] More specifically, a significant group of excavated manorial sites and associated churches and churchyards can be seen to follow a consistent pattern of development from the

[48] Costen, op. cit. in note 23; P. J. Fasham, D. Farwell and R. Whinney, *The Archaeological Site at Easton Lane, Winchester* (Winchester, 1989).
[49] Blair, op. cit. in note 47, 69–77.
[50] J. Parkhouse and J. Short, 'A late Saxon cemetery at Milton Keynes village', *Records of Buckinghamshire*, 38 (1996), 199–221; R. Canham, 'Excavations at Shepperton Green, 1967 and 1973', *Trans. Lond. Middlesex Archaeol. Soc.*, 30 (1979), 97–124.
[51] S. Leigh Fry, *Burial in Medieval Ireland 900–1500* (Dublin, 1999), 43–7.

10th century. At Goltho (Lincolnshire), Faccombe Netherton (Hampshire), Trowbridge (Wiltshire), Raunds (Northamptonshire) and Portchester Castle (Hampshire), for example, the manorial accommodation is primary, followed by a chapel, with burial a tertiary development in the sequence.[52] In summary, it might be suggested that simple 'burials' recorded in late Anglo-Saxon charter bounds represent the last vestige of burial geography in the 'pre-manorial' age, with the possibility that field cemeteries continued in use for a significantly longer period in certain localities prior to the building of an estate church and the acquisition of burial rights.

DISCUSSION

The thesis of boundary burial in the post-Roman period in England was formulated around a restricted body of material: furnished inhumation cemeteries and individual burials of the 5th to 7th centuries A.D. The view current during the gestation period of the Bonney thesis, and during the development and refinement of the Final Phase concept, was that burial in enclosed churchyards was a more-or-less immediate development by English populations following the Conversion to Christianity.[53] Recent research has revealed a clearer understanding of the archaeological dimension to the process of conversion, which provides a stark contrast to the traditional understanding of the development of churchyard cemeteries. Instead of viewing the 7th-century landscape as one littered with enclosed churchyard cemeteries, it now appears that there was an intermediate period, strongly marked between the 7th–9th centuries, where varied burial rites and burial foci existed contemporaneously. As noted above, John Blair has done much of the work on defining the Christian burial places of the 7th–9th centuries, whereas Helen Gittos (see this volume) has examined the evidence for churchyard consecration ritual. The present author has researched the evidence for the burial of social outcasts and the resultant overview presents a complementary picture of events.

To summarize, an over-simplified view of the relationships between Early Anglo-Saxon communities and the cemeteries that served them has led to a long-held consensus that the pagan Anglo-Saxons regarded settlement and burial as distinct spatial entities, whereas it is now increasingly recognized that early Anglo-Saxon communities frequently buried their dead in cemeteries either within or adjacent to their settlements.[54] Although there are many examples of cemeteries without evidence for adjacent settlements, antiquarian excavations and the sole concern for emptying graves may account for at least a proportion of such sites. Furthermore, the limited areas excavated at many cemetery sites have ensured a partial record which has

[52] Reynolds, op. cit. in note 5, 111–57.

[53] See, for example, the account of parish church origins in J. Godfrey, 'The emergence of the village church in Anglo-Saxon England', 131–8 in T. Rowley (ed.), *Anglo-Saxon Settlement and Landscape* (BAR Brit. Ser., 6, Oxford, 1974). For a discussion of the transition from furnished to unfurnished burial during the 7th and 8th centuries, see A. Boddington, 'Models of burial, settlement and worship: the Final Phase reviewed', 177–99 in E. Southworth (ed.), *Anglo-Saxon Cemeteries: A Reappraisal* (Stroud, 1990).

[54] A. L. Meaney, *Gazetteer of Early Anglo-Saxon Burial Sites* (London, 1964), 20; Welch, op. cit. in note 20, quotes an early realization of an intimate relationship between certain Early Anglo-Saxon cemeteries and settlements in M. Bell, 'Saxon settlements and buildings in Sussex', 36–53 in P. Brandon (ed.), *The South Saxons* (Chichester, 1978), at p. 46.

restricted an understanding of the extent and cultural setting of individual sites. Examples where a close relationship is found include Spong Hill (Norfolk), West Stow (Suffolk), Bishopstone (West Sussex) and Mucking (Essex), in addition to lesser-known sites such as Market Lavington (Wiltshire) and Carlton Colville (Suffolk).[55] In the context of such a settlement pattern, theoretically there is scope for the existence of liminal burials, but the archaeological evidence gives little if any support to this scenario. In fact, early Anglo-Saxon cemeteries are commonly notable for containing at least a handful of burials of a non-normative type, including prone burials, decapitations, multiple burials, bodies weighted down with stones and, occasionally, amputations. Moreover, early Anglo-Saxon cemeteries rarely give the appearance of having been formally bounded, which might suggest that the grave itself represented an all-containing receptacle for the deceased. Such a concept provides a plausible context for the 'safe' inclusion of 'deviant' burials within otherwise normal community cemeteries.

There are still insufficient data from excavated cemeteries from 7th–9th century contexts for us to be in the position to present as clear a picture as may be drawn for the early and late Anglo-Saxon periods. There are indications, however, from the known corpus of archaeological data that suggest a gradual move toward a ubiquitous exclusion of social outcasts to peripheral burial grounds by the 10th century. At Yarnton (Oxfordshire), for example, a female had been buried prone in a ditch associated with the Middle Anglo-Saxon settlement there, whilst at Cottam (East Riding of Yorkshire) a weathered skull from an 8th-century pit might indicate the former display of the head of an executed deviant.[56] In a similar vein, the corpse of a woman, possibly drowned, found on the Thames foreshore at Bull Wharf in London provides a further example of a deviant burial in close proximity to settlement, be it in rural Oxfordshire or on the London waterfront.[57]

The three examples just cited indicate a change in the way that deviant burials were treated. It can be observed in each case that the remains are either peripheral to or completely removed from any normative cemetery context. The two groups of deviant burials discovered at Sutton Hoo (Suffolk) during Martin Carver's excavation campaign appear to originate as a type in the 7th century, although the majority of the burials most likely belong to the 10th century and later.[58] The Deben Estuary, above which the Sutton Hoo cemetery lies, forms a natural boundary to the site, but one which came to serve as part of the boundary of the hundred of Wilford by the Late

[55] R. Rickett, *The Anglo-Saxon Cemetery at Spong Hill, North Elmham, Part VII: The Iron Age, Roman and Early Anglo-Saxon Settlement* (East Anglian Archaeol., 73, Gressenhall, 1995); S. West, *West Stow: The Anglo-Saxon Village* (East Anglian Archaeol., 24, Ipswich, 1985); M. Bell, 'Excavations at Bishopstone: the Anglo-Saxon period', *Sussex Archaeol. Collections*, 115 (1977); H. Hamerow, *Excavations at Mucking. Volume 2: The Anglo-Saxon Settlement* (English Heritage Archaeol. Rep., 21, London, 1991); 'Excavation and fieldwork in Wiltshire 1990', *Wiltshire Archaeol. Nat. Hist. Mag.*, 85, 156–62, at 160; R. Mortimer and J. Tipper, 'Excavation of an early-middle Saxon settlement at Bloodmoor Hill, Carlton Colville, Suffolk', *Lowestoft Archaeol. Local Hist. Soc. Ann. Rep.* 31 (1998–9).

[56] I am grateful to Gill Hey, Oxford Archaeological Unit, for providing me with details of the Yarnton burials prior to publication; for Cottam, see J. Richards, 'Cottam: An Anglian and Anglo-Scandinavian settlement on the Yorkshire Wolds', *Archaeol. J.*, 156 (1999), 1–110, at 92–3.

[57] B. Nenk, S. Margeson and M. Hurley, 'Medieval Britain and Ireland in 1991', *Medieval Archaeol.*, 36 (1992), 184–308, at 228.

[58] M. Carver, *Sutton Hoo: Burial Ground of Kings?* (London, 1998), esp. 135 and 137–53.

Anglo-Saxon period. A reference to the site of a gallows (*gabulos*) in a set of Latin charter bounds for Little Bedwyn (Wiltshire) provides further evidence of middle Anglo-Saxon date to indicate a conscious move toward boundary burial during this period.[59] The charter is dated 778 and the '*gabuli*' lie on the northern boundary of the extensive Wiltshire hundred of Kinwardstone, probably itself a middle Anglo-Saxon territory. By the late Anglo-Saxon period, the model for conscious boundary burial is fully developed with a clear set of concepts relating the range of social, religious and legal perceptions of the various dead to the landscape.

The ideological implications of boundary burial are of considerable interest. Thomas Charles-Edwards's discussion of boundary burial in late pagan Wales and Ireland emphasized the powerful role played by liminal interments in concepts of protection and legal ceremony. To quote: 'It is, therefore, possible that in pagan Britain the burial upon the boundary had the same function as in pagan Ireland: the dead warded off the outsider from the land and thus protected the rights of their heirs; and this belief provided the basis for the part of the procedure for claims to land which showed the basis of any lawful claim, hereditary right'.[60] I would suggest that the English evidence is different in emphasis, at least during the Christian period. The focus would appear to have been very much more upon the individual interred rather than any outward effect that the corpse might have. The nature of liminal burial in an English context appears rather more negative and concerned with the exclusion of social deviants to the limits of territories. Here, consigned to inhabit boundaries and not the sphere of the living and to unconsecrated plots and the malevolent underworld, the named individuals can be interpreted in a legal context if related to forfeited property, whilst the heathen burials represent a broader range of social outcasts.

In view of the observations made above, the question must accordingly be re-formulated to address the concept of boundary burial but with a refined understanding both of the burial data that can be incorporated into such a study and of the chronology of boundary development in England. All too little consideration has been directed to an understanding of boundary hierarchies and the possibilities that such an approach provides for exploring the notion of purposeful boundary burial and of the various ideological and theoretical questions that arise. Whilst a landscape without any meaningful territorial divisions is difficult to imagine for any period, the basic frame of the medieval countryside is, apparently, largely a product of the 'New Geography' of the late Anglo-Saxon centuries.

CONCLUSIONS AND RESEARCH DIRECTIONS

Ultimately, it is necessary to stress that the interpretations presented in this paper remain provisional, awaiting further developments in our understanding of English landscape history. I have attempted to relate explicitly documented burial sites into

---

[59] Sawyer, op. cit. in note 2, no. 264. The authenticity of this charter is long-held, but see also H. Edwards, *The Charters of the Early West Saxon Kingdom* (BAR Brit. Ser., 198, Oxford, 1988), 59–62, who notes a comment by the late Julian Brown that the palaeography of the document could belong to the 10th century. An authentic basis for both the charter and its bounds is not in doubt.

[60] T. Charles-Edwards, 'Boundaries in Irish Law', 83–7 in P. H. Sawyer (ed.), *Medieval Settlement: Continuity and Change* (London, 1976), at p. 87.

what is known from archaeological and broader historical sources about modes of burial in the Christian period, but the subject is advancing rapidly and much significant work is in progress. The analysis of boundary-types in relation to different categories of burial sites has provided a firmer footing upon which to explore the nature of the material, with both the 'heathen burials' and named individuals in particular emerging as clear groups.

It remains to suggest some directions for further research. In the first place, there is an increasing need for a computerized GIS database of Old English charter bounds. Whilst the boundary clauses form a core body of evidence for landscape history, the landscape context of individual categories of boundary marks requires a comprehensive analysis. A second approach to the material would be to select certain documented burial sites for archaeological excavation. A sufficient number of such sites can be located with a high degree of accuracy in the modern landscape and a test-pitting programme at several of these should yield useful results. A third body of data that lies substantially untapped is records of undated burials or cemeteries in county SMRs. John Blair has examined the material for Oxfordshire,[61] whilst the present author has analysed aspects of the Wiltshire data. Bruce Eagles is currently taking this study further in the latter county. A full characterization of SMR data is vital in order to tackle what is a substantial archaeological resource.

In summary, the data provided by documentary sources provide a series of criteria that can be judged against those exhibited by excavated burial sites. Up to the present, efforts to reconstruct the geography of burial in the later Anglo-Saxon world have relied almost wholly on archaeological material without reference to the significant body of contemporary evidence from charter bounds.

ACKNOWLEDGEMENTS

I am grateful to Sarah Semple for her help in checking my own list of charter terms against the Toronto Microfiche Concordance of Old English. The list was further checked and augmented by Audrey Meaney with regard to linguistic aspects of the various terms and I am indebted to Dr Meaney for her notes on the material, which are incorporated in this paper. Joy Jenkyns provided much useful material from her database of Anglo-Saxon charter bounds and I am grateful to her for this. I should also like to thank Alex Langlands who produced the line drawings and Henry Escudero for providing information at short notice on the Sussex charters. John Blair and Sam Lucy read the manuscript in draft and suggested various improvements, although responsibility for the final version rests firmly with the author.

APPENDIX

A HANDLIST OF BURIAL PLACES IN ANGLO-SAXON CHARTER BOUNDS

The burial sites in this handlist were collected by reference to the Toronto Old English Concordance[62] and supplemented by a search of the database of Anglo-Saxon charter bounds maintained by Dr Joy Jenkyns at Oxford. Sites are listed alphabetically, ostensibly in chronological order within each category, with a running numerical

[61] Blair, op. cit. in note 49, 72.
[62] R. L. Venezky, *A Micro-fiche Concordance to Old English* (Newark, 1980).

sequence for the whole series. The purported date of the charter to which each set of bounds is attached is given, along with the modern name of the estate in question. Where known, the status of the boundary upon which each site is located is noted and references to Sawyer's 1968 handlist are provided. References are also given to the published source for each charter in the editions of Birch, Kemble or otherwise.[63] Certain sets of bounds exist in isolation (that is without an accompanying charter and therefore undated) and these examples are listed last within each category. R = term repeated in later or adjoining boundary clause. Instances of more than one burial site in a set of bounds is indicated thus: 1st of 2, 2nd of 2 etc.

Heathen burials

1. **in hæþenan byrigels** (acc sg), . . . **on þæne hæþena byregels** (acc sg), A.D. 759 for 774. Pyrton (Oxfordshire). Boundary: estate. S104 (Birch 216). R46.

2. **to þam hæðenan byrigelse** (dat sg), A.D. 816 (11th C). Hawling (Worcestershire). Boundary: hundred. S179 (Birch 356).

3. **to ðem heþenum birigelsum** (dat pl), A.D. 826. Droxford (Hampshire). Boundary: hundred. S276 (Birch 393).

4. **to þæn æþænan byrigelsæ** (dat sg), A.D. 856. *Æscesbyrig* (West Berkshire). Boundary: hundred. S317 (Birch 491). R16 and 27.

5. **oþ þone hæðenan byrgels** (acc sg). A.D. 903. Risborough (Buckinghamshire). Boundary: hundred. S367 (Birch 603).

6. **Þæt to þæm heþenan byrigelse** (dat sg). A.D. 909. Overton (Hampshire). Boundary: hundred. S377 (Birch 625).

7. **Swa norð of þone æþena byrigels** (acc sg), 'so north[wards] from'. Early 10th C. Crawley (Hampshire). Boundary: hundred. S381 (Birch 629).

8. **up to þam hæþenan byrgelsan** (dat pl). A.D. 921. Collingbourne Kingston (Wiltshire). Boundary: hundred. S379 (Birch 635).

9. **Ærest on þone stan æt þæm hæðnan byrgelsan** (dat pl). . . . **Þonne of þæm stan beorge on þone hæþenan byrgels** (acc sg), 'First to the stone at the heathen burial-places . . . Then from the stone barrow as far as the heathen burial-place'. A.D. 931. Watchfield (Oxfordshire). Boundary: hundred. S413 (Birch 675).

10. **on þa hæþenan byrigelsas** (acc pl). **Þonne of þam byrgelsum** (dat pl). A.D. 931. Cold Ashton (Gloucestershire). Boundary: hundred. S414 (Birch 670).

11. **on ðone æþenan byrigæls** (acc sg), **of ðam byrigelsæ** (dat sg). A.D. 934. Enford (Wiltshire). Boundary: estate. S427 (Birch 705).

[63] W. de G. Birch, *Cartularium Saxonicum: A Collection of Charters Relating to Anglo-Saxon History* (London, 1885–93), 3 vols.; J. M. Kemble, *Codex Diplomaticus Aevi Saxonici* (London, 1839–48), 6 vols.; T. Hearne, *Hemingi Chartularium Ecclesiae Wigorniensis* (Oxford, 1723); P. Sawyer, *Charters of Burton Abbey* (Anglo-Saxon Charters II, Oxford, 1979).

12. **ut to þan hæþanne byrgelse** (dat sg), 'out to the'. A.D. 937. Burcombe (Wiltshire). Boundary: hundred. S438 (Birch 714).

13. **Andlang dic to þam æþænan byrigelsum** (dat pl) A.D. 939. Droxford (Hampshire). Boundary: hundred. S446 (Birch 742). R3.

14. **oð ðone hæþenan byrgels** (acc sg). **Of þam byrgelse** (dat sg). A.D. 944. BA.D.by (Northamptonshire). Boundary: estate. S495 (Birch 792). R42.

15. **to þon hæþenum byrgelsum** (dat pl). A.D. 944 (for 942?). Blewbury (Oxfordshire). Boundary: estate. S496. (Birch 801). See also 73.

16. **to þon æþænan byrigelsæ** (dat sg). A.D. 944. *Æscesbyrig* (West Berkshire?). Boundary: hundred. S503 (Birch 796). R4 and 27.

17. **on þa hæþenan byrgylsas** (acc pl). A.D. 945. Brightwell (Oxfordshire?). Boundary: hundred. S517 (Birch 810). R18.

18. **Of þa hæþenan byrigelsas** (acc pl). A.D. 947. Brightwell (Oxfordshire?). Boundary: hundred. S523 (Birch 830). R17.

19. **to ðam haþenum byrgelsum** (dat pl). A.D. 955. Chalke (Wiltshire). Boundary: hundred. S582 (Birch 917).

20. **Ærest of þam æþenan byrigelsæ** (dat sg) . . . **Of þam stane æft to þam æþænan byrgelse** (dat sg). A.D. 956. *Ellendune* (Wiltshire). Boundary: estate. S585 (Birch 948). See 56.

21. **Þonene adune rihte on ðone hæðenan byrgels** (acc sg). **Of þan hæðenan byrgelse** (dat sg) **on þone stanigan beorh,** 'as far as the stony barrow'. A.D. 956. Wilton (Wiltshire). Boundary: hundred. S586 (Birch 1030). R12.

22. **Þonne on ðone hæþenan byrgels** (acc sg). A.D. 956. Bayworth (West Berkshire?). Boundary: estate. S590 (Birch 932). R23.

23. **Þær on ðone hæðenan byrgels** (acc sg). A.D. 956. Abingdon (Oxfordshire). Boundary: estate. S605 (Birch 924). R22.

24. **oðða ða dunæ ufewearde on þa æþenan byrigelsas** (acc pl), 'as far as the upper part of the hill as far as'. . . A.D. 956. *Wudetune* (Staffordshire). Boundary: unknown. S608 (Birch 969).

25. **Þonon on þone ealdan weg,** 'from there as far as the old road', **up to ðan hæþenan byrgelse** (dat sg). A.D. 957. Stanton St Bernard (Wiltshire). Boundary: estate. S647 (Birch 998). 1st of two. R32.

26. **to þam hæþenan byrgelse** (dat sg). A.D. 957. Stanton St Bernard (Wiltshire). Boundary: estate. S647 (Birch 998). 2nd of two. R33.

27. **up on þone æþænan byrigels** (acc sg), 'up as far as' . . . A.D. 958. *Æscesbyrig* (West Berkshire?). Boundary: hundred. S575 (Birch 902). R4 and 16.

28. **on hæðennan byriels** (acc sg). **Of þan hæðenan byrielse** (dat sg). A.D. 958. Cern (West Berkshire?). Boundary: hundred. S651 (Birch 1035).

29. **to þan hæþan byrgeles** (dat sg). A.D. 958–9. Longworth (Oxfordshire). Boundary: estate. S673 (Birch 1047). 1st of two.

30. **to þam þorn stybbe aet cingtuninga gemære,** 'to the thorn stump at the boundary of Kington', **þonne to þan heaþan byrgelese** (dat sg); **þonne on þa meardic** 'then as far as the boundary ditch'. A.D. 958–9. Longworth (Oxfordshire). Boundary: hundred. S673 (Birch 1047). 2nd of two.

31. **Þon norð andlang mearce on þa hæþenan byrgenan** (acc sg or pl), 'then north along the boundary as far as'. . . . A.D. 955–9. Bathingbourne (Isle of Wight). Boundary: unknown. S1662 (Birch 1024).

32. **on þone ealdan weg up to þam hæþenan byrgelse** (dat sg). A.D. 960. Stanton St Bernard (Wiltshire). Boundary: estate. S685 (Birch 1053). 1st of two. R25.

33. **to þam hæþenan byrgelse** (dat sg). A.D. 960. Stanton St Bernard (Wiltshire). Boundary: estate. S685 (Birch 1053). 2nd of two. R26.

34. **on þone hæþenan byrgels** (acc sg); **of þam byrgelse** (dat sg). A.D. 961. Ringwood (Hampshire). Boundary: hundred. S690 (Birch 1066).

35. **to þam eþenan byrigelsan** (dat pl), **andlang mearce,** 'along the boundary'. . . . **Of þam æþenan byrigelsan** (dat pl). A.D. 961. Easton (Hampshire). Boundary: hundred. S695 (Birch 1076). R36.

36. **andlang mearce to ðam hæþænan byrigelsan** (dat pl). **Of þam hæþenan byrigelsan** (dat pl) **andlang mearce eft on ða ealdan byrig,** 'along the boundary again as far as the old fortified place'. A.D. 961. Avington (Hampshire). Boundary: hundred. S699 (Birch 1068). R35.

37. **Of þam hæþnan birigelsan** (dat pl). A.D. 966. Newnham Murren (Oxfordshire). Boundary: estate. S738 (Birch 1176). (NB: begins the circuit).

38. **on þane haþene berielese** (acc sg) **on middan þane punfald,** 'as far as the middle of the pound'. A.D. 966. Up Piddle (Dorset). Boundary: estate. S744 (Birch 1186).

39. **on þæt hæþene byrgils** (acc sg, neut). **Of þan hæþene byrgilse** (dat sg). A.D. 972. Kennet (Wiltshire). Boundary: estate. S784 (Birch 1285).

40. **Swa** 'so' **on ðone hæðenan byrgels** (acc sg), **lið** 'lies' **on hæðenan byrgels** (acc sg). A.D. 973 x 74. Crondall (Hampshire). Boundary: estate. S820 (Birch 1307). See 60.

41. **Þon norð andlang mearce** 'from there north along the boundary' **on þa heðenan byrgena** (acc sg or pl). A.D. 1003. Bengeworth (Worcestershire). Boundary: hundred. S1664 (Kemble 1299). R51.

42. **Andlang gemæres** 'along the boundary' **on þa hæþenan byrgelsas** (acc pl); **of ðam byrgelson** (dat pl). A.D. 1021–1023. Newnham (Northamptonshire). Boundary: estate. S977 (Kemble 736).

43. **Swa on Ælgares hagan æt** 'so as far as Ælfgar's enclosure at' **ðam heðanan byrigelsan** (dat pl). A.D. 1046. Hoddington (Hampshire). Boundary: hundred. S1013 (Kemble 783).

44. **on þæne hæþenan byriels** (acc sg). A.D. 1047 x 1070. Little Hinton (Wiltshire). Boundary: estate. S1588 (Birch 479).

45. **on þonne heþenan byrgels** (acc sg); **of þon heþenan byrgelse** (dat sg). No date. Oundle (Northamptonshire). Boundary: hundred. S1566 (Birch 1129).

46. **innan þæne hæþenan byrgels** (acc sg); **of þan hæðenan byrgels** (dat sg). No date. Pyrton (Oxfordshire). Boundary: estate. S1568 (Hearne). R1.

47. **to þam hæðenan byriggelse** (dat sg). No date. Shipston-on-Stour (Worcestershire). Boundary: hundred. S1573 (Hearne).

48. **locum quod appellatur hethene burieles** (acc sg). No date. Dauntsey (Wiltshire). Boundary: estate. S1580 (Birch 458). 1st of two. See 63.

49. **le hethene burieles** (acc sg). No date. Dauntsey (Wiltshire). Boundary: estate. S1580 (Birch 458). 2nd of two. See 63.

50. **le heðene buryels** (acc sg). No date. Rodbourne (Wiltshire). Boundary: hundred. S1587 (Kemble 632).

51. **on ða æðenan byrielse** (acc sg). No date. Twyford in Norton-and-Lenchwick (Worcestershire). Boundary: hundred. S1599 (Kemble 1368). See 66. R41.

Named individuals

52. **into Bernneardes byriels** (acc sg). **Of Byrnærdes byrielse** (dat sg). A.D. 693 (11th century). Battersea (Greater London). Boundary: estate. S1248 (Birch 82). R57.

53. **on Beahhildæ byrigels** (acc sg). A.D. 856. *Æscesbyrig* (West Berkshire?). Boundary: estate. S317 (Birch 491). R55.

54. **andlang straet thaet on Fridan byrgilis** (acc sg)**; of tha byrgelse** (dat sg) **on grenan byorh,** 'along the street as far as Frida's burial-place; from the burial-place as far as the green barrow'. A.D. 901. Chiseldon (Wiltshire). Boundary: estate. S366 (Birch 598).

55. **on Beaghildæ byrigels** (acc sg), **þonon on þonæ ealdan weg**, 'from there as far as the old road'. A.D. 944. *Æscesbyrig* (West Berkshire?). Boundary: estate. S503 (Birch 796). R53.

56. **on ðone hric weg** 'as far as the ridge way', **to Ealhæræs byrgelse** (dat sg). A.D. 956. *Ellendune* (Wiltshire). Boundary: hundred. S585 (Birch 948). See 20.

57. **to Bernardes byrieles** (acc sg). A.D. 957. Battersea (Greater London). Boundary: estate. S645 (Birch 994). R52.

58. **þonne to Tatemannes beorgelese** (dat sg); **of þan beorgelse** (dat sg). A.D. 963. Washington (West Sussex). Boundary: estate. S714 (Birch 125).

59. **wið Hoces byrgels** (acc sg), 'up to Hoc's burial-place'. A.D. 968. Bedwyn (Wiltshire). Boundary: estate. S756 (Birch 1213).

60. **þær Ælfstan lið on hæðenan byrgels** (dat sg). A.D. 973 x 974. Crondall (Hampshire). Boundary: hundred. S820 (Birch 1307). See 40.

61. **to Wures byrgylse** (dat sg). . . . **eft to þan byrgelse** A.D. 975. Fyfield (Hampshire). Boundary: estate. S800 (Birch 1316).

62. **on Scobban byrygels** (acc sg). A.D. 990. Wootton St Lawrence (Hampshire). Boundary: hundred. S874 (Kemble 673).

63. **ab eodem loco usque Strenges buriels** (acc sg). No date. Dauntsey (Wiltshire). Boundary: estate. S1580 (Birch 458). Separate burial in same bounds as 48 and 49.

64. **andlang stret on Eallistanes byrigels** (acc sg). No date. Evesham (Worcestershire). Boundary: hundred. S1591a (Kemble iii, 395–6). R66.

65. **on Ealhmundes byrigenne** (dat sg). No date. Tardebigge (Worcestershire). Boundary: estate. S1598 (Hearne).

66. **on Ælfstanes byriels** (acc sg). No date. Twyford in Norton-and-Lenchwick (Worcestershire). Boundary: hundred. S1599 (Kemble 1368). Separate burial in same bounds as 51. R64.

Other specified cemeteries

67. **to ðan þorne þer ða þeofes licgan,** 'to the thorn where the thieves lie', A.D. 1008. Rolleston (Staffordshire). Boundary: hundred. S920 (Sawyer in note 63, 59).

68. **Of Æcenes felda ðær ða cnihtas licgað . . . And fram ham ðe ða cnihtas licgað on matseg.** 'From Æcenes field where the lads lie . . . And from the village where the lads lie'; **matseg** not in Dictionary. A.D. 1044. Witney (Oxfordshire). Boundary: hundred. S1001 (Kemble 775).

Field cemeteries

69. **to þam byrgelsan** (dat sg); **of þam byrgelsan** (dat sg). A.D. 775 (for ?725). ?Preston (Sussex?). Boundary: unknown. S43 (Birch 144).

70. **to þare burgilsan** (dat sg (fem)). A.D. 903. Stanton St Bernard (Wiltshire). Boundary: estate. S368 (Birch 600). Equates to 33.

71. **Þonne on þa byrgelsas** (acc pl). A.D. 939. East Overton (Wiltshire). Boundary: unknown. S449 (Birch 734).

72. **swa on þa byrgelsas** (acc pl). A.D. 943. Burghclere (Hampshire). Boundary: hundred. S487 (Birch 787).

73. **on þone byrgeles** (acc sg). **Of þam byrgelse** (dat sg). A.D. 944, ? for 942. Blewbury (Oxfordshire). Boundary: hundred. S496 (Birch 801). Separate burial in same bounds as 15.

74. **on þa byrgelsas** (acc pl). A.D. 951. Chieveley (West Berkshire). Boundary: estate. S558 (Birch 892).

Creating the Sacred: Anglo-Saxon Rites for Consecrating Cemeteries

By HELEN GITTOS

A parish church, surrounded by the tombs of congregations past, is an archetypal feature of the northern European landscape. Cemeteries are specially reserved spaces where the dead may safely await their resurrection. They are both present within this world, yet removed from it, and set aside in anticipation of the world to come. The process by which churchyard burial became ubiquitous is little understood and its archaeology is peculiarly problematic. A further approach to the question is to begin, not with the archaeology, but with the rituals by which the church exerted control over burial practices. The development of a rite for consecrating cemeteries is a fundamental element in understanding the period during which places of burial came to be associated with places for worship.[1]

Cemeteries can only be consecrated by bishops and this was the case throughout the Middle Ages, just as it is today. Dedication rites, therefore, are found primarily in pontificals, a type of liturgical manuscript comprising the services specifically reserved for bishops. The ceremony for churchyard consecration is always located after the rite for dedicating a church, amongst associated rites for blessing various liturgical objects and for reconciling places and altars which had been violated by bloodshed or murder.

Anglo-Saxon rites for consecrating a cemetery involved ritual purification and demarcation of the designated area, articulating its transformation into a sacred space. The ceremony comprised four elements. First, the bishop and his clergy processed around the churchyard, sprinkling holy water in order to cleanse and purify the designated area. This was followed by a second procession in which the bishop said a prayer in each corner of the cemetery. In the Egbert pontifical (?s. x^2 or c. 1000, west country) this second procession proceeded in a clockwise direction from the east end.[2] The others, Anderson (s. x/xi, ?Christ Church, Canterbury), Dunstan (s. x^2, ?Christ Church, Canterbury) and Archbishop Robert (s. x^2, ?New Minster, Winchester), specified that the prayers were to be said at the east side, followed by the West, South

[1] The best discussions of the development of churchyard burial in early medieval Europe are: D. Bullough, 'Burial, community and belief in the early medieval West', 177–201 in P. Wormald (ed.), *Ideal and Reality in Frankish and Anglo-Saxon Society* (Oxford, 1983); C. Treffort, *L'Église Carolingienne et la Mort* (Collection d'histoire et d'archéologie médiévales, 3, Lyon, 1996); R. Morris, *The Church in British Archaeology* (CBA Res. Rep., 47, London, 1983), 49–62. For the consecration of cemeteries: B. H. Rosenwein, *Negotiating Space: Power, Restraint, and Privileges of Immunity in Early Medieval Europe* (Manchester, 1999), 178–83.
[2] *The Egbert Pontifical*, ed. H. M. J. Banting, *Two Anglo-Saxon Pontificals* (Henry Bradshaw Soc., 104, London, 1989), 57–60.

and North, tracing a cross through the cemetery.[3] The rites became elaborated in the later 11th century with additional antiphons and another procession: Cambridge, Corpus Christi College, MS. 146 (s. xi[1], ?Winchester or ?Christ Church, Canterbury), London, British Library, Add. 28188 (s. xi[2], Exeter) and London, British Library, Cotton Vitellius A. vii (?s. xi[1] or s. xi[med], ?Exeter).[4] All provided for a fifth prayer in the centre of the cemetery. The additional material was added in the margins of Anderson and is also found in Cambridge, Corpus Christi College, MS. 44 (s. xi[med], Christ Church, Canterbury).[5] The majority of the texts culminate in the celebration of mass, probably at a portable altar set up within the churchyard.[6] In form, the ceremony was closely related to those for dedicating churches, which also involved procession around the perimeters of the space, sprinkling holy water, prayers in the centre and concluded with a mass.[7]

There was a well-established tradition of churchyard consecration in England by the late 10th century, when the earliest relevant manuscripts survive. It is found in ten of the thirteen manuscripts known to the author which include a rite for church dedication, and where one would therefore expect to find instructions for the consecration of a cemetery. The books which omit the latter are the Leofric Missal,

[3] *The Benedictional of Archbishop Robert*, ed. H. A. Wilson (Henry Bradshaw Soc., 24, London, 1903), 101–3; *The Dunstan Pontifical* and *The Anderson Pontifical*, ed. A. M. Conn, 'The Dunstan and Brodie (Anderson) Pontificals', (unpublished PhD thesis, University of Notre Dame, 1993), 76–80, 227–31. Dunstan is described in V. Leroquais, *Les Pontificaux Manuscrits des Bibliothèques Publiques de France*, 4 vols (Paris, 1937), II, 6–10.

[4] Cambridge, Corpus Christi College, MS. 146, pp. 90–4; M. R. James, *A Descriptive Catalogue of the Manuscripts in the Library of Corpus Christi College, Cambridge*, 2 vols (Cambridge, 1909–12), I, 332–5; London, British Library, Add. 28188, ff. 56[v]–60[v]; A. Prescott, 'The structure of English pre-Conquest benedictionals', *British Library J.*, 13 (1987), 118–58; London, British Library, Cotton Vitellius A. vii, ff. 54–56; J. Brückmann, 'Latin manuscript pontificals and benedictionals in England and Wales', *Traditio*, 29 (1973), 391–458, at 437.

[5] Conn, op. cit. in note 3, 227–9. Cambridge, Corpus Christi Collge MS. 44, pp. 165–74 (s. xi[1] or xi[med], Christ Church, Canterbury); James, op. cit. in note 4, I, 88–90.

[6] The following manuscripts included a mass: *The Benedictional of Archbishop Robert*, (s. x[2], ?New Minster, Winchester), ed. Wilson, op. cit. in note 3, 101–3; *The Egbert Pontifical*, (?s. x[2] or c. 1000, west country), ed. Banting, op. cit. in note 2, 101–3; *The Dunstan Pontifical* (s. x[2], ?Christ Church, Canterbury) and *The Anderson Pontifical* (s. x/xi, ?Christ Church, Canterbury), ed. Conn, op. cit. in note 3, 76–80, 227–31; London, British Library, Add. 28188, ff. 59[v]–60[v] (s. xi[2], Exeter); London, British Library, Cotton Vitellius A. vii, ff. 54–56 (s. xi[med], ?Exeter); Cambridge, Corpus Christi Collge MS. 44, ff. 165–74 (s. xi[med], Christ Church, Canterbury); Cambridge, Corpus Christi College, MS. 146, pp. 90–94 (s. xi[1] and xi/xii, ?Winchester or ?Christ Church, Canterbury). The following manuscripts have no provision for a mass: *Claudius Pontifical I* (c. 1000, ?Worcester or York) ed. D. H. Turner, *The Claudius Pontificals* (Henry Bradshaw Soc., 97, London, 1971), 60–1; *The Lanalet Pontifical*, (s. xi[1], west country), ed. G. H. Doble (Henry Bradshaw Soc., 74, London, 1937), 21. In the late medieval period, burials were occasionally made in conjunction with the consecration of a cemetery: G. Oliver, *The History of Exeter* (Exeter, 1821), 89; J. Wickham Legg (ed.), *English Orders for Consecrating Churches in the Seventeenth Century* (Henry Bradshaw Soc., 41, London, 1911), 188.

[7] For the Anglo-Saxon rites see: Turner, op. cit. in note 6, xxii–xxiv; W. H. Frere, *Pontifical Services Illustrated from Miniatures of the XVth and XVIth Centuries* (Alcuin Club Collections, 3, London, 1901), 1–54; H. Gittos, *Sacred Space in Anglo-Saxon England: Liturgy, Architecture and Place*, unpublished DPhil thesis, University of Oxford, forthcoming), ch. 5.

which is considerably earlier than the others,[8] and two Anglo-Saxon copies of an Ottonian pontifical.[9]

Given the number of surviving Anglo-Saxon documents containing consecration rites, one might expect to find a similar number in continental sources. There were, however, no Roman *ordines* for the rite of churchyard consecration,[10] nor any references to it in the early continental sacramentaries or early saints' lives.[11] Neither is the rite contained in any 9th- and 10th-century European pontificals,[12] with one important exception, to which I shall return. The earliest continental rites are found in recensions of the Romano-Germanic Pontifical (hereafter RGP). A type of pontifical, the RGP was compiled in the mid-10th century in the monastery of St Alban, Mainz.[13] It comprised a substantial compendium of *ordines*, including Roman rites which had previously circulated as individual documents, with the addition of a substantial body of Gallican material. Many copies were made and spread rapidly across Europe during the late 10th and 11th centuries. Most though not all, copies of the RGP included a rite for consecrating a cemetery. There was no one archetype from which all the others were derived. Instead, it continued to evolve as new material was added and older rites were adapted.[14] The earliest manuscripts that survive do not include a consecration

[8] *The Leofric Missal*, ed. F. E. Warren (Oxford, 1883), 218–22. For the reassessment of the date and provenance of this manuscript: N. Orchard (Henry Bradshaw Soc., London, forthcoming).
[9] Cambridge, Corpus Christi College, 163, described by James, op. cit. in note 4, I, 368–9 and discussed by M. Lapidge, 'The origin of CCCC 163', *Trans. Cambridge Bibliographic Soc.*, 8 (1981), 18–28, who dates it to the mid-11th century. M. Gullick, 'The origin and date of Cambridge CCC ms. 163', *Trans. Cambridge Bibliographic Soc.*, 11 (1996), 89–90, suggests that it was produced in Worcester and argues for a date in the last quarter of the 11th century. London, British Library, Cotton Vitellius E.xii (s. xi²); M. Lapidge, 'Ealdred of York and ms. Cotton Vitellius E.xii', *Yorkshire Archaeol. J.*, 55 (1983), 11–25.
[10] There are no rites listed in M. Andrieu (ed.), *Les Ordines Romani du Haut Moyen Âge*, 5 vols. (Spicilegium Sacrum Louvaniense, 11, 23, 24, 28, 29, Louvain, 1931–61).
[11] Bullough, op. cit. in note 1, 185–90; cf. B. Effros, 'Beyond cemetery walls: early medieval funerary topography and Christian salvation', *Early Medieval Europe*, 6:1 (1997), 1–23, who argues that the Merovingian church did exert some control over burial practices.
[12] Bullough, op. cit. in note 1, 199 n. 57. C. Vogel, *Medieval Liturgy: an Introduction to the Sources*, rev. & trans. W. G. Storey and N. K. Rasmussen (Washington, 1986), 227–9; K. Gamber, *Codices Liturgici Latini Antiquiores*, 2 vols. (Spicilegii friburgensis Subsidia, 1, 2nd edn, Fribourg, 1963, 1964), nos. 1550–75; idem., *Supplementum, Ergänzungs-und Registerband* (Spicilegii friburgensis Subsidia, 1A, Fribourg, 1988) lists the principal 9th- and 10th-century primitive pontificals, of which I have checked editions or lists of contents in Andrieu, op. cit. in note 10, and Leroquais, op. cit. in note 3. In addition, of the 11th-century pontificals which Leroquais lists, the only ones which contain a rite for the consecration of a churchyard are copies of the Romano-Germanic Pontifical.
[13] Vogel, op. cit. in note 12, 233–7; C. Vogel and R. Elze, *Le Pontifical Romano-Germanique du Dixième Siècle*, 3 vols (Studi e Testi, 226, 227, 269, Rome, 1963–72), III, 3–55.
[14] Vogel, op. cit. in note 12, 236.

rite,[15] and those that have one are later than the earliest English examples.[16] The rite was not known in Rome until the adoption of the RGP.[17]

The form of the rite in the RGP was less elaborate than that which is found in the Anglo-Saxon manuscripts. It provided for the singing of the seven penitential psalms, the placing of four candles around the cemetery, which was not a typical feature of the Anglo-Saxon *ordines*, and a procession around the churchyard.[18] There were, however, no rubrics for a second procession, nor for prayers in each corner of the cemetery. Only the first three of the five or six prayers in the early Anglo-Saxon rites were included and there was no provision for a mass in the churchyard.

It is unlikely that the Anglo-Saxon church adapted the rite from the Mainz model, as the RGP seems to have been adopted relatively late in England. Of the six surviving manuscripts which were almost certainly used in Anglo-Saxon England, none have been dated earlier than the mid-11th century.[19] This does not seem to be merely a product of the differential survival of evidence, given the number of insular pontificals which survive from the late 10th and 11th centuries.[20] It would appear that the Anglo-Saxon church did not feel the need to import such material when they had their own well-established traditions. In any case, none of the surviving Romano-Germanic pontificals from pre-Conquest England included a rite for churchyard consecration.[21]

The only 10th-century continental manuscript which contains the rite is the Sacramentary of Ratoldus. This manuscript was written for the Abbot of Corbie between 972 and 986.[22] It is chiefly known for containing the earliest extant recension of the second English coronation *ordo*.[23] It has long been argued, on the basis of the inclusion of this rite, along with a number of other English elements, that the pontifical

---

[15] The earliest recension is Lucca, Bibliotheca capitolare, cod. 607 (960x1000, Lucca). Other manuscripts which omit the rite are: Pistoia, Archives du Chapitre, cod. 141 (s. xi[1]); Paris, Bibliothèque nationale de France, cod. lat. 820 (xi[2], ?Angers); Vienna, Österreichische Nationalbibliothek, cod. lat. 701 (s. xi[1], Mainz); London, British Library, Ms. Add 17004 (s. xi[2], ?Bamberg); Wolfenbüttel, Herzog-August Bibliothek, cod. lat. 603 (s. xii[in], ?Ausbach); Bamberg, Staatliche bibliothek, cod. lit. 53 (s. xi[1], ?Bamberg); Pontifical of Gondekar II, Eichstätt, Episcopal Archives (1057x1075). For the contents, date and provenance of the manuscripts see Andrieu, op. cit. in note 10, I; Vogel, op. cit. in note 12, 203–31, 233–5.

[16] Rome, Bibliotheca Vallicelliane, cod. D.5 (s. xi[med]); Monte Cassino, Bibliothèque de l'Abbaye, cod. 451 (1022x1035, Monte Cassino), thought to have been copied from a manuscript produced 996x1002; Rome, Bibliotheca Alessandrina, cod. 173 (s. xi[in], ?Rome), though this has only the first prayer: Vogel, op. cit. in note 12, 230–1; Vogel and Elze, op. cit. in note 13, III, 6–19, 65–71; Andrieu, op. cit. in note 10, I.

[17] For the date of the adoption of the RGP in Rome, see Vogel, op. cit. in note 12, 238.

[18] No. LIV in the edition by Vogel and Elze, op. cit. in note 13, I, 192–3. The only Anglo-Saxon pontifical to provide for the use of twelve candles is Cambridge, Corpus Christi College, MS. 44, pp. 165–74.

[19] J. L. Nelson and R. W. Pfaff, 'Pontificals and Benedictionals', 87–98 in R. W. Pfaff (ed.), *The Liturgical Books of Anglo-Saxon England* (Old English Newsletter Subsidia, 23, Kalamazoo, 1995), at pp. 96–8; Lapidge, 'Ealdred', op. cit. in note 9, 21; see also the references in note 9.

[20] Most are discussed in Nelson and Pfaff, op. cit. in note 19; cf. D. N. Dumville, *Liturgy and the Ecclesiastical History of Anglo-Saxon England: Four Studies* (Woodbridge, 1992), 66–88.

[21] The principal examples are listed in Nelson and Pfaff, op. cit. in note 19, 96–7.

[22] Paris, Bibliothèque nationale de France, lat. 12052, ff. 9[r]–10[r]; V. Leroquais, *Les Sacramentaires et les Missels Manuscrits des Bibliothèques Publiques de France*, 4 vols (Paris, 1924), I, 79; Gamber, 'Codices', op. cit. in note 12, no. 923. The rite is described by Treffort, op. cit. in note 1, 141–2. I am grateful to Professor Michael Lapidge for the loan, on behalf of the Henry Bradshaw Society, of copies of the manuscript.

[23] J. L. Nelson, *Politics and Ritual in Early Medieval Europe* (London, 1986), 361–9.

contained within the manuscript was copied from an English exemplar.[24] The rite for consecrating a cemetery must also have derived from the same English source.

The date at which the pontifical was incorporated into the manuscript is contentious. Christopher Hohler has argued that the source is most likely to have been brought from England by Louis IV in 936, when he returned from his exile at the court of Æthelstan in order to be crowned, and that the coronation *ordo* was subsequently used by him.[25] However, it is also possible that a pontifical containing an old coronation *ordo* could have been incorporated into Ratoldus at any point up until the death of the Abbot in 986.[26] Whichever date is to be preferred, the Ratoldus Sacramentary provides one of the earliest witnesses to the rite, and may preserve a primitive version of the Anglo-Saxon *ordo* similar to that which was used in the RGP.

This suggestion is supported by the form of the rites themselves. The rite in Ratoldus is identical to that in the RGP, except that Ratoldus does not specify aspersion with holy water. In Anglo-Saxon England, however, the rite became increasingly elaborate during the late 10th and 11th centuries. The Egbert pontifical (?s. x^2 or c. 1000, west country) specified four prayers and a mass; Lanalet (s. xi^1, west country) and Claudius I (c. 1000, ?Worcester or York) included five prayers but no mass; Dunstan (s. x^2, ?Christ Church, Canterbury), Archbishop Robert (s. x^2, ?New Minster, Winchester) and Anderson (s. x/xi, ?Christ Church, Canterbury) provided for five prayers and a mass;[27] and the four 11th-century manuscripts have six prayers, additional antiphons, a third procession and a mass.[28] In addition, Cambridge, Corpus Christi College, MS. 44 (s. xi^1 or xi^{med}, Christ Church, Canterbury) specifies the use of twelve candles, three aspersion processions, a final blessing and four additional prayers in the mass. It is possible, therefore, that Ratoldus preserved a primitive form of an English rite, akin to that from which the less elaborate *ordo* in the RGP was derived. A detailed comparison of the texts demonstrates that Ratoldus was not the source for the rite in the RGP, though it does provide an example of an Anglo-Saxon manuscript being copied on the Continent during the relevant period. Ratoldus was not unique, given the number of pre-Conquest manuscripts which are known to have been

[24] C. Hohler, 'Some service-books of the later Saxon Church', 60–83, at 64–9, in D. Parsons (ed.), *Tenth-Century Studies: Essays in Commemoration of the Millennium of the Council of Winchester and* Regularis Concordia (Chichester, 1975); A. Prescott, 'The text of the Benedictional of St. Æthelwold', 119–47 in B. Yorke (ed.), *Bishop Æthelwold: His Career and Influence* (Woodbridge, 1988), at pp. 135–42; Turner, op. cit. in note 6, xxx–xxxiii.
[25] Hohler, op. cit. in note 24, 64–9; N. Brooks, *The Early History of the Church of Canterbury Christ Church from 597 to 1066* (London, 1984), 164–5.
[26] Prescott, op. cit. in note 24, 135–42, argues for a date 965x980.
[27] For references to editions see notes 2, 3 and 6. Treffort, op. cit. in note 1, 142 n.89, 150 n.94, refers to another manuscript which has a rite of the Anglo–Saxon type: Paris, Bibliothèque nationale, lat. 1686, ff. 61^v–62^r. The manuscript, of uncertain provenance, is a highly miscellaneous compilation largely dating from the late 11th to 12th century, though with some material of the 9th century: *Bibliothèque Nationale Catalogue Général des Manuscrits Latins* (1939, Paris), II, 124–5.
[28] London British Library Cotton Vitellius A.vii (s. xi^{med}, ?Exeter); London, British Library Add 28188 (s. xi^2, Exeter); Cambridge, Corpus Christi College MS. 44 (s. xi or xi^{med}, Christ Church, Canterbury) and MS. 146 (s. xi^1, ?Winchester or ?Christ Church, Canterbury). Most of these additional elements are also added in the margins of the Anderson Pontifical (s. x/xi, ?Christ Church, Canterbury), ed. Conn, op. cit. in note 3.

exported to the Continent, sometimes as little as fifty years after their production.[29] By the 12th century, the divergence between the two traditions was even more marked. The English rites were more complex than the latest Anglo-Saxon rites,[30] whereas the 12th-century Roman rite was based on the RGP, and by the 13th century it consisted of a single prayer.[31] It is difficult to be sure that the compilers in Mainz were using Anglo-Saxon sources but the evidence is certainly suggestive.

In most of the Anglo-Saxon manuscripts the rite is followed by a mass for the dead. This mass was intended to be used in association with the rite. In the partial list of contents which prefaced the Dunstan Pontifical, it is described as *'consecratio cymiterii cum missa conpetenti'*.[32] In Anderson and Archbishop Robert the masses have the rubric *'incipit missa'* and in Egbert *'missa in cimetirio'*, in the form of rubrics rather than headings, and in London, British Library, Add. 28188 it is entitled *'Missa in consecratione cymiterii'*.[33] The mass in the Egbert Pontifical is found in the Gallicanised-Gelasian and Frankish-Gelasian sacramentaries as a mass for the dead.[34] It is also found in later manuscripts, contemporary with Egbert, such as the Fulda Sacramentary and the Leofric Missal.[35] This mass seems to have been chosen because it was the only one which specified that it was to be celebrated in the churchyard, and was therefore appropriate as a symbolic burial in the newly consecrated ground.[36] The mass that is found in the other Anglo-Saxon pontificals appears to be unique.

This is a classic example of the way in which the liturgy developed during the early medieval period: elements borrowed from elsewhere, adapted to suit a specific purpose, to which new material was added. It fits in with a wider pattern that is beginning to emerge of Anglo-Saxon influence on the liturgy of western Europe.[37] Perhaps the Anglo-Saxon church was in a uniquely powerful position to initiate such change. It is also possible that the explanation for the evolution of this rite in England may derive from differences in the development of Christian burial. Where traditional burial grounds, particularly those close to martyrial shrines, continued to be used into

---

[29] Examples of Anglo-Saxon liturgical manuscripts known to have reached the Continent in the 11th century include the *Missal of Robert of Jumièges*, ed. H. A. Wilson (London, 1896) (s. xi[1], ?Ely/ ?Peterborough); *The Egbert Pontifical* (?s. x[2] or c. 1000, west country), ed. Banting, op. cit. note 2 and *The Dunstan Pontifical* (s. x[2], ?Christ Church, Canterbury), ed. Conn, op. cit. in note 3; Dumville, op. cit. in note 20, 83–4.

[30] *The Pontifical of Magdalen College*, ed. H. A. Wilson (Henry Bradshaw Soc., 39, London, 1910), 125–7.

[31] M. Andrieu, *Le Pontifical Romain au Moyen Âge*, 3 vols (Studi e Testi, 86–88, 99, Vatican City, 1938–40, 1941), Vol. I: *Le Pontifical Romain du XIIe siècle*, 285–6. One of the manuscripts on which Andrieu based his edition, Lyon, Bibliothèque Municipale, cod. 570, contains two rites, one based on the RGP and another which is comparable with the Anglo-Saxon sources.

[32] Conn, op. cit. in note 3, 24.

[33] For references see notes 2, 3 and 4.

[34] The prayers are listed in E. Moeller, I. M. Clément and B. C. Wallant (eds.), *Corpus Orationum*, 12 vols. (Corpus Christianorum Series Latina, CLX, Turnhout, 1992–2000), II, 147–8 (no. 1170); VI, 40–1 (no. 3789); II, 162 (no. 4642); 164 (no. 1210). The mass is listed in P. Bruylants, *Les Orasions du Missel Romain*, 2 vols. (Louvain, 1952), I, 203 (no. 624.15).

[35] All the prayers were included in two adjacent masses, nos. 444 and 445: G. Richter and A. Schönfelder (eds.), *Sacramentarium Fuldense Saeculi X* (rpr. Henry Bradshaw Soc., 101, London, 1977), 309–10, though there are slight discrepancies between Fulda and Egbert; *The Leofric Missal*, ed. Warren, op. cit. in note 8, 98.

[36] In most of the manuscripts the mass is entitled *missa in coemeterio*: Bruylants, op. cit. in note 34, I, 203.

[37] See particularly M. Lapidge (ed.), *Anglo-Saxon Litanies of the Saints* (Henry Bradshaw Soc., 106, London, 1991), 1–61.

the early Middle Ages, there may have been no need to conceive of sanctifying burial by consecration.[38]

Although the earliest surviving liturgical evidence dates to the later 10th century, the homogeneity of the prayers suggests that it was already an established custom. This is supported by other evidence for consecrated cemeteries. The earliest relevant reference in the Anglo-Saxon law codes refers to the exclusion of criminals from consecrated ground and dates to the early 10th century (II Æthelstan 26).[39] By the time of Cnut, burial in consecrated ground was considered to be a Christian right.[40] The concept of soul-scot, the burial tax paid, usually at the grave-side, to the minster church, is intimately bound up with institutional control over burial. It is therefore unfortunate that its history is so little understood. The earliest references to soul-scot are in two charters, of Worcester and Winchester, from the 870s, although references to it did not become common until the later 10th century, and it does not seem to have been legally codified until the early 11th century.[41] The Anglo-Saxon evidence for the collection of soul-scot is far earlier than anything comparable on the Continent.[42] Quite why the Anglo-Saxon Church took such an initiative is unclear, but it does provide a context for the creation of a rite for consecrating graveyards. If burial taxes were being collected from the late 9th century, at least in areas in close proximity to major cathedrals, then it is understandable that there would be a concomitant desire to define burial places liturgically. Consecration ensured that the church had jurisdiction over burial rites, which became an increasingly important source of revenue during the 10th century. Paradoxically, it arose out of a desire for inclusivity, to provide burial *ad sanctos* for the entire Christian community, inevitably resulting in the exclusion of the unbaptised, criminals and suicides.[43]

A parallel development in the codification of sacred space is also manifested in the changing definition of sanctuary, the provision whereby a person accused of a

---

[38] P. Ariès, *The Hour of Our Death*, trans. H. Weaver (London, 1981), 39, 53, draws a contrast between the Roman concept of the tomb as a holy place and the medieval idea of the entire cemetery as a sacred space.

[39] Ed. F. Liebermann, *Die Gesetze der Angelsachsen*, 3 vols (Halle, 1903–16), I, 165; for discussion see, P. Wormald, *The Making of English Law. Volume I: King Alfred to the Twelfth Century* (Oxford, 1999), 307–8, 339–40.

[40] I Canute 22.5: ed. Liebermann, op. cit. in note 39, I, 304–5.

[41] J. Blair, 'Introduction: from minster to parish church', in J. Blair (ed.), *Minsters and Parish Churches: The Local Church in Transition 950–1200* (Oxford, 1988), 1–19, at p. 8; P. H. Sawyer, *Anglo-Saxon Charters: An Annotated List and Bibliography* (London, 1968) nos. 1275, 1279; A. J. Robertson (ed. and trans.), *Anglo-Saxon Charters* (2nd ed., Cambridge, 1956) no. xiv; W. de Gray Birch, *Cartularium Saxonicum: A Collection of Charters Relating to Anglo-Saxon History*, 3 vols. (1883–92), II, no. 580. The laws are V Æthelred 12.1, VIII Æthelred 13: ed. Liebermann, op. cit. in note 39, I, 240–1, 265. For discussion, see P. Wormald, *The Making Of English Law. Vol II: From God's Law to Common Law* (Oxford, forthcoming) and J. Blair, *The Church in Anglo-Saxon Society* (Oxford, forthcoming). I am grateful to Patrick Wormald and Dr John Blair for these references.

[42] Wormald, op. cit. in note 39.

[43] For the exclusion of execution victims: A. Reynolds, 'The definition and ideology of Anglo-Saxon execution sites and cemeteries', 33–41 in G. de Boe and F. Verhaeghe (eds.), *Death and Burial in Medieval Europe* (Zellik, 1997).

crime could claim the protection of a church.[44] The concept is first attested in the early
Kentish laws, but Wendy Davis has argued that, whereas the early Anglo-Saxon laws
specified the period of time during which sanctuary could be claimed, the 10th-century
law codes display a growing concern with defining sanctuary rights in spatial terms.[45]

The liturgical evidence fits well with the legal sources, but it is more difficult to
assess the archaeological evidence for the development of churchyard burial. The
nature of burial practices in the crucial period from the mid-8th to the early 11th
centuries is poorly understood. The Anglo-Saxon Church seems to have placed little
emphasis on the importance of churchyard burial, and there is no canon law that
forbids the use of traditional local cemeteries.[46] There are cases of 8th-century burials
in the vicinity of minster churches, but this does not necessarily indicate that
churchyard burial had become normal practice.[47] It is possible that it did not become
common until the early 10th century and in some areas possibly even later.[48] Bede
makes reference to cemeteries at the monasteries of Barking (HE IV.7), Ely (HE IV.19)
and Lastingham ((HE III.23), and monastic cemeteries are rarely found to be confined
to one sex.[49] Nevertheless, there is no evidence to suggest that monastic cemeteries
ever served a parochial function, and they appear to have been the exclusive preserve
of the monastic community, its benefactors and dependants.

The development of a rite for consecrating cemeteries was not related to the
control of burial at monastic sites, but was intimately associated with control over the
burial of the laity, as it became increasingly common to be buried in association with a
parish church. The consecration of an area of open ground, marking it out as a sacred
space appropriate for burial, necessitates the definition of that area by some form of
boundary, and bounded cemeteries seem to have been a product of the shift towards
burial close to churches.[50] Although there are many examples of enclosures around
individual graves or family groups in late pagan and early Christian burial sites,

[44] There is no modern study of English sanctuary. J. C. Cox, *The Sanctuaries and Sanctuary Seekers of Medieval England* (London, 1911), is the best source, though he concentrates primarily on chartered sanctuaries. C. H. Riggs, *Criminal Asylum in Anglo-Saxon Law*, (Gainesville, 1963), and J. H. Baker, 'The English law of sanctuary', *Ecclesiastical Law J.*, 2:6 (1990), 8–13, examine it from a legal perspective. See also D. Hall, 'The sanctuary of St. Cuthbert', 425–36 in G. Bonner, D. Rollason and C. Stancliffe (eds.), *St. Cuthbert, His Cult and His Community to AD 1200* (Woodbridge, 1989). For the Welsh material: H. Pryce, *Native Law and the Church in Medieval Wales* (Oxford, 1993), 163–203, and W. Davies, 'Adding insult to injury: power, property and immunities in early medieval Wales', 137–64 in W. Davies and P. Fouracre (eds.), *Property and Power in the Early Middle Ages* (Cambridge, 1995).

[45] W. Davies, '"Protected Space" in Britain and Ireland in the Middle Ages', 1–19, in B. E. Crawford (ed.), *Scotland and Dark Age Britain* (Aberdeen, 1996). Davies has traced a parallel development in the codification of the Welsh concept of *nawdd*: W. Davies, 'Property rights and property claims in Welsh *vitae* of the eleventh century', 515–33 in *Hagiographie Cultures et Sociétés IVᵉ–XIIᵉ siècles* (Paris, 1981) at p. 524. For the establishment of areas of immunity at Cluny in the 10th and 11th centuries, see Rosenwein, op. cit. in note 1, 163–83.

[46] Bullough, op. cit. in note 1, 185–90.

[47] A. Boddington, 'Models of burial, settlement and worship: the Final Phase reviewed', 177–99 in E. Southworth (ed.), *Anglo-Saxon Cemeteries: A Reappraisal* (Stroud, 1990).

[48] Blair forthcoming, op. cit. in note 41.

[49] *Bede's Ecclesiastical History of the English People*, ed. and trans. B. Colgrave and R. A. B. Mynors (Oxford, 1969).

[50] J. Kieffer-Olsen, 'Christianity and Christian burial', 185–9 in C. Jensen and K. Høilund Nielsen (eds.), *Burial and Society: The Chronological and Social Analysis of Archaeological Burial Data* (Århus, 1997) discusses Scandinavian parallels.

boundaries around the perimeters of the site do not seem to have been a common feature.[51] Susan Hirst has argued that this may not have been the case because few excavations locate the edges of a cemetery, many were not dug under modern conditions, and structures such as fences may not be archaeologically visible.[52] She cites the example of Bidford-on-Avon (Warwickshire), where a row of graves was possibly aligned on a N.–S. barrier and a series of ditches were found, though the closest was 9 m to the east of the cemetery.[53] At Finglesham (Kent) a trackway formed the boundary on one side, though the excavation did not extend beyond it.[54] Hirst's arguments urge caution, but there are few, if any, convincing examples and in most cases the burials sprawled towards the peripheries, suggesting a lack of confinement. The few excavated examples of monastic cemeteries also do not seem to have been enclosed, though Monkwearmouth (Tyne and Wear) may be an exception.[55] It is therefore unlikely that monastic cemeteries provided a paradigm for the enclosure of local burial grounds.

Very few complete churchyards have been excavated, though those which have suggest that the need for an enclosure was required only at the point of fusion between the places of burial and worship. The excavated church at Raunds Furnells (Northamptonshire) provides an excellent illustration of this process. In the mid-10th century a tiny chapel was constructed immediately to the East of a manorial enclosure.[56] A series of post-holes appears to delineate the eastern and southern sides of the churchyard, although they were too irregular and widely-spaced to have supported a fence. Half-a-century later, at the turn of the 11th century, a chancel was added and the first phase of burial began, and it was at this point that a ditched boundary was constructed.[57] There is a parallel for this at Rivenhall (Essex), where a church was erected in the 10th century on the site of a Roman villa. Soon afterwards, the church was replaced by a stone structure, at which point the site then became

[51] E. O'Brien, *Post-Roman Britain to Anglo-Saxon England: Burial Practices Reviewed* (BAR Brit. Ser., 289, Oxford, 1999), 17–21, 114–16, 122–3, 135–9; Boddington, op. cit. in note 47, 177–99. The extensive extra-mural cemetery at Poundbury, Dorset, had boundary ditches in the 4th century, when it has been interpreted as a Christian cemetery: D. E. Farwell and T. L. Molleson, *Excavations at Poundbury, 1966–80. Volume II: The Cemeteries* (Dorset Nat. Hist. and Archeol. Soc. Mon., 11, Dorchester, 1993), 18–9. Cannington (Somerset), which was in use from the late Roman period to the 8th century, appears not to have had any: P. Rahtz and L. Watts, 'The end of Roman temples in the West of Britain', 183–201, in P. J. Casey (ed.), *The End of Roman Britain* (BAR British Series, 71, Oxford, 1979). In the context of the Roman Empire bounded cemeteries are relatively uncommon, and it is difficult to identify patterns in the British evidence: J. M. C. Toynbee, *Death and Burial in the Roman World* (London, 1971), 91–4; R. F. Jessup, 'Barrows and walled cemeteries in Roman Britain', *J. British Archaeol. Assoc.*, 3rd series, 22 (1959), 1–32; E. W. Black, 'Romano-British burial customs and religious beliefs in South-East England', *Archaeol. J.*, 143 (1986), 201–39.
[52] S. Hirst, *An Anglo-Saxon Inhumation Cemetery at Sewerby, East Yorkshire* (York, 1985), 20–4.
[53] Ibid, 20–4; J. Humphreys, H. W. Ryland, F. C. Wellstood, E. A. B. Barnard and T. G. Barnett, 'An Anglo-Saxon cemetery at Bidford-on-Avon, Warwickshire: second report on the excavations', *Archaeologia*, 24 (1924), 271–88.
[54] S. C. Hawkes, 'Orientation at Finglesham: sunrise dating of death and burial in an Anglo-Saxon cemetery in East Kent', *Archaeol. Cantiana*, 92 (1976), 33–51.
[55] R. J. Cramp, 'Excavations at the Saxon monastic sites of Wearmouth and Jarrow, Co. Durham: an interim report', *Medieval Archaeol.*, 13 (1969), 21–66, at 31–4.
[56] A. Boddington, *Raunds Furnells: The Anglo-Saxon Church and Churchyard* (English Heritage Archaeol. Reports, 7, London, 1996); for the revised chronology, M. Audouy, *North Raunds, Northamptonshire: Excavations 1977–87* (forthcoming).
[57] Boddington, op. cit. in note 56, 14.

enclosed.[58] This pattern of development may also account for the growing number of examples of Anglo-Saxon burials which are found in association with early churches, yet lie beyond the current churchyard boundary.[59]

Those churches which had no burial rights may never have been enclosed. The late 10th-century laws of Æthelred classified churches into head minsters, medium rank churches, small sites with graveyards, and those without cemeteries which were termed *feldcircan*.[60] Lawrence Butler has argued that there may have been many small chapels, citing the number which were recorded in the 11th-century *Domesday Monachorum*.[61] As at Raunds, it is likely that they were literally located in fields with no surrounding boundaries. At East Coker (Somerset), where the church preserves Anglo-Saxon fabric, the western edge of the cemetery, bordering the grounds of the medieval manor, was not enclosed until the 1970s.[62] Similarly, at Barton-upon-Humber (North Lincolnshire), the late Anglo-Saxon church and graveyard were situated to the West of what is thought to be a pre-Conquest manor. The manor site was enclosed by a curvilinear ditch which was filled in when the first graves were cut. No evidence was found in the excavation for any subsequent boundaries between the church and manor.[63] Even the royal chapel at Cheddar (Somerset) had no distinct precinct of its own.[64] There are parallels for this in modern Greece and the southern Balkans, where virtually the only non-monastic churches with defined boundaries are those which have attached cemeteries. In Georgia, village cemeteries are typically located on a hill just beyond the settlement, and the only ones that are bounded are those surrounded by cultivated land. It is unclear whether a pre-10th-century cemetery would ever have been consecrated; in the pontificals, the rite stands alone, but always follows the ritual for the consecration of a church. It seems likely, therefore, that churchyards were consecrated only when they were newly created or when boundaries were erected. Older sites, such as minster churches, may never have been sanctified. Barbara Rosenwein has suggested that this may still have been the case in France in the late 11th century, citing the number of cemeteries that were consecrated by Pope Urban II.[65]

---

[58] W. and K. Rodwell, *Rivenhall: Investigations of a Roman Villa, Church and Village, 1950–77*, 2 vols. (CBA Res. Rep., 55 and 80, York, 1985, 1993).

[59] M. Adams, 'Excavation of a pre-Conquest cemetery at Addingham, West Yorkshire', *Medieval Archaeol.*, 41 (1997), 151–91; Morris, op. cit. in note 1, 59; O'Brien, op. cit. in note 51, 103.

[60] VIII Æthelred 5.i: ed. Liebermann, op. cit. in note 39, I, 264.

[61] L. Butler, 'The churchyard in eastern England, AD 900–1100: some lines of development', 383–9 in P. Rahtz, T. Dickinson and L. Watts (eds.), *Anglo-Saxon Cemeteries 1979* (BAR Brit. Ser., 82, Oxford, 1982), at p. 385.

[62] B. and M. Gittos, 'The surviving Anglo-Saxon fabric of East Coker church', *Somerset Archaeol. Nat. Hist. Soc.*, 135 (1991), 107–11, at 110. The current parish church contains Anglo-Saxon fabric and may have been founded as an estate church. Until 1975 there was no boundary on the western side adjoining the manor house (B. and M. Gittos, pers. comm.).

[63] W. and K. Rodwell, 'St Peter's church, Barton-upon-Humber: excavation and structural study, 1978–81', *Antiq. J.*, 62 (1982), 283–315.

[64] P. Rahtz, *The Saxon and Medieval Palaces at Cheddar* (BAR Brit. Ser., 65, Oxford, 1979), 193–216. The chapel had no graveyard and the extensive excavations in the surrounding area found no evidence for an enclosure.

[65] Rosenwein, op. cit. in note 1, 179–83.

There was, however, one corner of western Europe which was different, which may have considerable implications for the archaeological paradigm of an early Anglo-Saxon monastery. In Ireland the concept of sacred space, and of protective boundaries, was a recurring feature of saints' lives[66] and a defining characteristic of the archaeology of ecclesiastical sites.[67] This may not simply reflect the differential survival of evidence. The early 8th-century *Collectio Canonum Hibernensis* contains several canons concerned with holy places.[68] Book XLIV, '*De locis consecratis*', is of particular interest, because it is explicitly concerned with defining the attributes of a holy place. Drawing extensively on Old Testament references to the precincts around the Tabernacle and the Temple of Solomon, it defined the number of boundaries around a sacred place and those who were permitted to enter them: '*Primus vocatur sanctus, secundus sanctior, tertius sanctissimus*' (XLIV.5).[69] These prohibitions were intended to protect the holy place from pollution; '*si quis violaverit templum Dei, disperdet illum Deus*' (XLIV.7).[70] The same section also described the way in which the boundary of the space was marked: '*Terminus sancti loci habeat signa circa se. Sinodus dicit: Ubicunque inveneritis signum crucis Christi, ne laeseritis. Item: Tres personae consecrant terminum loci sancti, rex, episcopus, populus*' (XLIV.3).[71] This was a recurrent motif in saints' lives, where the foundation of monasteries was described in terms of the saint making a mark, or tracing a circle, with his crozier. In the *Tripartite Life of St. Patrick* the saint measured out the rath at Armagh with 'the angel before him and Patrick behind the angel; with his household and with Ireland's elders, and Jesu's Staff in Patrick's hand'.[72] Similarly, the *Life of Brigit* by Cogitosus, possibly written just after the mid-7th century, described the monastic city at Armagh, '*in cuius suburbanis quae sancta certo limite designavit Brigida*'.[73] Scenes on the east face of the Cross of the Scriptures at Clonmacnoise and on St Tola's cross at Dysert O'Dea (Co. Clare) have

---

[66] L. Bitel, *Isle of the Saints: Monastic Settlement and Christian Community in Early Ireland* (Cork, 1990), 61–74.

[67] C. Thomas, *The Early Christian Archaeology of North Britain* (Oxford, 1971), 27–47; N. Edwards, *The Archaeology of Early Medieval Ireland* (London, 1990), 105–12; L. Swan, 'Enclosed ecclesiastical sites and their relevance to settlement patterns of the first millennium AD', 269–80, in T. Reeves-Smyth and F. Hamond (eds.), *Landscape Archaeology in Ireland* (BAR Brit. Ser., 116, Oxford, 1983); id., 'Monastic proto-towns in early medieval Ireland: the evidence of aerial photography, plan analysis and survey', I, 77–102, in H. B. Clarke and A. Simms (eds.), *The Comparative History of Urban Origins in Non-Roman Europe*, 2 vols (BAR Int. Ser., 255, Oxford, 1985).

[68] Ed. H. Wasserschleben, *Die Irische Kanonensammlung* (Leipzig, 1885). T. Charles-Edwards, 'The Penitential of Theodore and the *Iudicia Theodori*', 141–74 in M. Lapidge (ed.), *Archbishop Theodore: Commemorative Studies on his Life and Influence* (Cambridge, 1995), at p. 142 n. 5, dates the collection to 716x725.

[69] 'The first is called holy, the second more holy, the third most holy'.

[70] 'If anyone violates the temple of God, he banishes God'.

[71] Wasserschleben, op. cit. in note 68, 175; 'The boundary of the sacred place should have signs around it. The synod says: wherever you find the sign of the cross of Christ, do not violate it. Also: Three persons consecrate the boundary of a holy place: king, bishop, people'.

[72] W. Stokes (ed. and trans.), *The Tripartite Life of St. Patrick with Other Documents Relating to the Saint*, 2 vols. (London, 1887), I, 236–7; cf. ibid., 230–1; C. Plummer (ed.), *Vitae Sanctorum Hiberniae*, 2 vols. (Oxford, 1910), II, 301 §24. For a discussion of these sources and the concept of the holy city in Ireland, see C. Doherty, 'The monastic town in early medieval Ireland', in Clarke and Simms, op. cit. in note 67, I, 45–75.

[73] Doherty, op. cit. in note 72, 55–6; 'In whose suburbs, which holy Brigit marked out with a precise boundary'.

been interpreted as depicting this act of foundation.[74] As with the *Hibernensis*, Patrick and Brigit were not marking out a burial-ground, but defining an area of protected space. The same section of the *Hibernensis* (XLIV.8), however, also included a list of penances for violation of ecclesiastical burials, indicating that at least some burial grounds were considered to be sanctified.[75] There is an intriguing section in the mid-10th-century *Life of Adomnán* where he blessed a cemetery on Tory Island, apparently in an act of purification: 'Once as Adomnán was going around a burial ground in Tory, he scrutinized and blessed the ground, saying "The corpse of a pregnant woman is in the graveyard, a thing which is offensive to the saints. This place here is her grave. Open it and take her with you to the sea-shore"'.[76]

The Irish concept of sacred space appears to have been conceived independently of other models. The *Hibernensis* drew its authority from Old Testament parallels, in particular the cities *ad refugium* of the Levites.[77] Early medieval Ireland and Wales had well-developed concepts of legal immunity and ecclesiastical protection which were related to, but not cognate with, those in England and Brittany.[78] Several centuries before the earliest consecration rite, the Irish Church had a concept of defined sacred spaces, and also a ceremony for their definition which was closely related to that which was later practised throughout western Europe.

It is not necessary to argue that Irish traditions directly influenced later medieval rites, though it is possible that they were filtered through the Anglo-Saxon Church. Given that the earliest reference to consecrated churchyards occurs in the laws of Æthelstan, one wonders whether it could have been diffused through the close links which his court had with the Church in Ireland, Wales and Brittany.[79] There is, however, a possibility that it could have been influenced directly by the *Hibernensis*. Numerous recensions survive in manuscripts from the 8th to the 12th centuries, particularly in continental houses associated with the Irish Church.[80] Most of them, though, were abridged versions, and it is currently difficult to judge the extent of

[74] N. B. Aitchison, *Armagh and the Royal Centres in Early Medieval Ireland: Monuments, Cosmology and the Past* (Woodbridge, 1994), 266, 271, 275, 279, 280; Edwards, op. cit. in note 67, 83. They are illustrated in P. Harbison, *The High Crosses of Ireland: An Iconographic and Photographic Survey*, 3 vols. (Bonn, 1992), no. 54, II, 132–3; no. 91, II, 261–5.
[75] For discussion of the sources see O'Brien, op. cit. in note 51, 52–9.
[76] *Betha Adomnáin: The Irish Life of Adomnán*, ed. M. Herbert and P. Ó. Riain (Irish Texts Soc., 54, 1988), 54, lines 129–37. I am grateful to Dr Elizabeth O'Brien for this reference.
[77] For a general discussion of the interpretation of this Old Testament concept in Irish law: D. Ó Corráin, 'Irish vernacular law and the Old Testament', 284–307 in P. Ní Cháthain and M. Richter (eds.), *Irlund und die Christenheit/ Ireland and Christendom: The Bible and the Missions* (Stuttgart, 1987). A. D. S. MacDonald, 'Aspects of the monastery and monastic life in Adomnán's Life of Columba', *Peritia*, 3 (1981), 271–302, at 294–7, discusses in detail the Biblical references to the city of God in Adomnán's *Life of Columba*.
[78] Davies, 'Protected Space', op. cit. in note 45; for the Welsh material, Davies, op. cit. in note 44, 137–64. Most of the Welsh laws were compiled in the 13th century, though Pryce, op. cit. in note 44, 163–203, argues that they may have had earlier origins.
[79] D. N. Dumville, *Wessex and England from Alfred to Edgar* (Woodbridge, 1992), 155–62.
[80] P. Fournier, 'De l'influence de la collection irlandaise sur la formation des collections canoniques', *Nouvelle Revue Historique de Droit*, XXIII (1899), 27–78; R. Reynolds, 'Unity and diversity in Carolingian canon law collections: the case of the *Collectio Hibernensis* and its derivatives', 99–135 in U.-R. Blumenthal (ed.), *Carolingian Essays: Andrew W. Mellon Lectures in Early Christian Studies* (Washington, 1983). However, M. P. Sheehy, 'The Collectio Canonum Hibernensis – a Celtic phenomenon', I, 525–35 in H. Löwe (ed.), *Die Iren und Europa im Früheren Mittelalter*, 2 vols (Stuttgart, 1982), argues that Fournier's work distorted the influence of the *Hibernensis* in Europe.

interest in the relevant sections of the manuscript. There is no modern study of the recensions of the *Hibernensis*, and without detailed descriptions of their contents it is difficult to make a proper assessment. There are, however, three complete copies from the first half of the 9th century, two of which were copied in Brittany and one in St Gall.[81] During the 10th century, one of the Breton manuscripts came into the possession of Christ Church, Canterbury,[82] whose scriptorium produced many of the surviving Anglo-Saxon pontificals.[83] It was written in France in the late 9th century, but at Canterbury c. 1000.[84] Without a definitive study of the recensions of the *Hibernensis*, it is difficult to judge whether the rite of churchyard consecration could have been directly influenced by Irish traditions, but it must remain a point of conjecture. It is worth noting in this context that there was considerable Irish influence on the form of the Gallican ceremonies for dedicating churches.[85]

Archaeologically, it may be significant that Ireland, and perhaps also parts of Brittany and the far North and West of England, had a more precisely defined concept of sacred space several centuries before it began to emerge in Anglo-Saxon England. One ought to be cautious, however, about using Irish and Insular models to inform our interpretation of early Anglo-Saxon monastic precincts. The publication of the excavations at the early monastic site of Whithorn (Dumfries and Galloway) demonstrates the extent to which the Irish paradigm has shaped our conception of monastic boundaries, but it may be an inappropriate model.[86] One does need to think carefully about the extent to which bounded precincts were signifiers of the sacred at a time when the concept of consecrated ground was anachronistic. An embryonic concept of sacred space makes much more sense of the contemporary topographical descriptions of monasteries, which emphasized their isolation in terms of natural features, particularly water sources.[87] This may also provide a better context for the archaeological evidence for industrial and trading activity within ecclesiastical precincts. These boundaries were perceived in, rather than constructed on, the land.

---

[81] Orléans, Bibliothèque de la Ville, 221 (193) and Oxford, Bodleian Library, Hatton, 42 are thought to have been copied in Brittany; Saint-Gall, Stiftsbibliothek, 243 was produced at St Gall: Reynolds, op. cit. in note 80, 102–4.

[82] Oxford, Bodleian Library, Hatton, 42 was at Canterbury c. 1000 and at Worcester soon after: D. N. Dumville, *English Caroline Script and Monastic History: Studies in Benedictinism, AD 950–1030* (Woodbridge, 1993), 3, 49.

[83] Dumville, op. cit. in note 20, 91–4; cf. Nelson and Pfaff, op. cit. in note 19, 88.

[84] A 12th-century Worcester tradition associated it with Archbishop Dunstan, though this cannot be proven. Additional material was added at Canterbury c. 1000, and Dumville has suggested that it could have been in Canterbury whilst Dunstan was Archbishop: D. N. Dumville, 'Wulfric cild', *Notes and Queries*, 238 (1993), 5–9; Dumville, op. cit. in note 82, 3, 49.

[85] Andrieu, op. cit. in note 10, IV, 319–20.

[86] P. Hill, *Whithorn and St Ninian: The Excavation of a Monastic Town 1984–91* (Stroud, 1997).

[87] Bede described Selsey as surrounded on all sides by the sea, except for the West (HE IV.13); Melrose encircled by a bend in the river Tweed (HE V.12); Cuthbert's retreat, surrounded on all sides by the sea (HE IV.28); and Lastingham 'amid some steep and remote hills which seemed better fitted for the haunts of robbers and the dens of wild beasts' (HE III.23): Colgrave and Mynors, op. cit. in note 49, 374, 488, 434–6, 286. For a survey of the topographical locations of Anglo-Saxon churches, see J. Blair, 'Anglo-Saxon minsters: a topographical review', 226–66 in J. Blair and R. Sharpe (eds.), *Pastoral Care Before the Parish* (Leicester, 1992), at pp. 227–35; and for the minsters of the Thames valley, J. Blair, 'The minsters of the Thames', 5–28 in J. Blair and B. Golding (eds.), *The Cloister and the World: Essays in Medieval History in Honour of Barbara Harvey* (Oxford, 1996), at pp. 9–12.

The development of a rite for consecrating specific areas for burial marked a major change in perceptions of sacred space in the Anglo-Saxon landscape.

The reforming bishops of the late Anglo-Saxon Church embraced both liturgical innovation and conservatism. There is strong evidence to suggest that the rite for consecrating churchyards emerged during the early 10th century and had become codified and widely practised by the early 11th century. Anglo-Saxon bishops were at the forefront of that development, and may have been the architects of a rite that came to be practiced throughout the western church. The 10th century was a time of immense change in the organization of the Anglo-Saxon church, and the evolution of a spatial dimension to sanctity was part of that revolution.

ACKNOWLEDGEMENTS

I am indebted to Dr John Blair for his initial work on this subject and for detailed comments on earlier drafts. Patrick Wormald discussed the problems with me and provided assistance with legal matters. Dr Marie Conn generously sent me sections of her unpublished PhD thesis and Dr M. Bradford Bedingfield lent microfilms of unpublished manuscripts. Dr Robin Wrench and Dr Elva Johnston provided help with specific problems. Earlier drafts were read by Professor Donald Bullough, Moira and Brian Gittos, Jason Hartford, Dr Christopher A. Jones, Nicholas Orchard and Dr Andrew Reynolds and I am grateful to them all for their comments, though responsibility for views expressed and errors made remains mine alone. The material was first presented at the Church Archaeology Society Conference (Glasgow, 1998) and the Oxford Medieval History Seminar (1999). This research was supported by a grant from the Humanities Research Board of the British Academy.

Burial Practices in Northern England in the Later Anglo-Saxon Period

By D. M. HADLEY

Much has been written in recent years about the role of early medieval funerary display in the construction and signification of aspects of social identity, including 'class' or rank, stage in the life cycle, gender, ethnicity and so on. However, Anglo-Saxonists have largely confined their focus to cemeteries and burial practices of the 5th to early 8th century. Attention has occasionally been turned to burials of the late 9th or early 10th century which are allegedly of 'Viking' character, but on the whole there has been little discussion of the role of funerary display in expressing social identity between the mid-8th century and the 11th century. There appear to be two main reasons for this. First, the apparent lack of funerary evidence from that period, and second, the belief that the influence of the Christian Church on burial led to the abandonment of existing cemeteries and burial rites and encouraged unelaborate burial in churchyards, where funerary display was prohibited. In essence, it has long been thought that following conversion the Anglo-Saxons become archaeologically invisible in their burial practices. This paper challenges these assumptions through an examination of the continuing diversity of burial practices employed in northern England during the 9th, 10th and 11th centuries, and proposes that burial continued to be an arena for social display. It will also consider the supposedly 'Viking' burials of northern England in the context of the much wider body of funerary evidence for the period, which permits new insights into the nature of the Scandinavian impact on burial practices in the region.

THE ORIGINS OF CHURCHYARD BURIAL

In order to place later Anglo-Saxon burial practices in context, it is necessary to outline briefly the burial practices of the preceding centuries. As elsewhere, the cemeteries of many parts of northern England are characterized between the 5th and 7th centuries by cremation and inhumation with grave-goods. There are, however, some areas of northern England with no or few such cemeteries, and this has sometimes been explained by reference to the building of later churchyards on earlier cemeteries, thus obliterating the evidence. Others, however, have taken it as an index of the progress of 'Anglo-Saxon' settlement, whereas others have attributed it to indigenous, and/or Christian, influence on the burial traditions of the settlers.[1] Most authors have

---

[1] See, for example, R. A. Hall and M. Whyman, 'Settlement and monasticism at Ripon, North Yorkshire, from the 7th to 11th centuries A.D.', *Medieval Archaeol.*, 40 (1996), 62–150, at 119–20; P. R. Wilson *et al.*, 'Early Anglian Catterick and *Catraeth*', *Medieval Archaeol.*, 40 (1996), 1–61, at 52–3. The evidence is reviewed in S. Lucy, 'Changing burial rites in Northumbria AD 500–750', 12–43 in J. Hawkes and S. Mills (eds), *Northumbria's Golden Age* (Stroud, 1999); for Cumbria, see D. M. O'Sullivan, 'A group of pagan burials from Cumbria?', *Anglo-Saxon Stud. Archaeol. Hist.*, 9 (1996), 15–23.

then supposed that from the 8th century unaccompanied churchyard burial was more or less the norm, following the conversion of the Anglo-Saxons to Christianity. This interpretation was modified in the 1960s and 1970s when it was suggested that churchyard burial followed burial in large 'pagan' cemeteries via an intermediate phase of burial, dubbed 'Final Phase'; that is, the final phase of furnished burial. Such 'Final-phase' cemeteries were said to be comparatively small, and relatively closer to settlement sites than earlier cemeteries, and they contained only a few grave-goods which were intepreted as hang-overs from pagan burial.[2] Although some still adhere to the notion of the 'Final-phase' cemetery, it has been called into question by, amongst others, Richard Morris and Andrew Boddington. They have pointed out that there is a much wider range of archaeological evidence for burial and settlement location in the 7th century than the Final Phase model accounts for, that the evidence for dating the cemeteries is weak, relying as it does on few closely datable objects, and that the question of whether these cemeteries display pagan or Christian qualities is more complex than has been allowed for. Moreover, they have argued that the tendency to ascribe the Church a pro-active role in the transformation of burial rites and location is not supported by the available documentary evidence.[3] In addition, more recent excavation suggests that the transition to unaccompanied churchyard burial was not uniform, nor invariably immediate, and it seems increasingly likely that it was not until the 10th century that churchyard burial became the norm for most people.[4] Even so, this did not necessarily lead to a stable pattern of burial location, as cemeteries continued to come into and go out of use, as they had done for centuries. In sum, it is not as clear as was once thought that the so-called 'Final-phase' burials should be regarded as belonging to a distinctive, pre-churchyard phase of burial.

In northern England there is no doubt that the inhabitants of religious communities, bishops and kings were buried in churchyards, or within churches, from the mid-7th century: this is documented at, for example, York, Ripon, Whitby, Lastingham (all North Yorkshire), Monkwearmouth (Tyne and Wear), Lindisfarne (Northumberland), Crowland, Bardney (both Lincolnshire), and Repton (Derbyshire).[5] The aristocracy may also have sought to provide burial for their kindred in and around both these major churches (indeed, Bede says that other noble folk were

[2] See, for example, M. Hyslop, 'Two Anglo-Saxon cemeteries at Chamberlains Barn, Leighton Buzzard', *Bedfordshire Archaeol. J.*, 120 (1963), 161–200; A. L. Meaney and S. C. Hawkes, *Two Anglo-Saxon Cemeteries at Winnall, Winchester, Hampshire* (London, 1970). The phrase 'Final Phase' had first been coined by E. T. Leeds: *Early Anglo-Saxon Art and Archaeology* (Oxford, 1936).
[3] M. L. Faull, 'The location and relationship of the Sancton Anglo-Saxon cemeteries', *Antiq. J.*, 56 (1976), 227–33; R. K. Morris, *The Church in British Archaeology* (CBA Res. Rep., 44, London, 1983), 49–62; A. Boddington, 'Models of burial, settlement and worship: the final phase reviewed', 177–99 in E. Southworth (ed.), *Anglo-Saxon Cemeteries: A Reappraisal* (Stroud, 1990). See also D. Bullough, 'Burial, community and belief in the early medieval West', 177–201 in P. Wormald et al. (eds.), *Ideal and Reality in Frankish and Anglo-Saxon Society* (Oxford, 1983), at pp. 185–6; B. Effros, '*De Partibus Saxoniae* and the regulation of mortuary custom: a Carolingian campaign of Christianization or the suppression of Saxon identity', *Revue Belge de Philologie et d'Histoire*, 75, fasc. 2 (1997), 267–86.
[4] See, for example, J. Blair, *Anglo-Saxon Oxfordshire* (Stroud, 1995), 70–1.
[5] Discussed, with references, in D. M. Hadley, *The Northern Danelaw: its Social Structure, c. 800–1100* (London, 2000), 220–1, 234, 245, 241–2, 252, 262, 265–6; see also C. E. Karkov, 'Whitby, Jarrow and the commemoration of death', 126–35 in Hawkes and Mills (eds), op. cit. in note 1. Many of the sites and issues summarized in the first part of this paper are discussed in more detail in D. M. Hadley, 'Burial practices in the northern Danelaw, c. 650–1100', *Northern History*, 36 (2) (2000), 199–216.

buried at Whitby)[6] and the churches they were evidently building on their own lands.[7] In addition to the documentary sources, there is also architectural and sculptural evidence which suggests that many other churches served as burial grounds for the elite in northern England from the 8th century onwards. This includes evidence for crypts and mausolea (e.g. at Repton and Ripon), and also sculptural evidence: including grave slabs (e.g. Kirkdale (North Yorkshire)), sarcophagi and shrines (e.g. Wirksworth (Derbyshire), South Kyme (Lincolnshire) and St Alkmund, Derby), name-stones (e.g. Monkwearmouth, York and Hartlepool), and perhaps also crosses — we might note here the commemorative inscriptions on the 8th- or 9th-century cross-shafts at Hackness (North Yorkshire), Carlisle and Urswick (both Cumbria).[8] The use of stone sculpture to mark graves or commemorate individuals increased dramatically in the 10th century, and it is important to remember that while individuals may be buried in a comparatively unelaborate manner, their grave may still be marked, and they may still be commemorated, in an extremely elaborate fashion in northern England.

There is archaeological evidence to suggest that a sizeable number of people were being buried at some of the major religious communities in northern England in the 7th to 9th centuries, as we shall see, although this does not demonstrate that churchyard burial was extended to everyone.[9] Indeed, there is also evidence from across the region for elite burial in the 7th and 8th centuries at sites seemingly unassociated with a church, including the many burials in or near barrows of 7th- or 8th-century date in the Derbyshire Peak District, the Yorkshire Wolds and Cumbria, some of which included elaborate assemblages of grave-goods. While they may have been a 'defiant pagan reaction to the new Christian religion',[10] it is as plausible that they represent a perfectly acceptable Christian aristocratic alternative to churchyard burial.[11] Both barrow burial and churchyard burial share a concern for monumental

[6] *Bede's Ecclesiastical History of the English People*, ed. B. Colgrave and R. A. B. Mynors (Oxford, 1969) [hereafter *HE*], III, 24.

[7] For the attempts of a *praefectus* to gain burial for his wife in 'holy ground' (*in locis sanctis*) see Bede, *Vita S. Cuthberti*, ed. B. Colgrave, *Two Lives of Saint Cuthbert* (Cambridge, 1940), XVI; discussed in A. Thacker, 'Monks, preaching and pastoral care in Early Anglo-Saxon England', 137–70 in J. Blair and R. Sharpe (eds.), *Pastoral Care Before the Parish* (Leicester, 1992), at p. 148. There has been much debate about the very existence of 'local churches' or proprietary churches in the 7th and 8th centuries: see the contrasting views of Thacker, loc. cit., 145; J. Blair, 'Ecclesiastical organization and pastoral care in Anglo-Saxon England', *Early Medieval Europe*, 4 (2) (1996), 193–212.

[8] R. J. Cramp, *Corpus of Anglo-Saxon Stone Sculpture. I: County Durham and Northumberland*, 2 parts (Oxford, 1984), I, 51–2, 97–101, 110–12, 123–4; R. N. Bailey and R. J. Cramp, *Corpus of Anglo-Saxon Stone Sculpture. II: Cumberland, Westmorland and Lancashire North of the Sands* (Oxford, 1988), 84–5, 148–50; J. Lang, *Corpus of Anglo-Saxon Stone Sculpture. III: York and Eastern Yorkshire* (Oxford, 1991), 18–19, 60–7, 135–42, 146–8, 161–3; R. J. Cramp, 'Schools of Mercian sculpture', 191–233 in A. Dornier (ed.), *Mercian Studies* (Leicester, 1977), at pp. 218–25; P. Everson and D. Stocker, *Corpus of Anglo-Saxon Stone Sculpture. V: Lincolnshire* (Oxford, 1999), 248–51; M. Biddle, 'Archaeology, architecture and the cult of saints', 1–31 in L. A. S. Butler and R. Morris (eds), *The Anglo-Saxon Church* (CBA Res. Rep., 60, London, 1986), at pp. 16–22; Hall and Whyman, op. cit. in note 1, 63–5; M. Biddle and B. Kjølbye–Biddle, 'The Repton stone', *Anglo-Saxon England*, 14 (1985), 233–92.

[9] E.g. Ripon, Whitby, Kirkdale, Addingham, Pontefract, Crayke, York, Repton, Monkwearmouth and Jarrow.

[10] R. van de Noort, 'The context of early medieval barrows in western Europe', *Antiquity*, 67 (1993), 66–73.

[11] R. Morris, *Churches in the Landscape* (London, 1989), 256.

construction, and the presence of actual crosses in some of these burials (as opposed to cross-shaped decorations) may, as John Blair has observed, replicate the artistic repertoire of self-evidently Christian crosses in sculpture and manuscripts (although, on the whole, we should be cautious of attempts to determine religious belief on the basis of artefacts in graves).[12]

There is also evidence for much less elaborate burials in or near barrows, or other prehistoric monuments, in the 7th and 8th centuries, and perhaps later, which suggest that burial near barrows may not have been limited to elite display. Examples include Garton Slack (Green Lane), Sledmere (Garton Slack I), Cottam, Thwing (all East Riding of Yorkshire) and Milfield South (Northumberland).[13] Burials such as these are conventionally dated to the 7th or early 8th century, but it is not impossible that burial in such locations continued much later, and this may be a case where the 'Final Phase' model has discouraged further investigation, because it places them in a particular, but in truth often unsupported, chronological bracket. Indeed, there is a small body of evidence that suggests that burial in the vicinity of prehistoric monuments continued much later. The cemetery at Thwing, located within a series of Bronze-age enclosures, contains W.–E. aligned burials, without grave-goods, some with coffins or grave markers, and radiocarbon dates suggest that it may have been used as late as the 9th or 10th century.[14] At Ash Hill barrow, Swinhope (Lincolnshire) two skeletons were found in a barrow previously used in the Neolithic for burial, and radiocarbon dates suggest that they were buried there between the late 9th and early 11th century.[15] At Southworth Hall Farm, Winwick (Cheshire) some 800 graves have been excavated, and there were perhaps more beyond the excavated area, in a cemetery that was focussed on a Bronze-age barrow. There is little available dating evidence but the W.–E. alignments, the regular organization of the cemetery, and the presence of stones placed around the head of one individual, suggest that the site was in use in the later Anglo-Saxon period.[16] In Cumbria a number of, admittedly poorly recorded, burials have been excavated in barrows, which have apparently produced few grave-goods but which could date to any part of the Anglo-Saxon period.[17]

In short, while burial near to a church was becoming common for some groups within society from the 7th century, for others burial at a distance from churches, in sites previously used for burial, appears to have continued. Of course, we should remember that we are dealing with negative evidence and cannot prove that there was not a church or chapel at any of these sites. Nonetheless, what these sites do demonstrate, if nothing else, is that the 8th century did not witness the emergence of a general pattern of churchyard burial. Indeed, the transient nature of burial near to

[12] J. Blair, *The Church in Anglo-Saxon Society* (forthcoming). For a more cautious approach, see E. James, 'Burial and status in the early medieval West', *Trans. of the Royal Hist. Soc.*, 6th ser., 39 (1989), 23–40, at 26.
[13] J. R. Mortimer, *Forty Years Researches in British and Saxon Burial Mounds of East Yorkshire* (London, 1905), 246–57, 264–70, 336–7; H. Geake, *The Use of Grave–Goods in Conversion–Period England, c. 600–c. 850* (BAR Brit. Ser., 261, Oxford, 1997), 159, 172.
[14] Geake, op. cit. in note 13, 159.
[15] P. Phillips, *Archaeology and Landscape Studies in North Lincolnshire*, 2 vols. (BAR Brit. Ser., 208, Oxford, 1989), I, 5.
[16] D. Freke and A. Thacker, 'The inhumation cemetery at Southworth Hall Farm, Winwick', *J. Chester Archaeol. Soc.*, 70 (1987–8), 31–8.
[17] O'Sullivan, op. cit. in note 1.

known churches can be demonstrated at a number of sites in the region. For example, recent excavations at Flixborough (Lincolnshire) have revealed a so-called 'high status' site occupied from the 7th century into the post-Conquest period, and, while there have been debates about the nature of the site, there is no doubt that it included a church during at least part of its existence which was a short-lived focus for burial, as indeed was a small inhumation cemetery near to the settlement.[18] At Whitby recent excavations of the cemetery at Abbey Lands Farm, *c.* 200 m south of the medieval abbey church, have revealed a series of W.–E. aligned burials, many in narrow graves, suggesting shrouded rather than coffined burial for which evidence survives in the form of a single shroud pin. Evidence for at least six coffins has also been recovered in the form of wood, coffin stains, metal strapping and other coffin furniture. This, along with a coin of the early 8th century and a glass gaming piece suggest that this cemetery was in use some time between the 7th and 9th centuries. This site, and other burial areas to the North of the medieval abbey church, seem to have gone out of use some time during the later Anglo-Saxon period: the burials at Abbey Land's Farm, Whitby were sealed by a 13th-century layer, and overlain by ridge and furrow.[19]

At Hartlepool there appear to have been at least two cemeteries associated with the religious community founded in the 640s by Abbess Heiu, and ruled in the mid-7th century by Abbess Hild.[20] A number of N.–S. burials have been excavated at Cross Lane, some of which were accompanied by inscribed stones. 100 m to the North-West in Church Walk over 70 W.–E. aligned burials were excavated with no grave-goods, which have produced radiocarbon dates centring on the late 7th to late 8th century. A number of the graves were edged with pebbles, and some had coffin fittings; there appear to be distinct groups of burials in this cemetery which may relate to social, age-related (there is a concentration of infant burials in the south-east corner) or occupational status. The cemetery contained males, females and infants and was presumably a lay cemetery.[21]

At Yeavering (Northumberland) successive inhumation cemeteries, which appear to belong to separate phases of occupation, appear to date to the 6th to 8th century and one associated building has been identified as a church. The burials at this royal vill are remarkable for their lack of elaboration, and serve as reminders that the elite do not invariably mark their status through elaborate funerary displays, so much as through *where* they were buried. The site appears to have gone out of use by the 8th century, although close dating is not possible.[22] As we shall see, at many other sites burial grounds located near to known churches or chapels came into and went out of use during the middle and later Anglo-Saxon period.

---

[18] C. Loveluck, 'A high-status Anglo-Saxon settlement at Flixborough, Lincolnshire', *Antiquity*, 72 (1998), 146–61, at 159.

[19] For a review of the earlier excavations, see P. Rahtz, 'Anglo-Saxon and later Whitby', 1–11 in L. R. Hoey (ed.), *Yorkshire Monasticism. Archaeology, Art and Architecture from the 7th to 16th Centuries* A.D., (Brit. Archaeol. Assoc. Conference Trans., 15, Leeds, 1995); *HE*, IV, 23. Information on the recent excavations from the English Heritage web-page: www.eng–h.gov.uk/projects/whitby/wahpsae/index.htm.

[20] *HE*, III, 24; IV, 23.

[21] Geake, op. cit. in note 13, 148; R. Daniels, 'The Anglo-Saxon monastery at Hartlepool, England', 102–12 in Hawkes and Mills (eds.), op. cit. in note 1.

[22] B. Hope-Taylor, *Yeavering: An Anglo-British Centre of Early Northumbria* (London, 1977); 244–67; Geake, op. cit. in note 13, 172–3.

Thus by the start of the period with which this paper is chiefly concerned burial location was not necessarily restricted to sites near churches, nor were churchyards necessarily of great antiquity. Burial location was and, as we shall see, remained fluid. Furthermore, we shall also see that burial rite was not uniform in the 10th and 11th century, and the means by which the status of individuals could be signified, and the available forms of commemoration, were varied.

BURIAL LOCATION AND BURIAL RITE IN THE 9TH, 10TH AND 11TH CENTURIES

Numerous sites have produced evidence for burial of 9th–10th- or 11th-century date in northern England, although not all are near to churches and not all survived in use. Early religious communities in northern England, as elsewhere, are often characterized by the presence of numerous ecclesiastical and burial foci.[23] Relatively extensive excavations at both Ripon and Repton have revealed not only multiple burial grounds in use from at least the 7th to 10th centuries, but also evidence of a variety of burial rites. The changing forms of burial at Ailcy Hill, Ripon, suggest that the cemetery was used at different times for different groups within the local community. It has been suggested that from the 7th century the pre-existing cemetery was used by the monastic population, given the apparent restriction of burial to adult males and the appearance of chest-burials with complex iron fittings. The latest apparent phase of burial activity excavated at Ailcy Hill includes the burial of three individuals in a single grave — a burial form that has been associated with felons — and the burial of a severely deformed individual. It has been suggested that by the 9th or 10th century the cemetery had undergone a transition and was being used to bury the socially excluded.[24] This cemetery at Ailcy Hill is only one of a number of Anglo-Saxon burial sites at Ripon, which also include St Peter's church, and burials both inside and outside an undated two-celled church, the Ladykirk, where fragments of 8th- and 9th-century sculpture have been found. Some of these burials contained later Anglo-Saxon bone combs, and were possibly the burials of priests. Undated, but possibly broadly contemporary, burials have also been excavated at St Marygate, the Deanery Garden, and All Hallows Hill, which may be a continuation of the cemeteries at either St Peter's or the Ladykirk.[25]

At Repton, which had been the site of a church and associated cemetery from the later 7th century, there was a crypt, a sunken two-celled mausoleum and at least one cemetery from the 8th or 9th century.[26] Burials took place to the South and East of the crypt through the 8th and 9th centuries, and from the 10th century to the North. These later burials include coffined burials and burials with 'ear muffs' (stones set around the head), a burial form which seems to be a particular feature of later Anglo-Saxon cemeteries. Some of the burials in the vicinity of the crypt contained artefacts.

[23] This is a pattern identified elsewhere: J. Blair, 'Anglo-Saxon minsters: topographical review', 226–66 in Blair and Sharpe (eds.), op. cit. in note 7.
[24] Hall and Whyman, op. cit. in note 1, 120, 65–124.
[25] Ibid., 63, 124–44.
[26] Biddle, op. cit. in note 8, 16–22; M. Biddle and B. Kjølbye–Biddle, 'Repton and the Vikings', *Antiquity*, 66 (1992), 36–51.

One burial (grave 511) contained a necklace with two beads and a Thor's hammer, a buckle, a sword, a knife, a key, the tusk of a wild boar and the bone of a jackdaw. Two other burials contained an iron knife, there were two other possible weapon burials, and a male burial contained a ring and five silver pennies of the mid-870s.[27] These accompanied inhumations have been interpreted as the burials of Scandinavians, yet although Grave 511 is clearly distinctive and probably was the burial of a Scandinavian, the other inhumations do not provide *prima facie* evidence of Scandinavian burial, not least because burial with a few artefacts can be paralleled elsewhere in England in the 9th century.[28] As Julian Richards discusses elsewhere in this volume, the mausoleum to the West of the church had seemingly fallen into disrepair by the later 9th century, and it was used to inter the disarticulated remains of some 249 or more individuals.[29] Clearly, this deposit represents more than one phase of interment, as the radiocarbon dates reveal. However, the role of the Viking army which over-wintered in 873–4 is debatable. It is not unknown for bones to be exhumed and reburied in a single tomb in the Anglo-Saxon period, as Bede records that the nuns of Barking Abbey (Greater London) did this in their cemetery in the later 7th century.[30] The mass burial is not easy to parallel in Scandinavia, and it is difficult to envisage from where the Viking army might have acquired the bodies of its battle dead during the winter of 873–4.[31] Since it can take many years for bodies to decompose to the extent that they are easily disarticulated, in order to be able to stack up the bones according to type, they can hardly have been the dead of that winter. Finally, the historical context poses more problems than it solves: King Burgred lost his throne and fled to Rome, but he was replaced by Ceolwulf II who was probably a member of the rival Mercian royal family descended from Ceolwulf I (821–3).[32] This suggests that, as is documented elsewhere, the Viking foray led to involvement in internecine warfare involving rival royal dynasties.[33] This is not to deny that members of the army or later settlers were re-interred beneath the mound, but the 'mass-burial' may just as plausibly be a charnel house, added to over a long period of time, rather than a statement of 'Vikingness' or of Scandinavian conquest. Even the multiple burial at the south-west corner of the mound cannot easily be accepted as a 'sacrificial deposit',[34] given that it is paralleled in other 'Christian' contexts, at Ripon, as we have seen, and also at the Gilbertine Priory site in York (below). Whatever the significance of the burials in the mound at Repton, burial continued around and against the slopes of the mound indicating that it was quickly adopted into the funerary landscape of Repton. Clearly, in advance of final publication of the site one cannot make definitive judgements, but

[27] Biddle and Kjølbye–Biddle, op. cit. in note 26, 40–3.
[28] For discussion, see G. Halsall, 'The viking presence in England? The burial evidence reconsidered', 259–76 in D. M. Hadley and J. D. Richards (eds.), *Cultures in Contact: Scandinavian Settlement in England in the Ninth and Tenth Centuries* (York, 2000).
[29] Biddle and Kjølbye–Biddle, op. cit. in note 26, 42–8.
[30] *HE*, IV, 10.
[31] See also Halsall, op. cit. note 28.
[32] P. Wormald, 'The ninth century', 132–57 in J. Campbell (ed.), *The Anglo-Saxons* (Oxford, 1982), at p. 138.
[33] For parallels see N. Lund, 'Allies of God or Man? The viking expansion in a European context', *Viator*, XIX (1989), 45–59.
[34] Biddle and Kjølbye–Biddle, op. cit. note 26, 45.

it may be that this burial site may not have such a prominent place in discussions about the Scandinavian impact on England as has hitherto been suggested.[35]

At Crayke (North Yorkshire) a number of adult male and female burials have been excavated just outside the churchyard, and they have produced radiocarbon dates which suggest that burial took place there between the 8th and early 11th century. This cemetery may have been for lay people, given that it includes both adult males and females, although it should be noted that at least in the later 9th century the religious community had a female head and it may have been a mixed house. On the other hand, nothing more is known about the community and it had apparently gone by the 11th century.[36] These burials may have been associated with a church on the site of the present parish church. However, the excavators have suggested that there was once another (?earlier) church some 60 m further down the hill where fragments of a 9th-century cross shaft were found. The excavated burials were notably in alignment with the south-easterly slope of the hill rather than the parish church. Whether or not there was ever another church, the site clearly underwent a transition in the post-Conquest period when the excavated cemetery was abandoned, as it was covered with a layer that included late medieval pottery.[37] A similar change in location of a cemetery located near to an early religious community occurs at Dacre (Cumbria), which is almost certainly the site of a religious community referred to by Bede as the location of a miraculous cure effected by the relics of St Cuthbert in the late 7th century. Indeed, finds commensurate with such a community have been found in the form of a stylus, a gold ring, a textile mount and stone cross fragments.[38] A cemetery of over 200 graves has been excavated to the North of the churchyard of St Andrew's, where the largely W.–E. aligned burials contain no grave-goods, although there is some evidence for coffin fittings. The burials were sealed by a variety of features of 11th- to 13th-century date, and they appear to have no relationship with the later cemetery of St Andrew's, although excavated building activity and finds of Anglo-Saxon date in the later churchyard suggest that the religious community may have been located there.[39]

St Gregory's church, Kirkdale, contains two grave-slabs of 8th-or 9th-century date, indicating that it was the burial site of elite figures at that date. In addition, recent excavations have uncovered a series of graves in the field to the North of the churchyard, an area that was cultivated subsequently, and which has produced about 500 sherds of 11th- and 12th-century pottery. Other burials excavated near to the tower of St Gregory's church were on a different alignment from that of the church, but were on a similar alignment to the burials excavated in the northern field, suggesting that they were broadly contemporary and that at some point there was a major reorganization of the site.[40] This may have happened in the 11th century, to

---

[35] See, for example, P. Stafford *The East Midlands in the Early Middle Ages* (Leicester, 1985), 110.
[36] K. A. Adams, 'Monastery and village at Crayke, North Yorkshire', *Yorkshire Archaeol. J.*, 62 (1990), 29–50.
[37] Ibid., 39–44.
[38] *HE*, IV, 32; Bailey and Cramp, op. cit. in note 8, 90–3.
[39] Geake, op. cit. in note 13, 148; S. M. Youngs, J. Clark and T. Barry, 'Medieval Britain and Ireland in 1985', *Medieval Archaeol.*, 30 (1986), 127–8.
[40] P. Rahtz and L. Watts, 'Kirkdale Anglo-Saxon minster', *Current Archaeol.*, 155 (1998), 419–22.

judge from the famous sundial at Kirkdale which records that the church was re-built from its 'broken and fallen' state in the mid-11th century.[41] A stone sarcophagus was excavated at Kirkdale: close dating is not possible, but it has been observed that the sundial is carved on a re-used part of a similar stone sarcophagus, providing further evidence for the changes that had taken place at this site in the later Anglo-Saxon period.[42]

At both Jarrow (Tyne and Wear) and Monkwearmouth cemeteries associated with major religious communities have been excavated, and in both cases there was reorganization of the site at some point in the Anglo-Saxon period which led to the abandonment of at least part of the cemetery.[43] At Jarrow the eastern part of the burial ground associated with Bede's community appears to have been abandoned at some point in the later Anglo-Saxon period, with burial seemingly continuing until modern times to the West. Differences in alignment and the presence of a few grave-goods may suggest that there was a cemetery at Jarrow prior to the establishment of the religious community in 682. At Monkwearmouth a cemetery has been excavated to the South of the later church, which accompanied, and possibly in some instances preceded, the monastic buildings of the 7th or 8th century. Most of the burials were aligned with the head to the East, with no grave-goods, although a single Anglo-Saxon coin was found in two graves, a boar's tusk in another and gold thread in a fourth. There was also evidence for wooden coffins. It has been suggested that the excavated cemetery was for the laity — given the presence of females and infants — and that there must have been a monastic cemetery to the East. Given the presumption that the Viking raiders destroyed, or displaced, many religious communities it is often supposed that religious activity and burial must have ceased at such sites. This need not necessarily be the case, and burial does appear to have continued, although the virtual cessation of production, or acquisition, of monumental stone sculpture — of which much was funerary — at both Jarrow and Monkwearmouth, indicates that there was a transformation in funerary display at these sites which may, indeed, have come about as a result of Viking incursions.

At Addingham (West Yorkshire) a number of middle to later Anglo-Saxon burials have been excavated to the West of the present parish churchyard, which have produced radiocarbon dates ranging from A.D. 670–990. The graves in this cemetery contain no artefacts and there is no evidence for coffins or grave markers. Burial here appears to have ended by the 11th or 12th century, when the manorial centre to the West was extended over the cemetery.[44] There was probably an ecclesiastical community based at Addingham as this was an estate held by successive archbishops of York, and where Archbishop Wulfhere fled from disturbances in York in 867. However, the burials were probably those of a lay community, as they include adult

[41] Lang, op. cit. in note 8, 158–66.
[42] Rahtz and Watts, op. cit. in note 40, 422; L. Watts et al., 'Kirkdale — the inscriptions', Medieval Archaeol., 41 (1997), 51–99, at 89.
[43] R. J. Cramp, 'Excavations at the Saxon monastic sites of Wearmouth and Jarrow, Co. Durham: an interim report', Medieval Archaeol., 13 (1969), 21–66.
[44] M. Adams, 'Excavation of a pre-Conquest cemetery at Addingham, West Yorkshire', Medieval Archaeol., 40 (1996), 151–91. It is not unlikely that Addingham was the site of an early church: it was in the hands of Archbishop Wulfhere of York in at least 867 when he fled there to escape the turbulent situation in York, and the medieval church possesses a piece of stone sculpture of roughly that date.

males and females and infants. Given the short life of this cemetery, evidenced by the lack of inter-cutting of graves, it seems likely that there was a major shift in burial location in the 11th century, which may have included the abandonment of some burial areas, as occurred at other early ecclesiastical sites, as we have seen.[45] Excavation has revealed evidence for the role of re-interment in this cemetery. There are several empty graves in the western part of the cemetery, and a number which contain the remains of more than one individual, to the South and East, where the graves are set closest together. Max Adams has suggested that bodies were exhumed from the western part of the cemetery, which is supported by the presence of a few bones in those otherwise empty graves, and reburied in graves to the East, with the bones of either the original occupant or the newcomer being placed in a pile at one end of the grave. This appears to have happened more than ten times in a sample of 50 or so graves. One possible explanation is that there was some focal point to the East and burial close to this was regarded as desirable, and if it was not possible initially it was undertaken later. The removal of bodies from graves has also been identified at Raunds (Northamptonshire) where the re-use of stone coffins may have been the reason.[46] At Addingham it may be that some form of social competitiveness was being played out through the removal of bodies towards some focal point, if it was not simply because of the encroachment of some other activity on to the western part of the cemetery.

Excavations outside the western boundary of the churchyard of All Saints at Pontefract (North Yorkshire) have identified a large burial ground which radiocarbon dates reveal was established by the 7th or 8th century. It remained in use until possibly as late as the 11th or 12th century. The cemetery was associated with a church of later Anglo-Saxon date, which either accompanied or preceded the parish church of All Saints. The cemetery appears to have been partly truncated by the construction of the Norman castle, and the eastern part of the cemetery appears to have been encroached on by urban development of the 12th century.[47]

The variety of types of burial practice and forms of commemoration employed within cemeteries of later Anglo-Saxon date is particularly apparent from the excavations of the cemetery beneath the Norman cathedral at York Minster. In the 9th, 10th and 11th centuries both coffined and uncoffined burial occurred in this cemetery, there were also twelve burials that contained charcoal and one burial that appeared to have made use of parts of a boat. Some of the coffins have been interpreted as re-used domestic chests, and they had elaborate fittings in the form of locks and hinges.[48] One of the males buried in this manner was accompanied by a coin of 841–8, and an adolescent burial contained gold thread from a costume. The charcoal burials are enigmatic. The charcoal may have served a functional purpose — to soak up odours, or to mark the site of a burial — but it may also, or alternatively, have had some symbolic association with the penitential ashes on which monks were sometimes placed. Either way, the charcoal seems to signify that the deceased was someone of

[45] Ibid., 181–4.
[46] A. Boddington, *Raunds Furnells: the Anglo-Saxon Church and Churchyard* (London, 1996), 26–7.
[47] Adams, op. cit. in note 44, 186.
[48] B. Kjølbye–Biddle, 'Iron-bound coffins and coffin-fittings from the pre-Norman cemetery', 489–521 in D. Phillips and B. Heywood, *Excavations at York Minster, Vol. I*, ed. M. O. H. Carver (London, 1995).

status given the effort that had gone into the burial.[49] The York Minster cemetery also had a tradition of marking graves above ground, which had begun in the late 7th or 8th century with the provision of small, up-right incised grave markers, including the name of the deceased.[50] Nearly 12 per cent of excavated burials had decorated grave slabs above them, and some had decorated upright markers. Some of the markers found *in situ* had been re-used from previous contexts as they had been cut down to be used as head- or foot-stones. There are also a few grave-markers that incorporate Scandinavian iconography, suggesting that burial continued in the cemetery after the Scandinavian settlement, although whether by the indigenous populations or the newcomers, or both, is a moot point.[51]

The sites discussed so far had all attracted burial from long before the 9th century. There are many other churches near which burial appears to have begun in the 9th or 10th century. At St Mark's, Lincoln (Lincolnshire), extensive excavation allows us to see the diversity of burial rites and forms of commemoration in this small urban churchyard of probable 10th-century foundation. Many of the burials of the 10th and 11th century contained 'nail-like' iron finds, which may have been either nails for coffins or, possibly, shroud pins. There were also burials in stone cists and charcoal burials. There are many grave markers and stone slabs from St Mark's, and one upright marker was excavated *in situ* over the centre of a burial. Evidence for postholes suggests that wooden markers were also in use alongside stone grave-markers at St Mark's.[52] At the site of the Gilbertine Priory of St Andrew's (York), the first 10th- and 11th-century phases of the cemetery associated with an earlier church (probably the church of St Andrew's mentioned in Domesday Book) include a double burial (evidenced by the fact that the arms of one skeleton were wrapped around the other), two burials which may have been shrouded and one of which had been moved from an earlier grave, some evidence for wooden coffins in the form of nails (two of which still had timber attached), and a burial with an iron strap hinge with a bifurcated scrolled terminal across his chest which showed traces of mineralized textile, suggesting that the coffin had been covered with a pall. There was little evidence for grave-markers, although an infant was marked with a roughly hewn limestone slab. Another individual, who had been decapitated, was buried with cobbles cradling the skull, the only example from this site, which given the state of the deceased may have served a fairly functional purpose. One grave included three individuals — two adult males with a female placed diagonally across their chests — and a decorated buckle plate which may have been contemporary with the burial. Although there are grounds for suggesting that these three individuals and the decapitated adult male may have been interred in this way because they were felons of some sort, this seems unlikely given the

[49] C. Daniell, *Death and Burial in Medieval England* (London, 1997), 158–60.
[50] Indeed, one inscription specifically indicates that they might be erected above the graves of the individuals commemorated: '+ Here [beneath this?] turf [or tomb?] rest the [—-] of Wulfhere', even though none of these markers was found *in situ*; Lang, op. cit. in note 8, 60–73.
[51] Ibid., 58–9, 71.
[52] B. J. J. Gilmour and D. Stocker, *St Mark's Church and Cemetery* (The Archaeology of Lincoln, XIII–1, Lincoln, 1986).

churchyard setting and also because there is some evidence that they were buried within the church.[53]

At Newark (Nottinghamshire) recent excavations at the castle have uncovered a late Anglo-Saxon cemetery containing at least 70 burials and probably many more. It is not certain that there was an associated church, although a number of beam-slots suggest some sort of building activity on the site; the parish church is about 300 m away. All of the burials are aligned W.-E. and contain no grave-goods, but radiocarbon dates suggest that the burials belong to the 10th or 11th century. A few of the burials had ear muffs and several were outlined by stones. Some of the burials were cut by a ditch containing 11th-century material, and it appears that the earliest castle on the site, which the excavations revealed to have preceded the first stone phase of the castle built by Bishop Alexander of Lincoln *c.* 1130–40, appears to have occupied a site which was enclosed by a palisaded bank and a ditch, and at which burial had until recently taken place, or even was still taking place.[54]

Remains of wooden coffins have been excavated at a site at Swinegate in York which was probably the cemetery of St Benet's church until the 12th century when the cemetery was built over. There were 44 timber coffins, of which 40 were of plank construction, one was a dug-out tree trunk and there were two infant burials that had only a wooden lid covering the interment, one of which was distinguished by bearing a shallow inscription of the grid of the game 'Nine Men's Morris'. Of the plank coffins, most were held together by wooden pegs, and only one had nails.[55]

At Barton-on-Humber (North Lincolnshire) burial at the site of St Peter's must have begun no later than the 9th century. Burial began prior to the construction of the church which occurred no earlier than the later 10th century. Many of the burials were in wooden coffins, some of which were of clinker-built construction. Many of the burials, both with and without coffins, had stone ear muffs or pillow stones placed under the skull. None of the graves contained artefacts. One of the graves had post-holes at each corner and there was an associated foundation of rubble set in sand which was probably the base for a cross or some other funerary monument. At the west end of one grave a rectangular void measuring *c.* 35 by 4 cm had probably contained some sort of upright grave-marker. Unusually for Lincolnshire churches of that date no stone grave-markers or crosses were discovered. Prior to the construction of the church, probably in the later 10th century, over twenty burials were exhumed. It has been assumed that the earliest phase of burial must have been associated with another, as yet undiscovered, church. This is certainly possible, although the basis for the argument — that 'an orderly cemetery of coffined burials is perhaps unlikely to have existed here without a focus . . . an earlier church' — is not a strong one, since it

[53] R. L. Kemp and C. P. Graves, *The Church and Gilbertine Priory of St Andrew, Fishergate* (The Archaeology of York, 11, York, 1996), 76–80, 89.
[54] P. Dixon, P. Marshall, C. Palmer–Brown and J. Samuels, *Newark Castle Studies: Excavations 1992–1993* (Newark, 1994); J. Samuels, 'Newark Castle', *Current Archaeol.*, 156 (1998), 458–61.
[55] I am grateful to Cathy Groves for bringing this site to my attention and for allowing me access to the Timber Report produced by the English Heritage Dedrochronology Laboratory at the University of Sheffield.

is becoming clear that coffined burials in orderly cemeteries are to be found in many different locations in northern England, for which there is no evidence for a church.[56]

The relationship of this cemetery to the earlier cemetery at Castledyke, some 400 m to the South-West, is not clear. The Castledyke cemetery has inhumations accompanied by grave-goods which have been dated to the 6th and 7th centuries. It has been suggested that this cemetery was abandoned and a new one established by the 9th century.[57] The other possibility is that which has long been seen as abandonment of sites may be a figment of the archaeological evidence, and, in fact, we may be looking at 'shifting' cemeteries: a similar interpretation has recently been offered of the contemporary settlement evidence by Helena Hamerow, who has observed that gaps in the settlement record 'are frequently offered as explanations when incomplete excavation is more likely to blame', and this may be equally applicable to the cemetery evidence.[58]

A number of other churches built in northern England in the 10th or 11th century were built in existing cemeteries, for which there is no evidence of an associated church. At Barrow-upon-Humber (North Lincolnshire) another late Anglo-Saxon church was clearly preceded by a series of burials, and disturbed soil above some of the burial has produced two coins of *c.* 870.[59] At Holton-le-Clay (North-East Lincolnshire) traces of Middle Saxon domestic settlement (suggested by pottery and metalwork) were overlain by a Late Saxon cemetery, suggesting that a factor in the location of burials there was the close proximity of a settlement, albeit one that had presumably relocated to some extent by the 9th or 10th century. The excavated burials were aligned W.–E. and contained no grave-goods as such, although a shroud or tunic pin was found in one grave and has been dated to the 8th to 10th century. A *terminus ante quem* can be given by the footings of the church tower, cut in the later 11th century. There is no evidence for an earlier church, although it is not impossible that there was one, an argument strengthened by the survival of a fragment of a 10th-century carved stone grave slab built into the tower, since such pieces of sculpture are commonly found in association with contemporary churches.[60] These, and other examples such as Kellington (South Yorkshire), suggest that it is possible, although admittedly hard to prove, that churches built in the 10th and 11th centuries were sometimes built at existing burial grounds.[61] By the 10th century an important test of the status of a church was whether it had an associated cemetery, and it may not be too fanciful to suggest that churches may have been built in the middle of existing cemeteries for this reason.[62]

---

[56] W. Rodwell and K. Rodwell, 'St Peter's church, Barton-upon-Humber: excavation and structural study, 1978–81', *Antiq. J.*, 62 (1982), 283–315, at 308 for the quotation.
[57] G. Drinkall and M. Foreman, *The Anglo-Saxon Cemetery at Castledyke South, Barton-on-Humber* (Sheffield, 1998).
[58] H. Hamerow, 'Settlement mobility and the "Middle Saxon shift": rural settlements and settlement patterns in Anglo-Saxon England', *Anglo-Saxon England*, 20 (1991), 1–17, at 17. In the case of Barton, however, the limits of the Castledyke cemetery on the north-eastern side appear to have been excavated.
[59] J. M. Boden and J. B. Whitwell, 'Barrow-upon-Humber', *Lincolnshire Hist. Archaeol.*, 14 (1979), 66–7.
[60] J. Sills, 'St Peter's church, Holton-le-Clay, Lincolnshire', *Lincolnshire Hist. Archaeol.*, 17 (1982), 29–42.
[61] H. Mytum, 'Kellington church', *Current Archaeol.*, 133 (1993), 15–17.
[62] See, for example, Edgar's law-code at Andover (II Edgar), in D. Whitelock, ed., *English Historical Documents. Volume I, c. 500–1042* (London, 1955), no. 40.

The later 10th century witnessed large numbers of church foundations in some regions of northern England, and they seem typically to have had an associated graveyard at their foundation.[63] It cannot be coincidental that these regions are characterized by few mother-churches with large parishes, although whether the proliferation of 10th-century churches caused, or was the result of, the decline in the roles of mother-churches is unclear.[64] Whatever the cause, the period witnessed the increasing use of local churchyards by the elite to memorialize themselves, in the form of stone monuments (both grave-markers and the churches themselves). This, and the contemporary legislative efforts to protect the rights of mother-churches, may have been the factors which finally made churchyard burial the norm. Nonetheless, there are many sites in northern England, which are not in known churchyards, at which evidence has been found for inhumation burials which could conceivably date to the later Anglo-Saxon period. These inhumations are usually W.–E., unaccompanied by grave-goods or with only a few, in particular small knives, occasionally containing evidence for the presence of coffins, and they are often found in small numbers. Some sites are particularly intriguing, such as the inhumation burials at Swaby (Lincolnshire), where the only associated datable material was 11th-century and later pottery, and a bone comb of 'possible' Anglo-Saxon date,[65] or Fillingham (Lincolnshire) where over 20 skeletons have been excavated in graves aligned W.-E., without grave-goods and lined with rough cut stones, similar to the graves at Newark.[66] Other examples are known from elsewhere in Lincolnshire at Whitton, Torksey, Hackthorn and Norm-anby-le-Wold.[67] Further work on these sites, which is in progress, and the acquisition of radiocarbon dates combined with analysis of any associated artefacts and the stratigraphy of the site, should confirm whether these burials belong to the funerary landscape of the later Anglo-Saxon centuries.[68] When combined with the evidence from sites such as Winwick and Newcastle-upon-Tyne (Tyne and Wear) — where the stone castle built in 1168 was preceded by a cemetery of over 660 burials some with coffins, some with pillow-stones and others with stone cists, and with no obvious evidence for a church[69] — it raises the possibility that burial at a distance from churches may have continued into the later Anglo-Saxon period. This does not necessarily mean that such burial grounds were not controlled by churches. Contemporary burial both near and at a distance from churches has been suggested by John Blair at Bampton (Oxfordshire), where it can be shown that a large burial ground some distance from the mother church, but on land that belonged to it, was a satellite burial ground of that church. Around 2,000 inhumations have been uncovered, and three have yielded radiocarbon dates ranging between the mid-10th and mid-11th centuries. This is, as John Blair has stated, an unequivocal case of a minster controlling

---

[63] J. Barrow, 'Urban cemetery location in the high Middle Ages', 78–100, in S. Bassett (ed.), *Death in Towns* (London, 1992).

[64] Hadley, 'The Northern Danelaw', op. cit. in note 5, 287–8.

[65] N. Field, 'A possible Saxon cemetery at Swaby', *Lincolnshire Hist. Archaeol.*, 28 (1993), 45–6.

[66] N. Field, 'Fillingham', *Lincolnshire Hist. Archaeol.*, 18 (1983), 96–7.

[67] I am grateful to Jo Buckberry for providing me with this information.

[68] Excavation of a number of these sites by the Department of Archaeology and Prehistory at the University of Sheffield is underway, as is doctoral research in that Department by Jo Buckberry.

[69] Lucy, op. cit. in note 1, 42–3.

a dependent cemetery which lay three miles away, and it suggests that a cemetery did not necessarily have to lie adjacent to a church for it to fall within its purview.[70]

'VIKING' BURIALS

The final group of burial sites of 10th-century date that need to be highlighted are those which have commonly been adduced as examples of 'Viking' burial. These include the cremation cemetery at Heath Wood, Ingleby (Derbyshire), the inhumations with grave-goods and the mass burial at Repton, the cremation burial with grave-goods in a mound at Claughton Hall (Lancashire), the inhumations and cremations in barrows from Cumbria (such as those at Hesket-in-the-Forest, Eaglesfield and Beacon Hill, Aspatria), the barrow burials at Cambois, Bedlington (both Northumberland) and at Camphill near Bedale (North Yorkshire), the burials accompanied by swords from Kildale and Wensley (North Yorkshire), and those churchyards which have produced artefacts which may have come from burials (such as the ring-headed cloak pin from Brigham (Cumbria) and the swords from Rampside, West Seaton and Heysham (all Lancashire)).[71]

In the context of the previous discussion, we cannot use the locations of these burials — in churchyards, outside churchyards, or under barrows — as evidence that these are Scandinavian burials because they are in similar locations to known pre-Viking burials. The cremations may, indeed, be those of Scandinavians — although we might note that cremations of probable 8th-century date have also apparently been found among inhumations at both Whitby and Thwing, but admittedly not on the same scale[72] — but the burials with grave-goods in barrows in Cumbria may continue an indigenous practice: in fact, it is hard to distinguish those that have been labelled as Viking from those that have been assigned earlier origins.[73] Of the rest, we appear to have a short-lived revival of elaborate burial display, accompanied or succeeded, by continuing elaborate above-ground display in the form of the monumental stone sculpture from the region (see below). Even grave 511 from Repton (see above), which seems likely to have been the burial of a Scandinavian, contained a wooden coffin and may have been marked above ground, to judge from a post-hole at the eastern end of the grave. Does this grave combine aspects of Scandinavian funerary custom (grave-goods) with English practices (adjacent to a church, coffin (rare at this date in Scandinavia, and widely regarded as a foreign import), and above-ground marker)? If so, it may be telling us something important about the acculturation process. It is increasingly difficult to uphold the argument that we can easily distinguish the Scandinavian burials of northern England from those of the indigenous population. The elaborate burials in the region that appear to date to a generation either side of A.D. 900 doubtless reflect a society undergoing major transition in political authority and in religious organization: studies of other regions and periods of early medieval

[70] Blair, op. cit. in note 4.

[71] J. D. Richards, *Viking Age England* (London, 1991), 115–16; J. D. Richards, M. Jecock, L. Richmond and C. Tuck, 'The viking barrow cemetery at Heath Wood, Ingleby, Derbyshire', *Medieval Archaeol.*, 39 (1995), 51–70.

[72] www.eng–h.gov.uk/projects/whitby/wahpsae/index.htm

[73] O'Sullivan, op. cit. in note 1, 20.

society have suggested that social crisis and competition for power was often manifest in elaborate burial displays.[74] If this is so, the tensions of the period around A.D. 900 in the northern Danelaw may not have been cataclysmic, and our evidence suggests that the elite had recourse to other means than burial display for establishing their authority.

It can be seen that the location of burial in the 9th, 10th and 11th centuries in northern England was varied and not particularly static. Many of the cemeteries of this date had not long been in existence, and some did not long survive in use. Of course, one factor in determining this apparent pattern is that cemeteries that remained in use are far less susceptible to archaeological investigation and we should not imagine that all or even many cemeteries of the later Anglo-Saxon period were ephemeral. Nonetheless, despite the evidence for fluidity it does appear to be the case that burial in a churchyard — even if the churchyard was liable to change in size — was common by the later Anglo-Saxon period, although there is little to suggest that burial near to a church was either expected or demanded much before the 10th century. Interestingly, this is when the earliest surviving legislative control over burial location, and the earliest evidence concerning the consecration of churchyards, is found.[75] The 10th century was also the time when certain individuals, who, for example, had been excommunicated or died without atoning for their sins, were forbidden Christian burial.[76] This is not to say, however, that the legislation was the catalyst for the transition to churchyard burial for most people, rather than it representing a response to a developing trend.

FUNERARY MONUMENTS

In analysing the range of burial practices employed in northern England in the 10th and 11th century, in addition to the excavated cemeteries, we must also consider the corpus of contemporary stone sculpture from the region. Much of this almost certainly had a funerary role although few examples have been found *in situ* above a grave. The corpus includes grave slabs, hogback monuments which are widely regarded as burial markers , and crosses, which while not certainly serving a funerary role, may well have done so in many instances given the depiction of lay figures on their shafts. Stone sculpture is found at five times as many places as in the 8th and 9th centuries and much more of the corpus clearly served a funerary purpose than earlier, as the number of grave slabs increases. This evidence qualifies the widely held view that prior to the later Middle Ages commemoration was understood to mean 'not monuments and material embellishments but prayers, anniversaries and obits'.[77] The presence of so many funerary monuments may have much to reveal about both the

[74] G. Halsall, *Settlement and Social Organization: the Merovingian Region of Metz* (Cambridge, 1995), 251–4, 264–7.
[75] Thacker, op. cit. in note 7, 148; Whitelock, ed., op. cit. in note 62, nos. 40, 44; J. Blair, 'Introduction', 1–19 in *idem* (ed.), *Minsters and Parish Churches: The Local Church in Transition 950–1200* (Oxford, 1988), at p. 8.
[76] Blair, op. cit. in note 12; Gittos, this vol.; Reynolds, this vol.
[77] A. Martindale, 'Patrons and minders: the intrusion of the secular into sacred spaces in the late Middle Ages', 143–78 in D. Wood (ed.), *The Church and the Arts*, (Studies in Church History, 27, Oxford, 1992), at p. 147.

role of the Church in providing suitable post-mortem commemoration and also about levels of social competitiveness in northern England. There is no doubt that the Church had suffered at the hands of Viking raiders and during the period of Scandinavian settlement, and that some churches had been attacked, and others had lost their movable wealth and landed possessions. Nonetheless, the Church did recover and in parts of northern England the number of churches proliferated in the 10th and 11th centuries. However, given the disruptions to the bishoprics and the loss of a number of major religious houses, which had, amongst other things, provided the training for priests, there may not have been sufficient ecclesiastical support for the souls of the deceased in parts of northern England, and this may begin, in part, to explain the reliance on commemorative displays in stone. Other factors may also be relevant, however. We should not overlook the fact that stone sculpture was already a much more common northern than southern phenomenon. In addition, the fact that many of the churches with stone sculpture in the 10th and 11th century may have been new foundations, combined with the disappearance or decline of many mother churches, may have been a factor in the use of stone sculpture as a symbol of the new seigneurial foundations, combined with a concern about the efficacy of these newer foundations.

Stone sculpture was a very visible manifestation of lordship, and much was seemingly created under secular influence to judge from the iconography, the proliferation and the distribution, which spread far beyond the sites of known mother churches. Its role in displays of social competition, and its use to signify status and political allegiances, in addition to its memorial function, have recently been highlighted, and it has been suggested that regional patterns in ornamentation, form and iconography may reflect not only the locations of schools of sculptural production, but also regional polities, in which lords signalled their allegiances and status through the commissioning and display of particular forms of sculpture.[78] In a recent study of 10th-century sculpture in Yorkshire and Lincolnshire David Stocker has suggested that since at most churches there is sculpture from only one or two monuments, that they were 'the founding monuments in a new generation of parochial graveyard'. However, there are a number of churches with many more sculptures. On the available evidence the distinguishing factor does not appear to be that these were the mother-churches of the region, but rather that these churches were located in trading places (usually riverine or coastal), such as Marton-on-Trent (Lincolnshire), Bicker (Lincolnshire, on the fen edge), St Mark's and St Mary-le-Wigford (in what has been dubbed the 'strand' of Lincoln).[79] These exceptional graveyards may, then, belong to unusual settlements with distinctive elite populations, with a sizeable number of newcomers (in the form of merchants) whose social competitiveness was played out, amongst other ways, through funerary display. Stone sculpture may also have been a means by which the Scandinavian settlers and the indigenous populations became acculturated to each other, as many of the images depicted may have had resonance for both Christian and

[78] P. Sidebottom, 'Viking age stone monuments and social identity in Derbyshire', 213–35 in Hadley and Richards (eds), op. cit. in note 26.
[79] D. Stocker, 'Monuments and merchants: irregularities in the distribution of stone sculpture in Lincolnshire and Yorkshire in the 10th century', 179–212 in Hadley and Richards (eds), op. cit. in note 26.

pagan viewers and demonstrate, once again, the ability of the Anglo-Saxon Church to respond to the aristocratic nature of society.[80]

Other forms of above-ground commemoration were employed in northern England in the later Anglo-Saxon period. As we have seen, burial in or near to a barrow continued to at least the 10th century in some cases, and burial near to, or even within, a church was an option for some members of society. Ecclesiastical law tried to prohibit intra-mural burial for the laity, but it clearly continued, as can be seen by the burial of Earl Siward in 1055 in the church he had built himself in York at 'Galmanho' (the former name of Bootham Bar), St Olaf's.[81] There is also, as we have seen, some evidence for wooden grave-markers — in the form of post-holes associated with burials — and for burial in various types of mausoleum. Commemoration, of whatever type, did not necessarily persist for long: there are, for example, many instances of the re-use and destruction of commemorative artefacts, including the re-carving or cutting down of stone markers, and for the abandonment or re-use of reliquaries, to judge from the disgarded lead plaques from reliquaries found at Flixborough and Kirkdale (and in the case of the latter it had been partially melted down).[82] There was clearly no aversion to re-using or disposing of such commemorative artefacts, neither was there any guarantee that the deceased would long rest undisturbed in their grave.

SYNTHESIS

What does this survey of material reveal about burial practices in northern England in the 9th, 10th and 11th centuries? Clearly neither burial rite nor burial location were uniform or static. The contraction or abandonment of cemeteries may be explained by reference to a decline in the numbers of people who needed to be buried there, perhaps because the church underwent a change in status, from that of a sizeable religious community, to that of, effectively, a parish church, or perhaps because of the foundation of other churches with cemeteries in the vicinity. Burial grounds also went out of use in the face of building campaigns, of castles, manorial complexes or houses. Of particular importance is the evidence that suggests that burial remained an opportunity for social display following the abandonment of grave-goods. However, it was now expressed through the use of wooden coffins with elaborate fittings, stone coffins, stone linings of graves, stone ear muffs, zoning in the cemetery or the use of different cemeteries for different groups, reliquaries, the re-burial of the dead, and the use and re-use of above-ground markers, in the form of churches, tombs, mausolea, wooden and stone markers and so on.[83]

These conclusions have several implications. First, they refute the notion that burial after the 8th century ceased to express social status and identity. Second, and a related point, they reveal that we should not only look at the grave in interpreting the 'meaning' of burial in later Anglo-Saxon society — or, arguably, at any time — but

[80] R. N. Bailey, *England's Earliest Sculptors* (Toronto, 1997), 77–94; see also J. Lang, 'Sigurd and Welland in pre–Conquest carving from northern England', *Yorkshire Archaeol. J.*, 48 (1976), 83–94; Stocker, op cit. in note 79.
[81] Whitelock, op. cit. in note 62, no. 1, s.a. 1055.
[82] Watts *et al.*, op. cit. in note 42, 52–64; Loveluck, op. cit. in note 18, 159.
[83] The possible significance of this is discussed in Hadley, op. cit. in note 5, 209.

also at the context: the ways in which the grave was marked above ground, its location in the cemetery, evidence for the movement of the dead between graves and so on. Third, they throw new light on the issue of 'Christian' burial. The notion that the presence of grave-goods indicates paganism must be rejected: in part because there is no evidence to suggest that grave-goods *were* un-Christian and they are, indeed, found in undeniably Christian contexts; and in part because even at an earlier date there is reason to doubt that grave-goods are used to signify paganism *per se*, as opposed to aspects of social or ethnic identity.[84] The fact that cemeteries of the middle and later Anglo-Saxon period are found outside churchyards does not mean that the individuals buried there were not Christian. It has become fashionable to discount the impact of Christianity on changing burial practices,[85] yet this seems implausible. The Christian Church placed great emphasis on what would happen in the 'afterlife', on the fate of the soul, on the need for a good death and on the importance of intercession.[86] Thus, Christianity may have focussed attention less on funerary display and more on the need to secure post-mortem prayers and remembrance for the soul, and on concerns for maintaining the integrity of the burial, which could be achieved through markers, mounds, charcoal and so on.

The fourth point raised by the foregoing discussion relates to efforts to identify Scandinavian burials. The recognition of a variety of cemetery locations and forms of burial means that previous attempts to chart the impact of the Scandinavian settlers on the basis of alien burial rite need to be modified, if for no other reason than that one of the prerequisites for such an analysis — the distinctiveness and uniformity of indigenous burial practices — cannot be met. The evidence discussed in this paper complements that analysed by Julian Richards in this volume. In addition to the lack of uniformity of burial practices in northern England on the eve of the Scandinavian settlement, we also have to remember that burial practice was not uniform in contemporary Scandinavia either, where cremation, inhumation with and without grave-goods, ship burial, and burial under cairns and mounds were all practised, often in the same region or even the same cemetery.[87] As Julian Richards demonstrates, there is certainly a handful of burials from the region that are almost certainly those of Scandinavians: in particular the cremation burials (although with the exception of Heath Wood, Ingleby, these are not well recorded) since cremation was seemingly no longer practised in England.[88] Whether, however, those few inhumations with grave-goods should automatically be assigned to the Scandinavians is debatable, as is the exclusion of the wealth of other burial evidence, not to mention the funerary sculpture, from the traditional map of 'Viking' burials.[89] An up-dated map of 9th- and 10th-century burials to include the latter would also contradict the oft-made claim that one of the reasons why we have so little evidence of 'Viking' burial practices is because of the problems of recovery of later Anglo-Saxon burial data in general: the claim that

[84] B. K. Young, 'The myth of the pagan cemetery', 61–85 in C. E. Karkov, K. M. Wickham–Cowley and B. K. Young (eds), *Spaces of the Living and the Dead: An Archaeological Dialogue* (1999), at pp. 72–4.
[85] E.g. Halsall, op. cit. in note 74, 246–7.
[86] Thacker, op. cit. in note 7, 148.
[87] J. Graham-Campbell (ed.), *Cultural Atlas of the Viking World* (New York, 1994), 68–73.
[88] Richards, op.cit. in note 71, 111–16.
[89] Ibid., 112, which reproduces Sir David Wilson's map of Scandinavian burials of 1976.

they all lie underneath later churchyards will no longer suffice. As seems to be the case in so many contexts, the Scandinavian settlers, or their leaders at any rate, proved themselves very adept at adopting indigenous practices and forms of lordship, and it may be this, and their desire to take control in parts of northern England, that rendered superfluous, and inappropriate, the shows of 'otherness' discussed elsewhere in this volume by Julian Richards. In northern England the impact of the Scandinavians may, ironically, have been to encourage the fashion for burial in churchyards and for local displays of status at thegns' churchyards, rather than in mother-churches, the *kudos* of which had been undermined by attacks on their property and resources and by their loss of saints' relics.

There is clearly far more evidence for the location and form of burial between the 9th and 11th centuries than has often been supposed. Moreover, social display did not cease to be expressed through the medium of burial following the decline and disappearance of the use of grave-goods, but it was transformed. It was increasingly to be above ground, in terms of ritual, ceremony and funerary monuments, that burial continued to be a dynamic arena for the expression of social identity. The potential to write more exciting social histories of later Anglo-Saxon England which incorporate funerary archaeology clearly exists, and it is to be hoped that this challenge is met in future research.

Constructing Salvation: A Homiletic and Penitential Context for Late Anglo-Saxon Burial Practice

By VICTORIA THOMPSON

This paper examines the different elements that constituted Christian burial practice in church contexts in England in the 9th to 11th centuries, considering those practices in the context of a range of documentary sources, primarily poetry, law codes and homilies. It also takes into account the development of the *ordo* for the dying and dead, and the changing modes of penitential practice. By these means, it provides the framework for understanding the intellectual and emotional context of these burials. It argues that the innovations in the treatment of the corpse in the late Anglo-Saxon period can be understood as the result of several different developments within society, most importantly the increased interest in penance and bodily purity which resulted from greater exposure to Continental religious thought.

While the later Anglo-Saxon Church was interested in burials in so far as it made money out of them, it was not interested in prescribing the form that those burials should take. Nor did the Church offer precise guidelines about what happened after death either to the body or to the soul. It is in this grey theoretical area, therefore, that we should locate the visible remains of belief about the fate of the body and soul, namely the burials themselves. From c. 800, burial practice begins to take on many different forms within a narrow and well-established range of parameters. While many graves remain simple — shallow, unfurnished — others become more complex and do so in a number of different ways. This appears to be the case throughout England as well as on the Continent: there is no obvious regional distribution to these practices.[1] Their commonest forms (which represent either new developments or a great increase in popularity for old ones) are charcoal burial, iron-bound wooden coffins, sarcophagi and stone-lined graves, and these crop up all over the country. Assuming that burial performs the function of communication as well as simply the practical function of disposal, are there therefore many different kinds of message being communicated here? Can this complexity be elucidated by examining contemporary discussions of death, burial and the body? It seems probable that it can, given that the documentary sources were generated by the same people who produced many of the burials under discussion: people associated with high-status monastic and episcopal centres. It is tempting to categorize these practices as 'Christian' and then simply move on, having considered this a sufficient analysis. However, as Frederick Paxton points out in his study of the development of Christian ritual for dying and death, 'most areas of religious life in Christian Europe were characterized more by diversity than by

---

[1] M. Durand, *Archéologie du Cimetière Médiéval au Sud-Est de l'Oise* (Revue Archéol. Picardie, 1988), 198–9; M. Colardelle, *Sépulture et Traditions Funéraires du Ve au XIIIe siècle ap. J-C dans les Campagnes des Alpes Françaises du Nord* (Grenoble, 1983).

uniformity before the twelfth century', and this is often the case within established groups as well as between them.[2] Paul Binski describes medieval thought about death as 'protean' while S. G. F. Brandon relates the wide range of beliefs he describes to the fact that: 'in the matter of eschatological doctrine the Church, while affirming belief in the resurrection and judgement of the dead, never attempted to define its teaching about them. . . Varieties of belief could be held which, on analysis, are found to be contradictory'.[3]

There were also rival ideologies at work within the Anglo-Saxon Church during this period. These are most visible at the time of the Benedictine Reform and Milton Gatch has drawn attention to the difference between the eschatological traditions drawn on in the earlier Vercelli and Blickling homilies, with their 'internal contradictions' and 'confused . . . incompatible pictures', and the more rigorous and consistent work of Ælfric and Wulfstan, as he understands them.[4] In considering the available data for the burial practices of later Anglo-Saxon England, therefore, one should not expect to encounter a single narrative or set of beliefs. Indeed, consistency should not necessarily be prized above contradiction when evaluating the evidence: dying and death are complex and highly variable biological processes, and are therefore amenable to many different kinds of interpretation even within the one culture. It is a salutary reminder that even when we understand the broad outlines of ritual practice it is not possible to apply a neatly algorithmic formula and thereby unlock the reasoning behind particular forms of mortuary behaviour.

THE RANGE OF BURIAL PRACTICES

The first part of this discussion outlines the burial practices under consideration, with the intention of giving a representative survey of the burial types under discussion, demonstrating their geographical range and showing that burials of this period are overwhelmingly found in association with churches. The majority of the examples come from urban or cathedral contexts: this represents a bias in the data, perhaps because of the monopoly on burial held by minster churches until late in the period, or perhaps because of the comparatively limited excavation of rural churchyards. This notwithstanding, it may be no accident that the early examples all seem to come from major monastic centres: as noted above, these are precisely the places where one might expect the purpose and process of Christian burial to receive most consideration.

Burials of this period present a particular set of challenges. In the first place, there are peculiar difficulties of access, in that they often form the lowest layer of churchyards, which are still or have been until recently in use. Furthermore, a millennium or so of continuous re-use results in a gallimaufry of intercutting graves. Thirdly, the digging of graves lifts and removes deposits from earlier stratigraphic contexts and scatters them around the surrounding area. Another complication is that many of the burial practices which emerge in the context of later Anglo-Saxon England

[2] F. Paxton, *Christianizing Death: The Creation of a Ritual Process in Early Medieval Europe* (Ithaca, 1990), 1.
[3] P. Binski, *Medieval Death: Ritual and Representation* (London, 1996), 214; S. G. F. Brandon, *The Judgment of the Dead: An Historical and Comparative Study of the Idea of the Post-Mortem Judgment in the Major Religions* (London, 1967), 113–14.
[4] M. Gatch, *Preaching and Theology in Anglo-Saxon England: Ælfric and Wulfstan* (Toronto, 1977), 7–8.

continue until the early 13th century and are therefore hard to date with precision unless sealed by a datable layer, as at York, where the Norman cathedral foundations and a cobbled area from c. 1080 lie above the Anglian and Anglo-Scandinavian burial ground.[5] In addition, there are particular challenges, such as modern road-widening, posed by urban cemeteries: these are usefully summarized by Julia Barrow.[6]

Bearing these caveats in mind, it is nonetheless possible to see that from the 9th century new types of burial emerge in Anglo-Saxon cemeteries. There is some continuity from the Middle Saxon Period, in that bodies continue to lie supine, with their heads to the West, in unfurnished graves: it is the nature of the graves themselves that changes. Each of these developments represents a different and experimental reaction to elements of contemporary belief about the body and soul after death, as will be discussed fully below. The changes fall into three basic categories:

1. burials in which a foreign substance, most commonly charcoal, is mixed with or scattered over the soil in the grave;
2. burials in which the body is buried in an elaborate container;
3. burials where the grave itself has been constructed from materials such as tile or stone.

Absolute dates for these changes are hard to establish, but the first of these new practices seems to be charcoal burial, which occurs from the 9th century at several sites, including Winchester (Hampshire), York and Hereford (Herefordshire).[7] In this kind of burial, charcoal is spread uniformly within the grave cut and the corpse, either coffined or uncoffined, laid on top. At several sites, including York and St Mark's, Lincoln (Lincolnshire), the practice with coffined burial was then to scatter or pack more charcoal around the coffin.[8] Charcoal burial is often found in combination with other kinds of innovative burial practice, such as iron-bound coffins or stones used to support the head. At some sites, such as Exeter (Devon), some 50 per cent of the burials use charcoal; at others, such as the parish churches of St Helen on the Walls, York, and St Nicholas in the Shambles, London, the genre is represented by only one example at each site.[9]

In many graves, it is impossible to be sure what the body was buried in: any shrouding material has long since disappeared (although the erratic occurrence of shroud pins points to wide use), as have most coffins constructed entirely of wood. That such coffins were used is known from Barton-on-Humber (North Lincolnshire), where 34 dating from the 9th to 10th centuries were found in a good state of

---

[5] D. Phillips, *Excavations at York Minster. Vol. II: The Cathedral of Archbishop Thomas of Bayeux* (London, 1985), 44–6; D. Phillips and B. Heywood, *Excavations at York Minster. Vol. I*, ed. M. O. H. Carver (London, 1995), 75–92.
[6] J. Barrow, 'Urban cemetery location in the High Middle Ages', 78–100 in S. Bassett (ed.), *Death in Towns: Urban Responses to the Dying and the Dead, 100–1600* (Leicester, 1992), at pp. 78–9.
[7] B. Kjølbye-Biddle, 'A Cathedral cemetery: problems in excavation and interpretation', *World Archaeol.*, 7 (1975), 87–108; B. Kjølbye-Biddle, 'Dispersal or concentration: the disposal of the Winchester dead over 2000 years', 210–45 in S. Bassett (ed.), op. cit. in note 6; R. Shoesmith, *Excavations at Castle Green, Hereford* (CBA Res. Rep., 36, London, 1980), 25.
[8] B. J. J. Gilmour and D. A. Stocker, *St Mark's Church and Cemetery* (Lincoln, 1986), 15–20.
[9] J. Schofield, D. Palliser and C. Harding, *Recent Archaeological Research in English Towns* (London, 1981), 36–7; M. O. H. Carver, *Underneath English Towns: Interpreting Urban Archaeology* (London, 1987), 95; W. White, *Skeletal Remains from the Cemetery of St Nicholas Shambles, City of London* (London, 1988).

preservation.[10] A variation on this appears at Norwich (Norfolk), where three burials appear to have been lined with planks, tightly constraining the skeletons found therein.[11] Thus, when iron coffin fittings first appear, it is hard to be sure whether the total number of coffins in use is increasing, or whether they are merely becoming more elaborate. Such coffins appear at Winchester in the mid-9th century, and at Hereford and elsewhere in the 10th century. A related practice is found at York, where four burials are in what appear to be domestic storage chests, complete with locks. A rare and expensive alternative to wood is the stone sarcophagus, of which examples have been found at Winchester, York, Raunds (Northamptonshire) and Kirkdale (North Yorshire).[12] Much more common is the practice of outlining and supporting the head with stones in a 'pillow' or 'ear muff' arrangement.

The third innovation involves constructing the grave in some enduring material: chalk or mortar floors at Lincoln, London and York; cist graves of stone or mortar at London, York, Hereford and Raunds; graves lined with stone or tile at Raunds, London and Rivenhall (Essex).[13]

It should be remembered, as noted above, when seeking an origin for these burial practices that they are not exclusive to England, although the contemporary evidence from the Continent is at least as complex and illegible as the English material. Pillow stones and anthropomorphic coffins have been found in French burials, but these can only be dated approximately within the period, and the excavator, Durand, goes no further in his analysis than the suggestion that 'il y a volonté de maintenir droite la tête du défunt'.[14]

SPECIAL PLACES FOR THE DEAD

What end could these innovative burial practices have been intended to achieve? What functions were they designed to perform? One common theme that the new kinds of burial emerging in this period all have is that they control and confine the body in new and more elaborate ways. Whether it is coffined, surrounded by stones, laid on charcoal or interred in a built grave, all these different structures serve the purpose of defining the area in which the body lies, both protecting it and imprisoning it. The cemetery as a whole, in both urban and rural contexts, was becoming a different kind of space, consecrated and bounded; it was during this period in England that proprietary churches were first established in any number, often with an area around the church enclosed for use as a burial ground.[15] Lawrence Butler stresses the

[10] I. Panter, 'Well-travelled coffins', *Interim*, 19: 3 (Autumn 1994), 26–35; W. Rodwell and K. Rodwell, 'St Peter's Church, Barton-upon-Humber: excavation and structural study, 1978–81', *Antiq. J.*, 62 (1982), 283–315.
[11] B. Ayers, *Excavations within the North-East Bailey of Norwich Castle, 1979* (East Anglian Archaeol., 28, Dereham, 1985), 18–19.
[12] A. Boddington, 'Chaos and disturbance in an Anglo-Saxon Cemetery', 27–42 in A. Boddington *et al.*, *Death, Decay and Reconstruction: approaches to archaeology and forensic science* (Manchester, 1987), at p. 30; P. Rahtz, and L. Watts, 'Kirkdale Anglo-Saxon Minster', *Current Archaeol.*, 155 (December 1997), 419–22.
[13] W. Rodwell and K. Rodwell, 'Excavations at Rivenhall Church, Essex: interim report', *Antiq. J.*, 53 (1973), 219–31.
[14] Durand, op. cit. in note 1, 198–9.
[15] W. Rodwell, *The Archaeology of the English Church* (London, 1981), 140–4.

importance of the churchyard boundary, marking 'the edge of resurrectible life', and he highlights the involvement of the community in maintaining the boundary in good repair.[16] So the new emphasis on the construction of the grave can be seen as an analogue of the boundary of the graveyard itself, a further demarcation of sacred space, both controlling and guarding the corpse.

At this period, therefore, burial practices are very sharply polarized: either one was buried as part of the Christian community in consecrated ground, or one was excluded from that community and buried in unconsecrated ground.[17] This polarity is as visible in the law codes as it is in the burial practice, unsurprisingly as high-ranking ecclesiastics such as Wulfstan, Archbishop of York, were the compilers of these codes.[18] From the late 9th century onwards, with the promulgation of Alfred's law code, Christianity was becoming ever more closely identified with the English state. By the reign of Edgar (959–975) it is hard to distinguish between the secular and sacred institutions, with their aims and interests, officially and rhetorically at least, becoming identified — 'all sins became crimes, and all crimes sins', as Frank Barlow puts it.[19] Unrepentant sinners could be punished by exclusion from Christian burial, as it says in the code Wulfstan compiled for the Northumbrian priests: 'If he die in his sins, then he forfeits clean burial and God's mercy' (cap. 62).[20]

One might expect that this and other similar laws would serve as a winnowing process, successfully keeping the bodies of the pagan or the sinner out of consecrated ground, and that therefore the bodies of those buried *within* the Christian community would be less problematic than the corpses of those who were excluded. However, this does not seem to have been the case, in life or death. Katherine O'Brien O'Keeffe has examined the ways, in 10th- and 11th-century law, in which the death penalty was with increasing frequency replaced with mutilation, a punishment which did not harm the soul and left the living scope for repentance.[21] As a result, there must have been many people bearing the signs of punishments such as amputation, an embodied and highly visible reminder of sin and its penalties. Even for those who escaped state-inflicted retribution, the relationship between soul and body was a spiritual minefield. A reading of the contemporary sermons and homilies suggests that there was a great and ever-growing mistrust of the body, applied both to the living body and its appetites, particularly sexuality, and to the dead body. This is also demonstrated by the penitential tradition as well as by the complex ritual practices that were developing

[16] L. Butler, 'The churchyard in eastern England 900–1100: some lines of development', 383–8 in P. Rahtz, T. Dickinson and L. Watts (eds.), *Anglo-Saxon Cemeteries 1979* (BAR Brit. Ser., 82, Oxford, 1980).
[17] A. Reynolds, 'The definition and ideology of Anglo-Saxon execution sites and cemeteries', 33–41 in G. De Boe and F. Verhaeghe, (eds.), *Death and Burial in Medieval Europe*, Vol. 2, (Zellik, 1997).
[18] D. Whitelock, 'Wulfstan and the Laws of Cnut', *English Hist. Rev.*, 63 (1948), 433–52.
[19] P. Wormald, *The Making of English Law: King Alfred to the Twelfth Century. Vol. I: Legislation and its Limits* (Oxford, 1999), 449–51; F. Barlow, 'The Holy Crown' in F. Barlow, *The Norman Conquest and Beyond* (London, 1983), 6.
[20] *Gif he þonne on ðam unrihte geendige, þolige he clænes legeres 7 Godes mildse*. 'Northumbrian Priests' Law of 1020 x 1023' in D. Whitelock, M. Brett and C. N. L. Brooke (eds.), *Councils and Synods of Great Britain with Other Documents Relating to the English Church. Volume 1, Part 1. 871–1066*, (Oxford 1981), 455. All translations are my own unless otherwise specified.
[21] K. O'Brien O'Keeffe, 'Body and law in Late Anglo-Saxon England', *Anglo-Saxon England*, 27 (1998), 209–32.

around the death bed. It is this mistrust, I suggest, that provides the rationale for the burial practices that emerge in the later Anglo-Saxon period.

THE LITERARY CONTEXT

The next section looks at attitudes to the body in homilies and in one poem that occurs in a homiletic context. The homilies fall broadly into two categories, the first being the anonymous, early 10th-century group in the Blickling and Vercelli manuscripts, the second the body of work produced by Ælfric, Abbot of Eynsham and Wulfstan, Archbishop of York, in the late 10th and early 11th centuries.[22] All the homilists draw heavily on the work of Carolingian scholars and treat at length the topics of penitence and eschatology. The earlier homilies, however, do not mention the subject of *public* penance, and their tone is more lurid and sensational.[23] One of the great achievements of the Benedictine Reform, therefore, may have been to create an agreed standard of regulated confession and penance, a set of guidelines on this most important and frightening matter, that was profoundly reassuring.

In *Sauwle Þearf* (Soul's Need), the eighth Blickling homily, the anonymous homilist enjoins his congregation: 'and above all, remember that they [i.e. the rich] will never return here, but their bodies shall lie in the earth and turn to dust, the flesh become foul and swarm with worms and pour down and ooze at all the joints'.[24]

Although the predicament of the corpse in the grave is a common theme in Old English writing — and generally in medieval Christianity — this description is a particularly graphic one for the period, with its vivid image of the flowing body. The context is a sermon on the renunciation of earthly pleasures. The homilist is referring particularly to the rich, and the contrast between their worldly splendour and the disgusting fate awaiting them. He makes his point in particular by contrasting the control exercised by the wealthy man while alive — his ability to choose rich clothes, maintain wives and concubines, to entertain lavishly and support hosts of flattering hangers-on — with the total loss of control in the grave. The homilist's description emphasizes two forms of decay: the external attack from the worms and the internal catabolic processes generated by the treacherous body itself.

In concentrating on the wealth of the rich man and that wealth's inevitable departure, the homilist omits the fact that the poor and virtuous will be subject to the same process of decay. In general, the association between virtue and incorruptibility is strong in the thought of this period. In the poem *Soul and Body*, this association runs

---

[22] *The Blickling Homilies of the Tenth Century*, ed. R. Morris (EETS 58/63/73, London, 1880); *The Vercelli Homilies*, ed. D. Scragg (EETS OS 300, Oxford, 1992); Ælfric, *Ælfric's Catholic Homilies: The First Series*, ed. P. Clemoes (EETS SS 17, Oxford, 1997); Ælfric, *Ælfric's Catholic Homilies: The Second Series (Text)*, ed. M. Godden (EETS SS 5, Oxford, 1979); Ælfric, *Ælfric, Homilies: A Supplementary Series*, ed. J. Pope, 2 vols (EETS 260, Oxford, 1968); Ælfric, *Ælfric's Lives of Saints Volume I*, ed. W. Skeat (EETS OS 76, 82, repr. as one volume, Oxford, 1966); Ælfric, *Ælfric's Lives of Saints. Volume II*, ed. W. Skeat (EETS OS 94, 114, repr. as one volume, Oxford, 1966); Wulfstan, *The Homilies of Wulfstan*, ed. D. Bethurum (Oxford, 1957).
[23] A. J. Frantzen, *The Literature of Penance in Anglo-Saxon England* (New Jersey, 1983), 157.
[24] *& ofor þæt næfre efngemyndige hider eft ne cumaþ, ah heora lichoman licggað on eorðan & beoþ to duste gewordne, & þæt flæsc afulað, & wyrmum awealleð, & neþer afloweþ, & beoþ gewitene from eallum heora gefogum.* Morris (ed.), op. cit. in note 22, 101.

headlong into the unpalatable fact that the bodies of the good also tend to rot, with the result that the author of the poem argues himself into a corner, interpreting decay both as as the result of sin and as the result of a natural process. The poem is preserved in both the Vercelli and the Exeter Books; it is extremely rare for an Old English poem unconnected with Bede to survive in more than one version, which suggests that culturally it may have been a highly significant text.[25] In the Vercelli version of the poem, though not in the Exeter one, the damned soul's address is followed by a much shorter speech by the saved soul. In the first part, common to both manuscripts, the damned soul returns every week to the body, blaming the latter's animal lusts for the soul's fate. Because of the body's weakness, the soul is in hell and the body is condemned to decay. It is devoured by 'many mould-worms' with needle-sharp teeth, whose leader is personified as Gluttony, one of the besetting sins of the body while alive. Decay here is not something natural or intrinsic to the body: it is visualized in terms of external attack, penetration and punishment. It is also something that can happen to the soul as well as to the body: in the Exeter Book poem *Christ III*, the damned souls will undergo the process of decay for all eternity, enduring *wyrma slite/ bitrum ceaflum* (1250b–1251a) — the bite of worms with sharp teeth — and in *Be Domes Dæge* the teeth have become burning tusks (*brynigum tuxlum*, 211).[26]

At this point in the Vercelli continuation the poet is confronted by a problem. In the first part of the poem he has equated decay, particularly in the form of worms, with punishment but in the second part (dealing with the saved body and soul), he also mentions worms attacking the body. Here, clearly, they cannot be a concomitant element of damnation and instead become nothing more than an unpleasant part of the common experience of burial. As a result, the saved soul is presented as apologetic and reassuring, full of regret that it cannot rescue its body before the Last Judgment. It sorrowfully contrasts its own state, 'adorned with beauty, wrapped in mercy' (*fægere gefætewod . . . arum gebunden*: lines 137–8), with the wretched condition of the body, 'for worms yet nibble you' (*þeah ðe wyrmas gyt/ gefre gretaþ*: 135–6). The implicit conclusion is that, even when dead, the body is ambiguous and disturbing, with the bodies of the virtuous as well as the vicious manifesting signs of decay. The result is that the quest for a reliable indication of virtue is doomed to failure: the fact that decay happens even to the good adds to the sensation of unease and mistrust that characterizes these accounts of body and soul.

Only by being a saint — and a virgin saint at that — might one escape the horrors of decay altogether. In Ælfric's *Lives of the Saints*, he gives two examples who were preserved incorrupt because of their virginity rather than any other virtue; it is noteworthy that they are both English, Eadmund of East Anglia and Æthelthryth of Ely. Of Eadmund, Ælfric says: 'His body, which lies undecayed, tells us that he lived in this world without fornication and journeyed to Christ with a clean life'.[27]

---

[25] G. Krapp (ed.), *The Vercelli Book* (New York, 1932), 54–8; G. Krapp and E. Dobbie, *The Exeter Book* (New York, 1936), 174–8. I am writing as if both the 'damned' and the 'saved' sections of the poem were indisputably by the same poet; this is debatable but does not affect my argument here.

[26] Krapp and Dobbie, op. cit. in note 25, 37; J. Lumby (ed.), *Be Domes Dæge* (EETS 65, London 1876), 15.

[27] *His lichama us cyð þe lið unformolsnod þæt he butan forligre her on worulde leofode and mid clænum lofe to criste siþode.* Skeate (ed.), op. cit. in note 22: Ælfric, *Lives of Saints. Vol. II*, XXXII, lines 186–8.

Of Æthelthryth, he points out that her incorrupt body is a demonstration of the truth of the general resurrection at the Last Judgment and goes on to say that her perpetual virginity is an example, not to monks, but to the laity, giving the example of a thane and his wife who renounced sex after having three sons and thereafter lived together chastely for thirty years. As a result, when the thane died: 'the angels of the Lord came at the time of his death and carried his soul with song to heaven'[28] — a reward normally saved for the saints, whose earthly bodies are already perfect and fit for heaven. In seeing virginity or chastity as desirable for everyone, not just for monks and nuns, Ælfric is in tune with the thought of reformed monasticism, as exemplified by the work of Odo, Abbot of Cluny (926–44). This is a change from earlier thinking: Alcuin, in the early 9th century, had been quite clear that chastity is the earthly equivalent to the angelic life, and that only monks should try because it would be far too demanding for the ordinary Christian.[29] In Ælfric's writings, by contrast, the stakes are raised for everyone, the boundary between purity and corruption redrawn.

I will come back to the concept of the resurrection body shortly, but first must return to the subject of fear of burial. The note of horror is sounded elsewhere in the Vercelli Book, in Homily IX, which lists five earthly experiences which are thought to give a foretaste of damnation, these being exile, extreme old age, death, burial and torture. In context, burial is clearly presented as an experience which one should anticipate undergoing and from which one can learn. The homilist says: 'Then the fourth likeness of hell is called burial, for the roof of the house is bowed down over his breast, and he is given the least part of all his treasure, that is, someone sews him into a length of cloth. After that three bedfellows have him, and they are dust and mould and worms'.[30]

This picture of a shabby, oppressive, dirty place is one of the most detailed portraits of the grave in Old English literature. It is highly emotive and affective, presenting the corpse in the grave as sentient and still aware of its predicament, and inviting the audience to imagine themselves sympathetically in the corpse's place. The blessed or damned state of this corpse's soul is not mentioned; here burial is equally hellish for everybody.

The picture is also a fairly literal description. The mention of the grave-roof over the breast is reminiscent of the one stone marker found *in situ* at St Mark's, Lincoln, which was over the chest area of the burial. There is almost no surviving fabric evidence for the use of shrouds in late Saxon burial, with the exception of a female skull from an otherwise simple burial from St Nicholas Shambles in London which had a fragment of cloth adhering to it.[31] However, shroud pins have sometimes been found, and the manuscript illuminations of the deaths of patriarchs from British Library Cotton Claudius B. iv and the depiction of the death of Edward the Confessor

---

[28] *And drihtnes englas comon eft on his forð-siðe and feredon his sawle mid sange to heofonum.* Skeate (ed.), op. cit. in note 22: Ælfric, *Lives of Saints. Vol. I,* XXI, lines 128–30.

[29] P. Jestice, 'Why celibacy? Odo of Cluny and the development of a new sexual morality', 81–115 in M. Frassetto (ed.), *Medieval Purity and Piety: Essays on Medieval Clerical Celibacy and Religious Reform* (New York, 1998).

[30] *Ðonne is þære feorðan helle onlicnes byrgen nemned, for þan þæs huses hrof bið [gehnæg]ed þe him onufan ðam breostum siteð, 7 him mon þonne deð his gestreona þone wi[r]sestan dæl, þæt is þæt hine [mon siw]eð on anum [hræg]le. Hafað him þonne syððan þry gebeddan, þæt is þonne greot 7 molde 7 wyrmas.* Scragg (ed.), op. cit. in note 22, 168.

[31] White, op. cit. in note 9, 18.

in the Bayeux Tapestry show the corpses closely swaddled.[32] The *Regularis Concordia*, the English monastic rule of the late 10th century, specifies that a monk is to be buried in clean clothing, specifying shirt, cowl, stockings and shoes.[33] The stress on *cleanliness* is noteworthy in this context, in contrast to the dirt and mould of the grave. There are a few other homiletic references to shrouds as well, as when Ælfric says: 'The dead body is wound with a shroud, but that shroud does not rise readily with the man, because a shameful shroud does not befit him but rather the spiritual garments that God provides for him'.[34] Here the contrast is between the earthly shroud, soiled by contact with the corpse, and the divinely pure raiment to be worn in heaven. The Vercelli homilist's association of shrouds with low status and Ælfric's understanding of them as 'shameful' or 'ignominious' (*huxlican*) give them strong penitential associations.

Ælfric makes the observation just quoted in the context of a discussion of the Last Judgment and the nature of the resurrection body. Although bodies, with their garments, are to be transformed at Doomsday, he nonetheless depicts revived bodies as recognizable individuals, in a tradition deriving ultimately from Tertullian, Jerome and Augustine.[35] Although he presents the body as transformed, it is still derived from the one that went into the grave:

Each person yet shall have his own height in the size that he was before as a person, or that he should have had, had he become fully-grown, those who departed in childhood or adolescence. Just as God shaped in soul and body, both male and female, and created them human . . . so he also at Doomsday raises them from the dead, both males and females, and they dwell ever so without any lust either good or evil, and no man after will ever take a wife, nor any woman take a husband, nor shall they beget children. Nor shall the holy ones who are to enter heaven have any blemish or ill-health, or be one-eyed, although he was before lame in his life, but his limbs shall be all sound to him, in shining brightness, and tangible in his spiritual body.[36]

It is worth noting his stress that, while there will be gender in heaven, there will most definitely not be any sexual activity. As touched on above, in his life of Æthelthryth, Ælfric recommended virginity even for the laity and there is a close connection between virginity in life and failure to rot after death. The resurrection body, the idealized self, has no fertility, disease or deformity: in fact it is no longer part of any biological process. At the perfect death bed, such as that of the great Benedictine reformer, Æthelwold, Bishop of Winchester, who died in 984, the fallible body is transformed into the perfect body:

---

[32] Gilmour and Stocker, op. cit in note 8, 16; F. Stenton et al., *The Bayeux Tapestry* (London, 1965).

[33] *induitur mundis vestimentis, id est interula, cuculla, caligis, calceis. Regularis Concordia: The Monastic Agreement*; XII, 65, T. Symons, ed. and trans. (London, 1953).

[34] *Man bewint þone deadan gewunelic mid reafe, ac ðæt reaf ne arist na ðe hraðor mid þam men, for ðan he ne behofað þas huxlican reafan, ac þære gastlican gyrlan ðe him God foresceawað.* Pope (ed.), op. cit. in note 22: *Ælfric, Homilies: A Supplementary Series. Vol. II*, XI, lines 339–42.

[35] C. Walker Bynum, *The Resurrection of the Body in Western Christianity, 200–1336* (New York, 1995), 11.

[36] *Ælc man hæfð swaðeah his agene lenge, on ðære mycelnysse þe he man wæs ær, oððe he beon sceolde, gif he fulweoxe, se ðe on cildhade oððe samweaxen gewat. Swa swa God gesceop on sawle and on lichaman ge [w]æpmen ge wifmen, and geworhte hi to men . . . swa he eac on Domes-dæg of deaðe hi ærærð, ge weras ge wif, and hi wuniað æfre swa, butan ælcere galnysse, ge gode ge yfele, and nan wer syððan ne gewifað næfre, ne wif ne ceorlað, ne hi cild ne gestrynað. Ne ða halgan ne beoð þe to heofonum sceolon on ænigre awyrdnysse, oððe wanhale, oððe anegede, þeah ðe he ær wære lama on his life, ac his lima beoð him ealle ansunde, on scinendre beorhtnysse, and grapiendlice on ðam gastlican lichaman.* Pope (ed.), op. cit. in note 22: *Ælfric, Homilies: A Supplementary Series. Vol. II*, XI, lines 308–25.

Those who were present [says Wulfstan Cantor, his biographer] have witnessed to us that the holy man's corpse was suddenly changed and renewed; it was suffused with a whiteness as of milk, and became lovely with a rosy redness, so that his face in a way looked like that of a seven-year-old boy; in this observed change of the flesh appeared even on earth some hint of the glory of the resurrection.[37]

Wulfstan presents Æthelwold's corpse in two lights: on the one hand it partakes of the asexual beauty of children; on the other it foreshadows the sexlessness of the resurrection body. The perfect corpse, therefore, is also one in which growth, change and decay are absent. One might therefore also expect to see this sympathy for the body and desire to protect it, and to make it perfect, manifest in the forms of burial practice under discussion here. Precisely such desires may be reflected in the range of burial practices which further separate the corpse from the soil, such as the mortar-lined graves and the stone sarcophagi. These constructions fall into a category I would term 'clean burial' (*clæne legere*, in the words of the Northumbrian Priests' Law, reminiscent of the *munda vestimenta* of the *Regularis Concordia*). This involves the creation of a drier, harder space around the body, separating it from the 'three bedfellows' of dust, mould and worms, particularly the last. Worms are not only intrinsically revolting but also a worrying intimation of the pains of hell, and the texts cited above attest to the horror of worms and their association with damnation.

PENANCE AND BURIAL PRACTICE

I want to conclude by looking in some more detail at the revival of penitential traditions in the English Church. Penance, particularly public penance, involves a paradox in that it requires a culture of ostentatious humility. I argue that this paradox provides a rationale for charcoal burial. By the time Æthelwold of Winchester died in 984, his Church was experiencing the culmination of the period of reforms originally set in motion by Alfred. For over a hundred years, Continental scholars working in England, such as Grimbald of Saint-Bertin and Abbo of Fleury, had been serving as a channel for Carolingian Reform ideas about the church, of which the institution of penance was one of the most important.

Although there had been an ancient penitential tradition in England from the 7th century, the structures of penance had to be reintroduced as part of the Alfredian reconstruction, very possibly by Grimbald of Saint-Bertin.[38] The proper practice of penance requires bishops who could oversee public penance and monastic scriptoria which could produce sufficient copies of the penitentials: both types of institution had been severely disrupted in England by the Viking invasions. On the Continent, however, the reforms of Charlemagne had revived public penance from 813 onwards and this was brought back to England through the Benedictine Reform. By the late 10th century, confession and penance had once again become, ideally at least, universal practices. Penance might be performed privately, on the instructions of one's

---

[37] *Testati uero nobis sunt qui ibi praesentes aderant exanime corpus sancti uiri subita inmutatione fuisse renouatum, lacteo candore perfusum roseoque rubore uenustum, ita ut quodam modo septennis pueri uultum praetendere uideretur, in quo iam quaedam resurrectionis gloria per ostensionem mutatae carnis apparuit.* Wulfstan of Winchester, *The Life of St Æþelwold.* M. Lapidge and M. Winterbottom (eds.) (Oxford, 1991), 62–3.
[38] Frantzen, op. cit in note 23, 127.

confessor, or publicly, under the supervision of a bishop. Whereas, as noted above, the earlier collections of homilies, Blickling and Vercelli, make no reference to public penance, by contrast Ælfric and Wulfstan both discuss it at length and by 1009 it is being used as a political tool: VII Æthelred prescribes three days of universal fasting, confession, psalmody and penance in response to invasion by one of the Viking 'great armies'.[39]

In step with this, the *ordo* for the dying and dead had become increasingly penance-oriented. The reforming monk Benedict of Aniane had regularized Carolingian commemorative practice in 816 and 817, by decreeing that all monastic houses should sing the seven penitential psalms for the dead. He also, as Paxton puts it, 'brought a new element of personal guilt and responsibility into the penitential quality of the prayers for the dead'.[40] In the Saint-Denis sacramentary of the late 860s, the seven penitential psalms are also to be sung around the bed of a dying monk or nun. It is this tradition that informs Chapter XII of the *Regularis Concordia*, which prescribes that, when a monk feels himself to be in his last illness, the entire community is to gather around him singing the penitential psalms, the litanies and the prayers. Should the brother die, the singing of these psalms is to accompany him to the grave and, still singing, the monks are to return to the church and complete the psalms prostrate before the altar (*prostrati coram sancto altari*). The position of the living brothers as they sing mimics the horizontal body of the dead brother, inviting further imaginative identification between living and dead. The penitential psalms continue to play a part for the week after the burial, as one of them is to be sung after each of the regular church offices. Although there is no such detailed description of lay practice, it is clear from the four surviving sets of guild statutes that there was a comparable ideal of gathering at the bed of the dying person, escorting him to the grave, and purchasing Masses and psalms for the dead man's soul.[41]

It is worth noting that in Psalm 102 (one of the seven penitential psalms), we find the verses 'For my days consume away like smoke and my bones are burned as a firebrand'. This may be an over-literal reading but it might have provided the basis for the idea that burnt oak brands — the usual wood used in charcoal burial, and the wood of the Cross as Birthe Kyølbe-Biddle points out — were an appropriate context for a burial.[42] Ashes were also an ancient symbol of the penitent, and in his homily for Ash Wednesday, Ælfric stresses the connection between the ash on the heads of the penitent and the dust to which they will return, beseeching: 'now let us do this, at least, at the beginning of our Lent, that we strew ashes on our heads to signify that we ought to repent of our sins'.[43] This is followed by the tale of a man who refused to be ashed and was killed in an accident shortly afterwards: 'He was buried then, and a great burden of earth lay upon him within seven days of him refusing that small amount of

[39] D. Whitelock, *English Historical Documents. Volume I*, c.*500–1042* (London, 1968), 409–11.
[40] Paxton, op. cit. in note 2, 140.
[41] See for instance the Exeter Guild Statutes of c. 900–950 in Whitelock, Brett and Brooke (eds.), op. cit. in note 20, 59.
[42] Kjølbye-Biddle, op. cit. in note 7, 231.
[43] *Nu do we þis lytle on ures lenctenes anginne þæt we streowiað axan uppan ure heafda to geswutulunge þæt we sculon ure synna behreowsian.* Skeat (ed.), op. cit in note 22: *Ælfric's Lives of Saints. Vol. I*, XII, lines 37–39.

ash'.[44] The ashes, which 'signify that we ought to repent of our sins' are again associated with burial: ashes may not be quite the same as charcoal, but they are not very different from it. Ash is thus an outward symbol of inner compunction and penitence, the cleansing of the soul. Here ash is explicitly contrasted with earth (*eorðe*); if ash signifies cleanliness and penitence (*to geswutulunge þæt we sculon ure synna behreowsian*), earth by implication represents sin and the absence of compunction.

By this period, the mechanics of penance and confession were complex and extensive, allowing the possibility for the penitent to turn to God, even at the moment of death. The ideal, for professional religious and layman alike, was the creation of a kind of spiritual hammock of confession, penitence, Mass, psalmody and prayer, which was constructed by one's community to carry the soul to heaven, an analogue to the bier which carried one to the grave. In this period, the concept of Purgatory had not yet been defined or institutionalized but there was nonetheless a very strong desire to help the souls of the dead.[45] By covering the body or the coffin with charcoal, symbol of penance, the mourners were hoping to extend the process of contrition into the grave.

To conclude, there are many different social, cultural and religious elements which make up the reasoning behind late Saxon mortuary behaviour. One underlying factor which could profitably be further explored is the context of increased stability and wealth in the period from the reign of Edward the Elder to that of Edward the Martyr, which might have encouraged more display in burial, the use of stone or iron-bound coffins for example. This is a factor apparently at odds with many of the arguments I have made for burial as a drama of penance and humility. But burial is often the locus of expression of conflicting ambitions. To have the kind of ostentatiously *humble* burial I have been discussing might itself be a sign of status: only the wealthy or well-connected would have access to the foreign visitors, the books and the travel which exposed them to the latest continental developments in religious thought.

The most important idea, though, is this ubiquitous sense of the body, both alive and dead, as something treacherous. At any stage in life, one's appetites, particularly sexual appetite, might betray one into damnation. Despite the efficacy of deathbed penance, body and soul still faced the unknown. The dead and decaying body was something out of control, a reminder of sin and temptation, that needed to be both controlled and protected. The range of different modes of burial represents a variety of experiments designed to guarantee salvation, in the absence of hard and fast guidelines from the Church itself. In charcoal burial, we see a desire for a display of humility, and a wish on the part of the survivors to extend the penitential process by proxy, even after death. In the elaborate coffins and constructed graves, there is a desire both to control the corpse and keep it in its proper place, and to protect it from the worst ravages of the worms.

[44] *He wearð ða bebyrged and him læg onuppan fela byrðena eorðan binnan seofon nihton þæs ðe he forsoc þa feawa axan.* Ibid., lines 56–58.
[45] J. Le Goff, *The Birth of Purgatory* (Chicago, 1984), 127.

Conquest, Crime and Theology in the Burial Record: 1066–1200

By CHRISTOPHER DANIELL

The arrival of the Normans seems to have had a negligible effect upon burial customs. Chroniclers of the time noted the changes sweeping society after the Conquest from major social changes of a new aristocracy to minor changes in appearance — the Normans being clean shaven whilst the Anglo-Saxons had moustaches.[1] There is nothing of note, however, mentioned in the chronicles about any new fashions concerning death and burial practices.

The archaeological evidence supports the lack of change for there seems to be no distinguishing features to enable Norman burials to be recognized — there is no 'black earth' horizon nor particular grave-goods. Lay burials seem to lack features which are now recognizable to distinguish Saxon from Norman, though at Winchester (Hampshire) it has been suggested that a certain type of stone and mortar grave may be a Norman style.[2] If this invisibility is real, then it has important consequences, for a whole invading people would have been lost archaeologically. Without the historical evidence the changes following 1066 could be seen as increased cultural interaction with the Continent, rather than as a successful invasion.

There are several potential reasons for this invisibility of Norman burials. The simplest is that in terms of burial practice, Anglo-Saxon and Norman cultures were very similar, both being from a Christian context with the same beliefs in the afterlife. There were therefore no unique Anglo-Saxon traditions for the Normans to compete with. Furthermore the lack of grave-goods may also show both Anglo-Saxons and Normans practising 'ostentatious humility' in burial.[3] This may also explain the difference between sometimes elaborate Anglo-Saxon burial ceremonies and the lack of wealth associated with the grave. Anglo-Saxon graves do not seem to have been often, or elaborately, marked in the mid-11th century, though there are some notable exceptions. The tomb of Cunni, the Earl's companion, at Winchester was marked with a headstone showing the hand of God, and within the tomb of Odda, the Anglo-Saxon founder of Deerhurst (Gloucestershire), was an Anglo-Saxon lead plaque with an inscription identifying him.[4] It is possible that the plaque was forged, but it does fit into an Anglo-Saxon tradition of identifying tombs by lead plaques, as discovered at St

---

[1] William of Malmesbury, *Gesta Regvm Anglorum*, ed. and trans. R. A. B. Mynors, completed by R. M. Thompson and M. Winterbottom, *The History of the English Kings*, Vol. I (Oxford, 1998), 565.

[2] B. Kjølbye-Biddle, pers. comm.

[3] See V. Thompson, this vol.

[4] B. Kjølbye-Biddle, pers. comm.; A. Williams, 'Land, power and politics: the family and career of Odda of Deerhurst', *Deerhurst Lecture 1996* (1997), 22, n. 11.

Gregory's Kirkdale (North Yorkshire), and in the tomb of Giso, Bishop of Salisbury.[5] In many cases, however, the evidence has probably been lost. Wooden crosses or markers associated with graves, for example, could be easily destroyed through decay, deliberate action, or later interments. Careful excavation, however, has revealed post-holes for wooden markers at Raunds Furnells (Northamptonshire) and at St Mark's, Wigford.[6]

Even with existing traditions — such as the Barnack School of grave cover design which has a postulated start date of c. 1050 — the Norman Conquest or the new lords who came into the area had no visible impact on the scale or number of the grave covers.[7] This is in contrast to the Vikings who discovered a carving tradition in the North of England, adapted it and made it their own.[8]

An alternative reason for a general lack of visibility of noble graves, whether Anglo-Saxon or Norman, is that monasteries and religious foundations played an important part in receiving wealthy Anglo-Saxon and Norman landowners in their declining years. This process is clearly illustrated by the later career of St Wulfstan's parents:

Meanwhile the young Wulfstan's father and mother had both grown weary of the world, and began to long and sigh earnestly for another habit and another way of life. Indeed old age and poverty lay before them. In no long time they satisfied their desire: the father took the monk's habit at Worcester, and his mother the nun's veil in the same city. The change of raiment called them to a better life . . . [9]

Similar sentiments are reflected in the various Anglo-Saxon law codes, such as the Laws of Cnut where cap. 73.3 states 'A widow is never to be consecrated [as a nun] too hastily' — indicating that the monasteries and convents served as places of retreat in old age.[10] Normans also retired to monasteries and Roger de Beaumont, the nobleman who had been left in charge of Normandy whilst William conquered England, entered the monastery of Preaux c. 1090 and died a few years later.[11] The result of this process was that monasteries received lands and money from the rich and powerful, but their graves would be simple ones within the monastic cemetery, thereby disguising the original status of the individual.

An alternative is that a large number of first generation Normans chose to be buried in Normandy. A number of cases have been explored with the conclusion that whilst some nobles who had settled in England were carried back to their homeland, 'many Norman lords chose to await the Last Judgement in [their own] English

---

[5] L. Watts, P. Rahtz, E. Okasha, S. A. J. Bradley and J. Higgitt, 'Kirkdale — the inscriptions', *Medieval Archaeol.*, 41 (1997), 51–99; S. Keynes, 'Giso, Bishop of Wells', *Anglo-Norman Stud.*, 19 (1996), 204.

[6] A. Boddington, *Raunds Furnells: The Anglo-Saxon Church and Churchyard* (English Heritage Archaeol. Rep., 7, London, 1996), 45–6; B. J. J. Gilmour, and D. A. Stocker, (eds), *St Mark's Church and Cemetery* (The Archaeology of Lincoln, XIII–I, Lincoln, 1986), 20–1.

[7] L. A. S. Butler, 'Minor monumental sculpture in the East Midlands', *Archaeol. J.*, 121 (1964), 118–25. As the dating is so imprecise (Butler gives both c. 1050 and 1066 as possible start dates) it may be that the tradition started because of Norman influence.

[8] R. N. Bailey, *Viking Age Sculpture* (London, 1980).

[9] William of Malmesbury, *Life of Saint Wulstan*, ed. and trans. J. H. F. Peile (Felinfach, repr. 1996), 10.

[10] D. Whitelock, *English Historical Documents. Volume I, c. 500–1042* (London 1979), 466.

[11] J. C. Holt, *Colonial England 1066–1215* (London, 1997), 152.

monasteries'.[12] However, the division of estates in either England or Normandy could cause a dilemma as to which side of the Channel to be buried — a decision which was still real over a century later. In 1189 the family of the last male de Mandeville buried him at the family abbey of Mortemar in Normandy rather than at his preferred choice of Walden in England. The stated excuse was the difficulty of the journey, although family politics probably intervened.[13]

The lack of visibility of Norman burials in England poses two further issues. The first is whether the Normans were deliberately following Anglo-Saxon methods of burial to emphasize the continuity. For this to be accurately assessed a detailed picture of Norman burial customs in Normandy is required — a task yet to be undertaken. The second issue is that looking at the grave itself the larger picture may be being missed: new churches themselves may have been an adequate symbol of power. Henry I built Reading Abbey for his interment, and Stephen built Faversham (Kent) as a mausoleum — on this scale there is no need to build an elaborate tomb or put things into the grave, as an impressive church visible from a distance stands as a powerful memorial.

CRIMINAL BURIALS

In one aspect, however, there does appear to have been a decisive shift in mortuary practice — the burial of criminals. Arguably at the Conquest there is a marked change in the archaeological record. Recent research has revealed the pattern of Anglo-Saxon gallows being placed on boundaries and the victims of the gallows, or other executions, being deliberately placed at these locations.[14] In addition, the concept of pushing criminals away from the centre of society to the very edge, to distance the crime and the punishment can be observed. It is noticeable, however, that such burials cease in the second half of the 11th century, as if the coming of the Normans saw the policy reversed. One of the Anglo-Saxon burials at Stockbridge Down (Hampshire) even had six coins dated 1065 concealed in the armpit, as if it were the last fling of the custom before the change the following year.[15]

In the later 11th century criminal burials disappear from archaeological view on boundaries, only to reappear in later centuries at a range of locations. The largest group of criminal burials discovered to date is at the parish church of St Margaret's in Norwich. Within its cemetery were a range of burial practices: at least ten corpses were orientated N.–S. or S.–N. (which is highly unusual, though not unique in a Christian cemetery) and some were buried W.–E.; 'many' were buried prone or face down, some with their arms behind their backs; and some had been buried hurriedly or in their clothes. The alternative medieval name for St Margaret's, was St Margaret's *ubi*

---

[12] B. Golding, 'Anglo-Norman knightly burials', 35–48 in C. Harper-Bill and R. Harvey (eds.), *The Ideals and Practice of Medieval Knighthood: Papers from the First and Second Strawberry Hill Conferences* (1986), at p. 48.

[13] B. Golding, 'Burials and benefactions: an aspect of monastic patronage in thirteenth-century England', 65–75 in W. M. Ormrod (ed.), *England in the Thirteenth Century: Proceedings of the 1984 Harlaxton Conference* (Grantham, 1985), at p. 67.

[14] See A. Reynolds, this vol.

[15] A. Reynolds, 'The definition and ideology of Anglo-Saxon execution sites and cemeteries', 33–41 in F. Verhaeghe and G. De Boe (eds.), *Death and Burial in Medieval Europe. Vol. 2* (Zellick, 1995), at p. 35.

sepeliunter suspensi ('where those who have been hanged are buried') and so it is not unreasonable to assume that some of the burials are of criminals, though an alternative explanation in certain cases is the burial of plague victims.[16] Parallels from elsewhere for practices found at St Margaret's include: the (undated) N.–S. grave in an Anglo-Saxon cemetery at Colchester (Essex) and another in the chapel of Colchester castle; a W.–E. burial, which had been decapitated, at St Andrew's, York, and a group of late Saxon prone burials at Beckery Chapel, Glastonbury (Somerset).[17]

Another possible criminal burial was discovered in a parish churchyard at Thetford (Norfolk) (burial F62). The man, who was aged 45 +, had been decapitated. It is unfortunate that so little additional information is available in the archaeological report, especially a date for the burial. The body was placed in the churchyard to the N. of the church at the W. end.[18] It is unlikely that being on the N. side was of significance as it is only right at the end of the Middle Ages, and especially in the 16th century, that the N. gains much significance in burial terms.[19] This theory is confirmed at Thetford as the burial is near some more prestigious graves. Little is known about the church itself, not even its name, though it is likely to have been operational in the 12th century.

Other possible indications of criminal punishment may show up in the archaeological record. At St Helen on the Walls, York, 'one [person] had apparently had his ear cut off, as the area [on the skull] was flattened and had become infected'.[20] This may of course have been an accident, though the cutting off of an ear was a punishment for petty larceny (theft of items less than a shilling) in the law codes of Henry II. If the crime was repeated, the other ear was cut off, and if again the gallows awaited. Punishments for theft of items of greater value were the loss on the thumb, hand or foot.[21] One possibility is that the man's ear in St Helen's graveyard had become infected as people were unwilling to medically assist him because he was a criminal.

As well as burial in the cemetery of the parish church, other possibilities for the locations of criminal burials opened up after the Conquest, for as the Anglo-Saxon tradition of boundary burials was discontinued, alternatives had to be found.

From the late 11th century onwards monasteries dramatically increased in number and after the Conquest it was not unusual for monasteries to have their own gallows. When this started is unclear, and for some monasteries the practice may have begun before the Norman Conquest.[22] In cases of monastic punishment, it is probable that the victims were buried in the local monastic graveyard or parish churchyard. Executed patrons, or nobles associated with monasteries, may also have been given

---

[16] B. Ayres, *Digging Deeper: Recent archaeology in Norwich* (Norwich, 1987) 13–14.
[17] P. J. Drury, 'Aspects of the origins and development of Colchester Castle', *Archaeol. J.*, 139 (1982), 302–419; R. L. Kemp and C. P. Graves, *The Church and Gilbertine Priory of St Andrew, Fishergate* (The Archaeology of York, 11/2, York, 1993), 157; P. Rahtz, *Glastonbury* (London, 1993), 121.
[18] C. Dallas, *Excavations in Thetford by B. K. Davidson between 1964 and 1970* (East Anglian Archaeol., 62, Gressenhall, 1993), 168–76.
[19] C. Daniell, *Death and Burial in Medieval England: 1066–1550* (London, 1997), 99.
[20] J. D. Dawes and J. R. Magilton, *The Cemetery of St Helen-on-the-Walls, Aldwark* (York 1980), 56.
[21] F. Pollock and F. W. Maitland, with additions by S. F. C. Milsom, *The History of English Law* (Cambridge, 1968), 497–8.
[22] A possible example is the hanging of the eight thieves at Bury St Edmunds. A depiction of the hanging is given in the 12th-century 'Miracles of St Edmund' (Pierpont Morgan Library 736).

prestigious burials within monasteries. At Glastonbury 'a wooden coffin with elaborate metal bindings, [and the] possibly mutilated bones of an adult male' were thought to be the bones of Humphrey Stafford, one of the Monmouth rebels, who was beheaded in 1469 at Gloucester.[23]

Some burials have items associated with punishment. Excavations at St Nicholas's Hospital in Lewes (East Sussex) have found bodies with their hands tied behind their backs, and one with an iron manacle around the leg.[24] Another burial with associated leg-iron was discovered at Old Sarum Cathedral (Wiltshire) in 1913, 'when clearance of the ambulatory uncovered several skeletons thought to have been thrown out of their coffins when the church was destroyed in the early 13th century; with one were . . . leg irons, thought to indicate a person of note'.[25]

As well as monastic or hospital complexes, criminal burials seem to be found in a variety of other locations, most obviously where there are prisons or gallows close to cemeteries, as at St Margaret's, Norwich (Norfolk). Some church cemeteries associated with castles have been dug, such as Trowbridge (Wiltshire), though in this case no evidence of capital punishment was discovered amongst the 286 skeletons excavated.[26] That castles were the scenes of such punishments can be seen from chronicles: Matthew Paris illustrates a hanging outside the walls of Bedford Castle in the reign of Henry III. The criminals are blindfolded, with their arms tied behind their backs and their bodies are suspended from a cross-beam which is supported by 'Y' shaped supports.[27] An example of possible execution burials within a castle chapel occurs at Colchester castle. In the chapel were an amazing array of graves: one had two skeletons within it, one on its back, the other face down upon it; another had a female skeleton on its side, in a third grave a skeleton lay on its face and in a fourth grave three people were buried together — one of whom may have been decapitated. Finally, three of the burials were aligned N.–S.[28]

There is, however, one widespread, nationally identified Christian place which was located on the edge of towns — often on the town boundary itself — which coped specifically with sinners who had spiritually and legally died: the leper hospitals. Whilst I am not aware of any evidence of criminal burials being reported in excavation reports, it may equally be that no one has looked. The largest leper cemetery yet excavated is that of St James and Mary Magdalene in Chichester (West Sussex). As might be expected, examples of leprosy, tuberculosis and osteoarthrosis were found, and also tantalizingly 'traumatic lesions'.[29] Another tantalizing piece of evidence

[23] Rahtz, op. cit. in note 17, 88.

[24] A. Reynolds, pers. comm.

[25] H. Thompson 'Iron Age and Roman slave shackles', *Archaeol. J.*, 150 (1993), 132–3; W. H. St J. Hope, 'Report on the excavation of the Cathedral Church of Old Sarum in 1913', *Proc. Soc. Antiq Lond.*, 26 (1914), 100–19.

[26] A. H. Graham, and S. M. Davies, *Excavations at Trowbridge, Wiltshire, 1977 and 1986–88* (Wessex Archaeol. Rep., 2, Salisbury, 1993), 32–41.

[27] Corpus Christi College, Cambridge, MS 16, f. 64r. The illustration is reproduced in J. Bradbury, *Stephen and Matilda The Civil War of 1139–53* (Stroud, 1996), 56. The structure and method has direct parallels with Anglo-Saxon practice as depicted in MS British Library Cotton Claudius B IV f. 59.

[28] Drury, op. cit. in note 17, 333.

[29] J. Magilton and F. Lee, 'The Leper Hospital of St James and St Mary Magdalene, Chichester', 249–65 in C. A. Roberts, F. Lee, and J. Bintliff (eds.), *Burial Archaeology: Current Research, Methods and Developments* (BAR Brit. Ser., 211, Oxford, 1989), 255.

occurs at the leper hospital of St Giles by Brompton Bridge (North Yorkshire). A female skeleton (burial 1710) was discovered beyond the hospital boundary ditch. This skeleton was the only one buried to the N., and on grounds of position alone the report postulated that it was the 'remains of a criminal or suicide'.[30] Suicide was rarely admitted in medieval society (the penalties were severe on the surviving family) and normally such deaths were categorized as mental illness with burial taking place in the cemetery.[31] A criminal burial is possible, and it is unfortunate (for the theory, if not the individual) that the few surviving bones do not have any marks of punishment on them. Burial of criminals in a leper hospital, on the edge of town and on a boundary, would provide a clear stepping stone from the Anglo-Saxon hundred boundary to the burials found later in the heart of towns.

This theory is backed up by an extraordinary piece of documentary evidence. In her account of medieval hospitals Clay discovered the following entry in the 1290 visitation returns for the leper hospital at Lincoln:

But strangest of all the residents in the hospital of the Holy Innocents was the condemned criminal Margaret Everard. She was not a leper, but had once been numbered amongst the dead. Mistress Everard, of Burgh-by-Waynflete, was a widow, convicted of 'harbouring a thief, namely, Robert her son, and hanged on the gallows without the south gate of Lincoln'. Now the law did not provide interment for its victims, but it seems that the Knights Hospitallers of Maltby paid a yearly sum to the lepers for undertaking this work of mercy at Canwick. On this memorable occasion, however, the body being cut down and already removed near the place of burial — the lepers' churchyard — the woman 'was seen to draw breath and revive'. We learn from the Patent Roll entry (1284) that pardon was afterwards granted to Margaret 'because her recovery is ascribed to a miracle, and she has lived two years and more in the said hospital'.[32]

The account is interesting in a number of ways. Although it is not clear whether Margaret lived in the leper hospital before her attempted hanging, her body was destined to be buried there, as a Corporal work of Mercy by the Knights Hospitallers of Maltby (South Yorkshire), and the annual sum paid for this service of the burial of criminals obviously meant a continuing tradition. The account also seems to reveal that Margaret was destined to be buried in the churchyard (rather than outside it) and that the bodies of executed women were (probably) treated in equal manner to male execution burials. It may even be that she was about to be buried next to her son in the cemetery.

As Clay further stated, the law not did provide interment for criminals. Burials of criminals were therefore organized on an *ad hoc* basis from place to place. This would tie in with the evidence emerging about the wide range of places where criminals were buried, whether parish cemeteries, hospitals or monasteries. This variation may also have resulted from local customs about the methods of execution, and hence burial. Holt describes the differences between the customs of Halifax and Wakefield (both West Yorkshire): 'If you escaped over Hebble Beck (which runs through Halifax) then you had the satisfaction of knowing that you might be hanged in Wakefield rather than

---

[30] P. Cardwell, 'Excavation of the hospital of St Giles by Brompton Bridge, North Yorkshire', *Archaeol. J.*, 152, (1995), 109–245.
[31] M. MacDonald and T. R. Murphy, *Sleepless Souls: Suicide in Early Modern England* (Oxford, 1990).
[32] R. M. Clay, *The Medieval Hospitals of England* (London, 1909), 101–2.

beheaded in Halifax', a tradition which Holt suggests was ancient in 1286.[33] With the combination of local traditions and no national laws about the burial of criminals it is not surprising to discover criminal burials in a wide range of graveyards.

Yet the question still remains why did the focus switch away from the traditional Anglo-Saxon boundary burial sites to churchyard cemeteries after the Norman Conquest? Perhaps the lack of accurate dating evidence may in reality reflect that it was a gradual change over the centuries. At Sutton Hoo (Suffolk) the gallows moved from the burial ground 'between the 10th and the 12th century'.[34] Yet the gut feeling is that there was a decisive shift with the arrival of the Normans.

DISCUSSION

There are a variety of possible different explanations. The simplest explanation is that boundary burial was not practised by Norman society, a theory that still needs to be tested. The Normans also emphasized their own dominance and control as evidenced by the large numbers of castles built around the country. Within this need for control lay the courts and the legal system. Whereas the older Anglo-Saxon system pushed the criminals to the edge, the new lords were individuals who wanted justice and punishment seen to be done in centres of population.

However, this approach does not take account of why burials of criminals were transferred from the boundary — presumably in unconsecrated ground — to the consecrated Christian churchyard, especially as the Hundred survived as a unit of organization. One answer may be in the nature and changing power of the Church. Religious and secular symbolism were fused together in Anglo-Saxon England in a remarkable way that was unknown after the Conquest.[35] The Anglo-Saxon boundary burials can be seen as a combination of local rulers or courts pushing criminals away from settlements as a secular punishment and at the same time the Church enforcing a religious punishment by burying criminals in unconsecrated ground. The unification of ideas between Church and State produced a totality about the concept of criminal burial.

A case can be made that after the Conquest this fusion was broken. New Norman influences and the continental reforms meant that combined ideology of Church and State were no longer so closely knit together, the ultimate clash being that between Henry II and Thomas Becket in 1170. If the thesis is correct — that Church and State were separated to a degree after the Conquest — then it probably had a dramatic impact on the burial of criminals. With the post-Conquest separation of the symbolism of Church and State there was no reason for a criminal to be buried in unconsecrated ground as the total symbolism of Church and State working together had been broken. One can imagine the Norman lords not particularly caring where a hanged criminal was buried.

---

[33] Holt, op. cit. in note 11, 20–4.

[34] M. O. H. Carver, *Sutton Hoo: Burial Ground of Kings?* (London, 1997), 142.

[35] For discussion about the Anglo-Saxon church and state I am indebted to Victoria Thompson and Andrew Reynolds for their insights. For a broad overview, see W. A. Chaney, *The Cult of Kingship in Anglo-Saxon England: The Transition from Paganism to Christianity* (Manchester, 1970).

There is also the issue of visibility of burials. Although some Anglo-Saxon gallows sites were in very visible locations it seems unlikely that a crowd would have watched the execution for few stray finds have been found around such sites. Rather, one gets the picture of a few key people attending in an isolated spot, which is re-enforced by the lack of evidence that hangings took place at the Hundred meeting places.[36] The isolation of Anglo-Saxon burials has a very different feel to hangings after the Conquest.

One such post-Conquest hanging is recorded by the Chronicler William of Malmesbury who gives a detailed description of the hanging of William de Aldery.[37] Godfather of William II, de Aldery was found guilty of treason. After his confession to Osmund, Bishop of Salisbury, he was scourged from church to church through the town. He then distributed his garments, frequently knelt upon the stony road, thereby drawing blood from his knees, and made a short speech declaring his innocence: 'Then the bishop, having spoken the commendation of the departing soul and sprinkled him with holy water, withdrew, and he was hanged, giving an admirable display of courage, for he uttered no groan at the prospect of death, no sigh in the moment of it'.

His punishment, and presumably death, took place within or close to the town. The presence of the Bishop, the scourging from church to church, and the sprinkling of holy water all give a Christian context to the punishment. It was also, however, a scene of maximum publicity, shame and visibility, for not only the bishop, but also the people followed him to the place of his death. Although William of Malmesbury does not say where he was buried, there is little doubt from the Christian references that it would have been in a Christian graveyard — 'ad sanctos' not 'ad paganos'.

There is another, wider, angle to this debate, a difference between cultures and mindsets. It is perhaps a truism to say that landscape was very important for the Anglo-Saxons. This is reflected in a large number of sources. Williams has highlighted and summarized the huge number of Anglo-Saxon burial sites which re-used previous monuments, as if asserting their own presence, but also identifying with the landscape they were living in.[38] Poems such as *The Ruin* also have a regard for past civilizations. The Anglo-Saxon mindset was focussed on the landscape around them. Centuries of Christianity lessened this in some ways (re-use of burial mounds faded out, possibly as church sites became more important), though boundary areas remained important and the horror of an isolated burial continued.

The Normans, however, had no such subtlety about the landscape. For them the landscape was to be used, changed and exploited, and the new monastic orders excelled at adapting the land to their own needs. Numerous castles were built across the country, not near the ancient and traditional places, such as burial mounds, but in the heart of settlements and in the best defensive positions. The thought of mapping castles against burial mounds has a slightly comic ring to it, exactly because it is a clash of mindsets.

[36] A. Reynolds, pers. comm.
[37] William of Malmesbury, op. cit. in note 1, 565.
[38] H. Williams, 'Ancient landscapes and the dead: the re-use of prehistoric and Roman monuments as early Anglo-Saxon burial sites', *Medieval Archaeol.*, 41 (1997), 1–32.

In many cases the Normans set about destroying the Anglo-Saxon landscape both in rural and urban areas. Marked examples of this include the destruction of cathedrals and their re-building (as at York), and even the location of Anglo-Saxon cathedrals could be moved: the cathedral church of East Anglia was moved from the rural site of North Elmham, to Thetford and then finally Norwich (all Norfolk).[39] The ending of Anglo-Saxon burial on boundaries can also be seen in the same light, of major actions being moved into centres of population.

The Normans were also very aware of the power of individual burials as political statements, though the local circumstances and responses varied from site to site. The power of burial as a political statement and the difference in mindsets is highlighted by the treatment of Harold's body after the Battle of Hastings. The accepted version of events is that Harold's body was taken to Waltham Abbey (Essex), but two Norman sources describe a very different tradition of Harold's burial. In his work *Gesta Guillelmi* William of Poiters described the Norman reactions to Harold: 'You have reaped the reward that you deserved, and have fallen bathed in your own blood; you lie in a tumulus on the seashore and will be an abomination to future generations of English no less than Normans'.[40]

The word '*tumulus*' is a general Latin word for a tomb (rather than its later association with a stone cairn or mound), but the concept of Harold being buried in a mound is also given in the *Carmen Hastingae Proelio*. The author, Guy, Bishop of Amiens, describes Harold's burial — first of all the body was wrapped in a 'fine purple linen' and William bore it with him to his camp so 'that he might carry out the customary funeral rites'. Harold's mother pleaded for the body, but this was refused by William 'swearing that he would sooner entrust the shores of that very port to him — under a heap of stones!'. William then 'commanded the body to be buried in the earth on the high summit of a cliff; and forthwith [one of Harold's comrades] swiftly took up the king's body and buried it, setting over it a stone, and he wrote as epitaph 'By the duke's commands, O Harold, you rest here a king That you may still be guardian of shore and sea'.[41]

The two accounts give a picture of Harold buried on a headland overlooking the sea. This is interesting as William the Conqueror is described as explaining such treatment as 'the customary funeral rites'. The question follows, customary for whom? Both the Normans and Anglo-Saxons were Christian and the Viking-style burial rite which included a mound of stones had probably not been used in England since the

[39] William of Malmesbury, op. cit. in note 1, section 338.
[40] William of Poitiers, *Gesta Guillelmi*, ed. and trans. R. H. C. Davis and M. Chibnall, *The Gesta Gvillelmi of William of Poitiers* (Oxford, 1998), 141.
[41] Guy of Amiens, *The Carmen Hastingae Proelio*, eds. C. Morton and H. Muntz (Oxford, 1972), 36-9. This description resonates with the burial of Beowulf, who was also buried on a headland overlooking the sea. There is considerable debate about the relationship between the *Gesta Guillelmi* of William of Poitiers and the *Carmen*. The authorship of the *Carmen* is also disputed. See R. H. C. Davis, 'Carmen de Hastingae Proelio', *Eng. Hist. Rev.*, (April 1978), 241–61 and L. J. Engels and R. A. Brown, 'The Carmen de Hastingae', *Anglo-Norman Stud.*, 2 (1979), 1–20. For the background to the Germanic/Viking practice of burial mounds see E. M. C. Houts, 'Scandinavian influence in Norman literature of the 11th century', *Anglo-Norman Stud.*, 6 (1983), 111.

formation of the Viking cemetery at Ingleby (Derbyshire) in the 9th century.[42] The Viking pagan past was closer for the Normans, but the Norman dukes had actively been pursuing a policy of encouraging Christianity for almost a century. The reference to such a burial may in fact be a slur upon Harold in that it was a customary burial rite for Viking leaders rather than the new Norman Christian leaders. This contrast is highlighted by William's action of founding Battle Abbey (East Sussex), emphasising his total commitment to the church.

There are other points of interest concerning Harold's burial. The isolation of the location can be seen as on a par with the isolated boundary burials of criminals. The seashore itself can be seen as boundary and his burial location places him in the most liminal position possible — between earth and sea, and air and water. The exposed open site, battered by storms, may also have been conceptually contrasted with the warmth and enclosure of the church and its cemetery and was therefore deemed to be outside the fold of Christianity. Harold was depicted as being buried in a way that the new Norman Conquerors would not have wanted for themselves. By contrast Edward the Confessor had built, and was buried in, Westminster Abbey, the greatest church in England. Moreover Edward was buried in heart of a royal complex which was teeming with the most important nobles who would have remembered Edward the Confessor by his physical presence and Westminster Abbey itself. Harold's burial on an isolated headland gave him no continuing status and his isolation meant that he would be of less political importance than those buried in the heart of royal power. Harold's burial 'on the seashore' and the horror associated with it may be the death-knell of the Anglo-Saxon tradition of isolated boundary burial.

The politics of burial and the treatment of Anglo-Saxon and Anglo-Scandinavian graves varied from area to area. At York the visible Anglo-Scandinavian graves were covered over and not destroyed.[43] This action can either be seen as an 'out of sight, out of mind' approach, or one of respect. However, the Normans were not always so conciliatory and at other churches Anglo-Saxon tombs and saints were attacked by new Norman incomers. Abbot Paul of St Albans destroyed the tombs of his venerable predecessors, the noble abbots, whom he described as *rudes et idiotas* and Abbot Walter of Evesham subjected the relics 'about which there was a doubt' to an ordeal by fire.[44] This destruction of Anglo-Saxon graves may have happened even at a local level: at Raunds Furnells (Northamptonshire) the new Norman church builders deliberately smashed graves of the previous Anglo-Saxons.[45]

Another Norman method of destruction was to place a castle on top of an Anglo-Saxon cemetery: examples of such practice have been excavated at Norwich,

[42] M. Posnansky, 'The Pagan-Danish barrow cemetery at Heath Wood, Ingleby', *Derbyshire Archaeol. J.*, 76 (1956), 40–56; J. D. Richards, M. Jecock, L. Richmond and C. Tuck, 'The Viking barrow cemetery at Heath Wood, Ingleby, Derbyshire', *Medieval Archaeol.*, 39 (1995), 51–70.
[43] D. Phillips and B. Heywood, *Excavations at York Minster. Vol. I*, ed. M. O. H. Carver (London, 1995).
[44] S. J. Ridyard, '*Condigna Veneratio*: post-Conquest attitudes to the saints of the Anglo-Saxons', *Anglo-Norman Stud.*, 9 (1987), 189.
[45] Boddington, op. cit. in note 6.

Barnstaple (Devon), York, Newark (Nottinghamshire) and Colchester (Essex).[46] In these cases the sanctity of a cemetery or church was forgotten in the haste for defence, though about fifty years later Roger, Bishop of Salisbury, was severely criticized for building part of his castle on the cemetery at Malmesbury (Wiltshire).[47]

As well as destructiveness, there was also the potential for the location of Norman burials to be highly aggressive in their pursuit of control and power. The case at Coventry (West Midlands) is highly indicative of this. The Bishop of Chester had long had his eye on the convent of Coventry, especially as it had been endowed by Earl Leofric and his wife Godiva of Mercia. The Bishop not only despoiled the church, but: 'he gave orders for his own interment at Coventry instead of Chester, in his own view leaving his successors in the position, not only claiming something which was not their due but of asserting their title to it as though it were a legal right'.[48]

The bishop was purposefully using his own burial not only to extend the boundaries of his own diocese, but also to claim the most prestigious convent in Mercia. The Bishop of Chester was viewed by contemporaries as particularly rapacious, but it cannot have been uncommon for a Norman lord or noble to have been buried in his most significant church as a sign of possession.

THEOLOGY: PURGATORY AND PENANCE

If the Anglo-Saxons were experiencing the pain of the Conquest, the whole of Europe was also beginning to experience a movement which has become known as the 12th-century Renaissance. The Normans, with their increased cross-Channel contacts, brought changes sweeping the Continent swiftly to England.

One of the features of the 12th-century Renaissance was the increasing emphasis upon the individual and it has been said that 'the discovery of the individual was one of the most important cultural developments in the years between 1050 and 1200'.[49] This increasing change led to the notions of individualism, freedom of choice (especially in love), and a greater consciousness about the self, which in turn led to emphasis upon portraiture, autobiography and romances. In terms of death and the afterlife the dramatic effect of this movement was on the increasing development of Purgatory as first an idea and then as a concrete notion of a physical place between Heaven and Hell. The fate of the individual soul moved to the forefront of interest rather than a far distant Final Judgement for all souls. The moment of death and its aftermath were now of greatest concern. Against this background the doctrine of Purgatory began to unfold.

The idea of the purgatorial flames was not a new one. The Anglo-Saxons understood the notion and Bede describes such a place — without using the term

[46] For Norwich see B. Ayers, *Excavations within the North-East Bailey of Norwich Castle 1979* (East Anglian Archaeol., 28, Gressenhall, 1985); for Barnstaple see T. Miles 'The excavation of a Saxon cemetery and part of the Norman Castle at North Walk, Barnstaple', *Devon Archaeol. Soc. Proc.*, 44 (1986), 59–84; for York see D. Evans 'The former female prison "skeletons in the cupboard"', *York Archaeol. Trust Interim Rep.*, 23/1 (1999), 17–22; for Newark see J. Samuels, 'Newark Castle', *Current Archaeol.*, 156 (1998), 458–61 and for Colchester see Drury, op. cit. in note 28.
[47] William of Malmesbury, *Historia Novella*, ed. E. King, trans. K. R. Potter (Oxford, 1998), 44–5.
[48] William of Malmesbury, op. cit. in note 1, section 341.
[49] C. Morris, *The Discovery of the Individual 1050–1200* (Toronto, 1995), 158.

purgatory — in the vision of Drycthelm.[50] The date of the impact of Purgatory across the ecclesiastical spectrum has varied according to authority: Platt sees the full impact of Purgatory being implemented at the Council of Lyons in 1274, whilst Le Goff in a carefully studied evolution of Purgatory sees its birth in the 1170s and 1180s and its flowering the early 13th century, with the Pope ratifying the significance of Purgatory in 1254.[51] The earlier date is supported by the growing number of chantry chapels from the early 13th century onwards, as at Wells Cathedral (Somerset), and at Lichfield Cathedral (Staffordshire) in the 1230s. From the 13th century onwards until the Reformation Purgatory was given great importance by the Church and laity alike.

The development of Purgatory was, I have argued elsewhere, a major factor in the subtle, but definite, change in burial practice between the late Anglo-Saxon/ Norman culture and the 13th century onwards.[52] By 1200 the most distinctive burial practices had practically disappeared — the charcoal burials, the 'ear muffs' and the majority of other such grave furnishings. In the later Middle Ages burials are more or less consistently uniform. This change in practice mirrors in time the theological change towards Purgatory. However, there is another theological change, which may have also influenced the decline in grave-goods: the notion of penance changed from an external display, to one of an internal emotion. Regular confession to a priest allowed for regular penance to be performed, rather than saving it for the grave.[53]

The two changes in theology — the growth of the importance of Purgatory and the increased emphasis upon internal penance rather than visible display — resulted in Purgatory taking over the visible symbols available for the laity. By the mid-13th century lay people were much more aware of the Purgatorial pains awaiting them and the best way to avoid the hellish punishments was for prayers to be said for the soul. This in turn resulted in the increasing visibility of tombs and effigies to catch the attention of the passer-by. Over the centuries effigies, and sometimes the skeletal bodies themselves in the cases of the transi tombs, literally rose out of the ground, demanding to be prayed for.

However, in the early and mid-12th century visible penance was still a key concern at the moment of death and a strong case can be made that the grave-goods in the 12th century, and by extension back into the Late Anglo-Saxon era, can be attributed to notions of penance. The normal medieval indications of monastic penance just before death were the Biblical themes of sack-cloth and ashes. There is good evidence of monks being laid on sack-cloth and ashes before they died,[54] and it may be that the ashes equate to charcoal burials. Historical sources often mention ashes (first used by Martin of Tours) and sack-cloth for religious burials, but lying on sack-cloth and ashes could also be a symbol of deep repentance by lay people. In a story by Walter Map, a noble man called Eudo became deeply penitent for his actions

---

[50] *Bede's Ecclesiastical History of the English People*, ed. and trans. B. Colgrave and R. A. B. Mynors (Oxford, 1969), V.12.
[51] C. Platt, *King Death* (London, 1996), 102; J. Le Goff, *The Birth of Purgatory* (London, 1984), 154–9, 283–4.
[52] Daniell, op. cit. in note 19, 177–82.
[53] P. Biller, 'Confession in the Middle Ages: introduction', 3–33 in P. Biller and A. J. Minnis (eds.), *Handling Sin: Confession in the Middle Ages* (York, 1998).
[54] Walter Daniel, *Vita Ailredi Abbatis Rievall*, ed. F. M. Powicke, *The Life of Ailred of Rievaulx* (London, 1950), 62.

which had indirectly led to the death of his first born son and 'In mourning garb he laid himself on a bed of ashes and haircloth'.[55]

A particularly interesting account details the actions of Henry II's son, the Young King, Henry. When the Young King lay dying he was put onto the usual sack-cloth and ashes, but also had stones under his head and feet, and the noose of a condemned criminal around his neck — all signs of penance and repentance. This account of the Young King is critical for two reasons — firstly because it shows that stones around the head in the grave, often called 'ear muffs', may be a sign of penitence, but secondly the noose of the criminal displays a direct symbol of justice being used in a death-bed scene, and by extension the grave. It may well be that he was depicting himself as the very lowest of the low as a sign of repentance. This example also causes a pause in thought between linking supposed 'criminal' attributes in a grave with criminals. Whilst I am not aware of any nooses being found in graves, a leg manacle has been discovered at Lewes and leg-irons were discovered at Old Sarum in association with a grave.[56] This obvious sign of a criminal burial may in fact be a sign of penitence: Walter Map recorded that an English hermit had an iron chain seven feet long, with an iron peg, attached to his leg. During the week he was absorbed in hymns, prayers and religious devotions but every Saturday he moved the peg and lived within its new radius for that week.[57] The chain was therefore part of the symbolism of religious devotion.

Similarly an iron band round the stomach of an undated skeleton was discovered at the Welsh monastery of Llandough (Vale of Glamorgan). The band was interpreted as a medical aid for a hernia or bad back.[58] This is a possibility, but the German medieval collector of miracles, Caesarius of Heisterbach, recorded two instances of sinful women who wore iron bands as a punishment. One woman, Clementina, 'committed a sin of the flesh' and when she died 'there were found round her body nine iron bands'.[59]

VISIBILITY OF DEATH AND BURIAL

As the 12th century progressed burials became more uniform and began to represent the burials of the later Middle Ages. One of the themes of this paper has been the visibility or otherwise of death and burial. The Norman burials themselves are virtually invisible to the present-day excavator, but a visible change was that of the burial of criminals from the boundary to Christian cemetery. Furthermore the very act of hanging seems to have moved from the boundary to close to settlements, as shown by the description of William de Aldery. With the increasing importance of Purgatory attention switched from signs of visible penance (such as sack-cloth and ashes) on dying

[55] Walter Map, *De Nugis Curialium*, ed. and trans. M. R. James, revised C. N. L. Brooke and R. A. B. Mynors, *Courtiers' Trifles* (Oxford, 1983), 337.

[56] Thompson, op. cit. in note 25. For references to both the Salisbury and the Lewes examples I am grateful to Andrew Reynolds.

[57] Walter Map, op. cit. in note 55, 131.

[58] S. Denison, 'Welsh monastery found to have Roman origins', *British Archaeol.*, 2 (4) (1995), 4.

[59] Caesarius of Heisterbach, *The Dialogue of Miracles*, eds. H. von E. Scott and C. C. S. Bland (London, 1929), 262–3.

and within the grave, to a greater concern for visibility above ground level with the increasing development of figural tomb sculpture to encourage prayers for the deceased.

Visibility, however, was also a feature of Anglo-Saxon death and burial and there may be elements of Anglo-Saxon practice in some remarkable 12th-century practices as given in the so-called Law Codes of Henry I.[60] As with any law code it is difficult to know whether the practices were idealized or used in reality, but these in particular stand out:

> If anyone kills a person in the course of a feud or in self-defence, he shall appropriate nothing at all for himself from the dead man's possessions, neither his horse nor his helmet nor his sword nor indeed any property; but he shall lay out the body itself in the manner customary for the dead, the head turned towards the west, the feet towards the east, resting on his shield, if he has one, and shall drive his spear into the ground and arrange his arms about it and put a halter on the horse (83, 6).

The concept of laying out the body 'in the customary manner', resting on the shield, and arranging his arms about the spear resonates with the type of grave-goods and arrangement found in Anglo-Saxon warrior graves. Moreover the completeness of the weapons is stressed ('nothing shall be appropriated from the dead'). Following the laying out of the dead in a very visible manner, the killer then has to declare the death, also making the death public and visible: 'He shall make this known at the nearest village and to the first person he meets, and also to the lord who has the soke, so that it may be possible for a case to be established or denied as against the slain man's relatives or associates (83, 6a)'.

By such actions the death can be quickly dealt with and punishments or compensation meted out. A very different procedure was for a murder victim with an unknown slayer, but once again a key issue is visibility: 'If the body of a murdered man is discovered anywhere, the hundred shall assemble at the spot with the reeve and neighbours; and whether it is identified or not, it shall be kept for seven days raised on a hurdle, with logs burning about it at night (92, 8)'.

The calling together of the hundred with the reeve and neighbours makes the murder public. The image of the hurdle and the logs burning in the night is a powerful one. Whilst they may have a subsidiary effect of keeping wild animals at bay, the burning logs fit in with making murder visible and public, as well as resonating back to earlier Anglo-Saxon society which used fire for cremating and making death visible.

---

[60] L. J. Downer, *Leges Henrici Primi* (Oxford, repr. 1996). In the original lecture behind this paper I highlighted the 'pyramids' at Glastonbury Abbey as described by William of Malmesbury. I am grateful to Victoria Thompson for pointing out that C. R. Dodwell, *Anglo-Saxon Art: A New Perspective* (Manchester, 1982), 113–18 gives a detailed analysis of these and other Anglo-Saxon 'pyramids'. One instance that Dodwell does not include is given in the Laws of Henry I: Law 83.5 states 'If anyone dares dig up or despoil, in scandalous and criminal fashion, a body buried in the ground or in a coffin or a rock or a pyramid or any structure, he shall be regarded as an outlaw'. Latham also gives examples of '(?) coffin lid c. 1180' or a 'hearse' at later dates for *pyramis*, in R. E. Latham, *Revised Medieval Latin Word-list* (London, 1989).

Summary

The volume brings together a series of studies concerned with aspects of the archaeology of burial in early medieval England and Wales during the period c. A.D. 400–1100. Previous work on mortuary behaviour has concentrated largely on furnished graves of the 5th to 7th centuries, but recent research has revised both our approaches to and understanding of burial archaeology throughout the early medieval period. The importance of this volume, therefore, is that it contains the most up to date thinking about previously well-researched material, but also that it represents one of the first attempts to draw together material relating to burial between the 7th and the 11th centuries. In addition, the volume is concerned with social aspects of early medieval burial. The demographic composition of cemeteries, burial rites and mortuary behaviour are considered alongside the political and landscape contexts of burial, all topics which are recent developments in the field of burial archaeology in Britain. Students and researchers will find the theoretical and methodological approaches of use to their own studies, whilst those seeking an understanding of trajectories of change in patterns of burial over the entire Anglo-Saxon period will find the first summary of its kind. Besides offering individual studies, the volume reviews the current state of early medieval burial archaeology in Britain and identifies areas for future research.

RÉSUMÉ

Cet ouvrage rassemble une série d'études consacrées à divers aspects de l'archéologie funéraire en Angleterre et au Pays de Galles, pour la période comprise entre 400–1100. Les travaux antérieurs sur les pratiques funéraires s'étaient largement concentrés sur les sépultures à mobilier du 5ème au 7ème siècle, mais des recherches récentes nous ont conduit à réviser notre approche et notre compréhension de l'archéologie funéraire tout au long de la période médiévale. L'importance de cet ouvrage tient au fait qu'il contient les réflexions les plus récentes sur des matériaux déjà bien étudiés et tente pour la première fois de rassembler tous les éléments concernant les pratiques funéraires du 7ème au 11ème siècle. Les aspects sociaux de ces pratiques au début du moyen-âge y sont également développés. La composition démographique des cimetières, les rites et les comportements funéraires sont évoqués en même temps que le contexte politique et environnemental des pratiques funéraires, objets de développements récents dans le domaine de l'archéologie funéraire en Grande-Bretagne. Les étudiants et les chercheurs y trouveront des approches théoriques et méthodologiques à exploiter dans leur propre recherche, tandis que ces pages fourniront les premiers éléments de réflexion à ceux qui cherchent à comprendre les trajectoires du changement dans les pratiques funéraires de la période anglo-saxonne. Cette collection propose des études individuelles, passe en revue l'état actuel de l'archéologie funéraire du début du moyen-âge en Grande-Bretagne et identifie les domaines intéressants pour l'avenir de la recherche.

ZUSAMMENFASSUNG

Der Sammelband umfasst eine Reihe von Studien, die sich mit verschiedenen Aspekten der Gräberfeldarchäologie des frühen Mittelalters von 400 bis 1100 n.Chr. in England und Wales befassen. Bisherige Arbeiten zum Totenbrauchtum konzentrierten sich größtenteils auf beigabenführende Gräber des 5. bis 7. Jahrhunderts, doch haben neue Ansätze in der Forschung unser Verständnis für die Grabkultur des frühen Mittelalters verändert. Die Bedeutung dieses Bandes besteht daher in der Neuinterpretation bekannten Materials und in dem erstmaligen Versuch eines Überblicks über das Totenbrauchtum des 7. bis 11. Jahrhunderts. Zudem werden soziale Aspekte der Grabkultur des frühen Mittelalters behandelt. Themen sind nicht nur Bestattungsriten, Grabsitten und demografische Untersuchungen zu Gräberfeldern, sondern auch politische und geografische Zusammenhänge — allesamt neue Forschungsbereiche in der Gräberfeldarchäologie Großbritanniens. Während die theoretischen und methodischen Ansätze für die Fachwissenschaft von besonderem Interesse sind, bietet der Band denjenigen, deren Interesse den übergreifenden Zusammenhängen in der Entwicklung der Grabsitten der angelsächsischen Periode gilt, erstmals eine Zusammenfassung dieser Art. Der Sammelband enthält neben individuellen Studien eine kritische Beurteilung des Forschungsstandes zur Gräberfeldarchäologie des frühen Mittelalters in Großbritannien und zeigt neue Forschungsbereiche auf.

RESUMEN

El presente volumen presenta una recopilación de artículos sobre la arqueología funerariade Inglaterra y Gales durante la época alto medieval (400–1100 d. C.). Mientras los estudios tradicionales se han centrando en los enterramientos con ajuar de los siglos V–VII, en la actualidad se le ha dado un nuevo enfoque e impulso a este tipo de arqueología. La importancia del presente volumen reside no solo en que reconsidera con nuevos enfoques material que ya había sido estudiado, sino que presenta por primera vez el estado actual de conocimiento sobre las prácticas funerarias entre los siglos V y VII, explorando además su dimensión social. Aspectos tales como la composición demográfica de los cementerios, ritos funerarios y el contexto político de los mismos, son temas que han surgido sólo recientemente en la arqueología británica. El libro será de interés no sólo por el contenido teórico y los aspectos metodológicos, sino porque además ofrece la primera visión de conjunto sobre el cambio y evolución en las prácticas funerarias del periodo anglosajón. El libro presenta tanto casos individuales como una revisión del estado actual de la arqueología funeraria alto medieval en Gran Bretaña, identificando temas de interés para las investigaciones futuras.

SAMMANFATTNING

Den här boken innehåller ett antal arkeologiska undersökningar av gravar och gravfält från tidigmedeltida England och Wales (mellan c. 400 och 1000 e. Kr.). Tidigare arbeten om gravskick har framförallt inriktats på gravar med gravgåvor från 400–talet till 600–talet. Senare tids forskning har dock ändrat både våra forskningsansatser och vår kunskap om gravar och gravskick från tidig medeltid. Boken är värdefull

eftersom den tar till vara de allra senaste rönen och tankarna kring tidigare
välundersökt material, men också för att den är ett första försök att sammanföra
gravmaterial från 600–talet fram till 1000–talet. Dessutom behandlas sociala aspekter
av tidigmedeltida begravningar. Gravplatsernas demografiska sammansättning,
begravningsriter och gravskick diskuteras parallellt med politiska och landskapliga
kontexter. Alla dessa områden utgör nya landvinningar inom brittisk arkeologi. De
teoretiska och metodologiska ansatserna är värdefulla för studenter och forskare. Även
den som söker förstå hur begravningsmönster förändrats under hela den anglosaxiska
perioden får en första sammanfattning i sitt slag. Förutom separata undersökningar,
ger boken en översikt över det nuvarande brittiska forskningsläget om medeltida
gravar och gravskick. Dessutom anges viktiga områden för framtida forskning.

INDEX